D0078623

Disaffected Patriots:
London Supporters of Revolutionary America, 1769-1782

Disaffected Patriots

London Supporters of Revolutionary America 1769–1782

JOHN SAINSBURY

McGill-Queen's University Press
Kingston and Montreal

© McGill-Queen's University Press 1987
ISBN 0-7735-0556-3

Printed on acid-free paper

Legal deposit 1st quarter 1987
Bibliothèque nationale du Québec

Printed in Canada

Canadian Cataloguing in Publication Data

Sainsbury, John, 1946–
    Disaffected patriots : London supporters of
revolutionary America, 1769-1782
    Bibliography: p.
    Includes index.
    ISBN 0-7735-0556-3
    1. London (England) – History – 18th century.
    2. Government, Resistance to – England – London –
History. 3. United States – History – Revolution,
1775–1783 – Foreign public opinion. I. Title.
    DA682.S25 1987   942.1'2073   c86-094059-4

For my Mother and Father

Contents

Preface

The theme of this book can be simply stated. It sets out to trace the composition, activities, and motivation of a group of Londoners who were sympathetic to the colonial cause during the period of the American Revolution. This theme has not hitherto been examined in detail, and those historians who have acknowledged the existence of an extraparliamentary, pro-American movement in London have tended to underestimate its vitality and endurance, or have misconstrued its socioeconomic basis.

This study attempts, however, not merely to set the record straight, but also to provide an original perspective on the character of popular disaffection in eighteenth-century London – a topic that in recent years has attracted a great deal of scholarly attention. Pro-American activity was a clear manifestation of the high level of political awareness in the capital and of the extent of alienation from central government among a large proportion of London's citizens. Studying the pro-American movement helps to illuminate the ideological content of popular protest by revealing the response of disaffected Londoners to events that both agitated and clarified fundamental issues concerning representative government and the disposition of executive authority.

In adopting the revolutionary cause, the antiministerialists of the capital were not simply wielding a convenient stick with which to beat the government. In Parliament and the provinces, pro-Americanism was not an effective political movement, especially after the outbreak of the War of Independence. The persistence with which London's so-called patriots adhered to the American cause thus testifies more to their ideological conviction than to their political opportunism. It is wrong, moreover, to characterize the tradesmen of London – legatees as they were of a rich inheritance of civic political involvement – as merely the dupes of disreputable and charismatic opposition leaders such as John Wilkes. To depict them as such has no more basis than, for example, representing loyal backbench MPs from the English shires as invariably manipulated by government.

There were good reasons, deriving from their socioeconomic situation, why so many of London's commercial population adhered tenaciously to the patriot, pro-American interpretation of events. In its exploration, narrative and analytical, of this dimension of the relationship between ideology and social structure, the book can be regarded as a case study of a general concern that is currently, and properly, preoccupying scholars investigating popular political movements in the Anglo-American world of the eighteenth century.

In researching and writing this book, I have incurred many debts of gratitude. Research was supported by postdoctoral fellowships that I received from the University of New Brunswick and the University of Pennsylvania. The preparation of the final draft was assisted by financial support from the Research and Conference Grant Program of the American University in Cairo. This book has been published with the help of a grant from the Social Science Federation of Canada, using funds provided by the Social Sciences and Humanities Research Council of Canada.

My acknowledgments are due to Olive, Countess Fitzwilliam's Wentworth Settlement Trustees and the Director of Sheffield City Libraries for permission to quote from the Wentworth-Woodhouse Muniments; to Hertfordshire County Record Office for permission to quote from the Baker Manuscripts; to Houghton Library, Harvard University, for permission to quote from the Thomas Hollis Diary; to the New England Historic Genealogical Society for permission to quote from the Hancock Manuscripts; to Lord Dartmouth and the Staffordshire Record Office for permission to quote from the Dartmouth Papers deposited in the William Salt Library; and to the William L. Clements Library, University of Michigan, for permission to quote from its various manuscript collections. Some material in this study was originally published in my article, "The Pro-Americans of London, 1769 to 1782," *William and Mary Quarterly*, 3d ser., 35 (1978): 423–54.

Many individuals have helped in the writing of this book by offering hospitality, encouragement, and criticism. In particular my thanks go to Jack Blocker, Jr, Wallace Brown, Mary Maples Dunn, Richard Dunn, Roberta Jacobs, Mary Kickham-Samy, Barry Levy, Gary Owens, Stephen Patterson, Alice Prochaska, Frank Prochaska, Alvin Riggs, Hereward Senior, Ian Steele, and members of Ian Christie's seminar in eighteenth-century history at the Institute of

Historical Research, London. Above all, I thank my wife, Lisa, for her continuing encouragement and for quelling the domestic chaos sufficiently to enable this book to be completed.

Disaffected Patriots

CHAPTER ONE

The Transatlantic
Background to 1769

AMERICAN GRIEVANCES AND
BRITISH RESPONSES

In 1760, to a contemporary observer, the prospects for political
tranquillity in Britain and unity within the empire could scarcely
have seemed brighter. The war against the Bourbon powers had swung
decidedly in Britain's favour, and the mood of loyal enthusiasm thus
induced was further encouraged by the accession to the British throne
of a young Hanoverian monarch who proclaimed that he "gloried
in the name of Briton." But the prospect of continuing loyalty and
contentment, at home and in the colonies, was to prove illusory. Within
a decade, a large body of London's citizens had reverted, with renewed
intensity, to a familiar posture of antiministerialism, and, in America,
the colonists were resisting the authority of the British government
in an unprecedented way.

This growing discontent in London and the colonies was linked
by more than simultaneous occurrence. By 1769 inhabitants of the
capital were expressing in petitions the view that American grievances
were integrally linked to their own; and before this formal joining
of the issues of transatlantic discontent, emerging patterns of popular
disaffection in London and America were developing a significant,
though in England, largely unrecognized, congruency. This intro-
ductory chapter deals briefly with the analogous development of both
movements prior to 1769 in order that their subsequent fusion may
be properly understood.

In America, tension between imperial officials and colonists had
been virtually endemic in the colonies since the seventeenth century,
and the future possibility of American independence had been a matter
of speculation from an early date, but only after the middle of the

eighteenth century did colonial grievances begin seriously to threaten the continued survival of Britain's North American empire. The Seven Years' War marked the turning-point. Despite the effusive expressions of devotion to empire that it elicited from America, the war had weighty negative consequences for future relations between Britain and its colonies. The elimination of Bourbon power in mainland North America freed colonists from their dependence on the support of British arms; and the extension of British military, fiscal, and governmental intrusions into their daily activities, which successful prosecution of the conflict necessitated, gave many Americans an unpalatable initiation in the implications of their colonial status.[1]

The burning issues of American grievance in the 1760s, however, derived mainly from the attempt of the home government to organize empire on a more rational administrative and economic basis after the termination of the war. Such a policy, while finding some support in America, was increasingly interpreted by colonists, not as necessary imperial reform, but rather as the manifestation of an encroaching despotism. Americans had previously enjoyed a considerable development of their own political institutions, notably the provincial assemblies; thus they had a practical experience of representative government which they were anxious to defend. In addition, their familiarity with the traditions of English libertarianism – which seemed peculiarly appropriate to their own political circumstances – promoted a self-conscious adherence to government by consent, balanced constitutions, and judicial independence, and predisposed them to regard the imperial policy of postwar administrations with suspicion and misgivings.[2]

It was the attempt of the George Grenville administration to raise a revenue in America that created the first widespread alarm among colonists that their liberties were being violated. The Stamp Act, legislated in 1765, met with especially bitter opposition. Its passage and attempted implementation seemed to deny what was commonly considered as a fundamental right of free men: taxation only by consent of the governed. The repeal of the Stamp Act temporarily mollified colonial opinion, but the Declaratory Act which accompanied repeal claimed parliamentary supremacy over the colonies "in all cases whatsoever,"[3] and came in time to have sinister significance for American pretensions to legislative autonomy. The apparent contempt of the home administrations for colonial assemblies, implicit in the Declaratory Act, was lent further credence by Parliament's threat in 1767 to suspend legislative functions in New York until its assembly permitted quartering of troops in that province.

British attempts to raise a revenue from the colonies were revived in 1767 by the Townshend Act, which imposed customs duties on a range of items, including tea, imported by the colonists. The scheme thus avoided the internal taxation envisaged by the Stamp Act, and colonists had previously accepted – at least in theory – import duties as a necessary element in regulating the flow of trade within the empire.[4] But such taxation for the purpose of deriving a revenue was another matter, and the Townshend duties reignited the passions created by the Stamp Act. During the course of colonial protest against the new measure, further evidence seemed to emerge of British hostility toward colonial assemblies: in 1768 Governor Francis Bernard, on instructions from the colonial secretary, Lord Hillsborough, dissolved the Massachusetts Assembly, following its refusal to rescind a circular letter which had been sent to the other colonies protesting the Townshend duties.[5]

Many Americans were apprehensive that the independence of their judicial, as well as of their legislative, institutions was being eroded by British policy. Most colonial judges had never secured permanency of tenure like their English counterparts; they normally retained their appointments only during the pleasure of the monarch. In 1768 a potent rumour that judges' salaries would henceforth be paid by the crown, and not by local assemblies, suggested that the judiciary was to become further subordinated to executive power. The jury system was also felt to be under attack from that section of the Townshend Act which substantially increased the role of the vice-admiralty courts. Apart from the practical consideration that this reform threatened to curtail a lucrative tradition of smuggling, it created a more high-minded resentment, for in these courts verdicts were rendered, not by juries, but by judges whose integrity was becoming increasingly questioned.[6]

Thus by 1769 a growing number of American colonists felt themselves oppressed by accumulating grievances. Comforting notions that ministerial and parliamentary attitudes towards them may have been based merely on British ignorance, or misrepresentation by colonial officials like Governor Bernard of Massachusetts, became less tenable as government ministers, and Parliament itself, appeared unmoved by colonial appeals for redress. It seemed increasingly clear to the colonists that their sufferings were the result of an integrated ministerial conspiracy, sanctioned by a corrupted Parliament, to subvert their constitutional liberties. The literal embodiments of imperial authority only added to their discontents: the revenue officers who came to the colonies as a consequence of the Townshend Act appeared to the colonists (with some justification) not as the efficient agents of a benign imperialism, but as venal, petty despots; and in the British troops who arrived in Boston in 1768 to quell disturbances in the town, they witnessed, through their libertarian perspective, not the guarantors of law and order, but the harbingers of social upheaval.[7]

During the 1760s very few people in England, including members of the metropolitan opposition, sympathized with this body of American complaints, or with the perception of empire that prompted their expression. In 1767 Benjamin Franklin noted the general acceptance in England of the view that the American colonies should exist in a subordinate relationship to the mother country. "Every Man in England," he wrote, "seems to consider himself as a Piece of a Sovereign over America; seems to jostle himself into the Throne with the King, and talks of OUR *Subjects in the Colonies*."[8]

Even parliamentary groups traditionally regarded as friendly to American aspirations were narrowly selective and pragmatic in their approval of colonial demands. The Rockingham Whigs (after 1766 the largest faction of parliamentary opposition) retrospectively claimed the title of friends to America on the basis of their promotion of Stamp Act repeal; but the Declaratory Act which they drafted to accompany repeal was deliberately intended to convince Parliament that they were not endorsing American criticism directed at the constitutionality of Grenville's original measure. Indeed, Lord Rockingham's ministry was at some pains to assert that it was motivated by expediency, not by principle, arguing that repeal was necessary to reverse a depression in trade, which it erroneously attributed to colonial nonimportation agreements in response to the offensive legislation.[9] The continuation of the Stamp Act, the repeal statute declared, would produce "many inconveniences, and may be productive of consequences greatly detrimental to the commercial interests of these kingdoms."[10] After their departure from office in 1766, the Rockingham Whigs were largely inactive in opposing legislation condemned by the colonists; and in opposition they adhered to the principles of the Declaratory Act until 1778, when the circumstances of imperial conflict made such adherence no longer tenable.[11]

To help promote repeal of the Stamp Act, the Rockingham Whigs encouraged organized parliamentary lobbying by merchants from London and elsewhere. This group was concerned primarily with the implications of the act for Atlantic commerce, and it derived only embarrassment from the militancy of colonial opposition. In letters to the Bostonian, John Hancock, and his fellow traders, the London merchants chided the colonists for the violence of their proceedings. 'Is it just, is it tolerable, that without proof of Inconvenience, tumultuous force shall be encouraged to fly in the face of power established for the good of the whole?" they asked. The same letter went on to counsel "Gratitude and Affection to your Mother Country."[12] It would be incorrect to discern in this self-serving paternalism, the seeds of the future pro-American movement in London.

William Pitt, the earl of Chatham, and his supporters – at least while out of office – expressed a more vigorous support for the colonists than did the followers of Lord Rockingham. Chatham condemned the Stamp Act as "founded on erroneous principle," and declared, "I am glad America has resisted."[13] Because he regarded the internal taxation of America as unconstitutional, he also opposed the Declaratory Act, a measure which his political ally, Lord Camden, denounced as "absolutely illegal, contrary to the fundamental laws of nature, and contrary to the fundamental laws of the constitution."[14]

Even the Chathamites, however, when saddled with the responsibility of power in 1766, bridled at American resistance to parliamentary authority. Chatham fiercely resented New York's refusal to quarter troops, and it was his administration that drafted the legislation to suspend the province's assembly. He must also share responsibility, together with his supposedly pro-American colleagues like Gen. Henry Conway and the duke of Grafton, for permitting Charles Townshend to proceed with his disastrous legislation. Indeed, Chatham, while still effective head of the administration, betrayed no hostility to the idea of taxing the colonies externally. Already, in the 1760s, can be discerned the tragic contradictions in Chatham's imperial policy which made him the hope of many disaffected Americans and their domestic allies, yet also, before his death in 1778, the implacable advocate of renewed military effort to retain the colonies for the mother country. The incongruities in Chatham's American policy were echoed in those of his leading disciple, Lord Shelburne, whose reputation as an enigma is best explained by his difficulties in interpreting the Delphic guidance of his adopted patron.[15]

Although parliamentary groups were hostile, or at best fickle in their support, the colonists were not entirely without English friends in the 1760s. They received the enthusiastic and wholehearted support of that small, and self-consciously select, circle of radical intellectuals, who are usually referred to as the Real Whigs or Commonwealthmen.[16] This group is properly defined in terms of its beliefs, but many of its members kept a loose social connection. In London, dissenting chapels like Caleb Fleming's at Pinners Hall, or the one founded at Essex Street by Theophilus Lindsey (a unitarian refugee from the

Church of England), not only helped to promote the advanced religious views which characterized the Real Whigs, but sustained personal contact between them. A similar function was performed by the Club of Honest Whigs, where Benjamin Franklin and the young Bostonian, Josiah Quincy, Jr, mingled with such English friends of liberty as Joseph Priestley, Richard Price, and James Burgh.[17]

The cohesion of the Real Whigs as a group, however, derived not from their habits of social intercourse, but from their political philosophy. The description of republican has been applied to them, both by their contemporaries and by present-day commentators,[18] and the label is appropriate insofar as it helps to locate the Real Whigs as eighteenth-century celebrants of a political credo – derived from classical tradition and supposedly realized in the putative British constitution – which sought the reconciliation and maximization of civic virtue, personal liberty, and political stability. A few of them, moreover, were republicans in the precise and conventional sense that they were adamantly opposed to monarchy. This coterie included the young, hot-headed Sylas Neville and his friends, who displayed their contempt for kings by annually feasting on calf's head as a symbolic celebration of the anniversary of King Charles I's execution.[19]

Most Real Whigs, however, such as the historian Catharine Macaulay, were content to evince a more cautious republicanism by their veneration of the premonarchical constitutions of Greece and Rome;[20] and certainly to overstress their opposition to monarchy is to distort seriously the emphasis of their thought. It was not the problem of kingly power, *per se*, that vexed them, but the problem of political power itself. The Real Whigs regarded it as axiomatic that the executive branch of government, unchecked, would become despotic, and it was to counter this tendency that they advocated strict adherence to the principles of the Gothic or mixed constitution. This form of government is succinctly described in an early eighteenth-century pamphlet, Lord Molesworth's *The Principles of a Real Whig*, which Thomas Hollis, a leading Commonwealthman, took as his political creed. For Molesworth, proper government was based on "the *three estates* of king (or queen) *lords* and *commons*; the *legislature* being seated in all three together, the *executive* entrusted with the first but accountable to the whole body of the people, in case of maladministration." Molesworth went on to define further the proper balance of rights and obligations between governors and governed: "A true *Whig* is of opinion, that the *executive* power has as just title to the *allegiance* and obedience of the subject, according to *the rules of known laws enacted by the legislature* as the *subject* has to protection, liberty and property; And so on to the contrary."[21] Thus Thomas Hollis was able to include Queen Elizabeth I in his pantheon of political idols,[22] and the Real Whigs as a whole felt justified in defending the Revolution of 1688, and the Hanoverian Settlement – both of which implied a tempered approval of kingship – as being in accordance with their standards of constitutional rectitude.

In itself, their adherence to the external form of a mixed constitution hardly explains the exclusivity of the Real Whigs. After all, the politician Sir Robert Walpole and the philosopher David Hume – whose politics and principles eighteenth-century Commonwealthmen regarded as diametrically opposed to their own – had approved a roughly similar conception.[23] There was, however, a crucial distinction. To the Real Whigs, the nominal distribution of power among the different elements of the constitution represented an insufficient check against despotism; their operation had to be separate and untainted by mutual influence – a contrast, therefore, to the theory of Hume and the practice of Walpole. Otherwise, in Catharine Macaulay's words, "the form of the constitution may be preserved when the spirit of it is lost."[24] To their seventeenth-century progenitors – men like John Milton and Algernon Sydney – it was the royal prerogative that threatened the constitution; but for eighteenth-century Commonwealthmen a different and more insidious menace had emerged: pecuniary corruption by the executive of the integrity and independence of the elected branch of the legislature "in which the security and safety of the people necessarily depend."[25] Mrs Macaulay – whose *History of England* represented the historiographical orthodoxy of the Real Whigs – thought that the achievements of the Glorious Revolution had been almost immediately infected by such corruption, which had come in time to poison the entire body politic. And the Real Whigs mooted elements of parliamentary reform, not from democratic instincts, but as the proper antidote to restore the constitution.[26]

These aspects of the political philosophy of the Real Whigs are important for understanding the nature of their sympathy for colonial grievances and aspirations throughout the period of the American Revolution. Apart from a few uninfluential adherents like Sylas Neville, they were no mere king-haters who rejoiced vicariously in the colonists' painful progress towards independence and republicanism.[27] Their justification for colonial resistance to the British government was based on the conviction that the administration was engaged in a despotic plan, connived at by a corrupted Parliament, to subvert personal liberty and the integrity of judicial and representative institutions in America. In short, they endorsed a principal theme in the colonial interpretation of the developing imperial crisis. The Real Whigs were warm in their praise of American pamphlets contesting British authority and argued that these publications echoed the spirit of the seventeenth-century Commonwealthmen. Thomas Hollis said of James Otis's, *The Rights of the British Colonies Asserted and Proved* (1764): "All of the great and generous Principles of government, that is of the public good, which ever warmed Milton, Locke, or any patriot head, are familiar to the author, and applied to his own particular argument in a way they had not thought of, but would have honoured and approved." Catharine Macaulay praised Otis's literary efforts in the same spirit and rewarded him with a copy of her partially completed *History of England*.[28]

The Real Whigs did more than offer to the colonists private expressions of sympathy and praise. They were largely responsible for mounting a campaign in England against what was assumed to be a ministerial plot to impose episcopacy in America, following the elevation of Thomas Secker to the primacy in 1758. Thomas Hollis was in the forefront of this domestic opposition to colonial bishops. His sympathies were probably enhanced by the close links which his family had maintained with New England throughout the eighteenth century. Hollis's great-uncle had been a generous benefactor of Harvard University, and Thomas had developed the family tradition by sending the institution libertarian tracts and books, as part of his grand scheme to spread the gift of British constitutional freedom. Hollis secured the publication in London of the antiepiscopacy pamphlets of Jonathan Mayhew – Hollis's main American contact until Mayhew's death in 1766 – and encouraged his friends to write pieces for the press exposing the potential evils of a church hierarchy in America.[29]

In part, of course, the domestic campaign against an American church establishment was generated by a natural desire of English nonconformists to protect the interest of their coreligionists across the Atlantic. But it also had a deeper political motive. The Real Whigs suspected that the main function of an American ecclesiastical establishment would be to serve the dubious ends of the secular executive. Thus Francis Blackburne, himself an Anglican minister, feared that "the crown was to have an interest in these bishops, distinct from the interest of the public; and should it appear in process of time that the limited powers with which these bishops should be sent out at the first, would be insufficient for the political purposes of the crown, can it be doubted but that they would be immediately enlarged?"[30] The threat to liberty inherent in the supposed alliance between high church episcopacy and a domestic administration is the connecting theme in *A Collection of Letters and Newspapers in Favour of Public Liberty,* which Blackburne edited from newspaper contributions submitted by himself and his fellow Commonwealthmen.[31] Other press contributors lent corollary support to the notion that bishops would serve as the administration's agents by claiming that the whole scheme of American taxation was itself designed to maintain an army of place-holders committed to supporting the government.[32]

The threat of an American episcopacy appeared to many colonists and their Real Whig sympathizers as one more element in a general and coherent scheme of repression; but, in itself, it never became a major American grievance for the simple reason that the project was never implemented. The English friends of liberty, however, were just as fervent, if not as well organized, in opposition to the more significant manifestations of colonial policy. Thomas Hollis opposed the Stamp Act from its inception on constitutional grounds, unlike the parliamentary converts to repeal who were moved by political and economic expediency. He was informed of likely American response to the measure by Jonathan Mayhew, and he communicated this intelligence to the act's author, George Grenville, in a futile attempt to change government policy. It is doubtless not an unrelated fact that in 1765 he was supplying his friends with material from the American press and recommending them as correspondents to William Strahan of the *London Chronicle.*[33] One of Francis Blackburne's group of newspaper correspondents, writing under the pseudonym of "An Unchangeable Whig," saw the Stamp Act, together with the domestic grievance of general warrants, as the prelude to some grand design of transatlantic tyranny.[34] The same association was made in English cartoons dealing with the Stamp Act, suggesting that they were inspired – perhaps even commissioned – by the Hollis circle.[35]

The Real Whigs regarded other issues of contention between colonists and government with a similar perspective. They allotted guilt exclusively to the administration; the reactions of the colonists, however violent, they saw as legitimate expressions of outraged virtue. On reading of the anticustoms riots in Boston in 1768, Thomas Hollis lamented "that the people of Boston, the most sensible, worthy of them all, and best affectioned to [Glorious] Revolution principles, and the settlement in the House of Hanover, should now prove most uneasy and disgusted!" He later recorded in his diary that "the whole Equity lies on the side of the North Americans, and that the Bostonites in particular have acted as became an outraged, free ... People."

Timothy Hollis (Thomas's first cousin once removed) and his friend Sylas Neville expressed their sentiments with a more militant ardour. They thought the threat to suspend New York's legislature "most tyrannical" and they expressed the wish that "the honest New Yorkians will not submit to it, but will draw their swords in defence of their Liberty."[36]

The individual held chiefly responsible by the Real Whigs for the iniquities of government policy and the sufferings of the colonists was Lord Bute. His supposed influence in the closet explains why the Real Whigs were able to identify a continuity and scheme in ministerial action in the 1760s, despite the frequent changing of administrations. Their choice of *deus ex machina* was perhaps inevitable. The unfortunate Scottish nobleman – the companion of the youthful George III and head of the unpopular and short-lived ministry that concluded the Treaty of Paris in 1763 – was *persona non grata* throughout virtually the entire political world and a scapegoat for a multitude of ills. Even his complete detachment from public life in 1766 failed to stem the torrent of hostility and abuse against him.[37] But if the Hollis circle only shared in a prevailing sentiment, they surpassed it in the extent of their paranoia. In February 1766 Thomas Hollis wrote to a friend that "the Scotchman has been striving with the jacobites and papists . . . to throw us all into parties and confusion, and to get the stamp-act enforced; and the colonists . . . declared rebels." Seven years later, Hollis congratulated himself that he had anticipated at an early date "that it would become necessary to the hate and subversions of *that Favorite* [i.e., Bute], *to sting* the People of Boston and New England *into madness!*" In 1767 Sylas Neville gravely recorded a rumour that "Bute intends making himself King, pretending to be descended from an elder branch than the banished [i.e., Stuart] family." And Caleb Fleming, mentor to young Sylas and his friends, was convinced in April 1768 that Bute and George Grenville (a most unlikely combination) were conspiring "to send Bishops to America and absolutely enslave that country."[38]

Thus during the 1760s the Real Whigs were producing an explanation of the developing imperial impasse, at once rational and mythical, incorporating heroes and villains, and corresponding neatly to that view of politics and the nature of power which they and their progenitors had derived from English experience. But they were only a very small group; and although their perception of the colonial situation would come to be shared by a substantial portion of public opinion in the capital, support for disaffected Americans, until at least 1769, was an esoteric not a popular cause there.

The repeal of the Stamp Act did produce celebrations in London, but only, it seems, because the City's inhabitants felt that the prevailing economic depression would thereby be ameliorated.[39] In the general election of 1768, opposition candidates in the capital did not embrace colonial grievances. The future leader of the metropolitan opposition, John Wilkes, who made a premature bid for a City seat, failed to mention America in his address to the London electors.[40] And although Barlow Trecothick – a former resident of Boston who had led merchant representation against the Stamp Act – was elected as a City MP for the first time, his American background was not a conspicuous advantage to him in the campaign.[41] Indeed, several newspaper correspondents questioned Trecothick's credentials to represent the capital's commercial interests in the light of news from America that the incorrigible Bostonians were again engaging in nonimportation agreements, this time in protest against the Townshend duties.[42] Even the London publisher, John Almon – a friend of Thomas Hollis and normally an enthusiastic pro-American – was reluctant to espouse the colonial cause. In an attempt to conciliate George Grenville (the author of the Stamp Act, but now the leader of an opposition faction), Almon's *Political Register* contained a list of suggested pledges that candidates might be asked to make. They included the following: "I do declare, that I will maintain, to the utmost of my power, the entire legislative authority of Great Britain over her colonies."[43] The interest of America for opposition groups at this juncture was clearly subordinate to the narrower, tactical interests of party manoeuvre.

A DISGRUNTLED METROPOLIS

By 1768 the American issue had not entered the orbit of London politics, but a metropolitan opposition to government was growing rapidly, based in many respects on a perception of political events and their causes which was analogous to that emerging in the colonies. The movement was both a revival and a development of a long tradition of antiministerialism in the capital. Although they were frequently in opposition to the king's ministers, however, the capital's disaffected inhabitants invariably cast themselves in the role of patriots. Their posture was in part a device to divert accusations of disloyalty in an age when sustained political opposition was not accommodated by constitutional practice;[44] but it also reflected a persistent fear on the part of London's independent tradesmen that central government would sacrifice native interests to alien ones. In this latter respect, the patriotism of Londoners frequently verged on xenophobia.

London's inhabitants had been prominent in the opposition to Charles I, and the first Lord Shaftesbury found considerable support there in his efforts to exclude the Catholic duke of York (later James II) from the English throne. Following the Glorious Revolution, however, and extending into the eighteenth century, a new urgency was engendered in the antiministerial politics of the capital by the economic and social changes effected by the so-called Financial Revolution. The central feature of this development was the emergence of an elaborate structure of public credit that enabled Britain to engage successfully in eighteenth-century wars of imperial expansion. But many of London's smaller merchants, retailers, and craftsmen, though normally bellicose advocates of war with France and Spain, were not disposed to regard favourably the financial innovations which facilitated the arrival of their nation as a leading world power. Like the Tory squires of the provinces, they perceived the creation of the national debt, the rapid growth of moneyed companies, and the practice of stock-jobbery as pernicious developments which benefited only a small financial elite (composed, they alleged, mainly of Jews and foreigners), but which operated to the detriment of the community as a whole. These tradesmen repeatedly complained that government competition for funds diminished the supply of circulating currency and that the service of the public debt necessitated burdensome taxation.[45]

This pessimistic perception was not, of course, universally shared; and the beneficiaries of the Financial Revolution – the wealthier merchants and financiers who essentially comprised the City under its economic, as opposed to its civic, definition – were not surprisingly among the government's most devoted supporters; but the very conflict of economic interest within the commercial community itself helped to focus the hostility of opposition.[46] Lord John Hervey put the point bluntly when he wrote that Sir Robert Walpole – the foremost eighteenth-century consolidator of the new financial structure – was "hated by the city of London, because he never did anything for the trading part of it, nor aimed at any interest of theirs but a corrupt influence over the directors and governors of the great moneyed companies."[47] The Common Councilmen of the City – democratically elected by London freemen who were mainly excluded from the advantages of financial innovation – remained in stubborn opposition to Walpole's long administration. Their hostility was increased in 1725 when Walpole endorsed legislation ratifying the claim of the City aldermen (who at this time represented the moneyed interest) to exercise veto power within the Common Council.[48]

The resentment felt in London towards the assumed machinations of successive administrations and the City's commercial elite was compounded by the inadequate representation of London and its suburbs in the House of Commons: at mid-century the metropolitan area contained 676,250 people, over 10 per cent of the total population of England and Wales, but it was represented by only ten MPs.[49] At the same time London's rich merchants were tending to shy away from the capital's civic affairs, thus increasing the local political control of smaller merchants and shopkeepers – a process which sharpened expressions of economic and class antagonism.[50] The American War of Independence would further intensify the clash of interests within the capital, and the assertion that this conflict was inspired by a conspiracy between the government and an elite group of financiers and materièl contractors was to become a persistent theme of London's disaffected patriots.

Ironically, the revival of metropolitan opposition to government in the 1760s derived from a period during the Seven Years' War of uncharacteristic concord between the City and the central administration. Under the aegis of Alderman William Beckford (a very rich sugar planter, but nonetheless a forceful spokesman for lower middle-class aspirations), the City, in both its mercantile and popular aspects, had forged a mutually cherished alliance with the great war minister William Pitt (later Lord Chatham) which was sustained by the profits and patriotic glory of successful conflict with the Bourbon powers. Pitt's resignation from the ministry in 1761, however, followed by the negotiation of a peace treaty widely regarded as unnecessarily indulgent to France and Spain, brought antiministerialism in London to a new pitch.[51]

It was in the wake of the unpopular conclusion to the Seven Years' War that John Wilkes emerged as the personality who was to dominate the political life of the metropolis for the next dozen years, becoming both the popular scourge of government and the most celebrated victim of its allegedly despotic tendencies. Wilkes made his initial reputation as a patriot by his slashing attacks in the opposition periodical, *The North Briton*, on the Peace of Paris and the ministers responsible for it. His subsequent persecution has been often described and requires recounting here only to the extent that the congruency might be emphasized between the issues it raised and those which were being mooted in America.

Wilkes's arrest for libel in 1763 on the basis of a general warrant issued by the secretaries of state, and the seizure of his personal papers to provide prosecution evidence, were portrayed by Wilkes and his supporters as a blatant ministerial assault on proper justice and the liberty of the subject.[52] Wilkes continued to press these two contentious issues after he returned from a four-year exile in 1768, although they had been largely settled by the courts and Parliament in his favour.

In his election address to London's electors in March 1768, he emphasized "the two important questions of public liberty, respecting *General Warrants* and the *Seizure of papers*."[53] His tactic worked its effect on the public mind and the recollection of the methods employed by the ministry in his original detention came to vitiate the subsequent legal proceedings against him, which culminated in June 1768 with the Court of King's Bench sentencing him to a £1,000 fine and twenty-two months in prison. General warrants were an especially relevant issue in the transatlantic context: they bore a sinister resemblance to writs of assistance employed by the colonial customs authorities, which had provoked controversy in 1761 and which in 1768 threatened to become a grievance again as a result of an (abortive) section of the Townshend Act.[54]

Even the question of general warrants, however, paled into insignificance compared with the reaction of the House of Commons to the triumph of John Wilkes at the polls in the election of 1768. After his initial rebuff by the City electors (his campaign had too little time to work its effect, and too many opposition votes had already been pledged to William Beckford and Barlow Trecothick), Wilkes secured election for the county of Middlesex. In February 1769 the Commons – exercising their legal omnicompetence in adjudicating their membership – expelled him from the House. They thrice repeated this vote after his successive reelection by the Middlesex freeholders, and then, in April 1769, they took the fateful decision to declare Wilkes's most recently defeated opponent, Henry Luttrell, the duly elected member for the county. The reaction of public opinion was not uniform: the various sections of opposition to the ministry drew different interpretations and favoured a variety of responses; but for metropolitan radicals and disgruntled Americans the message was clear enough: the House of Commons, by voting for the exclusion of a freely elected member, had shown itself to be corrupted to the point at which it had become, no longer a responsible and independent body, but the tool of a vindictive ministry.[55]

The popular demonstrations that attended Wilkes's adventures gave rise to further complaints of irregular justice and also revived a latent antipathy to the activity, indeed the very existence, of a standing army in peacetime. On 10 May 1768, following a riot in St George's Fields near the King's Bench Prison where John Wilkes was being held in custody, a young man, William Allen, was killed in a cowshed by some grenadiers. There were other victims of the soldiers' bullets, but the circumstances of Allen's death particularly rankled. He was apparently innocent of any riotous behaviour, and his assailants, as fate would have it, were all Scots – a people who in like manner to their notorious compatriot, Lord Bute, were at this time popularly identified in London as the enemies of English liberty. One of Allen's suspected assailants was indicted and found not guilty at the Surrey Assizes, but it was commonly supposed that the grenadier responsible for the actual shooting had escaped with the tacit approval of his superiors. Suspicions of ministerial complicity in the affair were lent credence by the publication of a letter of commendation from the secretary of war, Lord Barrington, to the officer in charge of the troops who attempted to control the riot of 10 May. Wilkes capitalized on this indiscretion by securing and publishing instructions sent to magistrates by Lord Weymouth, a secretary of state, counselling active deployment of the military in controlling crowd disturbances.[56] The incident of St George's Fields was not quickly forgotten, and two years later its recollection influenced the response in London to the news of a similar confrontation between troops and civilians, the so-called Boston Massacre.

A further example of discriminatory justice was the pardon granted to two Irish chairmen, who had been found guilty of murdering a young Wilkite lawyer during riots attending a by-election in which John Glynn, a political ally of Wilkes, was elected as an MP for the county. Such leniency, of course, contrasted starkly with the treatment to which Wilkes himself was subject.[57]

Popular grievances in London during the Wilkite troubles were thus closely parallel to those which the colonists were articulating. There were the same complaints of ministerial abuse of elected assemblies, legal chicanery, and excessive use of military force, all of which were felt to be the result of a systematic plot by despotic ministers and a corrupt Parliament against the liberty of the subject and his right to proper representation and the protection of the law. Before the 1770s, however, on each side of the Atlantic, the king was virtually immune from any criticism of executive policy;[58] or at least the time-honoured constitutional fiction was employed that he was the innocent dupe of secret and pernicious influence. It was to his prerogative to dissolve Parliament and dismiss his ministers that claimants for redress appealed, once the House of Commons, as constituted, was felt to be past redemption.[59] One pamphleteer, Stephen Sayre, an American resident in London, even advocated the strengthening of the king's constitutional authority over colonial administration in order to curb Parliament's claim to imperial omnipotence; and the inscription on William Allen's tombstone contained the proverb: "Take away the wicked from before the king, and his throne shall be established in righteousness."[60]

The apparent conformity of colonial and domestic grievances, in

origin and manifestation, was quickly appreciated in the colonies
where the cause of Wilkes was enthusiastically adopted by disaffected
Americans. His return from France and attempt to secure a parliamentary seat offered them passing hope that virtue had not entirely fled British political life; his imprisonment, expulsion from the
House of Commons, and subsequent failure to secure redress, confirmed traumatically a fear that it had.[61] The colonists' obsessive
interest in the politics of the metropolis was not immediately reciprocated by a corresponding absorption among the generality of
London's inhabitants in the affairs of America; but even before 1769
an ideological association had been established between the American
cause and metropolitan protest by the approval which the Real Whigs
accorded to both movements. Not even John Wilkes's career as a
libertine, colourful as it was even by eighteenth-century standards,
deterred the sober-minded Real Whigs from supporting his cause.
His proclivity for debauchery and libel was generally felt to be
irrelevant to the libertarian defence he was so courageously making
against an overweening administration. For Thomas Hollis, Wilkes's
peccadilloes were mere "spots in the sun."[62] The austere Richard
Price took a more censorial view, but felt that "the question which
he [Wilkes] had been the occasion of moving was of such constitutional
magnitude, that his private character ought to have no influence
on the decision of it."[63] Caleb Fleming and Sylas Neville expressed
early doubts about supporting "an enemy to every obligation of
religion and morality," but were won over to Wilkes's cause, apparently by the influence of Thomas Hollis.[64]

The Real Whig enthusiasm for the Wilkite cause was reciprocated
by a growing tendency of the London opposition to perceive its own
heightened grievances, and those of the Americans, largely in the
context of Real Whig ideology. That such a perception was brought
to the level of full consciousness is indicated by the rhetoric articulated
on political platforms in the capital, the publications of popular
societies, and, in one specific instance, by the official civic honours
that were accorded to the most celebrated Real Whig theoretician
of the 1770s, Richard Price, for his best-selling pamphlet on the
colonial crisis. The development of Real Whig attitudes on a popular
basis owed something to the industry of individuals such as Thomas
Hollis and Francis Blackburne in publicizing their political ideas
through the media of newspapers, pamphlets, and prints; but such
efforts, in all likelihood, would have been ineffective had not Real
Whig ideology, with its emphasis on the venal, despotic, and cor-
rupting tendencies of modern government, provided a world view
which was thoroughly rational and persuasive to many of London's

tradesmen in the light of their perceived economic and political victimization by successive administrations.

An important practical consequence of the coalescence of Real Whig and metropolitan dissent was that a number of Commonwealthmen were prompted thereby to abandon their customary refuge in the purity of the past and instead exercise their talents in the rather disreputable world of contemporary London politics. John Horne and, later, John Jebb were two such figures; both were to become active in radical caucuses and on the political hustings of Middlesex and Westminster. Catharine Macaulay played a less conspicuous, but perhaps equally important, role through her pamphleteering and influence over her brother, Alderman John Sawbridge, a leading figure in the patriot party.[65] Granville Sharp was another parliamentary reformer and pro-American who enjoyed a family connection with City politics. His brother, James, was a Common Councilman, which probably helped Granville in his promotion of progressive causes among London's professional politicians.[66] With such adherents, metropolitan opposition to government during the period of the American Revolution did not lack for articulate protagonists of its platform, including the plank of colonial aspirations.

The adoption of Real Whig notions as the normative mode of expressing metropolitan dissent may at first seem curious, however, given the character of earlier expressions of political opposition in the capital. In the early eighteenth century antiministerialism in London, in its civic and popular aspects, was mainly Tory and to some extent high church in its orientation. The Tory, Lord Bolingbroke, found a ready audience in London, as well as among country gentry, for his acerbic criticisms of the Financial Revolution and his nostalgic appeals to the stable social order that allegedly preceded it.[67] Tory became a pejorative label in London in the second half of the eighteenth century, but this did not signify a fundamental movement in political attitudes there.[68] On the contrary, once the divisive issues of Jacobitism and church polity had receded from the political foreground (the epithet Jacobite surviving as a synonym for papist, or as a useful brickbat to hurl at authoritarian, or specifically Scottish, ministers), there could be found an area of substantial agreement in the attacks by radical Tories and Real Whigs on the administrations of Walpole and his successors.

Both opposition factions spoke the language of patriotism and adopted what has been defined as a country-party ideology. John Pocock, who has traced with subtlety the origin and continuities of this political credo, sees it as having "expressed in great detail the values of civil liberty, the moral and political conditions under which they flourished or decayed, and the interpretation of European and English history in which they were seen as developing and as increasingly exposed to threats of corruption; but that this [ideology] was obliged by its postulates to attack as corruptive a number of important trends which it isolated as those of a 'modern' world."[69] One such trend was represented by the phenomenon of the standing army, which was anathema to Commonwealthmen as well as to most Tories of the early eighteenth century. It represented not only a threat to traditional liberties but also the most sinister embodiment of the capacity afforded to executive power by the development of public credit. To curb this and other alleged excesses of government influence and power, elements of reform, such as a bill to exclude placemen from the House of Commons, had been supported by the City during its period of Tory proclivities as well as by Real Whigs.

The political distinctions that had once separated the various sections of the country-party opposition became blurred in the minds of contemporaries during the second half of the eighteenth century. This tendency is implicit in the history of the *Monitor*, an opposition journal sponsored by William Beckford. In 1755 the *Monitor* avowed a Tory bias; yet by the time of its demise in 1765, without any shift in its fundamental attitudes, it had become a Whig publication.[70] Perhaps the clearest evidence of the erosion of old political barriers, however, is the approval with which Bolingbroke came to be cited by Real Whig reformers and American revolutionaries. Bolingbroke had, after all, echoed the call for a mixed government with separation of powers, and his passionate denunications of corruption in the body politic strikingly anticipated those of Catharine Macaulay.[71]

Real Whig ideas, then, offered a framework within which the longstanding, if sometimes inchoate, patriot and country-party attitudes of the capital might be reaffirmed; but opposition ideology was not just a static perspective through which the political events of the American revolutionary period could be regarded; it was itself susceptible to change by the impact of those same events. This tendency is apparent in the evolution of programs for parliamentary reform. In the century following the Stuart restoration, the unrepresentative character of the House of Commons had been recognized as anomalous by a number of writers. But critics of Parliament had generally sought to secure a less corrupt legislature by means other than a reorganization of constituencies or an extension of the franchise; and the notion that equitable representation was in itself a fundamental constitutional principle had been scarcely broached. Country-party ideology stressed the need for an independent and virtuous legislature rather than one which was strictly representative. Hence

William Beckford's denunciation of rotten boroughs, in the climate of political uncertainty that followed George III's accession, constituted an important addition to traditional metropolitan demands for reform.[72] Agitation against unrepresentative constituencies was continued by anonymous press contributors, many of whom were members of the Hollis-Blackburne connection.[73]

The development of theoretical justification for reforming the structure of the House of Commons was probably influenced by American resistance to the Stamp Act more than by any other event. The colonists explicitly repudiated the notion that they were virtually represented in the House of Commons and thus liable to taxation. The American argument could be readily transposed to the English context in view of the lack of representation, or underrepresentation, of the major urban centres and populous counties such as Middlesex.[74] From the period of the Stamp Act crisis, detailed proposals began to appear in the press, notably in John Almon's *Political Register*, for the redistribution of parliamentary seats and the extension of the franchise.[75] Until John Wilkes's expulsion from the House of Commons lent the whole issue of representation an unusual urgency, this development could scarcely be designated as a popular crusade; but the extension during the 1760s of the traditional, limited demands for parliamentary reform suggested that the theoretical vanguard of opposition ideology was vital to the extent that it was receptive to external influence and capable of rejuvenation, and portended that the American Revolution was to become, not merely a cause for sympathy, but a dynamic influence on the evolution of domestic radicalism.

CHAPTER TWO

The Early Growth of the Pro-American Movement

THE INFRASTRUCTURE OF LONDON POLITICS

The development of a broadly based pro-American movement in London implies that certain social and political tendencies prevailed there. Specifically, it suggests the existence of a citizenry, that, by the standards of the eighteenth century, was politically well informed, accustomed to weighing issues of national significance, and disinclined to defer in judgment to Parliament or to the social elements of which that institution was composed.

These conditions clearly existed in the capital, having reached a peak of development during the Wilkite agitation. It is true that Londoners of the middling and lower classes did, on occasion, respond to the leadership of charismatic political outsiders. The first Lord Shaftesbury and William Pitt are notable examples of those who sought and received political support in the capital, and these alliances contributed significantly to the City's sense of national importance. But leading politicians, in order to retain a following in London, were obliged to flatter the political pretensions of London's citizens and resist the perquisites that central government had to offer. Pitt's acceptance of a peerage in 1766 was sufficient to undermine, severely and irrevocably, his popularity in the capital. Any alliances which Londoners undertook with their would-be social superiors derived from a sense of political advantage or compatibility, not from any instinct of deference. Indeed, Londoners were notorious for eschewing respectful compliance with modes of behaviour based on a recognition of social distinction. In March 1775 Dr Campbell, a visitor from Ireland, observed at the Chapter Coffeehouse, "a specimen of English freedom viz. a whitesmith in his apron & some of his saws under his arm, came in, sat down & called for his glass of punch & the paper, both which he used with as much ease as a Lord. Such a man in Ireland (& I suppose France too or almost any other country) wd. not have shewn himself with his hat on, nor any way unless sent for by some gentleman."[1] When London's tradesmen did recognize distinctions of rank, it was, more often than not, to denounce the allegedly unproductive elements at the top of the social ladder. In 1761 William Beckford spoke for London's "middling sort" when he declared, "The scum is as mean as the dregs, and as to your nobility, about 200 men of quality, what are they to the body of the nation? Why ... they are subalterns ... They receive more from the public than they pay to it."[2] The capital's tradesmen did not explicitly reject a constitutional role for the aristocracy; but they seem to have regarded this social group as an estate of the realm, coordinate with, but not superior to, the chartered commercial and civic community of the City.[3]

By the 1770s London's trading community was clearly not dependent on the tutelage of "grandees" for defining areas of local grievance and relating them to issues of national policy. The penchant of Londoners for political controversy was a subject of frequent comment. One commentator sneered that "there is not a citizen, within the bills of mortality, but what is capable of filling the first offices in government, the veriest drudge, who now wears a leathern apron, can tell how far a secretary of state's power ought to extend; and expatiate on the illegality of General Warrants with the perspicuity of a *Camden*." A London pamphleteer stated in 1765 that "every man, woman, and child, is by instinct, birth, and inheritance, a politician," and that "men are more solicitous about the integrity of a lord commissioner of the treasury, or of a secretary of state, than the fidelity of their own wives, the chastity of their daughters ... or their own honour and virtue."[4]

The political consciousness of Londoners was encouraged by an elaborate infrastructure which facilitated both the spread of political information and public responses to it. This infrastructure included the numerous coffee houses and taverns of the capital, where tradesmen, apprentices, and artisans – all who could afford the beverages offered – might receive news and engage in political argument.[5] These centres also accommodated the numerous clubs and societies of London, many of which were overtly political. John Wilkes patronized several of them, and their numbers expanded with the development of his cause.[6] In many of these societies, matters of national controversy, such as the developing crisis in America, were agitated. For example, in the Robin Hood Society, a tradesmen's debating club, speakers avowed support for America. One Will Chatwell declared there in 1770, "I love the Americans because they love liberty!" and he excused riots in the colonies as "the ebullition of liberty."[7] Sympathy for the colonists was more predictable in another long-standing society, the Club of Honest Whigs, whose membership was predominantly composed of latterday Commonwealthmen.[8]

Of a somewhat different character was the Society of the Supporters of the Bill of Rights, formed at a meeting in the London Tavern on 20 February 1769, and the most famous and important of the organizations to spring up in the wake of the Wilkite agitation. Its immediate raison d'être was to pay the considerable debts of John Wilkes, though it quickly developed wider political objectives and came to function as the inner caucus of metropolitan opposition to government. The society included John Glynn and John Horne, who was largely responsible for promoting the group's formation, but most of the original members were wealthy men, such as Sir Joseph Mawbey, who shared the political, if not the economic, frustrations of London's shopkeepers and craftsmen.[9] The society was riven by internal feuding following the release of Wilkes from prison, when its membership almost completely changed, but throughout its existence it was to remain consistent in its advocacy of the colonial cause.

In a real sense, the most active and important political clubs in London were the City's organs of local government, which, despite their medieval origins, allowed for a considerable degree of popular participation. The involvement of tradesmen and craftsmen in this institutional structure encouraged their feelings of political virtue and significance. The City administration also offered a model of political practice with which the alleged decadence of the central government might be invidiously compared.

From the complex of courts which made up the City's constitution, two in particular – the Court of Common Council and the Court of Common Hall – functioned both to mobilize and express prevailing political sentiment in the metropolis. The Court of Common Council consisted of 236 Common Councilmen, who were characteristically independent craftsmen and shopkeepers, and twenty-six aldermen including the lord mayor. This body was elected in the individual wards of the City by the ratepaying freemen of the London companies; the Common Councilmen were elected annually and the aldermen for life. Both sections of the Common Council had to be composed of freemen of the City, but the Common Councilmen, unlike the aldermen, were required to reside in the wards they represented. The aldermen, as well as being magistrates, retained some separate executive powers, such as the privilege of selecting the lord mayor from two candidates elected by the London livery; but their right to veto measures supported by a majority of the Common Council as a whole was removed by Act of Parliament in 1746.[10]

The character of the Common Council was considerably affected by the impact of Wilkite radicalism. During 1769 a majority of Common Councilmen had resisted the popular tide. In May 1769 they stymied an early attempt to call the London livery and petition the throne on Wilkes's behalf. But the situation changed with the ensuing elections for the Common Council, when several antipetitioners were replaced by Wilkites.[11] Thus, insofar as Wilkite radicalism came to embrace American causes, the colonists were guaranteed a sympathetic party within London's central governing institution. Nor was the Common Council inhibited in debating and criticizing the government's handling of colonial affairs. In a Common Council debate on the eve of the American Revolution, a ministerial alderman, Benjamin Hopkins, requested wistfully "that the members of that court should confine themselves to their natural and proper sphere, that of watching the city, pavements &c &c.," but he was in a hopeless minority, and during the same debate even Alderman Thomas Harley, the senior government supporter in the City corporation, was drawn into a heated discussion of imperial policy.[12]

The dramatic and sudden shift in the political affiliation of the Common Council was less marked among the aldermanic bench, and the ministry retained throughout the period of the American Revolution a powerful interest within the latter group. But the type of alderman who was being elected was nonetheless changing. Political affiliation came to be of more consequence for the electorate than commercial prominence. George Onslow, MP – a jaundiced opponent of the City's political pretensions – noted the tendency: "They have adopted aliens instead of citizens; and in stead of the fat, inactive, commercial alderman, they have chosen patriots, as Shakespeare says, not sleek-headed men, and such as sleep of nights."[13] Representative of the new type was John Wilkes himself, who was elected alderman for Farringdon Without Ward in January 1769, and took his seat, after much legal quibbling, on his release from prison in April 1770. The next two vacancies on the aldermanic bench were filled by John Sawbridge (the brother of Catharine Macaulay) and James Townsend. Both were patriots, members of Parliament, and leading lights in the newly formed Society of the Supporters of the Bill of Rights; their motives for joining the City government were transparently political. The trend continued in the years prior to the outbreak of war with the colonies, and helped to ensure a substantial body, if not a majority, of support for America at the highest level of London's administration. The election for Cordwainer Ward of George Hayley – Wilkes's brother-in-law, and commercial agent for the Bostonians, John Hancock and William Palfrey – is noteworthy in this context, but even this event was to be surpassed by the elevation to the aldermanic bench of an American, William Lee, a few days before the news of the engagements at Lexington and Concord reached London.[14]

The institution of Common Hall, like that of Common Council, had a political significance beyond that of its purely civic function. Its members were the liveried freemen of the City companies (collectively denoted as the livery) whose prerogative it was to select from among the aldermen two candidates for lord mayor – the final choice resting with the vote of the aldermanic bench. In addition, Common Hall elected London's chamberlain, the two sheriffs of the City (who also served as sheriffs for Middlesex), and the four members of Parliament for London. In periods of political calm these functions were performed without friction: aldermen were returned by rota for the mayoralty, and the senior members of that body were generally elected as members of Parliament. In times of controversy within the City, however – of which in the eighteenth century the Wilkes episode was the most sustained and dramatic example – these customs were liable to be suspended. At such times, moreover, Common Hall exceeded its role as merely an electoral body. In the six years prior to the outbreak of the American Revolution, Common Hall revived the practice of instructing London MPs as to their parliamentary conduct; in 1773 a further device was introduced of extracting from parliamentary candidates a pledge to support a list of popular demands; and the gathering of the livery also provided an opportunity to promote petitions and remonstrances on national issues.

In the midsummer Common Hall of 1773, at which the City members were instructed to support shorter parliaments, the Wilkite recorder of the City, John Glynn, asserted Common Hall's constitutional right to pontificate on matters of national concern. Some remarks on this occasion by an egregious Guildhall orator, Capt. M.B. Allen, illustrates the extent to which the livery were encouraged by their leaders to assume a posture of political sophistication. Allen declared that "the recent example of the Swedes, who lost their Liberties by the corruption of a profilgate Senate, should serve as a warning to us"; he went on to cite the opinion of Montesquieu, who, speaking of the English, declared it "impossible for them ever to lose their Liberties, unless betrayed by a corrupt Parliament."[15]

The implied sanction of Montesquieu and the legal opinion of

John Glynn notwithstanding, the extension of Common Hall's function into the arena of national politics did not go unopposed by ministerial supporters within the livery. This group particularly resented the summoning of special meetings of Common Hall, on requisition from one section of the livery, for political purposes other than that of election. In 1770 the Courts of Assistants of three City companies – the Goldsmiths, the Weavers, and the Grocers – forbade their members from attending such a gathering. This led to the disenfranchisement of the warden of the Goldsmiths, Alderman Samual Plumbe, although this decision was reversed in a Court of Error in 1775, and the legal precedent was established that the lord mayor had no authority to compel the attendance of livery companies at Common Hall for nonelectoral purposes.[16]

But, though the political claims of Common Hall were sanctioned neither by courts of law nor even by a section of the livery itself, the importance of the institution for organizing and expressing the radicalism of the metropolis was ensured for as long as the movement itself survived. And Common Hall's instructions, pledges, and petitions offered an ideal opportunity for publicizing colonial grievances which Americans in London and their friends were not slow to exploit. The Wilkite agitation, moreover, extended such practices beyond the confines of the City – to Middlesex, among whose electors Wilkes derived his original metropolitan support, and to Westminster, Southwark borough, and part of Surrey. In short, a network of organized and coordinated opposition to government was established throughout the entire urban and suburban area of London.

Individual livery companies only rarely took the initiative in political action, although the admissions policy of certain of them was deliberately intended to promote the Wilkite and pro-American infiltration of the City's institutions. The Joiners admitted John Wilkes, by redemption, to their freedom and livery in March 1768, thus enabling him to secure election as an alderman. His friend, Dr Thomas Wilson – a devoted admirer of Mrs Macaulay – joined the company shortly afterwards. Following their acceptance of John Sawbridge in June 1769, the Frame-work-knitters likewise admitted a number of patriots, including John Reynolds (Wilkes's attorney), Luke Stavely, Captain Allen, and Heaton Wilkes (John Wilkes's brother), as well as two Americans – Arthur Lee and Stephen Sayre.[17]

These newcomers to London politics found that the medieval prerogatives of the City, as well as its political constitution, could be employed for promoting popular causes. In 1771 Wilkes and his supporters, using the City's claim under its ancient charter to independent jurisdiction within its boundaries, manufactured a row with the House of Commons, which ended with the newspapers securing the *de facto* right, subsequently unchallenged, of publishing parliamentary debates. During the crisis with Spain over the Falkland Islands, Wilkes and his crony, Brass Crosby (lord mayor, 1770–1), led the popular party in challenging the authority of the navy to impress men within the limits of the City, on the grounds of the absolute immunity of London's citizens from arbitrary arrest. Wilkes also used his authority as a magistrate to free victims of impressment and harass naval officers engaged in the practice; and Common Council was induced to accept a motion calling for the prosecution of aldermen who endorsed press warrants.[18] This experience in employing the chartered rights of the City to obstruct necessities of state proved valuable when the Common Council attempted, by the same tactics, to undermine the military effort of Lord North's administration during the American revolutionary war.

The civic institutions of the City, with their potent blend of democratic operation and medieval prerogatives, were thus the main agency through which London politicians sought to play a national role and confront the government of the day. But the stimulation of controversy was also related to another important element in the capital's political infrastructure: the Londoner's unrivalled access to the written word of political debate. The immediate impact of such literature, of course, was limited to those able to read it, and unfortunately, information concerning literacy rates in the eighteenth century is severely limited. A student of this problem, however, has reached the vague but nonetheless revealing conclusion that among "the middling classes" of England, literacy levels stayed between 75 per cent and 85 per cent in the hundred years after 1675.[19]

Specifically political material appears to have been in heavy demand from this literate section in London. "The dullest Pamphlet may have a fair chance of getting some readers, provided it be a political Pamphlet," wrote one contemporary commentator.[20] On the eve of the American Revolution there were about 150 people involved in selling pamphlets in London, of whom nearly one-third dealt in controversial literature about colonial affairs – a topic that increasingly dominated the pamphlet presses as the imperial crisis reached its peak. These tracts were sold mainly in bookshops along Fleet Street and the Strand, a main artery of the City and Westminster where a wide market could be reached. Altogether, the American revolutionary crisis stimulated in England the production of over 1,000 pamphlets – a figure which includes about eighty-five tracts first published in America or written by colonists resident in London. This English reprinting of American pamphlets was largely due to the industry of such committed pro-Americans as Thomas Hollis.[21]

Publication figures vary considerably for tracts relating to the revolution: 60,000 copies, in fourteen editions, were printed of Richard Price's *Observations on the Nature of Civil Liberty*, within a few months of its first appearance in February 1776; but this was an exceptionally successful pamphlet, most appearing in only one edition and with print runs of between 500 and 1,000. If the numbers for pamphlet production seem small, it should be recognized that readership figures in the eighteenth century greatly exceeded circulation figures. Contemporary estimates placed the number of readers for each copy at between twenty and fifty. Tracts were passed from hand to hand, borrowed from libraries, and perused by the patrons of coffee houses and taverns.[22]

Despite their importance, pamphlets probably ranked in significance below newspapers as a medium through which issues of public controversy were received and expressed. On the eve of the American war, four daily newspapers and nine triweeklies were published in the capital. In the 1760s and 1770s the intensity of political debate also engendered a number of short-lived periodicals. Of these, John Wilkes's *North Briton* achieved the greatest public attention, but publications of a similar format matched it in audacity, if not in wit or notoriety.

Some information is available concerning the circulation of newspapers. At one point, in early 1770, the *Public Advertiser* sold nearly five thousand issues. Thereafter its circulation remained above the three thousand level. The historian of the *Gazetteer* has estimated that daily newspaper to have been selling approximately five thousand copies in the early 1770s. As with pamphlets, the readership of newspapers undoubtedly far exceeded sales, because of the access to them provided in coffee houses and taverns.[23]

It would be wrong, on the basis of circulation statistics, to draw any hard and fast conclusions about the effect of newspapers in moulding attitudes – just as it would be conversely erroneous to assume that their content accurately reflected public opinion – but some additional sense of the political importance attached to the press can be adduced from the considerable extent to which opposition groups, as well as the government, used its columns to appeal to the public.[24] John Wilkes was probably unmatched among his contemporaries for his skill in using newspapers and magazines for political purposes. A feeble orator, he relied on the written word to publicize his grievances and promote his campaigns. The material he inserted in the press included anonymous paragraphs and pseudonymous essays by himself and his collaborators, copies of his speeches, and electoral propaganda.

This material was published in such quantity and to such effect that Wilkes's campaigns constituted, in the words of John Brewer, "a commercialisation of politics." Wilkes had no difficulties in finding editors prepared to accept his material. On the contrary, his contributions were eagerly solicited. The printer, John Miller, for example, wrote "to make a humble Tender of the *London Evening Post* to Mr. Wilkes, and his Cause; and at the Same Time most solemnly to assure him, that the Paper shall be at all Time devoted to the National Service with the most persevering Constancy."[25]

The press promotion of the Wilkite cause helped ensure a similar promotion of the colonial viewpoint, once the issues of Wilkes and America had become intimately associated. Americans in London – notably Benjamin Franklin and Arthur Lee – also had direct access to newspaper space for publicizing American grievances in pseudonymous essays.[26] In addition, many newspapers, such as the *London Chronicle*, began in the late 1760s to reprint large extracts from the American press as a matter of consistent policy.[27]

A further guarantee that the American cause would be adequately represented in newspapers, as well as pamphlets, was the fact that a number of booksellers, publishers, printers, and journalists had an active bias in favour of antiministerial and pro-American causes. Such men included the brothers Edward and Charles Dilly, whose City bookshop and publishing-house was a social centre for patriots and visiting Americans.[28] But the industry of the Dillys on behalf of the colonists was surpassed by that of John Almon, a leading journalist, publisher, bookseller, and editor. Almon was an energetic and ubiquitous figure in the various sections of the patriot camp. He cooperated with Thomas Hollis in reprinting American tracts, and he was an early zealot in the cause of John Wilkes. His publications included two periodicals: the *Political Register*, which ran from 1767 to 1772, and the short-lived *London Museum of Politics, Miscellanies and Literature*, which commenced publication in 1770. In the early 1770s he acquired a managing interest in the *London Evening Post* and wrote the newspaper's parliamentary reports. This newspaper – like the *London Courant* which Almon helped to establish in 1779 – was unequivocally pro-American and radical in its editorial policy.[29]

There was a considerable element of self-interest and opportunism in Almon's career: he made a handsome fortune in the business of political controversy, and, like the Dillys, he avoided allowing his political principles to compromise his desire for profit. He occasionally wrote on both sides of a newspaper debate to stimulate public interest; and he evaded libel suits – often at the expense of his associates

– by disguising the extent of his involvement in indicted publications.[30] Nevertheless, there is no doubting his diligence (with the
exception of his one lapse during the election of 1768) in support
of the colonists. His reputation as a pro-American was first established
during the agitation for Stamp Act repeal, which he promoted by
his writings and publications; Americans thereafter sent him material
for reprinting in London. Almon's own writings were coloured by
his interpretation of the government's colonial policy. He held "that
all the British measures against America, originated not in the
ostensible ministers, but in a junto of American and English traitors.
There was a junto in London, in the pay of the natural enemy, and
another in Boston, in the pay of the English junto. With these, he
said, originated the stamp-act and every other fatal measure."[31] Almon
was able to lend authority to such a version of events by his
extraordinary facility for securing American intelligence and by his
diligence in accumulating and publishing documents relating to
colonial affairs.[32] His edited collections of American materials were
characteristically a potent blend of accurate transcription interpolated
with incisive polemical comment.[33] Through the vicissitudes of the
imperial crisis, the activity of John Almon and others ensured that
at the very least the American cause would not be lost by default.

THE WILKITES DISCOVER AMERICA

The newspapers, societies, and civic institutions of London provided
the means whereby an extraparliamentary, pro-American movement
could be promoted and organized. But this political infrastructure
could not, of itself, create popular support for the colonists and
sympathy with their complaints. This development followed on the
heightened antiministerial sensibilities created in the capital by the
Wilkite crisis of the late 1760s. In such a situation London politicians
and their American allies were able to argue persuasively that colonial
and domestic grievances were similar in character and that they were
the product of the same despotic tendency in central government.

John Wilkes himself played an active role in linking American
aspirations with the other libertarian causes which his activities
inspired. Historians, though, have disagreed profoundly about the
extent of his contribution and the degree of his sincerity in support
of the colonists. Two of his more sympathetic biographers have no
doubt that his efforts on behalf of America were genuine and
substantial,[34] while other commentators claim that he felt contempt
for Americans and dismiss his professed regard for them as a

hypocritical and cynical response to their flattering overtures.[35] The latter judgments seem to derive mainly from the testimony of John Horne, who declared in 1771 that Wilkes "always hated the Americans, was always the declared foe of their liberties, and condemned their glorious struggles for the rights of humanity."[36] But these remarks were made during the course of a bitter newspaper controversy between Wilkes and Horne – the principal antagonists of internecine conflict within the popular movement – and their value as evidence should not be, therefore, uncritically accepted.

There is, however, more credible evidence which might lead to a conclusion that Wilkes was indifferent to the plight of the Americans. His political career as a whole was characterized by opportunism, albeit of a courageous kind, and his early interest in North America reveals him, in characteristic style, pursuing a place in the name of a principle. At the end of the Seven Years' War, he conceived the ambition of becoming the first British governor of Quebec, in order, he stated, "to have reconciled the new subjects to the English; and to have shewn the French the advantages of the mild rules of law, over that of lawless power." During his exile he nursed hopes of another governorship, that of Jamaica. In this instance, his declared aim was "to extinguish party in that island, and to give real strength to government."[37] While in Paris, Wilkes was kept informed of events in the mainland colonies, but he seems to have had little sympathy for American opposition to the Stamp Act. "There is a spirit little short of rebellion in several of the colonies," he wrote in November 1765.[38]

Back in London and enjoying the comforts of King's Bench Prison, Wilkes was bombarded with adulation and gifts from colonists who saw in him the champion of universal liberty. Wilkes was too well-imbued with the civility of eighteenth-century manners not to reply with equally fulsome tribute to his new admirers.[39] In his first reply to the Bostons Sons of Liberty, Wilkes pledged his support for the colonies which he described as the "propugnacula imperii." In subsequent correspondence he praised the rectitude and quality of American literary productions. "If Europe can furnish an answer to the Farmer's letters," he wrote, "it is more than Europe has yet been able to do." He also pressed his American correspondents to send him the Boston newspapers, which, he said, "I love to read." He commiserated with the Bostonians on the dispatch of troops to their town and admired their restraint in the face of the army's provocation which had "prevented the effusion of blood, which we have seen by the military in St. George's Fields." Wilkes expressed no equivocations in his support for American resistance to British legislation. He wrote in September 1769, "You have many warm friends here, who will never give up your cause, nor rest till the *declaratory bill*, as well as *all the late duties* are absolutely repealed. I am proud to be one of the foremost in that cause."[40]

Some of the visitors that Wilkes received in prison, however, were not convinced of his enthusiasm for the New World. One disappointed Bostonian, John Boylston, complained that "he [Wilkes] often with a Sneer enquires after his Friends in the Howling Wilderness as he terms us."[41]

The case for Wilkes's hypocrisy might appear damning; but there is counterevidence to suggest that he did develop a genuine sympathy for American grievances. The sarcasm which so offended John Boylston was directed by Wilkes at friends and foes alike, and other visitors to the King's Bench Prison received a contrary impression from that of Boylston. Benjamin Rush, for example, described Wilkes as an "enthusiast for AMERICAN Liberty."[42] Moreover, during his incarceration, Wilkes anonymously defended colonial causes in the newspapers; as he reasonably argued, "In no other way could I be useful in a prison."[43] After his release from jail Wilkes spoke up consistently in support of the colonists: his resumed parliamentary career, for example, was dominated by pro-American speeches.[44] And in his remarkably candid correspondence with his daughter Polly, he occasionally showed interest in the colonists' aspirations and a humane concern for their plight.[45] None of his extant letters reveals for the colonial cause the cynicism which he sometimes displayed for parliamentary reform and for the political pretensions of his lower middle-class supporters.[46]

Whether Wilkes was genuine in his professed sympathies for disgruntled Americans will presumably remain a challenging problem for his biographers. But in terms of his reasons for espousing American grievances, and the effects of that espousal, it is perhaps a question of only secondary importance. Whatever the sincerity of his feelings for the colonists, it is unlikely that Wilkes would have adopted their cause had it not been at least potentially acceptable to his metropolitan followers. He was wary of any course of action that might jeopardize his standing as a patriot, but he was in no danger of compromising his credentials in this respect by becoming a pro-American. On the contrary, it is clear from the acrimonious exchange of letters between Wilkes and Horne that support for America had become a kind of touchstone of patriot integrity.[47]

The consequence of Wilkes and his associates incorporating colonial grievances in their platform was profoundly important for the development of the pro-American movement, as the rest of this book will attempt to make clear. But an immediate effect of Wilkes's adoption of the American cause was to consolidate the sense of political kinship which radicals in Boston, and elsewhere in the colonies, felt with their political exemplar in the metropolis. This union of sympathies helped to sustain the hope that the iniquities of the British government might be countered by the cooperative action of patriots in London and America.

The leading enthusiast for this enterprise was Arthur Lee, a young, energetic, and ambitious member of the famous Virginia family. Lee had been educated at Eton and the University of Edinburgh, and in 1768 he returned to Britain to study law and engage in radical politics. Even before he left Virginia, Lee was contemplating a scheme for uniting the causes of Wilkes and America. After his arrival in England he sought out and befriended the more extreme opponents of the ministry, those whom he dubbed constitutionalists, who, unlike the Rockingham Whigs, sought not only the ejection of the government, but also fundamental parliamentary reform. He assumed that a reformed House of Commons, uninfluenced by the executive and responsible only to its electors, would spell the collapse of authoritarian policies at home and in the colonies. Catharine Macaulay was one of the compatible spirits whose company he cultivated. He also pursued an acquaintanceship with Lord Shelburne; but, although this nobleman reciprocated Lee's friendly overtures, he showed little inclination to promote the Virginian's projected constitutional upheaval.[48]

Members of the London opposition proved more cooperative. Lee quickly won the confidence of John Wilkes, and the two men were frequently in each other's company, both during Wilkes's tenancy of King's Bench Prison and after his release. Wilkes, in 1786, was to remember Lee "as one of the *greatest* this Country ever saw ... his *first* and *best* friend";[49] and insofar as Wilkes developed a sympathy for the American cause, the Virginian's personal influence was probably mainly responsible. Lee, for his part, had no doubts about Wilkes's integrity.[50] Lee's main instrument for influencing City politics was the Society of the Supporters of the Bill of Rights. Although he was not a founding member ("my purse does not equal my inclination to support the Bill of Rights," he wrote to his brother, Richard Henry, in March 1769),[51] he later became very active in its counsels.

Arthur Lee was assisted in his political activities by his brother, William, and Stephen Sayre, a financial and political adventurer from Long Island. Together they formed a close association with Dennis deBerdt, the septuagenarian agent of the Massachusetts Assembly, and assisted him in his lobbying activities. The connections of this group were further strengthened by business ties between Dennis deBerdt and his son (Dennis deBerdt, Jr), William Lee, and Stephen Sayre.[52]

The partisan activity of Arthur Lee and his compatriot friends in the capital represented a profound change in the process by which colonists sought to influence imperial policy. As the American crisis increasingly came to be seen as an argument over constitutional issues, attitudes hardened between Whitehall and the representatives of the colonies. It became increasingly difficult for colonial agents to proceed on the assumption that the empire was composed of harmoniously balanced interests. Both sides were being pushed into opposed ideological commitments.

Few colonial agents, however, shared Lee's enthusiasm for the politics of confrontation, although two of them, William Bollan (agent for the Massachusetts Council) and William Samuel Johnson (agent for Connecticut), approved of the London opposition's activities and its growing support for America. Benjamin Franklin, by contrast, was hostile to the popular movement. He detested Wilkes and chided the colonists for supporting such a miscreant. Franklin's misgivings about the emerging American-Wilkite coalition were further compounded by the enmity which existed between himself and the Lee coterie. His appointment as successor to Dennis deBerdt as the Massachusetts Assembly's agent, a post coveted by both Arthur Lee and Stephen Sayre, did nothing to improve relations.[53]

Well into the 1770s Franklin continued to place faith in the meliorating influence of merchants trading to North America and organized dissent; but after 1768 the most vigorous expressions of support for the colonists were emanating from the electors of London and its suburbs, among whom Arthur Lee was starting to exercise influence.

The colonial issue was first incorporated into the Wilkite crusade in the instructions drawn up by two metropolitan constituencies obliging their representatives to protest, primarily, Parliament's treatment of Wilkes and the legal and constitutional violations related to his persecution. The electors of Middlesex and Westminster failed to mention America in the instructions which they delivered to their MPs in January 1769, but on 10 February the London livery instructed its representatives to try "to reconcile the unhappy Differences subsisting between the Mother Country and her Colonies, the Effects of which have, in Part, been severely felt by the Manufacturer and the commercial Part of this Kingdom."[54] Alderman Beckford was apparently influential in drafting the City's instructions, and, in the light of his parliamentary record, he was probably responsible for the inclusion of the clause relating to America. On 1 March the Southwark electors followed the London livery in pressing for conciliation between Britain and America.[55]

The mention of the colonies in the instructions of London and Southwark was politically bland, limited to commercial considerations, and not explicitly "pro-American." Arthur Lee, not yet a freeman of the City, played no apparent part in drafting these documents. He did, however, strongly approve the use of instructions as a means of binding representatives more closely to the will of their constituents. The electors of London and Southwark, moreover, had established an important precedent for raising the American issue in metropolitan gatherings, which partisans of the colonial platform, such as Arthur Lee, could in future exploit.

The Middlesex freeholders, prompted by the Society of the Supporters of the Bill of Rights, soon provided a further opportunity to assert colonial complaints. On 17 April 1769 – two days after the Commons voted to seat Luttrell in place of Wilkes – a large gathering of the county's electors (estimates varied between 1,750 and 2,500 people) established a committee of one hundred freeholders to prepare a list of their "Grievances and Apprehensions." Out of their deliberations emerged a proposed address to the throne, which on 27 April was accepted by a further gathering of the Middlesex freeholders chaired by the attorney, James Adair. John Sawbridge and James Townsend spoke in support of the document and the meeting gave thanks to "Mr. Horne, for his great trouble, care and judgment, in drawing up and preparing the petition."[56]

The address was eventually presented to George III on 24 May by John Glynn, accompanied by six county freeholders. It called for the dismissal of the king's ministers and listed over twenty complaints against them. Most of these concerned the prosecution and expulsion of Wilkes, and associated domestic grievances, but the following clause was also added: "The same discretion has been extended by the same evil counsellors to your majesty's dominions in America, and has produced to our suffering fellow subjects in that part of the world, grievances and apprehensions similar to those of which we complain at home."[57] Arthur Lee later claimed responsibility for securing the incorporation of this passage in the Middlesex petition. To have done so he must presumably have been in close contact with John Horne, who was given the credit for its formulation. According to Lee, the insinuation of the colonial issue "was not effected but with great difficulty ... The subject was novel ... and appeared to many of the leading men to be foreign to their purpose."[58]

Although the connection between colonial and domestic grievances had thus not yet become axiomatic for some metropolitan reformers, the initiative of the Middlesex electors was soon followed by the London livery in their midsummer Common Hall. The civic purpose of this gathering was to choose sheriffs for the forthcoming year, and John Sawbridge and James Townsend were overwhelmingly elected to that office. Even this patriot success, however, was incidental to the pressing objective of the assembled livery which was to promote a petition to the throne. After the official business of electing sheriffs had been concluded, Mark Lovell, a West Indian merchant, read a petition which the meeting adopted with only one person dissenting.[59] The list of grievances it contained was shorter than in the Middlesex petition, although the central issues of complaint were the same. The livery petition, however, contained a more specific recital of colonial grievances. It stated that "they [the ministry] have established numberless unconstitutional regulations and taxations in our colonies; they have caused a revenue to be raised in some of them by prerogative; they have appointed civil law judges to try revenue causes, and to be paid from out of the condemnation money."[60]

Mark Lovell informed the livery that he had prepared the petition "with the assistance of several Liverymen."[61] No American appears to have directly influenced its drafting. It seems correct, therefore, to identify in the City's petition early indications of a native sentiment in support of the colonists, unprompted by expatriate Americans. William Bollan, who was shown drafts of the petition the day before the Common Hall, was especially encouraged by the fact that "two ... draughts each express'd a regard for the welfare of the colon[ies], but the third which is settled by the comittee makers, I think the most favourable mentn of them." Four weeks after the adoption of the petition, John Wilkes wrote to William Palfrey in Boston that "the pulse of this nation never beat so high for liberty as at the present moment, & all the true friends of it applaud exceedingly the late proceedings of the patriots in America."[62]

The London petition produced an echo in Bristol where Henry Cruger, "a hot Wilkite" and Atlantic merchant, pressed that city's freemen to accept an address which included a vigorous denunciation of the government's colonial policy. American grievances, however, were not generally included in the nationwide petitions from counties, cities, and boroughs presented in 1769 and 1770. The Rockingham Whigs, who promoted several addresses, were anxious to confine complaint to the single question of violated election rights. Even the Society of the Supporters of the Bill of Rights changed its tactics of agitating a miscellany of issues. Its new policy was revealed in the brief Westminster petition of August 1769, which concentrated on the single grievance of the Middlesex election and called on the king to dissolve the existing Parliament and speedily convene another. The Westminster model was imitated in a number of subsequent petitions. In September 1770 Wilkes was making plans for "another [City?] Remonstrance upon the Subject of America only"; but they came to nothing.[63] The omission of colonial grievances from addresses to the throne, however, did not unduly discourage Americans and their supporters; they comforted themselves with the hope that once the ministry was dismissed, and Parliament dissolved, their afflictions would quickly be lifted.

Although American grievances ceased to figure in the petitions of 1769 and 1770, the intrinsic association between domestic and colonial distress continued to be stressed at political gatherings in the City. In October 1769 Beckford was persuaded by his friends to accept the mayoralty for the forthcoming year. Ministerial supporters opposed his nomination, on the basis of a City by-law which stated that no person could be rechosen as lord mayor within seven years of his former mayoralty. The opposition newspaper, the *Middlesex Journal*, expressed the suspicion that the initiative to implement this local statute derived from the same ministerial source that in February 1769 sought the revival of a law, passed in Henry VIII's reign, which would have allowed for the removal of indicted colonists to England to be tried by special commission.[64] Beckford himself expanded on this theme in his acceptance speech from the Guildhall hustings. He saw "a Comparison between the By Laws and the Statute of Henry 8 made before we had a Colony, and now applied to our Colonies. He declared that the Americans were at present in an absolute State of Slavery, and that our Day was but very little distant, if the present Mode of Trick and Law-Chicane was tamely submitted to by the People; that our Liberties were at an End, if the Rights of the Nation depended upon every unheard of Statute, and the new Law Quick produced by Ministers and ministerial prostituted Law-Officers; whilst every old Law and Precedent ... made for the People was declared of no Force."[65]

Beckford had earlier demonstrated his sensitivity to American grievances by helping to initiate a campaign against Governor Bernard of Massachusetts, who was held largely responsible by the patriots of that province for the misfortunes which had befallen them. Beckford, as a member of Parliament, had privileged access to letters from Bernard to Lord Hillsborough, the colonial secretary, which had been laid before the House of Commons. In these letters Bernard complained bitterly of the Massachusetts Council's refusal to cooperate in quartering troops and suggested that the council be rendered more dependent on the crown. Beckford passed a copy of this incendiary material to William Bollan, who in turn sent it to Boston, where it was published in the spring of 1769. More Bernard letters were dispatched to Boston by Dennis deBerdt, Sr, in the autumn of the same year. Meanwhile in July 1769 Wilkes had become involved in the growing rumpus by publishing in the London newspapers a deposition sent to him from Boston, stating that the collector of customs at Salem, Massachusetts, had received bribes and shared them with Governor Bernard.[66]

Following Bernard's return to England in August 1769, and his acceptance of a baronetcy, other members of the metropolitan opposition became involved in the campaign against him. Their efforts concentrated on supporting the attempt by the Massachusetts House of Representatives to lay charges against Bernard of misrepresentation and illegally quartering troops; their indictment was made in the form of a petition to be heard before the Privy Council. Dennis deBerdt, Sr, coordinated the prosecution, and Arthur Lee, writing under his favourite pseudonym, "Junius Americanus," kept up a virulent press campaign against the ex-governor.[67] John Glynn, who was approached by deBerdt to plead the Massachusetts petition, offered his services gratis, and proceeded to handle his brief with a zeal indicative of more than just a lawyer's professional interest. DeBerdt wrote in February 1770 that "Sargeant Glynn is so valuable a Councillor & Friend I shall be govern'd entirely by his advice." Glynn kept John Wilkes closely informed of progress in the case, and Wilkes felt sufficiently confident of its outcome to write to William Palfrey in Boston that "Westminster Hall will do you justice, and a great number of separate actions against him will make your late proud, despotic governor tremble."[68]

The petition against Bernard, however, was dismissed in March 1770, by the Privy Council, as "Groundless, Vexatious & Scandalous"[69] – in retrospect, the inevitable outcome. Wilkes, undaunted, attempted to have the last word on the affair. In Common Council on 25 May 1770 he reportedly suggested that the City's congratulatory address to the throne, on the birth of a princess, should not be fulsome in tone, but "very chaste, modest, reserved" because of the insults offered by the administration to the City, and because of the conferment of a pension and baronetcy on Bernard "merely because he was a t——nt, and universally detested by our brethren in America."[70]

The pernicious effects of extending military activity into civilian situations – a process in which Bernard was heavily implicated – were dramatically confirmed for radical opponents of the ministry by the arrival of information from New England, in April 1770, concerning the Boston Massacre – a confrontation between troops and townsfolk in which five civilians were killed. The news came at a time of widespread alarm in London at an apparent increase of army activity in the capital. The "massacre of St George's Fields" was still a fresh memory, and there had been subsequent rankling incidents involving the deployment of the military. Troops had been sent to Spitalfields during weavers' riots in 1769, and two leaders of this agitation were hanged locally to awe the population – a mode of proceedings fiercely protested by the then sheriffs, James Townsend and John Sawbridge. In December 1769 soldiers on their way to Spitalfields provocatively marched in front of the lord mayor's residence, "with drums beating and fifes playing; and made a very warlike appearance," according to William Beckford's description. In the spring of 1770 there was reported to be intensifying troop activity at military encampments on the fringes of London and elsewhere.[71]

In the light of all this there was considerable interest in the news from Boston and an inclination to treat sympathetically the colonial version of the incident. Even before word of the affair reached England one particularly rabid periodical, William Moore's *The Whisperer*, had commented that "we may soon expect, like the enslaved *Americans*, to be butchered at the will and pleasure of mercenary hirelings."[72] After being briefed by William Bollan on the circumstances of the "massacre," Barlow Trecothick and William Beckford raised the matter in the House of Commons, where the latter charged that the commission of Gen. Thomas Gage, the commander of British forces in America, was "unconstitutional, unlawful and inconsistent with your [i.e., the Massachusetts] Charter."[73] Articles in the London press about the incident mostly blamed the troops, exonerated the inhabitants, and drew grim parallels between events in London and Boston.[74] Mrs Macaulay sent her condolences to the Bostonians, though she drew consolation from the opportunity which the "massacre" had given them for exhibiting "a rare and admirable instance of patriotic resentment."[75]

The friends of liberty in London cooperated with their American contacts in ensuring that colonial pamphlets on the event were published and circulated. Thomas Hollis placed the Boston tract, *A Short Narrative of the Horrid Massacre*, in the hands of the Dilly brothers for reprinting, and he later gave them three guineas to induce them to add a ten-page supplement to it.[76] The Dillys also published John Lathrop's *Innocent Blood Crying from the Streets of Boston*. Such activity, the Boston town committee complacently reflected, was "establishing Truth in the minds of honest men, and in some measure preventing the odium being cast on the Inhabitants as the Aggressors in it."[77] They might well have added that the correlation of events involving troop activity in Boston and London had already enhanced the credibility of pro-American propaganda in the capital.

The Boston Massacre occurred on the same day (5 March 1770) that Parliament repealed the Townshend duties, with the exception of the duty on tea. The circumstances leading up to this conciliatory gesture serve to place in context the nature of the developing pro-American movement. At the same time as popular support for the colonists was growing in the capital, merchants trading to North America were manifesting reluctance to support colonial opposition to the Townshend Act. Despite American nonimportation agreements beginning in 1767, merchants only began to organize agitation for repeal of the Townshend duties in 1769, two years after the legislation had been introduced; and when at last they successfully petitioned Parliament against the legislation, they made it clear to the colonial agents that they had little sympathy for American resistance to imperial authority.[78] Their attitude was in interesting contrast to that of the Real Whig, James Burgh, who, writing to the press under the pseudonym "The Colonist's Advocate," urged the full repeal of the Townshend Act because, as the Americans claimed, it was unconstitutional.[79]

The hesitancy of the merchants was in part a response to ministerial intransigence, but it also reflected the buoyancy of non-Atlantic commerce and above all their irritation at colonial embargoes on trade as an automatic reaction to unpopular legislation. Many Atlantic traders were induced finally to press for repeal of the Townshend duties because of their difficulties in collecting debts while colonial trade was dislocated; but their problems in this regard could hardly have been conducive in promoting heartfelt sympathy for the colonists' situation, especially as their colonial correspondents were frequently tardy in making remittances even when there was no offensive tax legislation on the statute book.

It was not only larger merchants who felt themselves victimized by colonial recalcitrance. A sequence of letters from a London pewtersmith firm, Robert and Thomas Porteus, to John Hancock in Boston, illustrates the vexations of a small business seeking to extend its market to New England. On 28 May 1766 the company wrote, hopefully, that "as the Evil [of the Stamp Act] is now removed and nothing of consequence left for complaint, we hope every thing will be conducted in better regularity than has been lately." Such optimism, however, proved unfounded. On 6 February 1767 the pewtersmiths urgently requested remittances for goods long since dispatched, adding, "We are in very great want of Money." On 30 April 1767 they wrote more anxiously, "Though the Sum may not be a consideration with you of its being of that consequence to us it really is, we can assure you the want of it has been a very great disappointment." On 22 October 1767 they made their final appeal, complaining, "We cannot help thinking you have trifled with us long enough now." By January 1768 the account had at last been settled. The sum in question was £222.3.4.[80]

Such experiences were undoubtedly an obstacle to the diffusion of pro-American sympathies in the capital. The committed patriots laboured conscientiously to remove it by contending that ultimately the government, not the colonists, was to blame for the disruption of Atlantic trade. Their arguments were a development of a familiar theme: namely, that the colonists, like London's tradesmen, were the victims, not perpetrators, of commercial dislocation, which derived from the administration's indifference to the trading interests of all except the rich merchants and financiers with whom it was in a corrupt alliance. Mark Lovell expressed this theme in Common Hall on 24 June 1769 – the occasion of the livery's first official espousal of colonial grievances – when he declared: "Another very great grievance . . . which we, as a commercial nation, have reason to complain of, is the very little attention that hath been paid to extending our trade and commerce since the . . . most infamous peace of Paris . . . The keeping open a breach with our colonies . . . must in the end prove the ruin of this country."[81]

This perception of administration guilt and American innocence would be sorely tested by later episodes, such as the Boston Tea Party, but it is testimony to the depth of disaffection in the capital that so many of London's independent tradesmen accepted the patriot interpretation of events despite the strains sometimes placed on it by colonial behaviour.

SPLITS, FACTIONS, AND THE SUPPORTERS OF THE BILL OF RIGHTS

The development of a pro-American opposition in the capital, in response to Wilkes's activities, was not characterized by internal harmony. Indeed, the process was beset by internecine conflicts which threatened the continued existence of the movement itself. These problems were in part implicit in the general manner in which the Wilkite movement evolved. Its growth not only engendered heightened antiministerialism, but also a sense of political autonomy and self-confidence which brought the activities and attitudes of parliamentary opposition under sceptical appraisal. In the early 1770s there was a virtual purge of Rockinghamite and Chathamite influence in the capital, and London politicians who retained association with these parliamentary factions seriously compromised their chances of popular favour. Despite internal disruption, however, the metropolitan opposition, led by the Bill of Rights Society, cooperated with disaffected Americans in resisting what they perceived as a continuing challenge to the liberties of the king's subjects throughout the empire.

The centrifugal tendencies among the opposition as a whole were scarcely affected by the recognition of many opponents of government that cooperation was a *sine qua non* for changing the course of administration policy, if not the administration itself. There was an attempt in May 1769 to evolve a program of joint action in the petitioning campaign; but this attempt at cooperation foundered as the different ends of the parties became apparent. Later, in March 1770, William Beckford invited the leaders of parliamentary opposition to dine at the Mansion House, where he tried, unsuccessfully, to pledge them to a program of parliamentary reform. Beckford's gesture, however, was perhaps not so much an appeal for unity, as a demonstration of the City's capacity for political initiative.

The differences between the followers of Wilkes and the largest faction of parliamentary opposition, the Rockingham Whigs, were profound and various. In terms of national policy, they disagreed over America and parliamentary reform. The Rockingham Whigs, moreover, distrusted the political devices that the metropolitan opposition employed to inflame and mobilize public opinion. For their part, many of London's "middling sort," with characteristic class-consciousness, resented the aristocratic condescension with which the Rockingham Whigs attempted to assume the leadership of opposition. Wilkes recognized the temper of the capital and disassociated himself from the political ambitions of the Rockinghamites and factions of similar social elevation.[82]

Whatever political credit the Rockinghamites had established in London, from their mercantile policy while in office, had dissipated by the end of 1770. During that year they achieved their final successes in City elections: in June 1770 their protégé, Barlow Trecothick, became lord mayor following the death of Beckford, and two Rockingham supporters, William Baker and Joseph Martin, were elected as sheriffs; but Baker himself was fully aware of the waning influence of his friends in the capital.[83] The political differences between the Rockingham Whigs and the City opposition were given public expression in Edmund Burke's *Thoughts on the Present Discontents* (published in April 1770) and Catharine Macaulay's spirited rebuttal. Burke specifically repudiated the desirability of any constitutional reform, calling instead for a Whig reunion on Rockinghamite principles to counter the secret and pernicious influence of the court faction. This prescription for curing the nation's various ills was denounced by Macaulay (whom Burke dubbed our "republican virago")[84] as "founded on and supported by the corrupt principles of self-interest." She condemned the Rockinghamites as the "concealed enemies of public liberty"; and she warned the public to treat with extreme caution any petitioning movement led by this faction.[85]

The split between the patriots of the capital and the largest single party of parliamentary opposition had mixed consequences for the future of the American cause in Britain. It enabled the London party to adopt colonial grievances whole-heartedly, unencumbered by Rockinghamite adherence to the principles of the Declaratory Act, but it also helped to ensure that its opposition would remain ineffective in challenging the course of government policy.

The breach between the Rockinghamites and the London patriots was illustrated in the later career of Barlow Trecothick. As a merchant trading to North America, colonial agent, and MP, with political ties both to the City and to the Rockinghamites, he might have played an important part in coordinating opposition to the government's imperial policy. His vigilance on behalf of the Americans was undoubted; in April 1770, for example, he unsuccessfully pressed in Parliament for the removal of the surviving Townshend duty on tea. But his brief mayoralty ended with recriminations over his Rockinghamite associations and his lack of firmness in resisting naval impressment within the City. He showed his disenchantment with the popular movement by voting for the ministerial candidate in the mayoral election of 1771; and he played no further part in active political life before his death in May 1775.[86]

Like the Rockinghamites, the supporters of Lord Chatham found their influence in the City diminishing. Even Chatham's personal reputation as a patriot did not prove inviolable. His acceptance of a peerage in 1766 had deeply offended many of his middle-class supporters with their celebrated aversion to "grandees." Among the Real Whigs, Thomas Hollis retained his regard for Chatham,[87] but Catharine Macaulay, in 1772, thought his popularity had been justly eroded "by his Inconsistencies, & Fondness for a Title."[88] Wilkes, who received no redress from Chatham's ministry during his French exile, also bitterly condemned the "great commoner." Chatham's credit in the City revived a little with his parliamentary defence of the rights of electors, for which, in May 1770, he received the official thanks of the Common Council. But in November of the same year he was at odds with the metropolitan opposition over the question of naval impressment, which the Wilkites were resisting within the City. At this time one of his parliamentary speeches was reported in which he flattered the traditional prejudices of middle-class Londoners by referring to the "monied interest of the city" as "blood-worms ... of the constitution," and expressed his regard for "the middling citizens, who preferred law and liberty to loans and contracts";[89] but his influence was clearly waning, and in December Wilkes or one of his supporters anonymously declared that "the constant City phrase of him [Chatham] is, *The funeral Sir, is gone by.*"[90] Even Chatham's eventual conversion to the notion of triennial parliaments did little to revive his popularity.

The loosening of ties between Chatham and the City had important implications for the future of the pro-American movement in London. Despite the tarnished lustre of his image as a patriot, his triumphs during the Seven Years' War and his later support for American opposition to the Stamp Act had secured his reputation as the man who built and defended the modern empire while seeking to guarantee the liberties of its colonial inhabitants. For this reason, Chatham, despite some inconsistencies over imperial policy, was looked to by a wide spectrum of public opinion as the one person who might successfully conciliate the colonists and preserve America for the British crown. It was unfortunate, therefore, for the prestige and effectiveness of the pro-American lobby in London that differences should have emerged between the City and its erstwhile champion.

The waning of Chatham's influence in London was undoubtedly hastened by the death of his close collaborator, William Beckford, in June 1770. Beckford's death also robbed the pro-American movement of one of its earliest and most illustrious advocates – a loss which his replacement as alderman and MP by Richard Oliver, also an avowed pro-American, only partly mitigated.[91] In addition, without Beckford's unifying influence, divisions of interest quickly appeared among London's politicians. Two warring factions emerged to contest for control of popular opposition. One party, led by James Townsend, John Sawbridge, and John Horne, retained a close association with Lord Chatham's protégé, Lord Shelburne, and acted as his agents in City politics. They resented what they felt was Wilkes's exploitation of prevailing antiministerialism for his exclusively personal advantage. For their part, Wilkes and his supporters were determined to resist any outside interference in the politics of the capital, and they branded the unfortunate Lord Shelburne as a mischievous and dishonest intruder.[92]

Divisions in the leadership of the popular movement were brought to the attention of the public in October 1770, when, at a meeting of Westminster electors, Wilkes and Sawbridge disputed the best means of carrying on protest against the government; Wilkes favoured a motion instructing the MPs for Westminster to impeach Lord North as "the chief instrument of the tyranny we groan under, at home and in the colonies"; Sawbridge, supported by the general sense of the meeting, recommended a further remonstrance to the throne.[93] Shortly afterwards commenced the prolonged exchange in the press between Wilkes and Horne in which the festering issues of contention between the factions were given public and acrimonious expression. The two groups successfully joined forces during the "printers' case," but this triumph did not help to reconcile their differences. The extent of the rupture between them was illustrated in November 1771, when their refusal to cooperate in supporting mutually selected candidates for lord mayor led to the victory at the polls of a ministerialist, Alderman William Nash. For Wilkes and his supporters, it was a more satisfactory outcome than the triumph of one of the Shelburnite contenders, Townsend or Sawbridge. The following year, Wilkes himself secured most votes in the mayoral election, but the Court of Aldermen exercised their prerogative of choosing for lord mayor the second-placed candidate in the Common Hall poll, James Townsend. The bitterness engendered by this decision ensured the continuation of hostility between the supporters of Wilkes and the Shelburne faction in the City.[94]

To many observers, feuding among the City patriots adversely affected the political credibility of popular protest in London. For this reason, *Junius*, the anonymous scourge of the ministry, unavailingly urged Wilkes to forget past differences and to make common cause with John Sawbridge in the mayoral election of 1771. Samuel Adams, viewing the result of that contest from Boston, expressed deep concern that there should be a division among the friends of liberty, and predictably he credited the administration with contriving it.[95] But the deleterious effects of splits within the popular opposition can be exaggerated. As Simon Maccoby has pointed out, the patriots were still able to make trouble for the government even when they were divided; and their activity rendered them for long periods, especially during parliamentary recesses, "the only active political forces in the country."[96] Furthermore, the close ties of Townsend, Horne, and Sawbridge with Lord Shelburne made them especially vulnerable to criticism, and they were convincingly cast as a factious splinter group by Wilkes and his adherents, who, after 1772, were unquestionably the dominant influence in London politics.[97]

The disunion among the metropolitan opposition as a whole produced divisions within, and secessions from, the Society of the Supporters of the Bill of Rights. This feuding did not, however, undermine patriot support for America. On the contrary, it probably encouraged such support, as each faction attempted to outvie the other in demonstrating enthusiasm for the colonists' cause.

From its inception, the Bill of Rights Society exhibited an awareness of the imperial dimension. In the summer of 1769 it dispatched circular letters, encouraging the formation of similar groups throughout the empire.[98] One such society was, in fact, established in Charleston, and it was in this town of colonial Wilkites that an incident originated which was to advance the revolutionary consciousness of South Carolina and throw the American sympathies of the Bill of Rights group into sharp focus. In December 1769 the assembly of South Carolina voted to remit £1,500 "for the support of the interest and constitutional rights and liberties of the people of Great Britain and America."[99] In February 1770 the letter that accompanied the gift was laid before the society, which appointed a committee to draft a reply acknowledging the generosity of the Carolinians. The form which this reply should take was predictably the cause of a dispute between Wilkes and Horne. Wilkes favoured the letter prepared by the society's secretary, Robert Morris, which Horne denounced as ill-composed and longwinded. Horne accused Wilkes of desiring approval of Morris's unsatisfactory draft in order to humiliate the Supporters of the Bill of Rights, as well as the South Carolina assembly, because the £1,500 gift had not been sent directly to him. Wilkes repudiated the charge in a forceful declaration of his American sympathies.[100]

The Morris draft was not adopted by the committee, however, but instead one prepared by Horne and amended by Glynn and others. The letter unequivocally stated the indivisibility of colonial and domestic opposition to government. It assured the Carolinians that

the same spirit of union and mutual assistance which dictated your vote in our favour animates this Society. We shall ever consider the rights of all our fellow-subjects throughout the British empire, in England, Scotland, Ireland, and America, as stones of one arch, on which the happiness and security of the whole are founded. Such would have been our principle of action, if the system of despotism which has been adopted had been more artfully conducted; and we should as readily have associated in the defence of your rights as our own, had they been separately attacked.

But Providence has mercifully allotted to depraved hearts weak under-standings: the attack has been made by the same men, at the same time,

on both together, and will serve only to draw us closer in one great band
of mutual friendship and support.

The letter, however, raised the possibility that the government might
yet resort to tactics of divide and conquer:

Whilst the Norman troops of the first William kept the English in subjection,
his English soldiers were employed to secure the obedience of the Normans.
This management has been too often repeated now to succeed.

There was a time when Scotland, though then a separate and divided
nation, could avoid the snare, and refused, even under their own Stuarts,
to enslave their antient enemies. The chains which England and Scotland
disdained to forge for each other, England and America shall never consent
to furnish.

The letter invoked the principle of "no taxation without representation," which it artfully linked to the issue of violated election
rights in the mother country: "Property is the natural right of
mankind; the connection between taxation and representation is its
necessary consequence. This connection is now broken, and taxes
are attempted to be levied, both in England and America, by men
who are not their respective representatives." The letter went on,
seditiously: "Our cause is one – our enemies are the same. We trust
our constancy and conduct will not differ. Demands which are made
without authority should be heard without obedience."[101]
It is unlikely that the squabble between Wilkes and Horne reduced
the impact of the gift from South Carolina or the response to it.
One London correspondent wrote to that colony that its grant "will,
in all Likelihood, be the best laid-out 1500 l. that ever was applied
by you; for it has given a greater Shock to the mini[steria]l Operations,
for binding Liberty in Fetters, than any one Act of the Americans
since the Stamp-Act bounced out of Pandora's Box."[102]
In the autumn of 1770 Edmund Burke grudgingly conceded that
the Bill of Rights men had become the most effective opponents of
the ministry. He wrote to Lord Rockingham that the administration
"respect and fear that wretched Knot beyond any thing you can readily
imagine, and far more than any part or than all the parts of the
[parliamentary] opposition."[103] In early 1771, however, it seemed as
if the society might collapse from internal dissension. On 26 February
1771 Wilkes and his supporters contrived to secure a resolution that
no new subscriptions were to be opened by the Bill of Rights group
for any purpose other than the discharge of his debts. This blatant
attempt to narrow the society's political function proved totally

unacceptable to the already disgruntled Shelburnite faction, and on 9 April 1771 its adherents seceded to form their own organization, the Constitutional Society.[104] But though now bereft of most of its rich and illustrious members, the remnant Bill of Rights Society continued to receive popular support which enabled it to maintain, even increase, its influence in London politics.

Partly responsible for maintaining the vitality of the organization was Arthur Lee, who came to play an increasingly conspicuous role in its activities. In March 1771 he had written the society's letter of thanks to the London magistrates imprisoned during the "printers' case." Following the departure of the Shelburnites, Lee, in company with Stephen Sayre and a few others, succeeded in securing the annulment of the restrictive resolution of 26 February – which, ironically, had prompted the secession – thus enabling the society to continue functioning as something more than a personal charity for John Wilkes. Soon afterwards it was reported in the *Gazetteer* that the Bill of Rights men had appointed Lee as their new secretary.[105]

Though Lee personally regretted the split in the organization and retained his regard for Lord Shelburne, he drew consolation from his assessment in June 1771 that the Bill of Rights group "flourishes still" and was "the most popular Society."[106] By this time the society had sufficiently recovered its equilibrium to contemplate its most ambitious attempt to make a common cause of domestic and colonial grievances. On 11 June 1771 the Bill of Rights men appointed a committee to formulate a list of pledges to be submitted to parliamentary candidates at the next general election. Lee was a member of this committee, and he assured his brother, Richard Henry, that he would "endeavour to include the redress of American Grievances." The full scope of his intentions is revealed in a letter he wrote to Samuel Adams, in which he not only listed a number of pledges he was proposing, but also detailed his plans for subsidizing Bill of Rights members to organize provincial corresponding societies.[107]

Samuel Adams and his associates in Boston were impressed by these proposals. Adams responded by speculating on the possibility of extending Lee's plan to include colonial organizations based on the model of the Bill of Rights society and in correspondence with it. There was clearly an element of whimsy in Adams's idea – in his own words, it was "a sudden Thought and drops undigested from my pen." It did, however, form the seed of inspiration for a less ambitious, though remarkably effective, society, the Boston Committee of Correspondence. It reveals much about the transatlantic character of radical opposition to the ministry at this time that an organization which contributed to the secession of America from

Britain was inspired by the model of a British radical society.[108] That Adams was receptive to cues from the Supporters of the Bill of Rights, moreover, suggests that there was something other than paranoia in the charges of American loyalists, such as Peter Oliver and Thomas Hutchinson, that the Boston opposition caucus received its tutelage in radical activity from London.[109]

The Bill of Rights men responded to Samuel Adams's acknowledgment of their political significance by electing a number of Americans, including Adams himself, to membership of their society. But despite its cosmopolitan outlook, the group's committee was not prepared to promote Lee's plan for a national party adhering to a common platform. Instead, it simply recommended that independent electors seek to impose the society's program on prospective members of Parliament.[110]

Lee's influence, however, was far from curtailed. He was the author of the committee's pledges and their lengthy preamble. Although Wilkes agreed with *Junius* that Lee's production was pompous and rambling, he claimed that "the majority of the members were too impatient to have something go forth in their names to the public" for any revision to be made.[111] The final document proposed ten pledges. The one relating to the colonies stated: "You shall endeavour to restore to America the essential Right of Taxation, by Representatives of their own free election; repealing the Acts passed in Violation of that Right, since the Year 1763; and the universal Excise, so notoriously incompatible with every Principle of British Liberty, which has been lately substituted in the Colonies, for the Laws of Customs."[112] The Bill of Rights Society, with Lee's guidance, thus went beyond the livery's petition of 1769 by endorsing the principle of "no taxation, without representation," and with it the whole American critique of parliament's colonial legislation.

The list of pledges also incorporated clauses relating to parliamentary reform. These included the traditional country-party palliatives of a place bill and annual parliaments; but, in addition, there was a statement that prospective MPs should commit themselves to working for a full and equal parliamentary representation. This clause represented the embodiment in a political platform of those stirrings in favour of franchise reform which had begun in the 1760s, partly in response to the Stamp Act crisis. By the spring of 1770 Beckford had refined his attack on rotten boroughs into a specific demand for equal representation – a development that quickly won popular approval. The reform program of the Bill of Rights Society, which Arthur Lee drafted, was therefore far from unheralded; but Lee himself was a zealous advocate of franchise reform, and his influence within the society may well have been crucial in this regard. In addition, Lee's advocacy of pledges was itself a direct attack on the concept of virtual representation and hence on the existence of anomalies in the electoral system which such a concept accommodated. There was an American contribution to the evolution of the English reform program, just as the Boston radicals received much of their inspiration from patriots in London. The geographical divide of the Atlantic was no barrier to the bilateral movement of both tactical and ideological influences between opponents of the ministry in London and America.

The Bill of Rights Society's formulation of its political platform came at a time when Lord North's partial repeal of the Townshend duties was threatening to induce a lull in the controversy between Whitehall and the colonies. Old grievances still rankled, however, and in 1772 new ones obtruded to revive American opposition to the government. In September of that year news reached Boston that judges of the Massachusetts Superior Court would in the future be paid from the crown's Civil List, rather than by annual assembly grants. The newly formed Boston Committee of Correspondence led the protest against this apparent attempt to undermine further the judiciary of Massachusetts and to create additional office-holders upholding the despotic interests of the administration. The new grievance was included in the committee's "List of Infringements and Violations of Rights," which was circulated around the towns of Massachusetts and received wide publicity in England. This document was even paraphrased in the staid *Gentleman's Magazine* as a means of impressing that periodical's readership that "the discontents in America, that were thought in a great measure to have subsided, begin again to break forth with more virulence than ever."[113]

The fear of the administration's opponents in Britain and America that the government was engaged in a systematic plan to extend its patronage and unconstitutional influence throughout the empire was lent additional credibility by a parliamentary bill, in early 1773, to regulate the affairs of the East India Company. Arthur Lee acquired stock in the organization and, as a proprietor, helped to organize resistance to the impending change. The Common Council of London temporarily overcame its animosity toward moneyed companies to denounce the Regulating Act as a blatant ministerial assault on the liberties of chartered corporations. In Massachusetts, in September 1773, the Boston Committee of Correspondence urged colonial solidarity with the East India Company and the City of London against the incursions of the administration.[114]

Meanwhile the Bill of Rights Society was effecting a further and emphatic demonstration of the transatlantic basis of opposition to government. In the summer of 1773 the society's manipulation, combined with an element of luck, resulted in two Americans being elected to the shrievalty of London and Middlesex. For Arthur Lee – who a year previously had become a liveryman so that he could influence more effectively the politics of the City – it was vital that sympathetic sheriffs should be returned, for they would provide the "only security by their summoning impartial Juries, in the event of any violent proceedings under the form of Law."[115] A meeting of the Supporters of the Bill of Rights on 8 June agreed to recommend Alderman John Kirkman and Stephen Sayre to the City electors as suitable candidates for sheriffs. At a subsequent nomination gathering on 17 June, the livery caucus adopted the nomination of Stephen Sayre – following what the *Middlesex Journal* of 17–19 June 1773 described as a "very warm and sensible speech" on his behalf by Arthur Lee – but chose as his running mate William Plomer, a recently elected alderman, instead of Kirkman. At the Common Hall, a week later, Sayre and Plomer were duly elected, with Kirkman declining the poll.[116] Arthur Lee wrote elatedly to Samuel Adams: "We have just carried Mr. Sayre, Sheriff for London . . . in great triumph, solely on public ground, and in the interest of the Bill of Rights. No men can be more determined in the cause of Liberty, than the Livery of London."[117]

Another success was shortly to follow. Alderman Plomer fined rather than serve as sheriff. Paragraphs shortly appeared in the press recommending as his successor, William Lee, who hitherto must have been largely unknown to the livery.[118] At a Common Hall on 3 July, Lee was unanimously returned. In his acceptance speech, he pledged that he would resist "the arbitrary encroachments . . . on our rights and privileges." A declaration of his principles published a couple of days later included the increasingly familiar warning that "it is not accidental Violation of the Laws of the Land, that should alarm us; but a systematic Plan, utterly to subvert them." For his term as sheriff, he made a public display of his attitude to Anglo-American relations by including on the decoration of his chariot the figure of "Britannia holding a Laurel Branch to America."[119]

As sheriffs, and therefore returning officers for City elections, William Lee and Stephen Sayre were able to contribute to the next metropolitan victory organized by the Bill of Rights group of behalf of the Wilkite and pro-American forces. The death in October 1773 of Sir Robert Ladbroke, an MP for London, precipitated a by-election, which provided the Bill of Rights group with its first opportunity to implement its plan of returning a parliamentary candidate pledged to support a list of radical demands. At a nomination meeting on 3 November, the Wilkites chose as their candidate Alderman Frederick Bull, a wealthy tea-dealer and lord mayor-elect. So strong was the tide of popular feeling that Lord North advised the king "that every attempt to overturn Wilkes in Guildhall will, at present, be fruitless."[120] Notwithstanding, a loyalist contender, John Roberts, was forthcoming, although the first attempt to nominate him ended in an hilarious triumph for the Wilkites. The nomination meeting called by Roberts's friends was invaded by patriots, and after scenes of "most glorious confusion," largely orchestrated by Arthur Lee, Bull, not Roberts, was declared its nominee. Roberts, undaunted, pursued his candidacy and a vigorous and acrimonious electoral battle was joined.[121]

During the course of the campaign Bull stressed his sympathies with the colonists. He argued that "the restoration of the American liberties to our meritorious brethren in the new world . . . are points of extreme importance, which every member ought to endeavour to accomplish."[122] At a livery caucus on the eve of polling day, Arthur Lee took the necessary steps to ensure that Bull's future parliamentary behaviour would reflect his avowed sentiments: the meeting accepted Lee's proposal that Bull subscribe to a previously formulated pledge. The next day, at the Guildhall, the prepared document was read, and Lee stated that Bull was prepared to sign it or to give it any other sanction.[123] The pledge, for reasons which are unclear, was much briefer and contained fewer articles than the one originally produced by the Bill of Rights Society in the summer of 1771. Bull vowed that, if elected, he would refuse any emolument from the crown; he also undertook to promote shorter parliaments, the exclusion of placemen from the House of Commons, and a more equal system of parliamentary representation; by the fourth article he promised to try to "redress the Grievances, and secure the Constitutional Rights of my fellow Subjects in *Great Britain, Ireland*, and *America*."[124]

During the poll the advantage to Bull's candidacy of sympathetic sheriffs was amply demonstrated. An elector who made an apparently justified complaint that a voter for Bull was not a liveryman was seized by William Lee, put in the charge of a constable, and detained for several hours, while the illegitimate voter made his escape. Because of such incidents, the supporters of Roberts demanded a scrutiny of the final result – a narrow victory for Bull. The scrutiny was suspended, however, when the sheriffs refused Roberts's demand to be represented by counsel, and the result stood.[125] The tensions created by the contest between Bull and Roberts, and a heightened awareness of the connection between colonial and domestic grievances, coloured even the Common Council elections at the end of the year. One candidate for Farringdon Without Ward was denounced in the press as a turncoat for supporting Roberts in the recent poll: "Remember your wishes of revenge on your first hearing of the massacre at Boston," chided the anonymous correspondent.[126]

On the eve of the Boston Tea Party, the colonial cause was prospering in London. The Supporters of the Bill of Rights had expressed their full support for the ministry's opponents in America, while continuing to promote programs of parliamentary reform that were partly inspired by American examples and the apparent lessons of the imperial controversy. There were clear signs, moreover, that the agitation of the Bill of Rights members and their allies in the press was making an impression on London's population, many of whom required little persuasion that the government's habitually despotic tendencies were becoming manifest in North America. The activity of committed Wilkites, both American and British, was to ensure that when the imperial storm finally broke, not all Englishmen would be driven into the loyalist camp.

CHAPTER THREE

The Coming of War,
1774–1775

THE BOSTON TEA PARTY AND ITS AFTERMATH

The period of comparative tranquillity in Anglo-American relations which followed the partial repeal of the Townshend duties was shattered at the end of 1773 by an incident deriving from a seemingly innocuous transaction by Lord North's administration. In order to alleviate the financial distress of the East India Company, the government included a provision in the Regulating Act which excused the company payment of the ninepence duty on the tea it imported into Britain. The company was also permitted to by-pass the middlemen, who normally handled the reexport trade, and send the tea to America on its own account. By thus reducing the cost of the commodity it was hoped that the company's tea would find a wide market in the colonies.[1]

The threepence duty on tea imported into America – the surviving element of the Townshend duties – was, however, retained, thus provoking the wrath of colonial radicals who regarded the whole transaction as an insidious attempt by the government to confirm Parliament's right to impose external taxation. The colonial response was swift and dramatic. In Boston, patriots dumped the first shipload of tea dispatched under the new scheme into the harbour.

This Boston Tea Party was a blatant repudiation of the government's authority, and Lord North and his colleagues saw no alternative to a policy of retaliatory punishment, until appropriate redress was forthcoming from Boston. Even "moderates" in the government, notably the colonial secretary, Lord Dartmouth, favoured such a course of action. The coercive policy that the government attempted to impose was based on four pieces of legislation passed between March and June of 1774: the Boston Port Act, which closed the town's port; the Administration of Justice Act, which gave the governor of Massachusetts discretion to allow the transfer of trials to England; the Massachusetts Government Act, which stipulated that the province's council would henceforth be appointed by the king, rather than elected by the lower chamber, and that town meetings could be held only once a year, except by special permission of the governor; and the Quartering Act (applying to all the colonies), which allowed for the accommodation of troops in occupied dwellings.

The passage of this legislation was facilitated by a hardening of public opinion against the Americans which found a reflection in both Houses of Parliament. Two letters from Benjamin Franklin to Thomas Cushing, a colonial correspondent – one written before the Boston Tea Party and one after – illustrate the shift in popular mood. On 1 November 1773 Franklin wrote: "The general Sense of the Nation is for us; a Conviction prevailing that we have been ill-us'd, and that a Breach with us would be ruinous to this Country." But on 22 March 1774 he was writing: "I suppose we never had since we were a People so few Friends in Britain. The violent Destruction of the Tea seems to have united all Parties here against our Province."[2]

Franklin himself experienced at first hand the bitterness aroused by the activities of his compatriots. In 1772 he had acquired by devious means, and then sent to Boston, letters written by Thomas Hutchinson and Andrew Oliver which apparently showed that these two Massachusetts officials bore heavy responsibility for the unsympathetic attitude of the British government towards the province. The Massachusetts House of Representatives consequently petitioned the king for their removal. At a resumed session of the Privy Council committee to hear the petition – on 29 January 1774, a few days after the arrival of news about the Boston Tea Party – Franklin was excoriated by the crude wit of Alexander Wedderburn, the solicitor-general, whose performance clearly delighted the other committee members. The Massachusetts petition was rejected, and Franklin lost his sinecure as deputy post-master general for America. It is indicative of a growing polarization of attitudes that the treatment of Franklin gave him a status akin to a martyred hero in the colonies, whereas in England his case generated little popular sympathy.[3]

The political climate which led to the public disgrace of Franklin also inhibited the parliamentary opposition from making a frontal assault on the government's coercive policy.[4] The Rockingham Whigs, moreover, were hidebound by their continued adherence to the concept of parliamentary supremacy expressed in the Declaratory Act and by their own alarm at the militancy of colonial opposition. "The conduct of the Americans can not be justified," wrote Rockingham.[5] Hence the Rockinghamites scarcely resisted the passage of the Boston Port Act, although they did pursue a more vigorous, if ineffective, opposition to the Administration of Justice Act and the Massachusetts Government Act.[6]

The Shelburnites were similarly erratic in their response to the government's legislation. Lord Shelburne and his protégé in the House of Commons, Isaac Barré, even supported the Boston Port Act. Indeed, such was the attitude of Lord Shelburne and his friends at this stage that rumours gained currency that the group was about to join the administration. With subsequent legislation the Shelburnites shifted markedly from acquiescing in a policy of coercion, although, according to Horace Walpole, they did so only after their mentor, Lord Chatham, had clearly indicated his disapproval of the Boston measures.[7]

How far in early 1774 did public opinion in London diverge from that in the rest of the country and in Parliament? And to what extent did the City patriots escape the uncertainties of the parties of parliamentary opposition, and continue to assert a vigorous support for the colonists' resistance to imperial authority?

Many Londoners clearly shared the distaste of the rest of the country at the Bostonians' apparently wanton destruction of property, and there is little doubt that the Boston Tea Party was a serious, if temporary, check to the growth of the pro-American movement on a popular basis. It tainted the image of colonial innocence that was so central to the pro-American interpretation of the imperial impasse and threatened to produce a mass desertion of the commercial interest from the colonial cause. Although the London press continued to express support for the Americans, this was probably thanks to the energy of colonists such as Benjamin Franklin and was not the reflection of a widespread sentiment.[8] "There is not a more obnoxious character here at present, than that of a friend to America," wrote one observer from the metropolis in early 1774. A colonist in London reported that the inhabitants were so exasperated that it was scarcely possible to communicate with them.[9] William Lee, whose comments were presumably based on his observations of London society, took a rather less jaundiced view: he wrote to Samuel Adams that "in the middling ranks a great deal of the old English Virtue remains & among them your friends are numerous"; but he also thought that "the highest & lowest ranks ... are so totally debauch'd & tainted with Scotch principles that no good can be expected from them."[10]

Probably because of the limited support for the colonists in early 1774, the City, in its corporate capacity, did not petition against any of the four Coercive Acts during their legislative passage.

But although the Boston Tea Party checked the growth of the pro-American movement in London, it by no means destroyed it. The committed patriots kept the cause alive until public opinion in London was again receptive to their arguments. They refused to indict the Bostonians for destroying the East India Company's tea because, they strenuously claimed, the government had deliberately intended to provoke such a violent reaction in order to furnish a pretext for coercing Massachusetts. This interpretation of events was expressed in April 1775 by Frederick Bull, who, as a tea-dealer, might have been adversely affected by the circumvention of English merchants in the dispatch of tea to the colonies. He stated in the Commons: "I own I cannot be brought to believe that the Tea was sent to Boston to raise money for the Company, to get rid of their load of Tea, or to prevent smuggling, because each of these salutary ends might have been answered without injustice, or offence to any individual. - The purpose for which the Tea was sent to America, and the consequences, are evident now to every man's understanding."[11] Bull himself considered he had tested the good faith of the administration - and found it wanting - by offering, in collaboration with some other merchants, to indemnify the East India Company for more than twice the value of the tea destroyed in Boston. Lord North deemed the offer unacceptable, unless the merchants could make themselves responsible for the future peaceful conduct of the Bostonians - a condition which the merchants, not surprisingly, refused.[12]

During the debate on the Boston Port Act another patriot alderman, John Sawbridge - who was soon to rejoin the mainstream Wilkites - was the only member of the House of Commons specifically to deny that England had the right to tax America; his speech on this theme was persistently interrupted by coughing.[13] At times during the session Sawbridge's language became almost treasonable; in the debate on the administration of justice bill he declared: "I plainly foresee the dangerous consequences of this Bill; it is meant to enslave America; and the same Minister who means to enslave them, would, if he had an opportunity, enslave England; it is his aim, and what he wishes to do; but I sincerely hope the Americans will not admit of the execution of these destructive Bills, but nobly refuse them."[14]

Other MPs from the metropolitan opposition, who did not share Sawbridge's pretensions to parliamentary eloquence, attempted to help their American friends by promoting their petitions in the House of Commons. Their efforts were indicative of attitudes only, and not productive of results, because, in Michael Kammen's words, "In March 1774 the petition as a means of redressing Anglo-American distress began to gasp its last breaths."[15] The petitions to Parliament and the king against the coercive legislation came from two main sources: the native Americans in London, organized by the Lee coterie, and William Bollan, on behalf of the Massachusetts Council.

Bollan requested General Conway and then Sir George Savile to present his first petition against the Boston Port Act to the House of Commons; but both these Rockinghamites refused to do so, General Conway on the grounds that "violence & disorders in the Colonies laid difficulties in the way of their friends obtaining the relief they wanted." The City patriots, however, proved more accommodating to the Massachusetts agent. Frederick Bull "very readily & kindly promised to present" Bollan's petition, and, although the recently elected member for London later demurred because of his unfamiliarity with House of Commons procedure, the address was sponsored by another Wilkite, Sir Joseph Mawbey, and duly put before the House on 25 March, where it was read, laid on the table, and subsequently ignored.[16] A motion of 21 March by Sir Joseph Mawbey that Bollan be allowed to speak in support of his petition was disallowed. Bollan's next petition was offered to the Commons by Alderman Brass Crosby, but the House refused to receive it on the grounds that Bollan, as agent for only one section of the Massachusetts legislature, had inadequate credentials for seeking redress on behalf of the province.[17]

Subsequent petitions from Bollan and Americans in London against coercive measures were sponsored in the Commons by the Rockinghamites, Sir George Savile and William Dowdeswell, and in the Lords by the duke of Richmond, Lord Shelburne, and the earl of Stair.[18] But the belated support of the major groups of parliamentary opposition for colonial protest stood in revealing contrast to the consistent attitude displayed, in defiance of prevailing public sentiment, by the handful of metropolitan radicals in the House of Commons.

It is questionable, however, if the pro-American movement could have been reestablished by the Wilkites on a popular basis had it not been for a further piece of legislation, which, in motive, had no connection with the government's policy of coercion. On 2 May a bill "making more effectual provision for the government of the province of Quebec" was introduced into the House of Lords; it passed into law on 22 June. The main purpose of the legislation was to provide a permanent civil government for Canada and stabilize frontier relations with the Indians – problems which had remained unresolved since the acquisition of France's North American territories

during the Seven Years' War. But the good intentions prompting
the legislation were obscured for its critics by the nature of its content.
For the act – in keeping with the French traditions of the province
– vested legislative authority in a nominated council, allowed the
Roman Catholic church to retain its privileges, and restored French
civil law; the boundaries of Quebec, moreover, were extended south-
ward to the Ohio River.[19]

The Quebec bill provided a golden opportunity for the patriot
leaders to recover support eroded by the Boston Tea Party. The
government's intention to create an authoritarian and Catholic polity
to the north and west of the British colonies could be readily portrayed
as part of an overall scheme to impose despotic government on the
whole of North America. John Dunning, a Shelburnite, expressed
these suspicions in the House of Commons when he remarked that
the act "carries in its breast something that squints and looks
dangerous to the other inhabitants of that country, our own colonies."[20] The same misgivings were repeated "out of doors" in stronger
vein, with the additional, and inflammatory, patriot refrain that the
legislation was a capitulation to incipient popish tendencies within
the administration. William Lee thought that the measure might
prove "as fatal to Lord North as the excise scheme was to Sir R.
Walpole." Lee played his part in stimulating opposition "by keeping
a continual fire in the papers" against the act.[21] Wild rumours –
for some of which Lee may have been responsible – abounded in
the London press. The earl of Bute was predictably indicted as the
true author of the bill, and a story was even credited that the pope
would be sending "a letter of thanks to his Majesty for his piety
in promoting and establishing the Roman Catholic religion, as the
national church in America."[22]

During the passage of the bill the Common Council of London
echoed, and perhaps helped to stimulate, popular protest, by petitioning against it. At a Common Council meeting on 3 June only
"Alderman [Walter] Rawlinson, who however did not venture a single
word in support of his opinion," opposed a petition to the House
of Commons requesting that the bill should not pass into law.[23] After
its passage through both Houses of Parliament the Common Council
framed another, more forcefully expressed, petition to the king,
demanding that he withhold his royal assent to the bill. This address
described the Quebec legislation as "entirely subversive of the great
fundamental principles of the Constitution of the British Monarchy
as well as of the authority of the solemn acts of the Legislature";
it remainded the king that the Hanoverian line had been called to
the throne in order to exclude the Roman Catholic Stuarts and that

his acceptance of the bill would contravene his coronation oath; it declared further that vesting legislative power in Quebec in a royally appointed council was "repugnant to the leading Principles of the free constitution by which alone your Majesty now holds or legally can hold the imperial Crown of these Realms."[24] The two sheriffs attended the king to know when the City's petition might be delivered, and Stephen Sayre, according to his own account, "gave high offence ... by going out of the common Form, in telling his Majesty what was the Prayer of the Petition" before it had been formally presented.[25]

The twenty-second of June was assigned for receipt of the address – the same day that the Quebec bill was to receive the royal assent and Parliament to be prorogued for the summer recess. George III neatly evaded the necessity of replying to the City's petition by instructing the lord chamberlain to inform the petitioners that he could not "take Public Notice [of the bill] until it is presented to him for his Royal Assent in Parliament."[26] But the king could not so easily escape the attentions of the City mob. According to Horace Walpole,

the Anti-Court party in the City had intended a procession to affront and go before the King to the House, and had prepared to carry figures of the Pope and the Devil; but the Government getting wind of the design, it was laid aside. The mob, however was very abusive, and some persons, dressed at least like gentlemen, held out their fists at the King, and cried out 'Remember Charles I! Remember James II!' ... The King was so hurt and alarmed, that when he came to the Lords he trembled, he faltered, and could scarcely pronounce his Speech.[27]

It was also reported, by Thomas Young, a visiting American, that the mob cried out *"no Roman-catholic King: no Roman catholic religion! America forever!"*[28]

The Supporters of the Bill of Rights attempted to capitalize on the passions aroused over the Quebec Act by forcing on the livery two virtually unknown candidates, George Grieve and John Williams, for the shrievalty in the midsummer elections of 1774. A press campaign was quickly organized on their behalf which stressed the two men's opposition to popery in general and the Quebec Act in particular.[29] John Williams, at the opening of the poll on 24 June, played on the popular theme: he stated that he "stepped forth to offer his services to his country, in these perilous times, when Administration were attempting to overturn it, by introducing Popery to be established in a part of his Majesty's dominions."[30] Notwithstanding such appeals, however, John Hart and Alderman Plomer

– who had the combined support of the ministerial and Shelburnite factions and were well known in civic life – were returned for the office of sheriff.[31]

But although the Wilkites overplayed their hand in the shrieval elections, the antiministerial and pro-American attitudes generated by the Quebec Act gave no sign of quickly abating. On 28 July the Middlesex electors demonstrated their bellicose inclinations by toasting "a Smithfield warming to the Popish framers of the Quebec bill."[32] The offending legislation was not only denounced in itself; it also threw into a new, and more sinister, perspective the Coercive Acts, which at first had generally been received in London with indifference or even approval.[33] This shift in attitude was to find ample expression during the election campaign of 1774.

THE PARLIAMENTARY ELECTIONS OF 1774

The parliamentary elections of 1774 provided the metropolitan opposition with the opportunity to extend its influence in the House of Commons; and an analysis of the campaign enables historians to assess the impact of the patriot and pro-American platform on the electorate in London and elsewhere.

The announcement of dissolution on 30 September anticipated the natural expiration of Parliament by six months. The administration opted for a premature election in order to have a fresh legislature to deal with new American business and also to prevent opposition from properly organizing its electoral resources.[34] But it is difficult to see how the Wilkites' chances in the election would have been improved if Parliament had been allowed to run its full course. It is true that Arthur Lee was travelling in Europe at the time of dissolution and was thus prevented from playing a leading role in the metropolitan campaign, but the Supporters of the Bill of Rights had been ready for over three years with a political manifesto and list of pledges to be imposed on candidates. In addition, a meeting of the Bill of Rights Society on 23 August 1774 resolved that its Committee of Correspondence should communicate with the high sheriffs of counties and returning officers of boroughs – presumably with the intention of seeking opportunities to implement its program – and that correct parliamentary division lists on a number of public questions should be drawn up, so that the voting records of sitting members could be properly judged by the electorate. An early dissolution, moreover, reduced the chances of the government itself organizing an efficient campaign in the metropolitan constituencies, as Lord North, who had misgivings about the early election, had argued vainly with the king.[35]

The campaign of the metropolitan radicals opened in Middlesex. Sheriffs Lee and Sayre summoned a meeting of the county electors for 26 September, the advertisement for the gathering appearing ten days before the announcement that Parliament was to be dissolved.[36] It is not clear whether the meeting was convened in response to the prevailing rumours of impending dissolution, but it had the effect of forestalling any serious attempt by the government to challenge Wilkite domination in the county. The freeholders met in an atmosphere of crisis and imagined persecution. One of them expressed the hope that the electors would meet together as often as possible, "as it was very likely in a short time a stop would be put to their meeting at all." An interpretation of his remarks in the *London Evening Post* linked this prediction with the recent restrictions on town meetings imposed by the Massachusetts Government Act: "Under George the Third, the Select Men in America are forbid to assemble in their town meetings; so that the conjecture of a gentleman yesterday at the Mile End assembly room, who said we very probably may not in a little time be allowed to meet at all, is not without foundation, as oppressors never love their conduct to be examined into."[37]

Debate at the Middlesex meeting, attended by an estimated three hundred to four hundred people, focused on whether candidates should adhere to a previously prepared pledge, which was a briefer and substantially modified version of that prepared by the Supporters of the Bill of Rights in 1771.[38] The Middlesex engagement bound candidates, if elected, to seek to restore government to the form adopted at the Revolution of 1688; to promote parliamentary reform by shorter parliaments, the exclusion of placemen and pensioners from the House of Commons, and a more equitable distribution of seats; and to vindicate the injured rights of electors, presumably by reversing the decision which excluded John Wilkes from the House of Commons.

The most controversial plank, however, was that which bound candidates to promote repeal of the Coercive and Quebec acts.[39] Debate among the freeholders concerning this article of the pledge revealed majority, though not unanimous, support for the colonists and indicated that resentments aroused by the Boston Tea Party had not entirely abated. A Mr Staples, aggrieved because the Americans, in a past phase of nonimportation, had returned some of his goods to England, argued that repeal of the Boston Port Act would effectively ensure that Americans would make no contribution to the cost of empire. But his views received little support; he was interrupted by general hissing, and it was reported that "nearly every one present thought our taxing of the colonies illegal."[40] A following speaker argued that "the Americans were always ready to pay for their support, but they objected to the mode of paying under the taxation of the British Parliament; that the Boston Port Bill was not a money bill, but intended as a punishment upon a great number for the crime of a few, which their greatest enemies owned to be unreasonable, and excessively beyond the deserts of that few." Henry Maskall, an inveterate opponent of the ministry, condemned government policy more emphatically. He saw in the Quebec bill "the old Prostitute, the Whore of Babylon" and he denounced Lord North as a "Butcher of a Minister."[41]

After further debate the meeting resolved to bind the candidates to the articles of the engagement. Only six freeholders opposed this vote. John Wilkes and John Glynn were then nominated and accepted as candidates.[42]

Despite vague hopes on the part of the ministry that some government candidates might be found, nobody in the event had the temerity to oppose the joint nominees of the freeholders' meeting, and Wilkes and Glynn were returned as members for Middlesex on 20 October.[43] On this occasion the ministry made no attempt to prevent Wilkes from taking his seat, and he thus finally became the legal representative of the county for which he had first been elected over six years before. The *London Evening Post* of 18–20 October 1774 gave credit for this triumph to the Americans: "The reason of Mr. Wilkes not being opposed in Middlesex, did not arise from any remission in the politics of the cabinet, but the great cloud threatening themselves from the other side of the Atlantic, which will cut them out enough work this ensuing session, without raising a ferment at home; so that ... *the rights of the Freeholders of Middlesex are restored by the resistance, and spirit of the Americans.*"

The London patriots also achieved success in the election of MPs for the City, where support for the colonists was again expressed as a conspicuous feature of their program. The morale of the Wilkites had been boosted at the beginning of October by the triumph of John Wilkes in the mayoral contest. This success also brought with it practical benefits – "the Lord-Mayor having it in his power to ensure a certain number of votes in his interest" during a parliamentary election.[44]

The patriot campaign in the City was conducted in a mood of popular excitement. The *London Evening Post* of 29 September–1 October 1775 declared that "there never was a time when the citizens of London so universally inclined to the popular side," for which the paper credited the growing unpopularity of the American measures. To stimulate public opinion, as they appraised it, the same newspaper issue headed its columns with such slogans as, "No Popery Members; No Unrepealers of the Quebec and Boston Acts."[45] A potential ministerial candidate, Sir James Esdaile, was deterred from running by the expressions of support for the colonists which he encountered during a preliminary canvass; one elector - Mr Hudson, a cheesemonger - told him that "he would not vote for any popery in Canada and shutting up the port of Boston."[46]

On 3 October some two thousand liverymen met at the Guildhall to nominate parliamentary candidates.[47] The chairman of the meeting, Luke Stavely, a Wilkite Common Councilman for Bread Street Ward, declared in his opening speech "that the eyes of the whole nation were upon them," and he urged the livery to elect only "known friends to liberty, not by profession but experience." In the sole reference to contemporary political issues in his speech, he cited American resistance to ministerial tyranny as a proper model for imitation by the livery: "Were we only to cast our eyes to America, we should see to what a dreadful situation those brave people were reduced through the iniquitous conduct of the late corrupt Houses of Parliament; that the unanimity the Americans have shewn to resist all such arbitrary acts, and the noble struggle they make to preserve their liberties ought to be an example to us; that we might depend upon it the persons who wished to enslave America, would, if it lay in their power, shackle us." A list of pledges, drawn up by a committee of the livery, was then read, and signed by four of the candidates: Frederick Bull, Brass Crosby, George Hayley, and John Sawbridge. Sawbridge had previously been reconciled to John Wilkes and had not opposed him in the recent mayoral election. The test was longer than the one signed by Wilkes and Glynn. It contained the same clauses relating to parliamentary reform, and it also bound its signatories to promote legislation subjecting each candidate to an oath against using bribery to secure a seat in the House of Commons. In addition, it pledged prospective MPs to follow the instructions of the livery in their parliamentary conduct. The clause which bound candidates to promote the repeal of the Coercive and Quebec acts was identical to that in the Middlesex engagement, but the London test also required the promotion of a bill "for restoring to our fellow subjects in America the essential right of Taxation by Representatives of their own free election, and for repealing the universal excise, which has been lately substituted in the Colonies, instead of the Laws of Customs."[48]

Present at the same meeting was another parliamentary candidate,

William Baker, who had been sheriff in the Rockingham interest in 1770-1. He did not, however, sign the pledge for reasons which reflected the views of his political patrons. He declared that he agreed with the articles in favour of the Americans; his objection to signing was based on his opposition to the proposed exclusion of placemen and pensioners from the House of Commons and on the broader ground that an MP should be the keeper of his own conscience. His views received no sympathy from the livery, who interrupted his speech with cries of "sign or decline." William Lee, in retort to Baker, asserted that "when a person becomes your Representative he is your servant, and consequently ought to do as his masters direct."[49]

The meeting concluded with the nomination of the four signatories to the pledge, and the livery present agreed to support their candidature jointly. William Baker and the four Wilkite nominees in the election were later joined by two other aspirants: Richard Oliver, the Constitutional Society's candidate, and the ministerialist, John Roberts. Alderman Harley, who had represented the City since 1761, declined to stand, choosing instead to continue his parliamentary career from the tranquillity of Herefordshire.[50] Oliver signed his own pledge to promote limited parliamentary reform and promised never to accept any place or pension from the ministry. In addition, he published an advertisement in the press stating that he agreed with all the clauses of the Wilkite pledge, except the article which bound members to accept instructions from Common Hall. A public meeting which supported his candidature singled out for praise "his determined opposition" to the Quebec and Coercive acts.[51]

Thus, of the seven candidates for City seats, six can be classified as pro-Americans, although the political stance of two of them, Richard Oliver and William Baker, differed somewhat from that of the orthodox Wilkites. The poll was closed after seven days, on 15 October, with the sole ministerial contender, John Roberts, languishing at the foot of it. Sawbridge, Hayley, Oliver, and Bull were elected; Crosby was the only adherent of the Wilkite pledge not to secure a seat.[52]

The patriots achieved less success across the Thames in the borough of Southwark. Here one of the candidates was William Lee, whose term as sheriff had just expired. Lee, along with Nathaniel Polhill, a tobacco merchant, signed, at a meeting of Southwark electors, the same pledge as the City candidates. In a speech to the electors Lee reiterated his theme of the previous day that MPs should be totally subordinate to the wishes of their constituents. Lee, however, was unsuccessful in the contest, coming third in the poll behind Polhill and Henry Thrale, a Southwark distiller, who had refused to sign the engagement.[53]

A further check to patriot ambitions occurred in the democratic constituency of Westminster, where the Wilkites appeared to have a position of some strength. They chose two young noblemen – Lord Mountmorres and Lord Mahon – as their candidates. Even before the nomination meeting at Westminster Hall on 4 October, Lord Mahon promised, in a handbill soliciting support, to promote if elected the repeal of the Quebec and Coercive acts and the reestablishment of concord between Britain and its colonies.[54] At the nomination meeting Mahon and Mountmorres, together with Humphrey Cotes (a friend of Wilkes but running without the backing of the Wilkite machine), signed an engagement which was longer than the London and Southwark pledge, but identical to it on the question of America.[55] The meeting nominated Mahon and Mountmorres, but the government after some difficulty was able to find two formidable candidates – Lord Percy (the son of the duke of Northumberland) and Lord Clinton (the son of the duke of Newcastle) – to oppose them.[56]

Despite a vigorous campaign by Mahon, Percy and Clinton were eventually elected after a long and turbulent poll. Their success was probably due to the enormous patronage exercised by the crown and the Newcastle and Northumberland families in Westminster, and to well-organized electioneering by the government and its allies.[57]

There is evidence, however, that the American policy of the ministry was an embarrassment, not an asset, to its campaign in Westminster. During the election Lord Percy was serving with his regiment under General Gage in Boston, and this fact was exploited by his opponents. A paragraph in the *Gazetteer* of 15 October 1774 repeated a rumour "that a horrid butchery had been committed upon the poor inhabitants [of Boston]" and added "that Lord Percy, the Court Candidate, is second in command upon that expedition." Of more significance was the response by Percy's supporters to such innuendo: an advertisement on Percy's behalf declared that "his Lordship disapproved those very measures, which rendered the present service necessary," and his humanity toward the Bostonians was stressed by his promoters.[58]

London radicals also attempted to extend their influence outside the metropolis, but they met with only limited success. Their campaign was, however, in Bernard Donoughue's words, "perhaps the most interesting political feature of the elections ... because they almost alone raised the American issue."[59] Candidates subscribed to Wilkite, or similar, engagements in at least five constituencies outside

London, and there was patriot activity elsewhere. In Worcester, Sir Watkin Lewes, a Wilkite alderman, came near to victory after mobilizing the support of the freemen electors of Worcester resident in London and subscribing on the hustings to a radical political engagement. In the Bedford contest the leadership of the Constitutional Society attempted a similar tactic with more success: a gathering of the Bedford freemen resident in London, at which John Horne and Alderman Townsend were present, agreed to support the candidature of Sir William Wake and Robert Sparrow, on condition that they subscribed to a prepared test. Their election was carried mainly by the support of these nonresident freemen, although Sparrow was later disqualified on petition from his opponents.[60]

Other constituencies where candidates pledged themselves to support reform and oppose the American measures were Cambridge, where two Wilkite candidates were heavily defeated, and Surrey, where Sir Joseph Mawbey was narrowly beaten. In Newcastle the two unsuccessful candidates signed a pledge in favour of parliamentary reform and associated issues, but the American question was apparently not raised; in this constituency local grievances dominated the contest.[61]

The Wilkites achieved a success in Dover, a seat they had long coveted. Their candidate, John Trevanion, a friend of John Wilkes and a Supporter of the Bill of Rights, was returned unopposed.[62] There is nothing to indicate, however, that he subscribed to a radical engagement before his nomination.

The American issue was probably raised in a handful of other constituencies. It is probable that Stephen Sayre expressed opposition to the coercive measures in his campaign at Seaford; in this contest he secured a majority of votes, but these were adjudged on petition to be illegal and he lost the election. His defeat especially disappointed Frederick Bull, who felt Sayre "would have made the Treasury bench prick up their Ears ... if he had gain'd his seat."[63] In Milbourne Port, Temple Luttrell, an outspoken pro-American, fought a successful campaign in which he indicted the government's American policy, although it is doubtful if this aspect of his platform contributed in any way to his success.[64] In Bristol, by contrast, the American question was clearly important to an electorate so heavily dependent on colonial trade. Here the two successful candidates were an American, Henry Cruger, and Edmund Burke. Cruger behaved during the campaign like an outspoken Wilkite, although he later became a government pensioner and moderated his opposition to the administration's American policy.[65] Burke was supported explicitly for his conciliatory attitude towards America, but his position on the colonies differed markedly from that of the patriots. Unlike them he took pains to emphasize the absolute legislative supremacy of Great Britain over America. On the first day of his arrival on the hustings he declared: "I have held, and ever shall maintain, to the best of my power, unimpaired and undiminished, the just, wise, and necessary constitutional superiority of Great Britain. This is necessary for America, as well as for us. I never mean to depart from it."[66]

The evidence of the election campaign of 1774 tends to confirm that organized support for the colonists was largely confined to London. In most places, with a few exceptions such as Bristol, there is no evidence that colonial aspirations were treated with anything other than apathy or hostility.[67] The election left John Wilkes with about a dozen supporters in the Commons, which ensured that patriot opposition to the administration would remain essentially an extra-parliamentary force.

MERCHANTS AND DISSENTERS

With the new Parliament firmly under the control of Lord North, the best possibility for any reversal in government policy appeared to many to rest with the merchants trading to North America – the group that had played a key role (albeit under the tutelage of a sympathetic ministry) in repealing the Stamp Act. Expatriate Americans and their patriot friends sustained the hope, increasingly desperate though it became, that an appeal to the merchants' self-interest, if not to ideological conviction, would yet bring them into the pro-American camp. While this effort continued, other organized campaigns on behalf of the colonists went into abeyance.

With few exceptions, however, the merchants trading to North America – as distinct from the smaller merchants and tradesmen of the capital – proved reluctant to manifest any support for disaffected Americans. Letters from Americans in London lamented the absence of merchant sympathy, while at the same time they gave encouraging assessments of pro-American feeling among the population at large.[68] In 1774 the Atlantic traders made virtually no organized response of any kind to the government's colonial policy. Only the merchants trading to Quebec petitioned as a group against what they felt was obnoxious legislation, and their protest was limited to the single ground that the reestablishment of French civil law in Canada, under the Quebec Act, would inhibit their commercial enterprises.[69] Those trading to New England seemed especially reluctant to question government colonial policy. According to William Lee, there would "have been a full petition from the Merchts. and Traders in London [against the Boston Port Bill], had it not been from [*sic*] all the Boston Merchts., except Mr. [Thomas] Bromfield ... refusing absolutely to take the lead or any part in such petition."[70]

The quiescence of the merchants was puzzling and vexatious to the English friends of America. Edmund Burke wrote to Lord Rockingham in September 1774 that "the insensibility of the Merchants of London is of a degree and kind scarcely to be conceived. Even those who are the most likely to be overwhelmed by any real American confusion are amongst the most supine."[71] How, then, can one account for the merchants' inaction? An explanation sometimes proffered is that Atlantic trade was becoming relatively less important in the general context of Britain's overseas commerce and that there was, in consequence, less urgency for the merchant community to take a strong stand on behalf of American complaints. Colonial embargoes and the impact of the financial crash of 1772, so the argument goes, eroded commerce with America, at the same time as trade was expanding elsewhere, particularly with Asia.[72]

Statistics, however, do not bear out such an interpretation. From 1771 to 1774 (inclusive), over 18 per cent by value of total exports from England and Wales went to the mainland American colonies. This figure compares with just over 12 per cent for the period 1762-5 and 10.5 per cent for the period 1750-3. The financial crisis of 1772 certainly had a curtailing effect on exports, and it probably discouraged a number of merchants from extending easy credit to colonial customers, but in 1773 the colonists were still purchasing more British goods than in any year prior to the Seven Years' War.[73]

Imports from the American colonies (including the West Indies) similarly expanded from prewar levels. In 1752-4 the Atlantic empire provided just under 33 per cent by value of total goods imported into Britain; by 1772-4 it furnished over 37 per cent of British imports. Moreover, the expansion of Britain's trade with the Orient before the American war mainly involved the import of commodities which were not competitive with, or substitutes for, American products such as tobacco and naval stores; and while it may be true that the Second British Empire was portended even while the First British Empire was collapsing, such a phenomenon had little meaning for merchants still heavily committed to Atlantic trade.[74]

The inactivity of London merchants in 1774 was thus clearly not the result of indifference about the perceived impact of a possible breakdown in American commerce. On the contrary, most colonial traders dreaded, with good reason, the consequences of confrontation between government and the colonists. But they were not thereby induced to support American resistance, in part because few of them

even privately supported it.[75] Despite some misgivings about aspects
of administration colonial policy in the 1760s, the Atlantic merchants,
in general, did not share with smaller traders and craftsmen those
historical feelings of estrangement from central government which
encouraged pro-American attitudes in the capital. Apparently gra-
tuitous ministerial assaults on the interests of Atlantic commerce,
such as the Stamp Act, were anathema even to loyal traders; but in
the alignment of imperial interest groups, London merchants and
the British government could also combine to thwart the aspirations
of colonial businessmen. In 1764 the "hard money" policies of the
Board of Trade, together with the anxiety of metropolitan traders
to protect the value of their colonial credit, gave rise to the Currency
Act which extended prohibition against paper money to the southern
and middle colonies. This legislation posed great problems for some
colonial merchants and southern planters who were confronted with
a dire shortage of circulating currency. The controversy over paper
money, in the words of one commentator, manifested "the existence
of a direct and fundamental conflict of interest between the British
and American commercial classes."[76]

The money policy of Whitehall was one aspect of a system of
trade regulation on the continuance of which most Atlantic traders
assumed their prosperity depended. In the years following the repeal
of the Stamp Act, American challenges to British authority posed
an apparent threat to the legal basis on which this system was
constructed, even though the Acts of Trade were not formally challenged by the colonists until after the outbreak of the American War
of Independence. In the wake of the Boston Tea Party, William Knox,
an influential undersecretary at the American Department, concluded
a strongly argued pamphlet with the statement that "the continuance
of their [i.e., the English merchants' and manufacturers'] trade to
the Colonies, clearly and entirely depends on the laws of England
having authority there. It is their operation which binds the commerce
of the Colonies to this country. It is their operation which gives
security to the property of the trader sent thither. Give up the authority
of Parliament and there is an end to your trade, and a total loss
of your property."[77] In these years before free trade theories had begun
to be seriously promulgated, let alone broadly accepted, such a
vigorous defence of orthodox mercantilism must have seemed very
convincing to a wide section of the British commercial community.

Many merchants, moreover, were bound to the government by
considerations more immediate than broad philosophical agreement
over the proper legal basis for Britain's trading empire. They were
quite simply loath to criticize in any way an administration on whose

charity they might in the future have to depend. It was in the government's interest that stories should circulate about its intentions to assist financially merchants adversely affected by the colonial crisis. One such rumour appeared in the *Middlesex Journal*, where it was reported "that the subscription for the tickets in the ensuing lottery are to be given to the American merchants to make them recompense for the damage they will sustain by the three Boston bills."[78] Lord North himself reportedly hinted that the government would assume responsibility for the plight of traders – although presumably only those of a loyalist cast – who were affected by any breakdown in empire.[79]

In view of the grave prospects that confronted them, it is not surprising that Lord Dartmouth's correspondence contains a number of letters from merchants anxious to show their fundamentally loyalist disposition. William Molleson, who traded with the Chesapeake and succeeded in retaining a reputation as a pro-American, commenced a correspondence with that end in view in August 1774.[80] The most revealing case, however, is that of Dennis deBerdt, Jr, who, despite his parentage and affiliations with the Lee coterie, wrote to Lord Dartmouth in June 1774 to request a place and continued thereafter to press his attentions on the administration.[81] It was not generally prudent for merchants to be open in their avowals of support for the government, however, for fear of provoking their colonial correspondents into suspending debt repayments. American importers themselves recognized the full significance of this tactical card, and they made no secret of their willingness to play it.[82]

The political invisibility of most merchants in 1774 can thus be explained. They could afford to offend neither their potential benefactors, the government, nor their current debtors, the colonists. By declaring support for one, the merchants were running the risk of offending the other. But London's traders were not a homogeneous group. They included a few open partisans of the American cause as well as of the ministry. The sympathies of these two opposed groups, however, invariably derived from influences external to the immediate economic circumstances of Atlantic commerce.

In some instances, family connections spanning the Atlantic appeared to constitute a transcendent affiliation. In the case of William Lee, who imported tobacco from his native Virginia, kinship ties were buttressed by ideological conviction. The American sympathies of William Baker – one of the few surviving representatives of the Rockingham viewpoint within the mercantile community – might well have been reinforced by his marriage in 1771 to Juliana Penn, the granddaughter of Governor William Penn of Pennsylvania.[83]

The few merchants connected with the Wilkite movement were also involved in patterns of association that encouraged their support for America. In the case of George Hayley, it is unlikely that his activity as a merchant trading with New England in itself induced sympathy for the colonists. His commercial relationship with John Hancock was far from harmonious; in 1774 he shared a widespread suspicion that the Americans were using the political crisis as a pretext for delaying remittances, and he refused to honour Hancock's bills.[84] It was Hayley's participation in the metropolitan opposition, and the fact that he was Wilkes's brother-in-law, that shaped his pro-American posture as an alderman and MP.

The Atlantic merchants who took little pains to disguise their support for the administration were, in general, those who were least likely to suffer in the event of Anglo-American conflict, either because they could engage in alternative areas of commerce, or because they had expectations, not merely hopes, of government contracts in the event of war. They were not, therefore, under the same pressure as most Atlantic merchants to appease American opinion. John Blackburn, who traded with New York, was a prominent figure in this group.[85] He held provisioning contracts before and after the outbreak of war. Anthony Bacon was another merchant who had close contractual ties with the administration. This connection proved more compelling than his kinship links with America. He was born in Maryland and later traded with that colony, but he acted contrary to its interests by promoting as an MP the Currency Act of 1764. Before the American war he victualled British garrisons in Africa and furnished slaves to the British government in the West Indies. During the period of the American Revolution he used munitions contracts as the basis for a transition from merchant prince to industrial magnate. He received his first such order in 1773, and during the war he was the leading supplier of iron cannon to the Ordnance Board. He also supplied food and coal to the British army in North America.[86] In 1775 he explicitly revealed his attitude to imperial organization in a pamphlet which advised severe measures in dealing with recalcitrant colonists.[87]

One further group of merchants may be distinguished – the London Quakers trading primarily with Philadelphia. Their distinctiveness, however, did not lie in any partisan bias. Rather, their religious opposition to violence, and their sense of community with their coreligionists in the New World, made them foremost among the Atlantic traders who wished ardently that the dispute between Whitehall and the colonists might somehow be mediated and confrontation averted. Toward this end, one of their number, David

Barclay (who was a prominent banker as well as a merchant), together with a fellow Quaker, Dr John Fothergill, was involved, in the winter of 1774-5, in an abortive series of negotiations with Benjamin Franklin, designed to establish areas of fundamental agreement between government and colonists.[88]

When the merchants reasserted themselves as a political lobby in early 1775, three active groups could be thus distinguished within their collective counsels: spokesmen for disaffected Americans, such as William Lee, the supporters of administration, and the advocates of neutralism and reconciliation, among whom the Quakers were prominent. The merchants were eventually moved to action in response to the measures of the Continental Congress, which laid down that no British goods were to be imported after 1 December 1774 and that no American products were to be exported to Britain after 10 September 1775. The policy of the congress corresponded with the views of Americans in London - such as the Lees, Benjamin Franklin, and Josiah Quincy, Jr. - that trade embargoes would force the merchants to support the colonists out of necessity, if not inclination. The proposed delay in curbing American exports reduced somewhat the impact of the economic sanctions, and even offered attractive short-term prospects for a rising market in tobacco, but at least the merchants could no longer sustain the desperate hope that Atlantic commerce might continue unimpeded in spite of the intensifying imperial crisis.[89]

It was the pro-Americans, led by William Lee, who took the initiative in attempting to organize the mercantile community into a political lobby. They placed an advertisement in the newspapers on 22 December 1774, announcing a meeting of the merchants for the following day. But on 23 December another statement appeared, which stated that the proposed meeting did not have the approval of the principal participants in the Atlantic trade, and that instead the merchants should assemble on 4 January 1775.[90] A letter by John Blackburn explains this episode and shows the influence that the administration's allies were able to exert in merchant counsels:

The anonomous person having advertis'd a Meeting of the Merchants tomorrow, & it being shrewdly suspected that the late Sheriff Lee & *that* party were concern'd therein in order to counteract the Good design of His Majesty's Ministers by a Petition to Parliament I thought it my Duty to prevent such Meeting by all the Endeavours in my power - & accordingly I waited on several of the most Respectable Merchants concern'd with American Trade when it was agreed that an Advertisement should be put into the Papers disavowing the intent of such a Meeting as premature, until

we see the nature of the Petition [of the Continental Congress] to the King
& His Majesty's Answer – & as such Petition is to be presented tomorrow
– it was thought prudent to advertize a Meeting of the Merchants on the
4 Jan[y] but not with any View to disturb the operations of His Majestys
Ministers but to take the head from a factious party.[91]

At the meeting on 4 January, attended by three to four hundred
individuals having some connection with American business, the City
radicals played little part. The proceedings were largely dominated
by David Barclay, whose desire for a petition to the House of Commons
"on a *commercial ground*, leaving the political to those who should
best know how to discuss it," reflected the wishes of most of those
present.[92] To prepare the petition, the meeting appointed a committee
of twenty-three members who incorporated representatives of the
diverse factions among the merchants. It included ministerialists such
as John Blackburn and pro-Americans such as William Lee, William
Baker, and Thomas Bromfield. The Pennsylvania trade was represented on the committee by three Quakers – David Barclay, Daniel
Mildred, and William Neate. Mildred wrote to a Philadelphia
correspondent that "altho I am retiring from the Trade [I] was willing
to permit my Name therein that I might be so farr serviceable as
to keep any Very fiery Persons out which might hurt the Cause and
I believe the same Motive induced ... David Barclay to acquiecss
with the Appointment."[93]

The address which the committee produced dealt mainly with the
economic consequences of confrontation between government and
colonists. Censure of the administration was brief and veiled, con-
sisting of a reference to the retention of the tea duty and "other laws"
by which "the minds of his Majesty's subjects in the British colonies
have been greatly disquieted." Even the introduction of this allusion,
however, represented, in the opinion of Edmund Burke, a considerable
improvement on the original draft of the petition, which Burke
described as "cold and jejune." He credited William Baker with
securing the inclusion of the "distant reflections on the American
laws, and some compliment on the beneficial effects of the repeal
of the stamp-act" which the final draft contained.[94]

The petition was adopted by a general meeting of the North
American merchants on 11 January. At this gathering, a group of
politically committed merchants pressed unsuccessfully for the inclusion of a specific denunciation of the Quebec Act. The Wilkite
Common Councilman, James Sharp – who exported iron products
to the colonies[95] – "said, amongst other things, that Canada was
universally looked upon as a cudgel, in the hands of Government,

against the rest of the Americans." Three Quebec traders were added to the merchants' committee, presumably to appease this kind of sentiment.[96]

On 23 January Alderman Hayley presented the merchants' petition to the House of Commons, where it was referred to what Edmund Burke described as a "committee of oblivion," instead of to the committee of the whole House for considering the American papers. As a result, the merchants' petition was destined to have no direct influence on Parliament's deliberations on colonial matters, and specifically on the address to the throne which would contain the administration's policy statement on American affairs. A further meeting of the merchants, on 26 January, prepared another address, to be presented the same day, praying that their previous petition be considered before any resolutions on the American papers were entered into by the Commons. This appeal, however, was rejected and the following day the merchants' first petition was considered by the parliamentary committee to which it had originally been referred. A representative of the merchants, Thomas Woolridge (whose commerce was with the Carolinas and who was soon to become an alderman with Wilkite support), spoke at the bar of the House and waived the entitlement of the Atlantic traders to appear before such an inconsequential forum.[97]

Before the merchants trading to North America met again to consider their next move, the West Indian planters and merchants had also organized themselves to promote conciliation between government and colonists. The well-being of the British possessions in the Caribbean was especially threatened by the Continental Association's nonimportation of West Indian products and its planned blockade of vital exports to the islands.[98]

There were, among the West Indian lobbyists, a few confirmed pro-Americans such as Alderman Oliver and Samuel Estwick (the colonial agent for Barbados), who, in their attitude to American affairs, continued the tradition of the late William Beckford.[99] It was probably the stance of this faction which prompted the *Gentleman's Magazine*, before the election of 1774, to warn its readers not to vote for members of the West Indian connection because they "publicly deny the legislative power of Great Britain over our American colonies." From within the West Indies, the assembly of Jamaica, in December 1774, adopted a petition to the crown that expressed support for the mainland colonies and denied Parliament's supremacy over colonial legislatures.[100]

But like the traders to the mainland colonies, a large proportion of the West Indian planters and merchants were loath to censure directly the government for their current and prospective situation. Not only would many of them become dependent on the administration's bounty when war came, but they would also need naval convoys to protect their trade and squadrons to protect the islands.[101] The pressures on the West Indian lobby to acquiesce in government policy are exemplified in the attitude of Rose Fuller, a planter. In April 1774 he pressed in Parliament for the repeal of the colonial tea duty, but by January 1775, according to Edmund Burke, "old withered Rose" had "totally lost his hue," having capitulated to the blandishments of Lord North.[102]

It was Fuller who, at a meeting of the West Indian planters and merchants on 18 January 1775, moved that "a petition . . . be presented to Parliament representing the alarming state of affairs in the West India islands." He proposed that the address should confine itself to the economic consequences of a breakdown of West Indian commerce; there should be no political condemnation of either the government or the colonists. An example of the meeting's desire to avoid any overt partisan commitment is afforded by its debate over whether the American Continental Congress should be referred to by name in the petition. One person objected that to use the term "Congress" conveyed acknowledgement of its political pretensions. An alternative suggestion, to use the phrase "a meeting held at Philadelphia, *called a Congress*," was, on the other hand, rejected because it implied "an oblique censure on the Americans." Finally the meeting settled for the simple and uncontentious description, "A Meeting held at Philadelphia." A committee was established to prepare the address; its draft was approved by a further general meeting on 25 January, and on 2 February the petition was presented to the House of Commons by Alderman Oliver, where it was immediately referred to the "committee of oblivion."[103]

After this rebuff by the House of Commons, the "West Indians" and North American merchants formulated petitions to the House of Lords. Lord Rockingham presented both addresses on 7 February, but the House decisively rejected his plea that they be considered before any resolutions were adopted concerning America.[104]

Neither the merchants trading to North America nor the West Indian lobby had thus succeeded in deterring Parliament from approving the administration's policy of coercion. At this point the tactics of the two trading interests diverged. The West Indian interest, unlike the traders to mainland America, opted for a hearing before the Commons committee of the whole House assigned to consider petitions. Its case was presented by Richard Glover, the poet and merchant, who introduced the evidence of a number of planters and traders. Glover, in his summing-up, cogently pointed out the implications of a breakdown in trade between the continental colonies and the West Indies, not only for the internal economies of the islands, but for the whole integrated network of Atlantic commerce. He made, however, no indictment of government policy, except, indirectly, in his warning that the Americans were unlikely to abandon the Continental Association in response to coercion by the British government. But, despite Glover's eloquence and the evidence he presented, his case was ignored by Parliament in its deliberations on colonial policy. After this failure the West Indian merchants and planters made no more organized attempts to divert the course of the government's American policy before the commencement of hostilities.[105]

The merchants trading with mainland America, however, continued for a while to function as a political lobby. At a meeting on 8 February they discussed whether or not to petition the throne. Their debate further revealed the fundamental split between the nonpartisan advocates of reconciliation, represented by David Barclay, and the committed pro-Americans, represented by James Sharp, William Lee, Thomas Woolridge, and William Saxby (a Wilkite Common Councilman for Bread Street Ward). Because Parliament's address to the king had declared Massachusetts to be in a state of "actual rebellion," Barclay argued, it would be "unsafe" to sign an address seeking suspension of laws against the province. The meeting, however, accepted the pro-American demand for a petition to the throne. This decision, in its turn, was changed at a meeting a week later, on the basis of the merchant committee's recommendation to defer any more petitions until further colonial legislation was brought into Parliament as a result of the address of the two Houses to the king.[106]

Such legislation was soon forthcoming in the form of the New England restraining bill, which forbade New Englanders to trade anywhere except with Britain and the British West Indies and barred them from the North Atlantic fisheries after 20 July 1775. A merchants' meeting was held on 22 February, when a petition was prepared for presentation to the House of Commons by Alderman Hayley the next day.[107] William Lee described some of the conflicts within the merchants' committee about the form of the address. He criticized the New England merchants because they merely wanted "fishing prolonged to 1st Nov. next . . . that they may have a large remittance," and he excoriated Samuel Gist, a Virginia merchant, for wishing "to assent *indirectly* to the wicked and bloody address of the two houses, to the declaration that Massachusetts Bay was in rebellion, and that the other Colonies were aiding and abetting them." But the influence of the ministerialists seems on this occasion to have been effectively checked by William Lee and his friends; for the petition not only pointed out the economic dangers of the restraining bill, but also criticized the proposed legislation for further limiting trial by jury and for extending the jurisdiction of the Admiralty courts.[108]

The merchants were joined in their protest to the House of Commons against the restraining bill by the Common Council of London and by the Quakers. The City's petition was assertively partisan. It stated that the "Petitioners feel for the many hardships which Fellow Subjects in America labour under from the execution of several late Acts of Parliament evidently partial and oppressive and which seem to be extended and continued by this Bill." The Quakers' petition, drawn up at David Barclay's house in Cheapside, was by contrast politically noncontroversial; it stressed mainly the prospective plight of the inhabitants of Nantucket, nine-tenths of them Quakers almost entirely dependent on the North Atlantic fisheries for their livelihood.[109]

Evidence in support of these various petitions was presented at the bar of the House by David Barclay on 28 February 1775. Barclay, and the witnesses introduced by him, were politically uncontentious and confined themselves to economic and humanitarian considerations: they particularly emphasized the potential impact of the bill in disrupting the repayment of debts by New Englanders to City merchants. The restraining bill passed through the House of Commons, however, with only minor amendments which were unrelated to the London petitions against the legislation.[110]

The London merchants and the Common Council also petitioned against the measure during its passage through the House of Lords. William Lee claimed some responsibility for drafting the merchants' petition, which explains its vehemently partisan sentiments. Possibly, by this time, the ministerial and neutralist merchants had withdrawn from lobbying activity, thus leaving the field clear for the pro-Americans. After the bill had passed the Lords, the City and the merchants petitioned George III, requesting that he withhold his assent to it.[111] None of these addresses, it is scarcely necessary to add, had any effect on the bill's passage or final form; and after these rebuffs, the merchants trading to North America virtually ceased to function as a political lobby with any potential for influencing the course of imperial events.

The Quakers made their last appeal for reconciliation in the form of a petition presented to the king on 17 March 1775. The address was respectfully phrased, claimed that no subjects were "more loyal

and more zealously attached" to George III than the Americans, and
humbly requested the king "to stay the Sword." David Barclay,
however, had little hopes for the success of the petition. He confided
to James Pemberton, a Philadelphia correspondent: "I don't expect
... much Advantage to arise from yᵉ Petition further than that of
all others, *the most desireable*, a satisfaction to the Minds of those,
who wished to leave Nothing unassayed, that might have the most
distant prospect of doing good, and strengthening the hand of those
in the Ministry who are against sanguinary Measures."[112] The London
Quakers followed their address by counselling the Friends in Philadelphia that the Quakers' duty was to give "no just cause of Offence
to our lawfull Superior, by contending for our just Rights and
Liberties in any other way than by a patient Submission and respectful
Remonstrance." After the outbreak of war the London Quakers
withdrew from the political arena, adopting an official stance best
described as loyal pacifism, and privately hoping that the imperial
conflict would be quickly terminated by some shift in international
alignments or by the growth of "a pacific disposition" within the
ministry.[113]

The Quakers on the eve of war, however, had at least demonstrated
a more active concern for the welfare of the colonists than had the
other denominations of Protestant dissent. This statement, it is true,
runs counter to some authoritative assumptions that popular support
for America derived mainly from nonconformists.[114] But these assumptions, on close examination, are revealed as untenable. They are in
part the product of a circular argument. As one commentator has
noted, "Anyone sympathising with America was likely to be called
a Presbyterian."[115] (In a similar way, "Methodist" became quite
unjustifiably synonymous with "Jacobin" during the period of the
French Revolution.) There is a more plausible basis, of course, for
linking nonconformity with support for America. Undeniably, there
are connections between the traditions of dissenting religion and
political libertarianism. The Real Whigs were mainly nonconformists, and the Club of Honest Whigs was both a centre of Protestant
dissent and of pro-American attitudes.[116] But as Michael Kammen
has pointed out, "The prominent careers of such men as Joseph
Priestley, Richard Price, James Burgh, and Thomas Hollis have
perhaps diverted historians' attention from a significant trend. Less
famous but equally important dissenters steadily turned their backs
on America during the later 1760's and 1770's."[117]

Benjamin Franklin sustained the hope that dissent's historical
influence on political events might yet be revived, and it was
presumably for this reason that in 1774 he persuaded his friend, Joseph

Priestley, to compose a pamphlet addressed to English nonconformists, reminding them of their heritage and why it should lead them to support the colonists.[118] Priestley lectured the dissenters that *"religious liberty*, indeed is the immediate ground on which you stand, but this cannot be maintained except on the basis of *civil liberty*; and therefore the old *Puritans* and *Nonconformists* were always equally distinguished for their noble and strenuous exertions in favour of both."[119]

But Priestley's appeals had little or no effect. Contemporaries commented on the passivity of the nonconformists as a group. Many dissenting clergymen remained indifferent, even hostile, to the American cause, and the institutions of organized Protestant dissent evinced coolness toward colonial aspirations. Indeed, one reason that American dissenters were prepared to detach themselves from Britain was the poor treatment that their case was accorded by dissenting organizations in London. The Body of Protestant Dissenting Ministers of the Three Denominations (Congregational, Baptist, and Presbyterian) did not address itself at all to colonial questions during the period of the revolution; it was concerned primarily with the contemporaneous agitation for abolishing subscription to the Thirty-nine Articles. The Protestant Dissenting Deputies had supported colonial opposition to an American bishopric, but thereafter the colonies scarcely figured in their deliberations. On the eve of the revolution, they were preoccupied exclusively with domestic affairs. The composition of the organization suggests one reason why the colonists received no support from it: among the deputies were such prominent government supporters as James Bogle French, a rich contractor, and Thomas Wellings, a promoter of loyalist causes within the livery.[120]

It would, of course, be wrong to generalize about the attitude of religious dissenters toward America on the basis of these loyalist nonconformists, just as it would be erroneous to assume that every dissenter thought like Richard Price. The degree and nature of pro-American sympathies of most individual nonconformists depended largely on other considerations, external to religious denomination, of which the most important was the extent of their involvement with the Wilkite movement, which continued to embody the ideological connection between domestic and colonial grievances. The Wilkite movement itself was not entirely secular in its preoccupations. It incorporated a tradition of anti-Catholicism that became manifest during the opposition to the Quebec Act; but this tradition was part of an attitude of xenophobia – that warped dimension of English libertarianism which had little to do with the denominational

distinction between orthodox Anglicanism and dissenting Protestantism.

THE WILKITES REASSERT
THEMSELVES

The Wilkite movement in early 1775 was still very much alive,
although there has been a tendency among some historians to accord
it a premature demise.[121] Indeed, the worsening colonial situation
and the collapse of the merchant lobby prompted the City's institutions
to a further bout of antiministerial activity. Still guided by the Bill
of Rights coterie, the patriot tradesmen of London were the most
persistent and unequivocal source of support for disaffected Americans
as war impended.

John Wilkes himself emerged from a few months of political
dormancy, following his election as lord mayor and MP for Middlesex,
with two parliamentary speeches denouncing the administration. The
first of these, on 1 February 1775, was in support of John Sawbridge's
annual motion for shortening the duration of Parliament. In this
speech Wilkes attributed the contemptuous treatment the London
merchants were accorded by the House of Commons to the corruption
of MPs and conjectured that the latter's behaviour augured badly for
"our excellent fellow-subjects in *America*."[122]

Wilkes's next parliamentary effort, five days later, was a castigation
of Parliament's proposed address to the crown. For much of this
speech he expounded the axiom, "no taxation without representation"; he also criticized the address for driving the colonists toward
rebellion and independence; and he warned that America could not
be militarily suppressed.[123]

Wilkes's renewed concern about the colonial situation was echoed
in Common Council and Common Hall. It has been described how
the Common Council joined the protest against the New England
Restraining Act, but this was by no means the limit of its activities
in the months before the outbreak of war. On 31 January 1775
Frederick Bull laid before the Court a letter from Francis Maseres,
agent of the Protestant settlers in Canada, complaining about the
Quebec Act and entreating the City's governing institutions to renew
pressure for the legislation's repeal. At the next meeting of the
Common Council, on 10 February, a reply to Maseres was formulated,
which assured the Protestant settlers "that nothing in the Power of
the Lord Mayor Aldermen and Common Council shall be wanting
towards promoting so desirable a purpose as the obtaining Redress
respecting the late . . . Quebec Act"; the Court then went on to instruct

its members who were also MPs to promote repeal of the act in the Commons.[124]

At the Common Council on 21 February the first steps were taken to petition Parliament against the Restraining Act, but debate at the meeting mainly focused on two motions put forward by James Sharp. He called first for a resolution reprobating "the present measures of Administration ... towards America in general as improvident and impolitic"; he then moved that the Court officially condemn the four Coercive Acts and state that the Americans were justified in constitutional resistance to them. Subsequent discussion was lively and far-reaching. Progovernment spokesmen, such as Alderman Harley and John Jones of Cripplegate Without Ward, stressed the dignity and supremacy of Parliament in imperial matters, and argued that Lord North's conciliatory proposals of the previous day should be supported as the most effective basis for reuniting the empire. The pro-Americans countered by dismissing North's peace overtures as both futile and devious. They went on to stress the familiar themes that all obnoxious legislation derived from Lord Bute, and that, in John Sawbridge's words, "the distinction between freemen and slaves was the free enjoyment of our property, our privileges, and not to be taxed but by our own consent." After some minor amendments James Sharp's motions were passed with only ten opposing votes – a striking confirmation of the pro-American sentiment of Common Council at this time.[125]

A few weeks later it was the turn of Common Hall to express its support for the Americans and its opposition to the government's colonial policy. A preliminary meeting of a section of the livery, on 28 March, resolved "that a requisition be made to the Lord Mayor for convening a Common Hall with all convenient speed to Petition the Throne against the late proceedings against our brethren in America." Arthur and William Lee drafted an address, remonstrance, and petition, which was adopted by a meeting of the pro-American livery caucus on 4 April for recommendation to the Common Hall – summoned by John Wilkes in response to the livery's requisition – the next day.[126]

The numbers attending this Common Hall were variously estimated at two thousand – by William Lee – and from one hundred and fifty to two hundred – by a hostile, pseudonymous press commentator.[127] Those present were treated to lengthy harangues from John Wilkes, Henry Maskall, and Captain Allen. Wilkes, in an obvious attempt to establish Common Hall as the accepted voice of the City's commercial element, stressed the dire economic consequences of the government's colonial policy. Allen's speech was typically hyperbolic: he concluded by describing Lord North's govern-ment as "one of the most abandoned administrations that ever disgraced this or any other country."[128]

The address itself was eloquently rabid in the usual Lee style. After cursory mention of the economic implications of the colonial impasse, it continued: "Your petitioners, look with less Horror at the consequences, than at the purpose of these measures. Not deceived by the specious Artifice of calling Despotism, Dignity – they plainly perceive, that the real purpose is to establish Arbitrary Power over all America." A long recital of colonial grievances followed and the petition concluded with an entreaty to the king to "dismiss imme-diately and for ever" his ministers and advisers. After the address's virtually unanimous adoption, the livery passed a number of reso-lutions thanking MPs and members of the House of Lords who had opposed the passage of colonial legislation.[129]

John Wilkes and a large party of the City petitioners presented the address to the king at St James's on 10 April after an impressive march through the streets of London and Westminster. Two separate newspaper accounts refer to the vast crowds which observed the progress of the party.[130] According to the *London Chronicle* of 8–11 April 1775, "when they came into Pall-mall, the shouts of the populace testified their approbation of the petitioners' proceedings"; and the same newspaper claimed that although "on the countenance of many spectators there appeared a grin of contempt ... the majority of faces were marked with the smile of applause."

During the presentation of the address John Wilkes, according to Horace Walpole, conducted himself with such decorum "that the King himself owned he had never seen so well-bred a Lord Mayor." Despite Wilkes's good manners, however, the court did not mellow in its attitude to the City's importunities. The king replied to the London petitioners that "it is with the utmost Astonishment that I find any of my Subjects capable of encouraging the rebellious Disposition which unhappily exists in some of my Colonies in North America." The following day, the lord chamberlain dispatched a letter to John Wilkes informing him that the king had determined not to receive on the throne any more petitions from the City, other than in its corporate capacity (that is, from the lord mayor and Common Council). George III was constitutionally entitled to take such a position, although, as Horace Walpole accurately observed, by receiv-ing the City petition of 10 April the king "had established a precedent for what he now proscribed."[131] The king had also ensured a strong reaction from Common Hall at its next meeting on Midsummer day.

London's civic institutions were supported in their defence of the colonists by other opposition elements in the metropolis. At a meeting of the Supporters of the Bill of Rights on 4 March 1775, Frederick Bull, the treasurer of the society, was directed to furnish "Five Hundred Pounds, for the persecuted inhabitants of the town of Boston, and of the poor distressed fishermen of New England," who had been robbed of their livelihood as a result of "an unrelenting spirit of cruelty in a wicked administration." The Constitutional Society also raised money, which it sent via Benjamin Franklin, to succour the Bostonians.[132] There were other press reports of businessmen privately subscribing sums for the same purpose.[133]

Another indication of a reviving enthusiasm for the colonial cause was the appearance in January 1775 of a fanatically pro-American periodical entitled *The Crisis*. At the end of each issue it was stated that its printer and publisher was Thomas William Shaw of Fleet Street, but government investigations revealed that one Samuel Axtell was in fact the printer. William Moore – who had previously written and published another licentious periodical, *The Whisperer* – was strongly suspected of being its author.[134]

During the period of its publication *The Crisis* excoriated the king, his ministers, Parliament, and the policies of the administration.[135] It described the king as acting "like a Tyrant"; he was called "the greatest CRIMINAL in England," and "a national Executioner, [who] for a Scepter, carries a BLOODY KNIFE."[136] Lord North, Lord Mansfield, and, inevitably, Lord Bute were also singled out for special abuse.[137] The colonists, by contrast, were praised for their "*Virtue, Courage*, Firmness, and Resolution" in the face of tyranny, and their behaviour was cited as a proper model for imitation by Englishmen.[138] Nearly every issue of *The Crisis* contained a thinly veiled incitement to oppose the administration with violence. Troops leaving for the colonies were urged not "to BUTCHER their Relations, Friends, and Fellow-Subjects in America."[139]

In view of such vitriolic and seditious content it may at first seem surprising that *The Crisis* was allowed to continue publication until October 1776 with relatively little legal harassment, although its language was so extreme that possibly the administration felt it was unlikely to subvert anybody sufficiently literate to read it. The only issue to provoke official reaction was *The Crisis*, Number 3, which was addressed to the king, whom it attacked unmercifully. Parliament – after some disagreement between Lords and Commons over the wording of the charge – condemned this issue as a "false, scandalous and seditious Libel," and ordered the public hangman to burn it.[140] The popular response to this decision lent additional force to the argument that it was probably the wisest course for the government to remain indifferent to libellous publications. According to the *St. James's Chronicle*, people rushed all over London to purchase *The Crisis*, Number 3, after Parliament's condemnatory resolution.[141] On the occasion of the periodical's public burning outside the Royal Exchange a minor riot ensued. The *Morning Post* reported that "as soon as the fire was lighted before the Exchange it was immediately put out, and dead cats and dogs were thrown at the officers; a fire was made at the Cornhill, and the pelting still continued. Sheriff Hart was wounded in the wrist, and Sheriff Plomer in the breast with a brick-bat; Mr. Gates, the City Marshal, was dismounted, and with much difficulty saved his life. Three of the ringleaders were taken into custody, but were soon after rescued by the mob."[142]

There is considerable evidence, then, that the enthusiasm for the American cause in London, led by the Wilkites, and displayed in the election campaign of 1774, expanded in the months prior to the outbreak of war in April 1775. The petitioning by the City's institutions, the raising of money for the colonists, and the publication of *The Crisis* together with the public's response to its condemnation, all testify to this trend. One feature of the metropolitan pro-American movement remained constant, however: its continuing difficulties in combining effectively with other political elements – in particular the Rockingham Whigs – which also opposed the administration's colonial policy.

The vaguest indications of impending cooperation between sections of the opposition were observed with hopeful expectancy by the friends of America. Theophilus Lindsey, for example, wrote in February 1775 to a friend in Yorkshire that he "was glad to see my Lord Mayor's chariot about a week before at Sr Geo. Savile's doors." From the other end of the political spectrum, Thomas Hutchinson, the American loyalist, who clearly did not desire a closing of ranks against government, suspected in January 1775 that some opposition noblemen, including Lord Rockingham, were engaged in consultations with such undesirables as Josiah Quincy, Jr, and Arthur Lee.[143]

But Lindsey's hopes and Hutchinson's fears were unfounded. Relations between the metropolitan patriots and the Rockinghamites remained as strained as ever. Lord Rockingham's sponsorship of the City's petition against the New England restraining bill was the only sign of any active cooperation between the two groups, and in presenting this address to the Lords, Rockingham appeared to damn the London corporation with faint praise: "With regard to the city petition he observed, that it originated from a body, the Members of which demanded every attention, on account of their official respectability."[144]

Other Rockinghamites regarded any association with the City as damaging to their political credibility. Richard Champion, a Bristol merchant, for example, "saw the opposition in England discredited by the license of Wilkes and his friends, and urged the Americans not to be misled by support that they would receive from that quarter." Edmund Burke also became thoroughly disenchanted with the Wilkites after they withdrew support for his intended candidature for Westminster during the election of 1774. *Lloyd's Evening Post* reported that, during his famous speech of 22 March 1775, in which he introduced his resolutions for conciliating America, Burke remarked "there was nothing he would despise more [than the smiles of a corrupt ministry] unless it were the smiles of the Common Council of London" – a slur which brought John Sawbridge to his feet in angry protest. John Wilkes pointedly did not stay in the House to vote for Burke's plan of conciliation.[145]

The Rockinghamites still adhered, as war impended, to the theoretical supremacy of Parliament in colonial matters, which further reduced chances of cooperation between themselves and the City. Lord Chatham, however, held the view that Parliament's sovereignty over America was limited, and did not include the right – let alone practice – of taxation. On a fundamental principle of colonial policy, therefore, he was in accord with the metropolitan radicals and their American collaborators.[146] For this reason, and also because of his lingering national prestige, the Lee coterie made strenuous efforts to reintroduce Lord Chatham into the mainstream of national political life in cooperation with the Wilkites. From the summer of 1774 William Lee and Stephen Sayre kept Chatham informed of changing events in the colonies and especially of the proceedings of the Continental Congress.[147] The two Americans stressed the limited ends the colonists were seeking and their continuing commitment to the trade empire which Chatham was so anxious to preserve. Accordingly Sayre wrote to Chatham on 27 September 1774: "I can assure your Lordship, that I never heard or found an Idea from among them all [i.e., his colonial correspondents], which tended to assume the least right relative to the regulations of Trade. The Colonists have definitely more to fear, so far as respects their Commerce, from provincial Legislation than from that of the Mother Country."[148]

The delegates at Philadelphia did indeed concede Britain's authority to regulate trade, and the resolutions of the Continental Congress in general apparently reassured Chatham about the colonists' intentions. According to Arthur Lee – who with Stephen Sayre visited the ageing statesman on Christmas Day, 1774 – Chatham was "clearly for a full, solemn, authentick settlement of the dispute upon the conditions proposed by the Congress, and will assuredly support it with all his abilities."[149] Chatham's conciliatory proposals in the House of Lords on 31 January 1775 (preceded a few days before by his motion that all British troops be withdrawn from Boston) coincided with the demands of the Continental Congress in many important respects, including the denial of Parliament's right to tax the Americans, the proposed removal of legislation offensive to the colonists, and, above all, the recognition of Congress as a legally valid body. Stephen Sayre was satisfied that Chatham's proposals could form the basis of a settlement "should the necessities of state force him [Chatham] into the direction of its Councils."[150]

The Common Council acknowledged Chatham's renewed espousal of the American case by officially thanking him, on 10 February 1775, for his plan of conciliation; the livery in Common Hall likewise thanked Chatham on 5 April. John Wilkes in his speech of 6 February on the proposed address to the throne also paid tribute to Chatham's conciliatory proposals.[151]

But the significance of these events – although they signalled a definite improvement in relations between Chatham and the Wilkites – should not be overemphasized. Chatham was an old and ailing man whose chances of making a sustained impact on the political scene were yearly diminishing. Ill-health prevented him from presenting the first merchant petition to the House of Lords in 1775. Even William Lee was forced to concede that Chatham's infirmities reduced his political usefulness.[152] At most the temporary accord on principle between Chatham and the City lent something to the latter's prestige as dissensions within the empire finally erupted into war.

THE OUTBREAK OF HOSTILITIES

Shortly after the outbreak of hostilities in America, but before news of this event reached Britain, a ward election in London yielded further indication of continuing metropolitan support for the colonists: on 23 May 1775 William Lee was chosen as the alderman for Aldgate, beating his nearest rival, William Baker, by seventy-three votes to forty.[153] Lee in his acceptance speech did not confine himself to parochial issues:

As an American, he declared it his wish that the union between Great Britain and the colonies might be reestablished, and remain forever, but that constitutional liberty might be the sacred bond of that union.

He considered the attempts of the present administration against American liberty, as a plain prelude to the invasion of liberty in this country; but he trusted, that the virtue of the Americans, aided by the friends of freedom here, would teach the Tories of this day . . . how vain a thing it is to attempt wresting their liberties from a people determined to defend them.[154]

Four days later there arrived in England news from Massachusetts which suggested that Lee's confidence in the militancy of his fellow-countrymen was not misplaced: a ship, dispatched by American rebels from Salem, docked at the Isle of Wight on 27 May with copies of a Massachusetts newspaper, the *Essex Gazette*, which contained accounts of the fighting at Lexington and Concord.[155] These reports were reprinted in a special edition of the *London Evening Post* on 29 May and in other newspapers shortly afterwards.

Many of the military details of this first encounter between the redcoats and the provincial militia were accurately stated by the *Essex Gazette*, although the general tenor of the account was heavily biased against the king's troops. It claimed that hostilities were begun by the British soldiers "attended with Circumstances of Cruelty not less brutal than what our venerable Ancestors received from the vilest Savages of the Wilderness." The report went on to accuse the British of indiscriminately shooting the unarmed, the aged, women and children.[156]

The official account of the engagements did not reach London until 10 June, and in the meantime patriots in London, American and English, were able to exploit a temporary monopoly of colonial information. The ministry advised the public to disregard the *Essex Gazette* reports, but Arthur Lee countered by stating in the press that copies of the affidavits on which the newspaper's accounts were based were lodged for public inspection with the lord mayor.[157] Horace Walpole wrote to Sir Horace Mann on 5 June 1775 that "the public were desired by authority to suspend their belief – but their patience is out, and they persist in believing the first account." According to William Lee, "the sword of Civil War is . . . almost universally believed to have been first drawn by General Gages [*sic*] troops." The propaganda coup of the pro-Americans was so effective in the short term that Lord George Germain concluded on 30 May that "the many joyful faces" of the opposition evinced expectations "that rebellion will be the means of changing the Ministry."[158]

The first press accounts of the opening of hostilities led indirectly to the most extensive and vigorously conducted legal prosecutions during the course of the war of individuals involved in publishing antigovernment material. On the basis of the *Essex Gazette* reports, supported by private conversation with Arthur Lee, John Horne, on behalf of the Constitutional Society, wrote and inserted in nine

London newspapers an advertisement which stated that £100 had been raised for "the Relief of the WIDOWS, ORPHANS, and AGED PARENTS of our BELOVED American Fellow Subjects, who, FAITHFUL to the character of Englishmen, preferring Death to Slavery, were, for that Reason only inhumanly murdered by the KING'S troops at or near Lexington and Concord."[159]

The newspaper editors who printed the advertisement were soon after indicted, *ex officio*, by the attorney-general for seditious libel. Five of them were brought to trial before special juries, one of which was headed by Sir James Esdaile, a ministerial alderman; the prosecuted editors were duly found guilty and each was sentenced to pay a fine of £100.[160]

A more substantial punishment awaited John Horne, who was tried before Lord Mansfield at the Court of King's Bench in July 1777. At his trial Horne displayed all the qualities of courage, foolhardiness, arrogance, pedantry, and wit which charactetized his long career in the cause of liberty. He vigorously disputed the validity of *ex officio* informations; he claimed that his prosecution was based on a situation *ex post facto*, because the Americans had not been declared rebels at the time he wrote the advertisement; and he denounced the special jury which was to decide his case as biased in favour of the ministry. But his trial conduct was more of a provocation than a defence: he was found guilty and in November 1777 sentenced to a year in prison and a £200 fine; he was also obliged to lodge £400 as a security for future good behaviour.[161]

The affair of the Horne advertisement is important for a number of reasons: it provoked a government reaction which anticipated the sedition trials of the 1790s; and it confirmed Horne as the most zealous and dogmatic of the pro-Americans. But it also indicated in a negative way the waning enthusiasm for the American cause at the time the trials took place (a trend which will be discussed at length in chapter 5). Defence counsel for the newspaper editors pleaded in mitigation "the insignificant manner" with which the public was treating the affair; and Horne himself, in a letter to his lawyer, John Lee, after his trial, lamented his political isolation, the result of declining support for the cause he was upholding, and, though he did not state it, of his continuing unpopularity in London and detachment from the mainstream Wilkites.[162]

In the summer of 1775, however, the pro-American movement – stimulated by the news from Lexington and Concord – continued to flourish, and this was reflected in some hectic activity by London's political institutions. Instead of simply supporting colonial dissent, the pro-Americans were now of course aligning themselves with armed opponents of the crown. The escalation of events discouraged some of the less zealous friends of the disaffected colonies, but others remained undaunted in their opposition to the government.

The livery, in response to war, actually intensified its efforts on behalf of rebellious Americans. On 20 June its caucus met at the Half-Moon Tavern to formulate the agenda for the Common Hall on Midsummer day. Arthur Lee nominated Aldermen Hayley and Newnham as sheriffs for the forthcoming year, and his nominees were accepted by the caucus. In their support one speaker stated that "if any persons should be brought from the other side of the Atlantic; they would be lodged in the custody of the Sheriffs, who should be men of fixed, tried, and approved principles." The caucus also agreed to recommend that Common Hall again petition the king on the throne. Accordingly Arthur Lee produced an address, remonstrance, and petition, which he had written, and proceeded to defend it against objections. His draft was eventually accepted by the caucus with no dissenting votes.[163]

The petition itself was one of the most vitriolic yet penned by Arthur Lee. It lamented that "we have seen, with equal dread and concern, a civil war commenced in America, by your Majesty's commander-in-chief. Will your Majesty be pleased to consider, what must be the situation of your people here, who have nothing now to expect from America, but gazettes of blood, and mutual lists of their slaughtered fellow-subjects?" The petition went on to assure the king that the livery would "exert themselves, at every hazard, to bring those who have advised these ruinous measures, to the justice of this country, and of the much injured colonies."[164]

An estimated 2,500 liverymen in their midsummer Common Hall sustained the militant tone of the caucus meeting.[165] After the nomination of candidates for sheriff (to which office Aldermen Hayley and Newnham were elected after a poll) the livery listened to the letter from the lord chamberlain, which included the king's refusal to receive on the throne any more petitions from the City, except in its corporate capacity; the livery also heard Wilkes's reply in which he warned "that your Lordship's letter, immediately following His Majesty's unfavourable Answer to the Remonstrance [of 5 April], will be considered as a fresh Mark of the King's anger against all the faithful citizens of his capital." In response to this exchange the livery resolved that those who advised the king on his treatment of Common Hall's petitions were "enemies to the right of the subject."[166] The livery accepted Arthur Lee's petition with the proviso that it "be not presented to his Majesty but sitting on his throne." Among other resolutions adopted was one thanking the earl of Effingham

- a distinguished soldier and close friend of the reformer, Major John Cartwright - "for having consistent with the Principles of a true Englishman refused to draw the Sword against the Lives and Liberties of his Fellow Subjects in America, which has hitherto been employed to the Honour of his Country."[167]

The king, adhering to his decision of 11 April, expressed his willingness to receive the livery's petition at his next levee, but not on the throne. He told the inquiring sheriffs, "I am ever ready to receive addresses and petitions - but I am the judge where."[168] The livery's petition thus remained undelivered, and a further Common Hall was summoned for 4 July to consider the impasse.

At this assembly the livery adopted a number of resolutions, proposed by Luke Stavely, asserting the subject's right to petition the monarch (although this was a right which George III had scarcely denied; he had merely insisted on a voice in the mode of petitioning). It was then ordered by Common Hall that its address, remonstrance, and petition of 24 June should be published in the newspapers and that the livery's resolutions of its current and previous meetings should be delivered to the king by the sheriffs. Also, instructions were given to the City's MPs to move in Parliament "for an humble Address ... to His Majesty, requesting to know who were the advisers of those fatal measures which have planted Popery and arbitrary power in America, have plunged us into a most unnatural civil war, to the subversion of the fundamental principles of the English liberty, the ruin of our most valuable commerce, and the destruction of His Majesty's subjects." Once the guilty men were revealed the City MPs were to move for their impeachment, so "that by bringing them to public justice evil counsellors may be removed from before the King." George Hayley and Frederick Bull both intimated their willingness to comply with the livery's instructions.[169]

The meeting was also subjected to characteristic flights of rhetoric from John Wilkes, Captain Allen, and Luke Stavely, who, collectively and predictably, emphasized the political importance of the livery and denounced the administration and all its works. One government supporter, Walter Humphries, attempted to disrupt the pro-American consensus by criticizing the livery's remonstrance of 24 June as "disrespectful" and by arguing that Common Hall should desist from involvement in imperial politics "until the Sentiments of the Delegates in [the Continental] Congress are known."[170] His appeal, however, while winning the approval of George III, received short shrift from the assembled livery.[171]

The outbreak of hostilities in America also prompted the Common Council, like Common Hall, to renew its support for the colonists, though with more caution and qualification than the livery had displayed.

On 23 June 1775 John Wilkes laid before the Common Council a letter which he had received from the Committee of the Association for the City and County of New York. This missive denounced the government's policy as "a Despotism scarcely to the Paralleled in the Pages of Antiquity or the Volumes of modern times," and expressed confidence in "the most vigorous exertions of the City of London to restore union mutual Confidence and Peace to the whole Empire."[172] The appropriate response to the New York letter was to prove a considerable dilemma, as Thomas Hutchinson predicted:

The Address of the present powers of Government in New York, to the Corporation of London must, I think, be very difficult to manage. For the first City in the Kingdom to justify the Revolt of so great a part of the King's Subjects, would be a most daring defiance of the whole Power and authority of Government, and on the other hand, a disavowal or disapprobation of any part of the conduct of the Addressers, will be too great a mortification for Wilkes and his Supporters to suffer, if they are able to prevent it.[173]

Two meetings of the Common Council, on 5 and 7 July, failed to reach any decision on a response to the New York letter. The issue partly hinged on whether or not the Americans were in a state of rebellion: John Merry, a government supporter, claimed that they were; his arguments "were strongly confuted on the other side by Mr. [James] Sharp"; John Glynn, the recorder of the Court, was unable satisfactorily to resolve the problem. Common Council also rejected resolves in favour of the Americans offered by Luke Stavely and William Hurford, but it did accept, on 7 July, a motion for an address and petition to the king (though not, it should be noted, a remonstrance) praying that "his Majesty will be pleased to suspend Hostilities against our Fellow Subjects in North America and adopt such conciliatory Measures as may restore Union Confidence and Peace to the whole Empire."[174]

This petition, because it derived from the City in its corporate capacity, was received by the king on the throne on 14 July. It was respectfully phrased – in contrast to the strident productions of Common Hall – while still being assertively pro-American: it referred, for example, to the "destructive principles [which] have driven our American brethren to acts of desperation." The king thought the petition "certainly the most decent and moderate in words that has been for some time fabricated on that Side Temple bar," although this did not, of course, deter him from adamantly refusing its requests. (Alderman Harley also thought the petition "more moderate & decent than usual"; he offered this opinion to John Wilkes who replied in mock alarm that "he hoped the king would not smile upon him, for that would ruin him for ever.")[175]

The comparative restraint of the Common Council, however, offended some correspondents to opposition newspapers, who compared its behaviour unfavourably with that of Common Hall. They thought the corporation's petition timid and saw its presentation as a tacit acquiescence in the king's discriminatory attitude to the receipt of City addresses.[176]

On 21 July the Common Council once again considered the vexing problem of the New York letter. On this occasion a motion to acknowledge receipt of the letter, and send to New York copies of the corporation's recent address and the king's reply, was defeated by thirteen votes. The Common Council thus balked at identifying too closely with the colonial rebels, though without repudiating its pro-American posture. Its caution naturally provoked further criticism from the more extreme elements of the radical movement in London and also created surprise in America where a more militant stance had been expected from the City corporation. The Common Council continued its policy of restrained opposition, however, and in October 1775 delivered mildly expressed petitions to both Houses of Parliament praying for the cessation of hostilities.[177]

The Middlesex electors proved less inhibited than the Common Council in expressing their support for the colonists. At "their annual festivity to Liberty" on 27 July at Chiswick, many pro-American toasts were proposed, such as:

General Putnam, and all those American heroes, who like men nobly prefer death to slavery and chains.

To him who risques his life in the support of a good government, and would in opposition to a bad one.

Messrs. Hancock and Adams, and all our worthy fellow-subjects in America, who are nobly contending for our rights with their own.[178]

Soon afterwards it became a matter of potential risk to express such sentiments. The king's proclamation of 23 August 1775, for suppressing rebellion and sedition, placed in legal jeopardy "all persons ... in any manner or degree aiding or abetting" American rebels. In the short term metropolitan expressions of support for the colonists were not seriously affected; indeed the immediate effect of the proclamation was merely to confirm the residual antigovernment attitude of the London mob, who greeted its reading at the Royal Exchange with "a general hiss."[179]

Nevertheless the proclamation did articulate an important reality consequent upon the outbreak of war. Henceforth patriots in London could be readily cast in the same light as patriots in America – disloyal and rebellious subjects of the crown. Likewise, government supporters, in London as in America, could now claim exclusive use of the title loyalist with all that pejoratively implied about the conduct and character of their opponents.

This emerging polarity became evident when the Middlesex electors gathered (1,064 in number, according to the *London Evening Post*)[180] at the Mile End assembly rooms on 25 September 1775. This assembly had been summoned by Sheriff Plomer, following a requisition from John Sawbridge and nearly forty other freeholders for a meeting to consider the American situation.[181]

The electors were addressed by Stephen Sayre and Henry Maskall. Sayre repudiated a claim that the charters of the American colonies recognized a British right of taxation; he also made some gratuitously insulting remarks about Sir Francis Bernard. Maskall, in his usual high-blown way, lamented the encroachments of popery, the attack on trial by jury and electors' rights, and "the punishing and ruining such of our American fellow subjects as have taken a firm and decided part against the common enemy." Maskall concluded his speech by moving that the electors instruct their MPs as to their parliamentary conduct. Instructions, previously formulated, were consequently produced by William Lee and accepted by the meeting. After a long preamble they commanded John Wilkes and John Glynn to exert themselves "in preventing the further effusion of the blood of our innocent fellow-subjects in America, and to put a speedy end to the present unnatural and ruinous civil war"; the Middlesex MPs were also instructed to assist the City members "in bringing to the justice of their country" the king's secret advisers. The freeholders further approved a letter, produced by Henry Maskall, from themselves to the electors of Great Britain, calling on the latter to support the former in their struggle on behalf of the oppressed Americans.[182]

The Middlesex electors in their September meeting thus displayed much of the same zeal for the American cause that they had previously manifested for the cause of John Wilkes. But their proceedings were by no means unanimous. The statements and proposals of the pro-Americans were persistently questioned by a group of ministerial supporters, led by the Middlesex justices of the peace, who had themselves the previous day organized a meeting which produced a loyal Middlesex address to the throne. Furthermore, on 3 October the Middlesex loyalists delivered a protest – signed by fifty-one of their number – to Sheriff Hart, affirming their support for government policy, claiming that freedom of debate was inhibited at the meeting of 25 September, and arguing that the county's instructions to its MPs did not reflect the true sentiments of the freeholders.[183] Whether or not the loyalists' last claim was valid, they were beginning to organize in a way which soon would seriously challenge the pro-American movement.

Within the livery, too, there was to be a growing loyalist challenge, but at the Common Hall of 29 September (at which John Sawbridge was elected lord mayor) patriot resolve remained firm. The assembly accepted the recommendation of the livery caucus that, like the Middlesex electors, it adopt an address to the electors of Great Britain. In view of the king's August proclamation it was a bold document. It blamed "the unnatural War excited in America" on "the arbitrary & inexorable Spirit of his Majesty's Ministers, & Advisors"; the colonists were exonerated from all censure because their appeals for conciliation, including the Olive-Branch Petition of the Continental Congress, had all been ignored, and they were therefore justified in turning to the ultimate recourse "which Self preservation suggests against impending Destruction."[184]

John Wilkes also laid before Common Hall a letter from the Continental Congress, signed by its president, John Hancock, thanking the City of London for its stand in defence of "the violated Rights of a free people," and expressing the hope that "the Mediation of wise and good Citizens, will at length prevail over despotism, and Restore harmony and peace . . . to an oppressed and divided empire." The livery, possibly cognizant of the king's August proclamation, did not reply to this letter; they did, however, acknowledge its receipt by entering it in the City records and securing its publication in the newspapers.[185]

In the months following the outbreak of war, therefore, London's civic institutions withstood with fair success the blandishments of loyalism and continued to oppose the government's American policy. But old obstacles blocked a coordinated assault on the administration from the City and other politically disaffected groups. Each section of the opposition recognized the need for a common front against the government, but none was prepared to sink differences in order to accomplish it. In August 1775 Edmund Burke wrote to Lord Rockingham that he wanted to revive "the importance of the City of London by separating the sound from the rotten Contract-Hunting part of the Mercantile Interest, uniting it with the Corporation, and joining both to your Lordship." But in order to achieve this, he later explained, it was necessary "to keep the City, now and for ever, out of the hands of the Wilkes's, Olivers, Hornes, Mascalls [*sic*], and Joels." In similar vein, Sir George Yonge – a supporter of Lord Chatham and Lord Shelburne in the House of Commons – thought, in July 1775, that "the *Intemperance* of the City of London, has *kept back* the voice of the People in many other Parts." With such attitudes prevalent it is scarcely surprising that appeals from radicals like William Lee and Stephen Sayre to opposition noblemen, attempting to induce them to follow the political lead of the City, were not successful.[186]

Within the metropolitan opposition itself splits continued to exist, with more damaging effect than hitherto. On 27 November 1775 Alderman Oliver moved in the House of Commons for an address to the king requesting that he inform Parliament who advised the American measures. Oliver, as a London MP, was acting in accordance with the livery's instructions of 5 July, but he undertook the motion at an unpropitous time and without consulting his fellow City MPs. Frederick Bull, when he heard of Oliver's intentions, was furious; Oliver, he wrote, "proposes the whole Merit to himself, he wants to be a second Pitt and like him to be naked but not ashamed"; Oliver's actions revealed, according to Bull, "his Pride, Insolence, Vanity, Conceit, Self-suffituncy, Obstinacy, Malice, Envy, Independence of his Constituents, and of evry creature upon the face of the earth and above all Folly in the extreem." In the Commons the affair was a debacle for the opposition and a minor triumph for the administration. John Wilkes, George Hayley, and John Sawbridge spoke in support of Oliver with obvious reluctance, and nonmetropolitan opposition MPs were so embarrassed by the motion that they attempted to bury it by moving the previous question, and then the order of the day upon the previous question. But members of the administration in the Commons cleverly insisted that Oliver's motion be brought to a division in order to expose the factions within the opposition, and Oliver's brief attempt at parliamentary glory was defeated by 163 votes to 10.[187]

CHAPTER FOUR

The Spectre of
Insurrection

PLOTS AND RUMOURS OF PLOTS

The fate of Alderman Oliver's parliamentary motion of 27 November 1775 was one more illustration of the ineffectiveness of constitutional opposition to the war in its early phase. And with the parliamentary opposition in disarray, it seemed that intervention from outside Parliament was now the only means of reversing imperial policy. So it was largely for this reason that in 1775 both the hopes of the patriots and the fears of some members of government and its supporters focused on the possibility of a popular uprising in England against the administration.

Clearly, in evaluating the potential for insurrection in 1775, the observations of these partisans must be treated with some scepticism. Colonists in London – from an excess of wishful thinking or because they kept mainly sympathetic company – often tended to exaggerate the potentialities for revolution in England. William Lee, in particular, was persuaded that trade sanctions against Britain would produce economic malaise followed by armed insurrection. In January 1775 he wrote to America that "there is a fire kindling among the people that will blaze most furious in about a year," and that if the measures of the last Congress were continued "12 months must produce a Revolution here." Arthur Lee was less optimistic than his brother. He stressed from an early date that the colonists should expect, at best, only subsidiary support from Britain. But he, too, in early 1775, thought that domestic revolution was feasible. If America adheres to the Continental Association, he wrote to John Dickinson, then "a few months will carry more than Remonstrances to the Throne."[1] Other letters received in America cast the possibility of insurrection in more explicit and dramatic terms. One anonymous correspondent assured Dickinson in July 1775 that the ministry "will not hold their places 3 Months. The People at home will rise, and their Heads will be on Temple Bar before Xmas." Presumably it was because of such reports, and also because of the reprinting in America of bloodcurdling items from *The Crisis*, that the most extravagant rumours of revolution in Britain gained credence in the colonies in the summer of 1775.[2]

Some members of the administration feared the threat of domestic insurrection as much as the partisans of the revolution welcomed it. For example, for Lord Rochford, secretary of state for the Southern Department, the possibility of internal upheaval was a very real one. After the outbreak of hostilities he told his friend, Pierre Augustin Caron de Beaumarchais, the French playwright, "j'ai grand-peur, Monsieur, que l'hiver ne se passe point sans qu'il y ait quelques têtes à bas, soit dans le parti du roi, soit dans l'opposition."[3] The king's proclamation of August 1775 declaring the Americans in rebellion, addressed as it was principally to the threat of internal sedition, was presumably intended to head off any such domestic insurgency; but it is at least possible that the proclamation was the work of more sanguine minds in the administration – those who did not share Rochford's anxieties but deliberately raised the spectre of insurrection in order to nurture the growing loyalist sentiment.

In the event, of course, Rochford's gloomy predictions proved unfounded. No heads rolled, and the surface tranquillity of society was barely disturbed – in contrast, as Sir Nathaniel Wraxall pointed out, "with the terror and alarm ... that pervaded the firmest minds in 1792 and 1793, after the deposition of Louis xvi, and the commencement of the Continental war in Flanders."[4] The few scattered incidents of domestic violence and sabotage in the late 1770s scarcely justified Rochford's anxieties.

In Bristol, in January and February of 1777, a series of incendiary attempts was linked, as an intercepted letter from one of the arsonists shows, with support for the American cause. The incidents did not continue, however, following the dispatch of three troops of dragoons to Bristol. A more successful attempt at sabotage was carried out by James Aitken (alias James Hill, James Hinde, or "Jack the Painter") who in December 1776 and January 1777 managed to ignite in Portsmouth dock some rigging, a Jamaican ship, and a bookseller's warehouse. There is strong circumstantial evidence to support Aitken's claim in his trial confession that he was encouraged in his incendiary activities by Silas Deane, an American agent in Paris, and by Dr

Edward Bancroft, the celebrated American double-agent in London. It is probable that Aitken acquired the taste for revolutionary sabotage in America, where he had been living on the eve of war.[5]

Members of the pro-American movement in London were not implicated in either of these incidents. But one of their number, Stephen Sayre, was a principal in what seems to have been a genuine, albeit risible, attempt at domestic insurrection. Sayre was apprehended on 23 October 1775 for allegedly formulating a plot to kidnap George III while the king was on his way to open Parliament on 26 October. The case against Sayre was based on evidence sworn before Lord Rochford by Francis Richardson, an American who had recently become an adjutant in the Guards and who had considerable responsibility for the defence of the Tower of London, as Sayre apparently took pains to discover. Richardson claimed that Sayre had engaged him in private conversation at the Pennsylvania Coffee House on 19 October 1775 and told him of his scheme. The king, Richardson reported Sayre as remarking, "was at the bottom of all, for he believed Lord North was heartily sick of the business." The plan therefore was to imprison the king in the Tower before dispatching him to his German dominions. Meanwhile public order was to be kept by a *posse comitatus* raised by the lord mayor (John Wilkes) and the sheriffs, and proclamations were to be issued by a revolutionary council under the authority of the king's sign manual. Sayre allegedly claimed that a Major Labellier had already distributed £1,500 among the Guards "for the purpose of alienating their Affections from Government, and to prepare them for a Revolt." Richardson's role was to extend this subversion by insinuating the notion among the troops "that if a change of Government should take place, their Pay would be raised in proportion to the Dearness of Provisions"; and then on 26 October he was to assist in securing the king and seizing the magazines and arsenal in the Tower.[6]

Richardson's testimony was partially corroborated after Sayre's arrest in information sworn before Lord Rochford by Nicholas Nugent, also an officer in the Foot Guards. Nugent deposed that, prior to Richardson's meeting with Sayre, he, Nugent, had dined with "a Gentleman in Business," whom he refused to name, who questioned him closely about the possibility of an officer ingratiating himself with the common soldiers in order to exercise total influence over their behaviour. The inference of Nugent's testimony was clearly that Stephen Sayre was the anonymous gentleman. The businessman allegedly claimed that a friend, "Major Debrisere, or some such name," already had influence with the troops because of his generosity to them. This mysterious officer was probably the "Major Labellier" mentioned by Richardson; Horace Walpole also refers to "one Labelic, a poor mad enthusiast to liberty," who was arrested along with Sayre. The businessman further probed Nugent, according to the latter's testimony, to yield information about the regiment's adjutants, including of course Richardson. Nugent admitted telling his interrogator that in his opinion Richardson "talk'd too much about American affairs which the Informant said he was afraid might hurt him."[7]

It was on the basis of Richardson's testimony alone, however, that Sayre was arrested and his papers seized, among them a letter from Catharine Macaulay and a newspaper contribution addressed to the livery of London and signed "Barnard's Ghost." From the start the detention of Sayre was mishandled. The warrant for his arrest charged him with high treason, but the warrant to the Tower authorities for his committal accused him only of treasonable practices, which ranked only as a misdemeanour and usually entitled the accused person to bail. On the basis of the original warrant, however, Sayre was kept in close custody until 28 October and only his wife was permitted access to him.[8]

In a statement to Lord Rochford before his committal Sayre denied any treasonable intentions but made some interesting admissions. He agreed that he had conversed with Richardson at the time and place the latter had referred to in his testimony, and he thought that John Reynolds, the Wilkite lawyer and business associate of Sayre, may have been present during the interview. Moreover, Sayre admitted discussing with Richardson "the Mischiefs which must arise in consequence of the Contest now with America," and "that he declared to him [Richardson] that he thought nothing would save both Countries but a total Change of Men and Measures"; he recalled adding, however, "that he was afraid there was not spirit enough left in this Country to bring such a Measure about."[9]

After five days of incarceration Sayre, attended by John Wilkes, Arthur Lee, and John Reynolds, was brought on a writ of habeas corpus before Lord Mansfield, the chief justice, who admitted him to bail. No other proceedings were taken against him and he remained a free man. Later, attended by a phalanx of opposition lawyers, he was awarded damages of £1,000 against Lord Rochford for wrongful arrest. During the course of this action the government's incompetent handling of the affair was fully exposed. Owing to a legal technicality, however, Sayre never received any of the damages, and thus the suit did nothing to mitigate his bankruptcy which he claimed was the result of his arrest and consequent erosion of confidence in his banking house.[10]

There are still unanswered questions concerning the Sayre affair.

Just what was the extent, if any, of Sayre's involvement in attempted insurrection? And what does the incident reveal about the government's attitude toward the possibility of subversion and the larger problem of opposition during wartime?

On the sole basis of Francis Richardson's evidence the case against Sayre would seem rather meagre. Richardson was known to be habitually in debt, and his subsequent inclusion among the beneficiaries of the secret service dole dispensed by the secretary of the treasury, John Robinson, strongly suggests that his information against Sayre was calculated opportunism to ingratiate himself with the government in the expectation of financial reward. On the other hand, the testimony of Nicholas Nugent indicates that Sayre had at least investigated the possibility of subverting the Guards. Sayre, moreover, was not squeamish about the ultimate necessity of violent opposition: in April 1775 he had written to Samuel Adams that in order to save the Mother County "high Convulsions" were necessary, which if started in America might "prove salutary even to us in England."[11] Significantly, on the day of Sayre's arrest thousands of papers were distributed among the population in London encouraging them to rise up and prevent the opening of Parliament.[12] The coincidence of these two events strongly suggests the implication of Sayre and perhaps some of his political associates in attempted insurrection.

Lord Rochford, then, perhaps had more legitimate grounds for apprehending Sayre than some of his contemporaries were prepared to acknowledge. It seems unlikely that he concocted spurious grounds for Sayre's arrest as part of a scheme for purging political opposition in the capital, despite rumours that Sayre's detention was only the start of a general round-up of City radicals for allegedly abetting the rebellion in America.[13] There seems at this point to have been no coordinated policy within the administration about dealing with the reality or potentiality of subversion. Lord Rochford, when he detained Sayre, apparently acted alone, although he probably anticipated the subsequent support of his colleagues. Lord Mansfield and Lord Thurlow (the attorney-general) disassociated themselves from Rochford's action, however, and even the king reportedly considered the evidence against Sayre too insubstantial to merit his prosecution. The affair probably had an impact on future government policy. The ridicule heaped upon Rochford for his handling of the matter and the unease expressed even by government supporters were in all likelihood responsible for the government's subsequently cautious response to rumours of subversive activity. Significantly, Rochford was removed from the ministry in November 1775.[14]

Other members of the London opposition, besides Sayre, were implicated in illegalities on behalf of America. Although their actions scarcely rank as insurrectionary, they indicated a growing sense of the futility of constitutional opposition to the war and illustrate the lengths to which some individuals were prepared to go in support of the colonies. In 1776, for example, John Sawbridge, the lord mayor, freed an American rifleman from Bridewell prison and sent him to Philadelphia with some dispatches from Arthur Lee sewn into his clothing. Sawbridge's predecessor as lord mayor, John Wilkes, also engaged in some suspect activities. In 1774, according to an informant of William Knox, Wilkes had discharged a prisoner sent to London by General Gage for encouraging desertion and was training him "to start upon the first occasion."[15]

After the outbreak of the war Wilkes continued to be an object of suspicion. Beginning in September 1775 he maintained close contact with Beaumarchais, who despite his friendly links with Lord Rochford became in 1776 a secret agent responsible for channelling aid for American revolutionaries through France to America. Wilkes and Beaumarchais dined together frequently until May 1776; Arthur Lee – who from November 1775 was the confidential correspondent of the Continental Congress in London – was also present on a number of these occasions. In the summer and autumn of 1776 Wilkes and Beaumarchais corresponded weekly, their letters being carried by a M. Garnier.[16] The British ambassadorial staff in Paris was convinced that the purpose of this contact was to facilitate the transfer to France of "sums of money for the Rebels in America, from their Friends in England, in order to convey them in French Ships to the French Islands, and from thence to Congress."[17] No move, however, was made against Wilkes; either the conclusive proof of his activities was lacking, or the government did not relish the prospect of a further legal battle with its old antagonist.

John Wilkes's brother-in-law, George Hayley, was also suspected of helping to supply the colonists. In November 1775 John Robinson received information that cannon, ammunition, and military stores, shipped to Spain on Hayley's account, were intended for the eventual use of the American rebels.[18]

Later in the war Wilkes was invited to participate in another seditious scheme. In July 1779 he received a letter from William Lee (then in France) suggesting that he acquire and dispatch to Lee military and political intelligence. Lee even provided Wilkes with a code for this purpose. In return for his services as a spy Wilkes was to receive £200 a quarter plus expenses. It is not known whether Wilkes accepted this offer. He might have been tempted by it because about the time he received it he was once again in dire financial straits. But in December 1779 he finally secured the lucrative post of City chamberlain and started a new career as a pillar of the establishment. Even if he had initially responded to Lee's offer, therefore, his career as a spy was in all likelihood very brief.[19]

Wilkes's tempter, William Lee, had earlier, while in England, acted in a way which can only be described as treasonable. In March 1775 he was responsible for distributing a broadside (probably written by himself or Arthur Lee) addressed to the troops about to embark for America, exhorting them not to shed the blood of their fellow subjects in the colonies. Copies of the tract were conveyed to Ireland for distribution among soldiers embarking there; it was also reprinted in American newspapers. The government became cognizant of the affair when a letter from William Lee to Josiah Quincy, Jr, enclosing the broadside, was intercepted and sent to Lord Dartmouth's office.[20]

No action was taken against Lee, however, and in August 1775 he was again engaged in subversive activity. His efforts on this occasion were directed at persuading disaffected and striking shipwrights from the royal yards to emigrate illegally to America.[21] It is not clear, however, if Lee was the main organizer in the affair, or whether he merely involved himself in an established scheme. The government uncovered details of the matter when the master and employees of the Ship Tavern in Woolwich informed the secretary of state's office that two men had come to the public house to agitate among the shipwrights. One of the men was identified as Edward Richardson, a former deputy to the marshal of the City of London and a member of the pro-American London Association. Richardson was also active among the Chatham shipwrights whom he allegedly intended using to initiate a revolutionary uprising in London. According to a curiously expressed letter to the *Morning Post*, Richardson told the London Association that

he had ... offered money to the [Chatham] shipwrights who were turned out of the King's yard to come to town and follow him and his advice, and they would soon have an increase in their wages; but the cowardly dogs skulk'd and would not go with him; whereas if they had, I would have rendezvous'd them in Smithfield, displayed the *Orange Flag* – the Flag of *Liberty*, and the multitude would have readily joined the standard; you know then, my boys, the business would have been done; the Americans have peace offered to them on their own terms, the ministry, the jacobite tory rascals brought to condign punishment, and Lord Chatham, my *old friend*, steering the SHIP what course he pleased.[22]

At Woolwich, however, Richardson and his associate confined their activities to treating the shipwrights and convincing them that influential elements in the City were eager to support them. They also distributed leaflets which promised wages in America considerably higher than the half-crown a day the shipwrights were petitioning for in England, as well as "work plenty ... good accommodation, Provision plenty, & all possible Encouragement gave to them."[23] The leaflet further informed the shipwrights that two ships' captains – Lawrence and Read – could be contacted to secure passage to the colonies.

The ministry used this last piece of information to infiltrate the project. It sent spies to Captain Lawrence posing as shipwrights wishing to emigrate to New York with forty of their fellows on Lawrence's ship. Their investigations revealed that the leading proponents of the scheme were, besides Lawrence himself, James Searle (a merchant and friend of the Virginia Lees) and Alderman William Lee. Captain Lawrence promised that the shipwrights who emigrated would be received by the Committee at New York; he further expressed the hope that men who did not find work immediately would "join the Provincials in support of the common cause." The spies also acted as *agents provocateurs*: they feigned destitution "in hopes," ran the instructions to one of them, "that Lawrence would promise payment [for passage] by Alderman Lee; or some of the committee at New York"; both Lee and Lawrence were to be implicated "in the transaction as far as would be done." The ploy partially succeeded: Lawrence opined that Lee would assist the men's passage, and when the government agents secured access to Lee he reluctantly agreed to pay nine guineas on their behalf as passage money. Lawrence also reported that Lee had found a secret means of raising additional funds for the men. Otherwise Lee, perhaps suspicious of the would-be emigrants, behaved with caution: he refused to give the imposters "letters of recommendation to the Committee at New York, [because] as an Alderman of the City of London and expecting to be in Parliament, such letters were they brought to light would occasion a blaze in the City." He did, however, agree to write them a general testimonial. At one point in his interview with the men Lee asked if they could build houses. "They answered yes, and Gun Carriages too if wanted"; Lee refused the bait. At a second interview with the spies Lee erased his name from a paper of encouragement to the shipwrights; he had been included, along with Searle, as a possible benefactor for those unable to pay for the voyage.[24]

The most enthusiastic participant in the affair was Searle, who was himself planning to remove to America in Captain Lawrence's ship. He told the spies he had "sent many Men to America who had blessed him for so doing, and made no doubt but the Men now going would do the same." He even produced his wife's book of household expenses to show the cheapness of provisions in New York.[25] At a later meeting with Searle the men were promised generous help with their passage and subsistence.

No other names emerged from the government's inquiries, although Captain Lawrence made reference to a group of unnamed gentlemen sympathetic to the shipwrights. The whole affair ground to a halt at the end of August when Captain Lawrence announced that the ship of which he was master had been sold and would not be making the voyage to New York. Searle – clearly the most sanguine of the conspirators – informed the spies that he would transfer the forty guineas he had promised for their passage to any captain willing to transport them to America, and he promised to recommend them to contacts in Philadelphia. The government took no further action in the matter, although John Robinson pressed for William Lee to be prosecuted, and Alexander Wedderburn, the solicitor-general, even took preliminary steps in framing his indictment for treason.[26]

THE LONDON ASSOCIATION

Because the activity of William Lee was clandestine, it had no impact either in inspiring further subversion or in encouraging the loyalist backlash against the patriots. Of a different character was the behaviour of a group describing itself as the London Association – the only formally organized society that in the light of the king's proclamation could be regarded as subversive – which emerged in the summer of 1775 and kept a precarious existence until February 1777. Historians have hitherto neglected to examine the society, but the political backgrounds and avowed credo of the group's adherents lend particular importance to this organized expression of pro-American sentiment in the metropolis. Moreover, it played an unintended role in promoting the kind of loyalist reaction that the government was so eager to encourage.[27]

The society's ideology and intentions are stated in its miscellaneous output of publications and in its resolutions which were published in sympathetic newspapers. The circular letter of the London Association, which was dispatched to various parts of the country in the late summer and autumn of 1775, begins with a paragraph which indicates the main stimulus to the society's formation: "The *present awful* and *calamitous* situation of *Great Britain* and its *Colonies* cannot but alarm and grieve *every true Friend* to LIBERTY and his COUNTRY, who considers the *ruinous consequences*, inevitable to the most essential interests of this nation, its *commerce* and *freedom*, in the *alienation*, perhaps the *total loss* of *America*." The letter goes on to denounce the ministry for subverting the constitution established by the Glorious Revolution and Hanoverian succession. It explains that the London Association was instituted "conformable to ancient usage ... in support and maintenance of the principles confirmed at those two great and important periods."[28] Recipients of the letter were called on to form similar societies in their localities.

The London Association thus saw itself as embodying the ideology and adopting the methods of the Revolution Whigs. It stressed this connection by prefacing the later publication of its circular letter with Lord Molesworth's *The Principles of a Real Whig*. In newspaper paragraphs promoting this publication the London Association claimed "those genuine principles of a real Whig" as "the solid ground of all their resolutions." A further literary inspiration to the society was probably the recently published *Political Disquisitions* of James Burgh which called for a "Grand National Association for Restoring the Constitution." Burgh specifically suggested that the initiative for such an organization come from London.[29]

The London Association was also responsible for the distribution of a broadside headed "Sidney's Exhortation ...," a title which, in itself, is indicative of the group's source of historical inspiration. This tract strongly denounced the government for its refusal to redress American grievances and advocated violent resistance to arbitrary measures.[30]

A more detailed exposition of the London Association's attitude to contemporary events was contained in its lengthy and repetitive "Declaration of Grievances" which was published in the *London Evening Post* of 21-23 September 1775. Several of the declaration's fifty-two grievances related to America; they included the destruction of trial by jury, violation of colonial charters, and the arming of papists and appointment of a Catholic hierarchy in Quebec. The remainder of the document contained a comprehensive restatement of all the afflictions to which metropolitan patriots felt themselves exposed; most of these grievances fell within the general categories of governmental abuse of the legal system, ministerial interference with elections, attacks on press freedom, excessive use of military force in domestic situations, high taxes, and venal and corrupt use of public funds.

At its weekly meetings the London Association pontificated on matters of immediate concern and secured the publication of its

resulting resolutions in sympathetic newspapers. The alleged harassment of the press was one of its chief preoccupations: the group
passed a resolution to open a subscription in aid of the printers
who were prosecuted for publishing John Horne's controversial
advertisement; the society claimed at the time this resolution was
passed to have already contributed £100 to the printers' legal defence
fund.[31]

Other dangers to the constitution, to which the published resolutions of the London Association were designed to alert the public,
included the planned formation of a Scottish militia force under Lord
Mountstuart ("to be sent against our Fellow-subjects in America!")
and the modification of the Habeas Corpus Act, as a wartime
emergency measure. The latter issue, together with the general trend
of government policy, prompted another resolution from the society
which called for "the Nobility ... Representatives in Parliament, and
others, friends to the glorious Revolution, and the form of government
then established, calling to mind the deeds of their illustrious ancestors
in times of national distress and calamity, speedily to meet the Citizens
in Common Hall ... to consider of and support a general Remonstrance to the nation."[32]

But this and other grandiose appeals of the London Association
fell on deaf ears. There was an unsubstantiated claim that a branch
of the association had been formed in Newcastle,[33] but the propaganda
of the society, despite its protestations of loyalty to the king, mainly
served to antagonize country squires, JPs, and other local dignitaries,
who, acting in accordance with the king's proclamation, returned
the London Association's letter to the offices of the secretaries of state
with accompanying expressions of loyal outrage. In the opinion of
the mayor of Worcester the circular letter was "principally intended
to recommend and abett in this Country the Rebellion which now
exists in America." Rev. J. Craven, a Berkshire magistrate, sent the
circular letter to Lord Suffolk (secretary of state at the Northern
Department), describing it as "ye inclosed Treason" and declaring
that "sooner than engaged in such a rebellious & unconstitutional
association I w^d exchange my black Coat for red, & spend my genteel
independent Fortune in support of His Majesty's Crown & Dignity."[34]
Such sentiments must have cheered the government; Craven's letter
is annotated "read by the king" (doubtless with considerable pleasure),
and one especially eloquent expression of loyalist reaction to the
association's activities – from the Devonshire magistrates – was
published in the *London Gazette* of 10–14 October 1775.

Even within the familiar territory of London's taverns the association encountered hostility. The group held its early meetings in

the Standard Tavern in Leicester Square, where, in the past, political gatherings had been accommodated. Mr Tibbs, the landlord of the public house, developed scruples, however, as a result of the king's proclamation, and placed a statement in the press declaring that the intended use of his establishment for the receipt of the association's correspondence "must be injurious to his unsullied Character, and hurt the Reputation of his House, in the Eyes of the Magistrates"; accordingly he refused to receive any letters addressed to the society.[35] Thereafter the London Association conducted its affairs from the Globe Tavern, though here also its presence was reported to be unwelcome.[36]

Hostility was thus the main reaction to the London Association. It made no positive political impact. The group, however, merits further study for the information which an analysis of its membership yields concerning the motives and affiliations of London's pro-Americans.

The names of twelve of the association's members can be gleaned from various sources. Tibbs provided eight of them in his statement to the *Public Advertiser* of 4 September 1775. They are Atkinson Bush, Edward Banner, Richard Beere, and five others identified as Hunt, Hurst, Crompton, Thomas, and Willmott. It was later denied that Atkinson Bush was a member of the association,[37] but a letter from "Cassius" to the *Public Advertiser* of 11 October 1775 added the name of Edward Richardson to the group. In addition, the names of the society's officials are revealed from the various published resolutions which they signed: they are Thomas Joel, secretary; Henry Maskall, president; and Robert Turner and John Piper, treasurers.[38]

Three of the group – Hurst, Hunt, and Thomas – cannot be distinguished from the numerous individuals of those surnames in poll-books and directories, and no entries can be found for Richard Beere and Edward Banner. Information can, however, be obtained for the remainder.

Willmott was a signatory to the circular letter dispatched by the association where his Christian name is revealed as John.[39] He is probably the John Willmott, goldsmith of 86, St Margaret Hill, listed in Lowndes' *London Directory* for 1774.

Crompton was referred to in the press as a "paultry [*sic*] Turner in Cockspur-Street"; his true identity, however, was almost certainly either Benjamin Crompton, or his son John, who were not turners, but paper-hanging makers and upholders in Cockspur Street.[40] Both father and son were active in the Wilkite and pro-American movements: Benjamin was a member of the Bill of Rights Society and spoke on behalf of the Wilkite candidates at a nomination meeting for lord mayor in September 1774; John signed the pro-American petition of 11 October 1775, and accompanied the presentation of a livery petition to the king on 10 April 1775.[41]

The career of Edward Richardson was less consistent in the cause of liberty. In the early 1760s he had acted as agent for Lord Bute in the City. His services included protecting Bute's coach from the unwelcome attention of the London mob in 1761. Later he was given a job in the Customs Office from which he was dismissed in 1772, three years before his agitation among the disaffected shipwrights. Richardson's enthusiasm for libertarian causes was short-lived, however, and was conceivably just a perverse method of pressing his attentions on the government: in 1777 he wrote to Charles Jenkinson, his former contact in Whitehall, relating his past services to the administration and requesting compensation.[42]

The London Association's treasurers and president had sounder credentials in defence of liberty and support for revolutionary America. All three had well-established and continuing links with the Wilkite political machine. Henry Maskall, especially, was a prominent figure at political gatherings in London. His oratory, his zeal for radical causes, and his occupation as an apothecary invited epithets from his opponents: he was variously described in newspapers as "the Demosthenes of the Mortar," a "haranguer general of turbulent coalheavers," and "a dirty little apothecary on the road to Tyburn."[43] Maskall's closest senior associate in the Wilkite movement was Frederick Bull; the two men jointly purchased tenements in Enfield for £126 which qualified Maskall as a Middlesex elector and entitled him to a place on the county hustings.[44]

Maskall played a central role in the nomination meetings for the mayoralty which, in the palmy days of Wilkite domination in the metropolis, rendered a virtual formality the subsequent gatherings in Common Hall to elect the two final candidates for lord mayor. On 15 September 1774 he successfully recommended Wilkes and Bull as the livery's nominees for first magistrate; and a year later his candidates, Wilkes and Sawbridge, were similarly accepted by a caucus meeting in the Half-Moon Tavern.[45]

Maskall's main efforts and most vehement rhetoric, however, were reserved for the American cause. His belligerent denunciation of the Quebec Act and Lord North's colonial policy, at the Middlesex nomination meeting of 26 September 1774, is described above. Later, in March 1775, Maskall avowed himself the author of an advertisement for a meeting of the livery caucus which successfully called for a Common Hall to petition against the government's American measures. He spoke at the Common Hall thus convened and was a member of the party which presented its petition to the king.[46] Following its rejection Maskall read a further petition (written by Arthur Lee) at the ensuing midsummer Common Hall, preceded by a speech in which he denounced "those wicked and despotic Ministers, who would drive the colonists to desperation"; he further expressed the hope that "the Livery would take a decisive part in favour of the Americans." In September 1775 Maskall was one of the Middlesex freeholders who applied for a special county meeting to consider domestic and colonial grievances, and he played an active part in the assembly thus called.[47]

John Piper, a packer by profession, also had close links with the Wilkite political machine, although, unlike Maskall, he was not celebrated for hustings oratory. Piper had been a member of the Bill of Rights Society, and he maintained close personal links with John Wilkes. One squib referred to him as "Deputy Piper/Jack Wilkes's A——e wiper." On 25 September 1775 Piper chaired the nomination meeting for lord mayor and referred to the "good Consequences arising from the active Virtues of the present Chief Magistrate [Wilkes]."[48] At the subsequent Common Hall Piper moved for the pro-American address from the livery to the electors of Great Britain. He was also chairman of the committee formed to promote the election of Wilkes as chamberlain for the City in 1776. Moreover, until December 1777 Piper was a Common Councilman for Queenhithe Ward; within the corporation he used his vote and influence in favour of the American cause.[49]

The other treasurer of the London Association, Robert Turner, was also a Common Councilman. He was less active on the hustings or in caucus than Piper or Maskall, but like all the officials of the London Association he signed the pro-American petition of 11 October 1775. His colleague, both in a linen drapery business and as a Common Council member for Bread Street Ward, was Luke Stavely, himself an active Wilkite.[50]

Unlike his fellow officials, Thomas Joel, the secretary of the London Association, established his patriot credentials exclusively by his literary efforts. In the 1760s he had been one of the newspaper essayists engaged by Thomas Hollis to support libertarian causes.[51] Later, writing under the pseudonym "Hystaspes," Joel was a prolific contributor to the *London Evening Post*. His pieces were florid in style and violent in sentiment; one piece of invective against the ministry illustrates both characteristics:

O! Plunge the sword of Justice deep into their corrupt hearts. Imitate the example of Jehu. Pile up their Heads at the Palace Gate, and stop not till Victory is compleat ... Shall *one* wicked Minister be suffered to live, who

sports with the lives of millions? No. – I would have such a man divided
into fifty-two parts, and with each I would have proclamations in every
country, 'Behold! – this is the Head of an infamous Wretch, who, after having
ruined our Trade, and weakened our national Strength, by vain, though
sanguinary measures, would have brought us, and our children, under the
tyranny of a foreign yoke'.[52]

Joel's other pseudonymous contributions included a funeral oration
for the American victims of Concord and Lexington couched in
language similar to that of John Horne's notorious advertisement,
an ingenious comparison of Lord North with the earl of Strafford,
and exhortations addressed to the City's governing institutions, which
either praised them for their vigour or chided them for their desul-
toriness in support of the Americans.[53]
    Joel, a former schoolmaster, was also the author of a series of
essays and poems, published collectively under his own name, in
which two items, "Political Thoughts" and "Letters to Lord Mansfield," exhibit attitudes echoing those of the London Association's
resolutions, especially in their impassioned defence of press freedom.[54]
As with Edward Richardson, however, there is a suspicion that Joel's
endeavours derived from questionable motives. An anonymous correspondent to the *London Evening Post* claimed that Joel had sought,
and been refused, a government pension, and that he was the paid
hack of the duke of Richmond.[55]
    The London Association thus seems to have been largely composed
of small tradesmen, with the exceptions of Edward Richardson and
Thomas Joel who are probably best described as frustrated place-
seekers and professional agitators. None of the group appears to have
had any direct economic stake in the outcome of the American contest.
Except for Joel and Richardson, there is little room for doubting
the genuine adherence of the society's members to the "Good Old
Cause" and its contemporary expression in metropolitan radicalism.
The close Wilkite associations of some of the group, and the nature
of its program, inevitably created the suspicion that the London
Association was merely a continuation of the Bill of Rights Society
under a different guise. The Bill of Rights Society was inactive during
the London Association's existence, but there is no evidence of any
connection between the two organizations. Nor did the London
Association engage in the electoral politics of the City as the Bill
of Rights Society had done. It was also rumoured that John Wilkes
may have been the London Association's secret leader or patron.
Thomas Joel certainly appealed to Wilkes for encouragement and
furnished him with copies of the association's resolutions; but it does

not appear that Wilkes responded to these overtures.[56] The London Association seems to have been an autonomously organized society which raised the spectre, without threatening the reality, of insurrection. In national impact, as well as in ideology and membership, it typified in microcosmic form the metropolitan pro-American movement as a whole.

CHAPTER FIVE

Loyalty versus Opposition in London, 1775-1778

PARTISAN IDENTITIES AND THE INFLUENCE OF CONTRACTS

The response to the London Association and the desperate activities of some of the pro-American partisans testify less to the strength of the prorevolutionary movement than to its evident failure to affect the course of imperial events. Within London itself the pro-Americans were increasingly challenged by government supporters as it became more and more evident that Britain was involved in a genuine war with her colonies and not merely a protracted squabble punctuated by military skirmishes. The circumstances of warfare and American progress towards independence helped consolidate a simple and emotional basis for loyalism – the denunciation of rebellion abroad and disloyalty at home – while entangling the patriots in increasingly complex problems of strategy and commitment. In October 1775 the surge of loyalist sentiment in the capital gave rise to two addresses to the throne supporting the administration's colonial policy; at the same time, despite their difficulties, the pro-Americans in the capital were able to muster a petition highly critical of the government and calling for a unilateral cessation of hostilities.

The pro-American petition had 1,100 signatures and was presented to the king on 11 October 1775. It was the outcome of a public meeting held at the King's Arms Tavern on 4 October. William Baker chaired this assembly and probably composed the petition; but pressure to hold the meeting in the first instance apparently came from the London patriots. William Lee successfully moved at the meeting that the presentation of the petition should be attended by the four City MPs. The signers of the document were collectively styled as the "Gentlemen, Merchants, and Traders of London." They comprised a broad spread of occupations and made no claims to having any involvement with Atlantic trade, unlike the signers of previous merchant petitions relating to North America. The pro-American petition of 11 October thus represented a wider range of public opposition to the government's colonial policy than had hitherto expressed itself in this form.[1]

Meanwhile the loyal merchants and traders of London were promoting their own address to the throne. A meeting for this purpose was held on 4 October at the London Tavern with Isaac Hughes, a Turkey merchant, in the chair. The loyalist address attracted 941 signatures and was presented to a delighted George III on 14 October.[2] Perhaps inevitably it was condemned as unrepresentative of commercial sentiment by the pro-Americans, who claimed it had the support only of "Jews, Papists, Contractors, Justices, and the whole ministerial group of creatures and runners of the Ministry, who, to gratify their Lordlings in place, would endeavour even to extend discord, faction, and civil war, to still greater lengths."[3] To the further discomfiture of the pro-Americans, a loyalist group within the livery, headed by Thomas Wellings, produced their own progovernment address which was presented to the king on 20 October. This address clearly indicated a stiffening of resolve among the loyal livery, and an improvement in their organization, which augured ominously for the survival of Wilkite hegemony in the capital. One thousand and twenty-nine liverymen signed this document, in implicit repudiation of the pro-American posture officially adopted by Common Hall.[4]

The competing appeals to the throne in October 1775 illustrate the developing partisan struggle in the capital. And they also provide the historian with an opportunity to examine in detail the comparative economic and occupational circumstances, contractual associations, and voting habits of the contending factions.

It can be definitely established that 124 (over 10 per cent) of the identified progovernment addressers were, or would become, involved in supplying the war effort with various provisions and supplies.[5] But because the information concerning subcontraction is deficient, the real figure was certainly higher. The loyal addressers also included 167 men who would subscribe to the notorious government loans of 1780 and 1781, which, because of the high rates of interest they offered to selected creditors were widely (though probably wrongly) regarded in opposition circles as an important source of executive patronage.[6] In addition, the addresses were signed by fifty men who between them held fifty-two directorships of London's major moneyed companies, which traditionally retained close financial links with the administration and subscribed heavily to government loans.[7] As well as the contractors and financiers among their number, twenty-

five of the loyal addressers were under the immediate patronage of
the crown as purveyors to the Royal Household, or as professionals,
artisans, and sinecure-holders in the king's service. This group
included Charles Eyre and William Strahan (the crown printers) and
two liverymen, Kirkes Townley and Joseph Manwaring, who each
enjoyed an annual sinecure of £100 as gentlemen pensioners of the
king.[8]

Many addressers had connections with government in more than
one category. John Durand, for example, held during the war navy
contracts for shipping and Treasury contracts for provisioning the
king's forces in North America. He subscribed £20,000 to the government loans of 1780 and 1781, and he also enjoyed the perquisites
of pewterer to His Majesty's Household. Altogether, it can be established that at least 263 (24 per cent) of the identified loyal addressers
were connected economically with the administration during the
American War of Independence; and there were undoubtedly others
whose links are not revealed by the extant record.[9] It is possible,
moreover, that the contractors, government financiers, and placemen
were in a position to bring pressure on others to sign the loyal
addresses.

A relatively small number of the pro-American petitioners enjoyed
economic links with the administration. Only five of them can be
identified as receiving contracts or subcontracts for supplying the
war effort, one of which was a subcontract that a petitioner, John
Tappenden, and two others received in September 1775 for tools valued
at £3.19.6 – a sum presumably insufficient to encourage subsequent
commitment to the loyalist cause.[10]

Forty pro-American petitioners subscribed to the government loans
of 1780 and 1781. This figure appears to confirm the invalidity of
the parliamentary opposition's claim that the subscription was
allotted exclusively to friends of the administration; but, notwithstanding, the figure represents only 6 per cent of the identified pro-
American petitioners, which contrasts with the 15 per cent of
progovernment addressers who subscribed to government loans. In
addition, the pro-American petition was signed by only eight directors
of moneyed companies, most of whom had special reasons for
repudiating overt affiliation with the government. Two of them, John
Manship and Robert Gregory, were members of the General Court
of the East India Company: Manship was a conspicuously independent
director within this faction-ridden group, while Gregory was a
longstanding supporter of the Rockingham interest within the court.
The two directors of the London Assurance Company who signed
the pro-American petition – Silvanus Grove and Samuel Turner, Jr

– were both involved in Atlantic trade, as was Richard Neave, a petitioning Bank of England director.[11]

Unremarkably, nobody under the direct patronage of the crown, as a purveyor or placeman, jeopardized his position by signing the pro-American petition.

Comparing the petitioners and addressers by occupation rather than by interest also produces revealing results. Not unexpectedly, over half of the overseas merchants who signed the pro-American petition were involved directly in the various branches of the Atlantic trade. But this number constitutes only about 9 per cent of the identified pro-American petitioners and fails to include a number of merchants who had been involved in previous attempts to intercede with the government on behalf of their colonial clients.[12] Some merchants, presumably, had decided that no tangible benefits lay in supporting revolutionary Americans. Or they may have been alarmed by the partisan tone of the pro-American petition. There were, significantly, no Quaker merchants among the petitioners. Their absence was in accord with the recommendation of the Yearly Meeting of the Society of Friends that Quakers avoid any involvement "in the present Heats and Commotions."[13]

A fear of losing their assets in North America continued to haunt many merchants, and that may have been the principal reason why a number of them did in fact sign the pro-American petition. William Molleson explained his dilemma and that of his fellow traders in a letter to Lord Dartmouth:

I found myself under the disagreeable necessity of signing the petition – a great part of my fortune is in America. I found myself marked by the faction for opposing the Petition, and had I not signed it, from the American Principle of "he that is not with us is against us," I should have been deemed an Enemy to America, and probably the next News we heard from there, might have been, that My Property was confiscated, and my Debtors ordered not to pay their just debts. In this Situation have I been compelled for the preservation of my Property, to give my concurrence to a measure I do not approve, and I can vouch for this being the case with numbers besides myself.[14]

Molleson went on to assure Dartmouth that if a guarantee could be given that in the event of a British victory the credit in the colonies of British merchants would be secured, then the government "would find such a Majority in the City, as would baffle all Opposition." The North American trade interest was a reluctant as well as a small element within the petitioning faction.

It was clearly not overseas merchants and financiers who predom-

inated among the pro-American petitioners. Rather it was the wholesalers, retailers, and craftsmen of the capital. Sixty-six per cent of
those petitioners whose occupations can be ascertained fall into these
categories. The pro-American petitioners were thus largely drawn
from the same occupational class as the members of the London
Association and the pro-American majority in the Common Council.[15]

The proportion of tradesmen and craftsmen among the loyal
addressers was lower than among the pro-American petitioners. Forty-
four per cent of the addressers whose occupations can be identified
fall into this category. But in absolute terms more members of this
occupational grouping signed loyal addresses than signed the pro-
American petition. Many of these addressers, however, were not
independent tradesmen or craftsmen. At least seventy-five addressers,
who were tradesmen and craftsmen, enjoyed contractual links with
the administration during the war, and there were probably others
whose names have been lost to the record.[16]

One-third of the loyalists whose occupations can be ascertained
were merchants (despite the fact that only five merchants trading
to North America signed the progovernment documents). Many of
these merchants were contractors, and merchant support for the
administration was probably also buoyed by the continuing prosperity
of European and Oriental commerce in 1775. Significantly, the largest
bloc of loyal merchants whose regional trading interests can be
determined were those engaged in commerce with Northern Europe.
They stood to profit from the increased demands for naval stores and
other commodities from the Baltic region, following the suspension
of similar imports from North America.[17]

The economic situation of the loyal addressers was on the whole
healthier during the war than that of the pro-Americans. As a group
the loyalists probably possessed more fluid capital resources. Only
6 per cent of their number went bankrupt between 1775 and 1783
compared with 10 per cent of the pro-American petitioners.[18] Within
one occupation, banking, there were evident differences in the financial
viability of the two groups. Loyalist bankers like Francis Gosling
(of Gosling, Clive, and Gosling) were generally partners of well-
established institutions that subscribed to government loans and
normally had sufficient resources to weather the perils of a wartime
economy. The pro-American bankers, by contrast, appear to have
been less securely based. They included men like Richard Gravatt
(bankrupt in 1778), Thomas Plumer Byde (bankrupt in 1779), and
Stephen Sayre (bankrupt in 1776).[19]

As well as the differences in economic circumstances between the
pro-American petitioners and the loyal addressers, the two groups

also had contrasting histories of political affiliation. Of the 260 pro-American petitioners who voted in the mayoral election of 1772, 223 (86 per cent) voted for one or both of the patriot candidates, John Wilkes and James Townsend; of the 558 loyal addressers who voted in the same contest, 471 (84 per cent) polled for one or both of the ministerial candidates, Sir Thomas Hallifax and John Shakespear. In addition, many of the pro-Americans were avowed Wilkites but for various reasons failed to vote in the mayoral contest. This group included Arthur and William Lee (who had not been liverymen long enough to qualify for the franchise), Thomas Plumer Byde, John Crompton, Samuel Petrie, John Piper, Stephen Sayre, Luke Stavely, Robert Turner, Samuel Thorpe, and Heaton Wilkes. The evidence of the pro-American petition confirms that the Wilkite movement and support for America were integrally related.[20]

There is a further piece of evidence that points to prior differences in the political sympathies of the contending factions. One hundred and eighty-seven of the progovernment addressers had previously, at the height of the Wilkite disturbances in 1769, signed a loyal address to the throne; eighty-two of these became connected economically with the government during the war. Only ten pro-Americans had signed the address of 1769.[21]

Analysis of the petition and addresses of October 1775 thus suggests the continuation of a longstanding ideological and political rift in London based to a large extent on socioeconomic distinctions. The American Revolution did not create contending factions; rather it provided an issue which served to focus existing hostilities. Many independent tradesmen, habituated to opposition, signed the pro-American petition because, through their jaundiced perception of administration motives, they saw the war as an outcome of corrupt and despotic government policies. They had, moreover, good reason to fear the consequences of a conflict which threatened economic dislocation with no apparent compensatory benefits. The loyal addressers, on the other hand, incorporated members of an economic elite who traditionally supported the administration, and the outbreak of war provided them with a natural pretext for reaffirming their loyalty. The loyal addressers, in general, had less to fear from the war than the pro-American petitioners which made them correspondingly less critical of government policy. In this context, the receipt or realistic expectation of contracts played a crucial role in consolidating loyal support for the administration. Contractors and government financiers not only signed the loyal addresses of October 1775; they were active throughout the war in raising voluntary subscriptions for the king's cause.[22]

This analysis of the petition and addresses of October 1775 should conclude on a cautionary note. Even though some of the loyal addressers almost certainly enjoyed connections with government unrevealed by the historical record, it remains a strong, though unverifiable, possibility that many of them were indeed independent tradesmen, who expected neither perks from government nor economic benefits from the war, but were simply finding the emotional appeal to loyalty in wartime more persuasive than continued opposition denunciations of administration policy.

The Wilkites, however, admitted no such possibility. They attributed the resurgence of loyalism in the City – first expressed in the addresses of October 1775 – and the decline in their own fortunes solely to the influence of contracts. Some argued that the war was actually contrived and sustained by the greed of profit-seeking contractors.[23] It was also widely alleged that Scots held all the lucrative contracts. A paragraph in the *Public Advertiser* of 7 February 1776 even referred to the war as "this ruinous Scotch contest with the *Anglo Americans*." The circumstances of conflict thus rendered more strident an habitual complaint of the London opposition: that the administration, in alliance with job-hunters and aliens, was pursuing policies that were contrary to the true interests of the country – a patriot cry which resembled the more sophisticated lamentations of the Real Whig, Richard Price, about the economic and moral state of Britain.

This aspect of Wilkite rhetoric was a revealing expression of middle-class anxieties in the capital; but much of the opposition attack was quite clearly misdirected. The war was neither caused nor sustained by a quest for contractual profits. Nor was there any truth in the allegation that Scots received a disproportionate share of government largesse.[24] But the other, less sensational, charges levelled by the Wilkites cannot be dismissed so readily. Two related questions merit particular investigation: Did the government and its agents deploy contracts to secure political advantage? And was the dissemination of contracts and subcontracts responsible, not just for the consolidation of existing loyal support (a situation already confirmed by analysis of the addresses of October 1775), but for the actual erosion of Wilkite and pro-American strength in the capital?

The opposition analysis was simple and plausible: war disrupted normal commerce; manufacturers and tradesmen were hence forced to supply the military effort in order to remain in employment, which put them under the patronage of the government and its agents.[25] The leading contractors were stigmatized by the Wilkite opposition, not so much for their support of the government – most of them, after all, had been avowed loyalists *before* the war – but because, allegedly, they adopted a subcontraction policy deliberately calculated to corrupt hitherto independent, patriot citizens.

A society entitled the Associated Livery (but normally called the White Hart Association after the tavern at which its meetings were held) became the main focus of Wilkite suspicions. This organization, formed in early 1776, set out ostensibly to resist "the late repeated Attempts to violate the Freedom of Elections, to introduce Strangers to the most honourable and confidential Offices, to destroy all Order and Subordination ... and to throw this once happy Nation into Anarchy and Confusion"; and the association planned "to restore the great Metropolis to its ancient Dignity and Importance; and to the British Legislature its just and necessary Power and Supremacy." The Wilkites, however, claimed that the society was simply the instrument by which corrupted citizens were organized politically.[26]

On 1 March 1776 John Wilkes blamed his failure to secure election as City chamberlain on "the deluge of corruption which has ... gained not a small part of the Livery." He expanded on this theme in July 1776 after he was again thwarted in pursuit of the same office. On this occasion he lamented the transformation of the livery "into tame, mean, vassals, ignominiously courting, and bowing their necks to, the ministerial yoke." He continued: "We are ripe for destruction. If we are saved, it will be almost solely by the courage and noble spirit of our American brethren, whom neither the luxuries of an unprincipled Court, nor the sordid lust of avarice in a rapacious and venal metropolis, have hitherto corrupted."[27]

The evidence from private correspondence indicates that such charges were not merely a cynical excuse for political failure; they were genuinely believed by members of the opposition knowledgeable about London politics. Arthur Lee, writing to Wilkes in November 1779 to wish him well in his last (and successful) attempt to become chamberlain of the City, commented: "I am mortally afraid of [Alderman Thomas] Harley and his Contracts. He is Pharoah's great Magician." And in 1778 Granville Sharp circulated "a memorandum for the consideration of the citizens of London" which contained the following analysis: "Citizens, in general, have been, of late, so much injured in Trade, that their Spirits are broken by their reduced Circumstances! And the Influence of the Contractors is very great (their's being almost the only Trade remaining) for they employ many Citizens in different Branches; so it is to be feared a Common Hall, or even the Common Council will not appear so independent as formerly." Even Edmund Burke, who was no friend of the City patriots and therefore under no constraint to excuse their diminishing success, was convinced that the "Haut Gout of a Lucrative War" was undermining commercial opposition to the government as early as August 1775.[28]

Circumstantial evidence lends support to these opposition claims. For years patronage had clearly influenced political allegiances in the democratic constituency of Westminster. Here numerous trades-men depended on the royal court and its noble courtiers for their livelihood, and they usually returned the favour by electing govern-ment supporters as MPs for the constituency.[29] It is not unreasonable to suppose that the expansion of war contracting in the City of London contributed to a political climate there similar to Westminster's. Also, it is known that the administration keenly involved itself in civic and parliamentary elections in London. In the contest for lord mayor in 1774, for example, the government attempted unsuccessfully to prevent Wilkes from winning that office. And in the parliamentary election of 1780, the administration attempted to organize opposition to the candidature of John Sawbridge in London.[30] It might therefore be deduced that the ministry played some part in the electoral triumphs of loyalism from 1776; and it might further be conjectured that ministerial pressure on the subcontractors, exercised through loyalists such as Thomas Harley, was one aspect of the government's involvement.

There is, however, evidence that points in the opposite direction. Studies of Treasury and Navy Board policy during the War of Independence have shown conclusively that the administration's overriding concern in distributing contracts was to secure value for money.[31] This, in itself, does not preclude the possibility that the government expected the contractors to become their agents in marshalling political support; but contractors chosen for reasons of economic and logistical efficiency would presumably have felt under no pressing obligation to play such a role.

In addition there was apparently no basis for the specific charge, levelled by the parliamentary opposition, that special Admiralty licences, issued after the passage of legislation prohibiting normal commerce with the continental colonies, were instruments of cor-ruption. These licences were intended to facilitate the supply of supplementary provisions to British troops and loyalists in North America. The opposition charged, however, that the licences were granted to privileged friends of the administration (few of whom were regular North America merchants) in order to furnish them with a lucrative trade monopoly and enable them, in turn, to influence politically tradesmen with whom they placed orders for goods. After a thorough parliamentary investigation in 1776 that quieted the opposition, evidence emerged of administrative slackness in the Admiralty (many luxury items, for example, were permitted conveyance to North America) though not of any conscious scheme of corruption. Moreover, John Robinson, supposedly the arch-corrupter in the administration, earnestly reprobated the Admiralty on a number of occasions for the careless manner in which some of the shipping licences had been distributed.[32]

Ultimately, the only satisfactory way for the historian to evaluate the existence or extent of corruption is to establish the degree of correlation between receipt of contracts and shifts in political behaviour. Unfortunately, the inadequacies of the available record mean that only tentative conclusions can be drawn from such an approach. There is a dearth of surviving poll-books for the appropriate period – the proximate ones being for the mayoral contest of 1772 and a City by-election of 1781 – and the all-important record concerning subcontraction is very limited.

The lacunae are particularly frustrating because two of the leading employers of subcontractors were Alderman Thomas Harley and William Knox. Harley was responsible for remitting specie to America and providing the troops there with clothing, blankets, and miscellaneous items of camp equipment; Knox was a senior official in the American Department responsible from 1777 for supplying presents to Indian tribes allied with the British.[33] Both men were deeply involved in the partisan struggle, so they had, presumably, the inclination as well as the capacity to exert political influence over the subcontractors whom they engaged. But the available record, for what it is worth, reveals no pattern of corruption. The names of thirty-four subcontractors can be positively identified. Of these, only two, Daniel Fossick and Samuel Freeman, both subcontractors to William Knox, voted for Wilkes and Townsend in the mayoral election of 1772. There is no evidence that expecting or receiving contracts influenced the subsequent political behaviour of the two Wilkite liverymen. Neither of them signed the petition or addresses of October 1775; and in the City by-election of 1781 Daniel Fossick voted for the Wilkite, Sir Watkin Lewes, while Samuel Freeman did not register a vote. None of Thomas Harley's eighteen known subcontractors had any previous association with the Wilkite movement.[34]

There was a handful of cases of shifting affiliation among the Victualling and Ordnance contractors engaged directly by the administration. Four of these men – Matthew Wiggin, Sam Sanders, Richard Crawshay, and William Ayres – voted for Wilkes and Townsend in the mayoral contest of 1772, but later signed one or both of the loyal addresses in October 1775. Of the four, Wiggin, Sanders, and Ayres did not vote in the City by-election of 1781, though in the same contest Crawshay voted for the ministerial candidate, Richard Clarke.[35]

The career of one other political apostate, William Strahan, is also worthy of special mention. In the late 1760s Strahan had been a leading supporter of the colonies;[36] but by the outbreak of war he had become an advocate of their coercion – a volte-face which brought a stinging rebuke from his former close friend, Benjamin Franklin.[37] It is possible that Strahan's political conversion was connected with his appointment to the coveted position of crown printer. But his case is unusual in that he was a consistent opponent of the Wilkite movement,[38] and, indeed, he may have felt that the American cause had received a taint from its adoption by the London opposition.

Within the City corporation, the influence of contracts was negligible. Besides Thomas Harley, the only war supplier on the aldermanic bench was Sir James Esdaile (alderman for Cripplegate Ward and lord mayor, 1777-8) who supplied the army with a variety of paraphernalia.[39] Esdaile and Harley were both longstanding government supporters and the contracts they received at most reinforced their attitudes of loyalty.

There seem to have been few contractors among the Common Councilmen, and there is no clear pattern of partisan behaviour among those who did receive contracts. Charles Wilkins, a Common Councilman for Tower Ward, supplied the Ordnance Board throughout the war with brushes, mops, pitch, tar, resin, and turpentine, and he supported the loyalist cause by his votes in the City corporation. But Lake Young, Common Councilman for Cordwainer Ward, who received £389.8 for glazier's work at the Admiralty Office in 1774, was a Wilkite and pro-American. Robert Barneveit, Common Councilman for Billingsgate Ward, supplied the Victualling Board with cheese and butter, but he seems to have refrained from any overt partisan commitment.[40]

It is possible that Common Councilmen were generally reluctant to receive war contracts and thus expose themselves to the wrath of their colleagues who placed such a high value on independency. (The harsh treatment accorded in Common Council to the major contractors, Harley and Esdaile, would tend to confirm the prudency of such caution.) It is also possible that the government was reluctant to taint authentic independent opposition to Wilkes in Common Council with the stigma of corruption. Zealous government supporters, however, could expect to be rewarded after their retirement from civic life. For example, ex-Common Councilman Thomas Burfoot held Treasury contracts for supply rum and packaging supplies; he was a subcontractor to Thomas Harley for blankets and rugs; and he was also packer for the Great Wardrobe in the King's Household. To cap all that, he received £200 in 1779, on a secret service warrant, for some mysterious "City Expences."[41]

All in all it appears that the dissemination of contracts was a negligible factor in the political conversion of Wilkites, despite some circumstantial evidence to the contrary. It should be stressed that this is a qualified judgment based on incomplete information. One thing seems clear, however. Contracts mitigated the economic impact of war for a number of individuals which made them more disposed to participate in organized displays of loyalism. Most of the known contractors had records of loyalty before 1775, and so their attitudes of loyalty during the war involved a reaffirmation and not a reorientation of political attitudes. At the same time, as we shall see, there were circumstances, unrelated to the distribution of contracts, which were undermining the Wilkite and pro-American campaign in the capital.

PRO-AMERICAN ATTITUDES AND THE PRESSURE OF EVENTS

The war had a complex impact on the opposition campaign. In some respects the Anglo-American conflict served to intensify radical criticism of the administration and to clarify the ideological basis of opposition. But at the same time the Anglo-American conflict rendered support for the colonists vulnerable to loyalist criticism and reduced the opposition's political effectiveness.

Real Whig polemics continued unabated. Leading Commonwealthmen kept up the themes of government iniquity and American virtue. Before the outbreak of hostilities a characteristic Real Whig notion had been that liberty and morals were degenerating in Britain, but advancing in the colonies. The Real Whigs consoled themselves that America would become the refuge for victims of the decline of liberty in the mother country. As the colonial crisis developed into open hostilities, they asserted more persistently the themes of Britain's decadence and America's future role as an asylum for free men.[42] This perception found its most influential expression in Richard Price's celebrated *Observations on the Nature of Civil Liberty, the Principles of Government, and the Justice and Policy of War with America*, first published in London in February 1776. This tract has been correctly analysed as a largely orthodox defence of natural rights, government by consent, and the legitimacy of revolution,[43] but it was as a jeremiad on Britain's decline that it had its main impact. Price blended the style of an Old Testament prophet with the authority of a modern economist. He wrote that "an abandoned venality, the inseparable companion of dissipation and extravagance, has poisoned the springs of public virtue among us." The war with America compounded Britain's degeneracy by increasing the country's dependence on paper credit and enlarging the national debt while real wealth was being drained. A collapse of the British economy, Price thought, was imminent. In America, by contrast, Price witnessed "a number of rising states in the vigour of youth, inspired by the noblest of all passions, the passion for being free; and animated by piety."[44]

Price's views prompted mixed, but intense, reactions. The Common Council of London bestowed on him the freedom of the City. The public fundholders were so alarmed by the Reverend Doctor's predictions that the government engaged its pamphleteers to repudiate them. In America the publication of *Observations on ... Civil Liberty* enhanced Price's growing prestige and led the Continental Congress, in 1778, to invite him to become an American citizen and take charge of the public finances of the fledgling nation.[45]

Price's doom-laden warnings about the dissipation of English morals and the expansion of the national debt became more strident and apocalyptic as the war continued.[46] In one published sermon he drew an analogy between Sodom and contemporary England which implied that England was about to suffer Sodom's fate. Price did, however, soften the blow for his congregation, commenting: "Perhaps, you may be directed to some means of escaping from the common ruin; and a *Zoar*, or an *Ark*, may be provided for you, from whence you may view the storm, and find yourselves safe. Methinks, the friends of truth and virtue may now look across the *Atlantic*, and entertain some such hope."[47]

To leading Wilkites, and Real Whigs such as Richard Price, the corruption of the House of Commons symbolized, and at the same time sustained, the decadence of British political life. The causes of parliamentary reform and America became more firmly associated in the minds of English radicals as a result of the war. They reiterated the theme that the conflict was provoked by Parliament's unconstitutional taxation of unrepresented colonists; and James Burgh reminded his readers that such taxation was itself designed to extend executive influence in the House of Commons by providing more places and pensions for the ministry's creatures. John Cartwright, in 1775, compared the corruption of the British Parliament to the purity of emerging political institutions in America, where authority was vested in "*unplaced, unpensioned, and uncorrupted* delegates."[48]

Such comments echoed traditional themes of country-party agitation; but the conflict was responsible for encouraging the new shift in reformers' demands. The growing dissatisfaction with the state of representation found expression in a wartime motion, introduced by John Wilkes, that called for a radical extension of the franchise and a redistribution of parliamentary seats. Wilkes linked his appeal directly to the state of Anglo-American conflict. He calculated that 5,723 corrupted voters could elect a majority of MPs; and he therefore agreed with Americans who claimed that the "war is carried on, contrary to the sense of the nation, by a ministerial junto, and an arbitrary faction."[49]

Despite, however, the stimulus that war lent to the ideological intensity and theoretical innovation of radical opposition, the shifting circumstances of Anglo-American hostilities also served to demoralize the opposition and diminish its chances of political success. John Wilkes himself acknowledged the futility of his own reform motion.[50] It was the issue of American independence that more than anything compromised the friends of America. They themselves were embarrassed and dismayed (initially at least) by colonial rejection of British sovereignty. Before the war they had accepted that the colonists were resisting abuses, not the ultimate legitimacy, of imperial authority. In January 1775, for example, Edward Dilly wrote to John Dickinson that he had no doubts "of the warmth the Americans have for the Parent Country, and their Loyalty to the King." He went on that America was "the brightest and most inestimable Gem in the British Crown, and [that] those who endeavour by misrepresentation, to rob the Crown of that Jewel, are enemies both to their Prince and their Country, and must be considered as the worst of Traitors."[51]

Some Real Whigs were reluctant to recognize that by 1776 revolutionary Americans were wholeheartedly and deliberately opting for independence and republicanism. Joseph Priestley thought that the Declaration of Independence did not reflect "the general sentiment." Richard Price wrote in *Observations on ... Civil Liberty* that, among the colonists, "independency is, even at this moment, generally dreaded."[52] Thomas Paine's *Common Sense*, which urged Americans to adopt full independence, was not well received by the main body of the colonists' English friends. They were affronted by its message and downplayed its popular appeal. Sylas Neville and his circle liked some parts of the pamphlet, "particularly that where the author treats Geo. III as the dog deserves,"[53] but their reaction was not typical of the British patriot movement as a whole. In the summer of 1776 John Almon reprinted the pamphlet, together with James Chalmers's anonymous refutation, *Plain Truth*, prefaced by the following advertisement: "The public have been amused by many extracts from the Pamphlet entitled *Common Sense*, which have been held up as Proof positive that the Americans desire to become independent; we are happy in this opportunity of publishing *Plain Truth*; which we take to be as good a Proof that the Americans do not desire to become independent." One opponent of the war even accused Lord George Germain, the new colonial secretary, of promoting *Common Sense* in order to discredit the Americans.[54] It is difficult to find in the opposition press as a whole any laudatory comment about the pamphlet.

The friends of America continued to hope that the colonists might be reconciled to an imperial structure reconstituted on a federal basis[55] – an option that had appealed to leading American patriots before the war, but which was rapidly becoming unviable. Some Real Whigs advocated legislative autonomy for the American states on the same basis as that existing in Ireland.[56] The analogy they chose was rather inappropriate in view of the massive corruption of the Irish House of Commons, but it nonetheless enjoyed widespread appeal in patriot circles. On 29 April 1776 the Court of Common Council resolved that John Sawbridge, the lord mayor, should move in Parliament that the American colonies "be continued upon the same footing of giving and granting their Money as his Majesty's Subjects in Ireland are by their own Representatives"; Sawbridge duly complied with Common Council's request on 10 May.[57]

A few English radicals persuaded themselves that parliamentary reform would reconcile the Americans to British authority. Major Cartwright thought in 1776 that "immediate reformation ... might, – it would – but nothing else can, reunite us with our American colonies"; and in 1777 Granville Sharp, on the basis of a conversation with some Americans in London, was convinced that a redistribution of parliamentary seats would predispose the colonists to accept peace terms from the government.[58] On 14 March 1777 Sharp recorded in his diary how he had tried to impress Lord Dartmouth with this conviction: "I ventured to pledge my life upon the success of an attempt to bring back the American Empire to the allegiance of the Crown of Great Britain provided a proof of *Sincerity* in Treating with them was given and the proof which I proposed was the *Reformation of Parliament* at Home."[59]

Sharp, of course, failed to realize that over the questions of independence and attitudes to monarchy there had been an important parting of the ideological ways for colonial revolutionaries and their English friends. While the Americans erected a new state on the constitutional basis of republicanism, domestic radicals continued to press for parliamentary reform as the proper means of restoring the balance of the British constitution. The hostility to monarchy, in the person of George III, that progressively developed in the colonies, was scarcely echoed in England, except among factions (such as the friends of Sylas Neville and the authors of *The Whisperer* and *The Crisis*) which were in any case habitually antimonarchical.[60] The American Revolution, at least in the short term, did not promote republicanism as a significant ideological force in England.

Despite their reluctance to see the colonists depart from the empire, Real Whigs and Wilkites eventually reconciled themselves to the fact of colonial independence, and, at least in their public statements, they conveyed no sense of having been betrayed by their American friends. Chatham's clarion call in April 1778 for renewed military effort to retain the colonies evoked no discernible response from either group. The metropolitan opposition was loath to blame the Americans for choosing to detach themselves from Britain. The patriots reserved all their criticism for Lord North's government. John Wilkes declared in the House of Commons on 31 October 1776 that the administration "drove the Americans into their present state of *independency*." A year later he attributed the "civil war ... and perhaps the loss of half our empire" to the government's rejection of Congress's Olive-Branch Petition in 1775. Richard Price, in 1777, adduced three other major reasons why the colonists opted for independence: the Prohibitory Act of December 1775, the rejection of a City petition of March 1776 which called for the suspension of hostilities, and the deployment of foreign mercenaries against the Americans.[61] (This last issue particularly troubled the Wilkites: in February 1776, for example, Frederick Bull inveighed against the government's intention of engaging German hirelings to shed the blood of Protestant subjects in America.)[62]

The leaders of the pro-American movement thus recovered from the shock of colonial independence and sustained their attack on the administration, but there seems little doubt that the American decision eroded popular support for the metropolitan opposition and opened the way for a loyalist counterattack.

The ministry and its adherents had for some time been convinced – and made public their apprehensions – that the real intention of the colonial revolutionaries was to sever all political ties between Britain and America. This conviction found its most authoritative expression in the king's speech to Parliament on 26 October 1775, which stated that "the rebellious war now levied ... is manifestly carried on for the purpose of establishing an independent empire."[63] The government's view was supported by a host of newspaper writers and pamphleteers.[64] A ministerial writer, "Coriolanus," writing in the *Public Advertiser* of 8 April 1776, declared with reference to *Common Sense* that "the Mask is at last thrown off"; he went on to attribute the pamphlet to Samuel Adams. When the American Declaration of Independence was reprinted in England, it quickly became the target of loyalist abuse. The *Morning Post* of 20 August 1776 published a parody of the entire document which commenced as follows: "When, in the course of human events, *pride, hypocrisy, dishonesty*, and *ingratitude* stimulate a subordinate community, to shake off the duty and allegiance which in honour and in necessity they owe the *superiority* from whence they derive their existence: a fear of *universal* reprobation, renders it necessary that they should declare causes to the world, – no matter how ambiguous and salacious." For "Pacificus," writing in the *Morning Chronicle* of 22 August 1776, the American Declaration of 4 July confirmed "that a jealousy of Taxation was the plea, while Independency was the real object of the Congress."

Pro-American protestations that the colonists were cruelly driven to independence proved an inadequate rejoinder to this kind of propaganda. Samuel Curwen, an American loyalist in London, accurately commented, after reading *Common Sense*, that "independence which America now evidently aims at, makes it a difficult part for her friends to act." And in February 1777 Thomas Walpole, a prominent London merchant, complained to Benjamin Franklin that American independence deprived the opposition "of refuting the tales which have been imposed on the world by the artifice of administration and which have principally contributed to the delusion of the people of England."[65]

Not only did the London pro-Americans suffer as a result of their support for alleged ingrates and deceivers, they were also held responsible in some quarters for actually directing the colonists towards rebellion and independence. This accusation was strongly implied in the king's proclamation for suppressing rebellion and sedition, and it became a theme in early loyalist historiography of the American Revolution.[66] It was also given contemporary expression in John Wesley's widely read pamphlet, *A Calm Address to our American Colonies* (published in London in 1775), and in a number of newspaper essays.[67]

It was really over the meaning of patriotism – which in a sense subsumed the issues of parliamentary reform and American resistance – that the pro-Americans were most vulnerable to the challenge of loyalism. They fell victims to the administration's success in branding opponents of government policy, in Horace Walpole's phrase, as "self-

interested incendiaries of the War."[68] During peacetime the metropolitan opposition could claim the appellation patriot without too
much semantic strain, especially in view of the movement's belligerent
attitude towards France and Spain. In wartime, however, the title
patriot ill-suited an avowed supporter of His Majesty's declared
enemies. Samuel Johnson had, in 1774, already derided the patriotic
credentials of those who justified "the ridiculous claims of American
usurpation";[69] with the outbreak of hostilities this denunciation
assumed an enhanced force. J.H. Plumb has argued with cogency
that the dissociation of radicalism and patriotism was almost wholly
responsible for the erosion of incipient pro-American sentiment
among provincial industrialists, such as Josiah Wedgwood, and also
contributed to the decline of Wilkite power in the capital.[70] Loyalism,
moreover – until Gen. John Burgoyne's defeat at Saratoga in October
1777 – enjoyed all the attractions of an apparently winning cause.
The news of Gen. Sir William Howe's successes at New York enhanced
the ministry's popularity in the autumn of 1776, and confidence in
an ultimate British triumph continued well into 1777. It would require
military reverses before opposition to the war could vigorously and
extensively reassert itself.[71]

THE BATTLE IN THE CITY

The odour of factiousness and disloyalty that clung to the pro-
Americans helped to erode the strength of the metropolitan opposition
even within the civic institutions of London.

Common Hall – always the most politically volatile of the City's
institutions – virtually ceased to function as an agency of opposition
in the metropolis, a situation portended by the loyal livery address
of October 1775. The triumph of the ministerialist candidate over
Wilkes, in successive contests for the chamberlainship, was not the
only electoral success for the loyalists in 1776. In July Alderman
Plumbe, an avowed supporter of the administration, was returned
as one of the City's sheriffs. And in September Sir Thomas Hallifax,
the most senior alderman not previously to have been lord mayor,
was elected to the mayoralty. Hallifax was basically a loyalist, but
in his acceptance speech he reminded the livery that when he was
sheriff of London and Middlesex in 1768-9 he "stood undaunted
in Support of the violated Rights of Election, and the Constitution
as by Law established." His remarks were reportedly "received with
great Approbation by the Friends of Freedom, while the Associated
Livery with lengthened Faces muttered their Disappointment to each
other."[72] But despite Hallifax's unexpected declaration the Wilkites

had clearly lost control of the livery's electoral behaviour. With Hallifax's election the practice was reestablished of returning alder-men as lord mayor on a basis of seniority. In 1777 this led to the elevation of the contractor, Sir James Esdaile, to the office of first magistrate without the necessity for a poll.

Under these circumstances it is scarcely surprising that the Amer-icans ceased to receive any significant support from the livery in Common Hall during the late 1770s. It was reported in the *Gazetteer* of 30 September 1776 that Captain Allen had intended proposing an address, on behalf of the colonists, at the Common Hall the previous day, but "after reconnoitring the ministerial forces, and finding them very numerous" he had decided to drop his plan. There were also rumours in the spring of 1777 that a Common Hall would be called to remonstrate against the war,[73] but they proved unfounded. The pro-Americans, however, briefly reasserted themselves in the Common Hall of 29 September 1778: William Baker proposed that the City's MPS be thanked "for their steady and uniform opposition to the measures of a weak and wicked administration, whose injustice, obstinacy, and folly have rent the empire, and lost to Great Britain her most valuable possessions in America." The lord mayor, Sir James Esdaile, refused to put the question to the Common Hall, however, and dissolved the assembly. A remnant of the livery then hoisted Sir Watkin Lewes into the chair vacated by Esdaile and carried Baker's motion.[74] These subsequent proceedings were strictly unofficial; they are not mentioned in the City records and it is doubtful whether they indicated renewed support for the American revolutionaries among the livery as a whole. Not until December 1781 did Common Hall again officially produce a remonstrance against the government's war policy.

Common Council proved more resistant than Common Hall to the growth of loyalism. The White Hart Association attempted to organize the removal of Wilkites from the Court but met with only limited success.[75] Some idea of the changing balance of pro-American and progovernment forces within the Common Council can be readily ascertained. Of the pro-American petitioners of 11 October 1775, twenty-eight left the Court and twenty-two joined it between October 1775 and December 1778. (The worst year for the pro-Americans was 1777 when ten of their number – including Luke Stavely and Deputy John Piper – were dislodged from the corporation.) Of the loyalist addressers of October 1775, twenty left the Court and nineteen joined it during the same period. A shift in favour of loyalism within the Common Council was thus apparent, but it was slight: the relative numerical strength of the progovernment party increased by only five on the basis of the figures cited.[76] Very few members of the Common Council, moreover, switched their political allegiance during the period in question.

The survival of a large body of opposition within the Common Council helped to ensure that support for the American revolutionaries continued to find political expression in London despite the rise of loyalism. The war itself was criticized by the pro-Americans as well as the expediencies to which it gave rise; meanwhile resurgent loyalists in the metropolis demonstrated their support for the government by helping in various ways to sustain the war effort. The incompatible objectives of the two groups produced a number of clashes – within Common Council and outside it – which illustrate the extent to which the American issue had riven public opinion in the capital.

At a Common Council meeting on 14 March 1776, William Saxby successfully proposed that a further petition be presented to the king condemning the war. The document consequently formulated pleaded that peace terms should be offered to the Americans before renewal of military operations. It further warned, in language reminiscent of Richard Price's, of "that increase of the national debt, and of burdensome taxes, the loss of our most valuable resources, those distresses of our merchants and manufacturers, those deficiencies of the revenue ... that failure of public credit ... which must follow a civil war, so begun and pursued."[77]

Common Council not only echoed Richard Price's sentiments; it also accorded him the official thanks of the Court for his *Observations on ... Civil Liberty* and voted to award him "the Freedom of this City ... presented in a Gold Box of the value of Fifty Pounds."[78] Price gratefully accepted the honours bestowed on him and dedicated his *Additional Observations on ... Civil Liberty* to the lord mayor, aldermen, and Commons of London. The exchange of compliments between Price and the Common Council is an interesting demonstration of the close accord between the Real Whigs and active Wilkite politicians over the issue of America.

The Common Council was roundly abused by government supporters, including Samuel Johnson, for its pretensions in entering the literary debate over the American Revolution.[79] City loyalists also argued that the resolutions honouring Richard Price were secured by chicanery: the disgruntled opponents of the Wilkites claimed that eighty pro-American Common Councilmen were previously instructed by William Hurford (a Common Councilman for Castlebaynard Ward) to read Price's pamphlet; other Court members, meanwhile, were allegedly ignorant of the tract's contents and left the Common Council before the resolutions were considered; this left an estimated 121 members in Court, which guaranteed the victory of the pro-American party.[80] There was probably some justice in these loyalist complaints; there were significantly no voting divisions on the motions in question. The resolutions in honour of Richard Price, therefore, are perhaps a misleading indication of political opinion within the Court, but they at least demonstrate the continuing determination of Wilkite Common Councilmen to organize support for the Americans and their English sympathizers.

Common Council also opposed specific war measures. In February 1777 it presented a petition to the House of Commons criticizing a bill which enabled the crown to detain without trial persons suspected of high treason or piracy committed in North America or on the high seas. The City's petition argued that the legislation would in effect suspend habeas corpus. John Wilkes protested against the bill in the House of Commons – even after it had been amended to limit its effect – because it reduced the possibility of reconciliation with the American colonies.[81] Despite protests from the City and other quarters, however, the bill passed into law.

Common Council resisted another war measure, naval impressment, in a more sustained way and with some limited success. Impressment, of course, was never popular, especially with its potential victims, whatever national interests were at stake. The City aldermen, however, normally recognized necessities of state by endorsing the Admiralty's press warrants. In addition, the City traditionally offered bounties to volunteer sailors. During the dispute with Spain over the Falkland Islands in 1770 – when tension between the City and the administration was at a peak – the Common Council opposed impressment within city limits, but gave forty shillings to able seamen who engaged to join the Royal Navy.[82] No such bounty was forthcoming during the American conflict.

The Common Council made it clear that its refusal to assist in supplementing the fleet arose specifically from opposition to the government's prosecution of the American war. On 22 November 1776 the Court resolved that it "will at all time be ready to assist Government . . . to raise an Armament to oppose our natural Enemies whenever due Information shall be given that it is necessary."[83] When, in January 1777, a regulating captain chided the City aldermen for rendering the country defenceless before the fleets of France and Spain, Lord Mayor Hallifax replied that if the government did fear a war with continental opponents it should inform the London corporation which would then raise the necessary bounty.[84]

The City was supported in its stand by the Watermen's Company, which in previous wars had offered for service two hundred of its freemen in return for immunity from impressment for the remainder. By October 1777 only two of its members had been furnished by the company despite a request by the Admiralty for the fulfilment of the normal quota.[85]

The necessary Order in Council for the issue of press warrants was passed on 28 October 1776, two weeks before the expiry of John Sawbridge's term as lord mayor. With his background of opposition to the government's American policy, it is hardly surprising that Sawbridge should have offered such stubborn resistance to the operations of the press gang. He refused to back Admiralty warrants and ordered the City marshal and his assistants to apprehend any naval officers attempting to snatch London citizens. He could not prevent, however, the seizure by the press gang of fifty men in Billingsgate and four from the Fleet market on the basis of warrants unendorsed by the City magistrates.[86] (These incidents took place shortly before John Wilkes declared in the House of Commons that "no press-gangs have dared to make their appearance in London.")[87] Sawbridge was praised in Parliament for his endeavour by Lord Shelburne, who added, "If it was a war with France or Spain he [Sawbridge] would be pulled out of the Mansion-house, if he did not back the warrants."[88]

The Admiralty probably hoped for a more sympathetic response to its needs from Sawbridge's successor, Thomas Hallifax. On 10 November 1776 the Admiralty wrote to the new lord mayor, asking for "his countenance and assistance" to officers engaged in impressing for the fleet. Hallifax, in reply, protested his loyalty, but refused the Admiralty's request, ostensibly on the basis of a legal opinion given in 1770 by three lawyers, including Alexander Wedderburn who had subsequently become solicitor-general. Hallifax claimed that the lawyers had shed doubt on the legality of press warrants. In fact, their opinion confirmed the legality of press warrants issued by the Admiralty under the authority of the king in Council and advised that, although the lord mayor was under no binding obligation to back them, it was conducive to the peace of the City, and in conformity with precedent, for him to do so.[89] Probably Hallifax distorted the meaning of this judicial advice in order to guarantee a tranquil mayoralty, without constant criticism from Wilkite Common Councilmen. He intimated this in his letter to the Admiralty in which he stated that he would be "very cautious not to begin my Mayroyalty by promoteing a Measure I cannot support."[90] The experience of his successor Sir James Esdaile – who suffered abuse and recrimination from the Common Council and a section of the general public for his approval of impressment and other war measures[91] – confirmed the prudence of Hallifax's course of action.

Hallifax did make one small concession to Admiralty needs: shortly after his installation as lord mayor he gave orders to the City marshal to remove from the City's public houses "all suspected persons, that ... can give no account of themselves" and send them to serve the king.[92] But this gesture did not appease the ministry. At a meeting of the cabinet on 18 November 1776, it was determined, on the advice of the attorney-general and the solicitor-general, that the Admiralty should continue to execute press warrants within London, even though the lord mayor refused to back them. Reports of press-gang operations in the City subsequently became common in the newspapers. On one occasion a man was snatched from directly opposite the Mansion House.[93]

The government received some support for its action from the leading ministerialists on the aldermanic bench. On 10 December 1776, for example, Thomas Harley and Brackley Kennett backed a number of Admiralty warrants. But they acted independently, in defiance of the corporation's official policy. Harley and Kennett were roundly abused for their gesture by the Wilkite aldermen, and the lord mayor and other City magistrates reiterated their instructions to the City marshal and ward constables to seize members of gangs found pressing within City limits. These aldermen were officially thanked for their action by the Common Council as a whole.[94]

The controversy over impressment was stimulated, if not resolved, by a sequence of judicial contests between the Admiralty and the City. The Wilkites sought to defend a general principle – the illegality of impressment – in order to further a specific end, which was obstruction of the war effort. Such tactics evoke comparisons with past City battles over general warrants and freedom of the press.

On 4 November 1776 John Tubbs, one of the City's official watermen (that is, he attended the lord mayor at ceremonial occasions on the River Thames) was pressed near Gravesend. The City's waterbailiff applied to the Admiralty for Tubbs's return which was refused. He then petitioned the Court of Aldermen to help secure Tubbs's release. The Court responded by instructing the town clerk to write to the lords of the Admiralty insisting on Tubbs's immediate discharge. The Admiralty refused the town clerk's demand but strongly implied that if Tubbs's release had not been claimed "as a matter of right" its attitude would have been more conciliatory. On the following day the Admiralty consulted the opinion of the crown law officers who confirmed the legality of its refusal.[95]

A Common Council, summoned by Hallifax on 22 November,

reacted to the situation by forming a committee to manage the necessary business for securing Tubbs's release. The committee included one American – William Lee – and several other Wilkites, among them John Wilkes himself, Sir Watkin Lewes, Samuel Thorpe, and Luke Stavely. Its main goal was to effect, if possible, Tubbs's discharge on the ground of the illegality of impressment and not on the basis of his special status. For this reason, at the committee's second meeting on 23 November 1776, a proposal that the City solicitor apply for a writ of habeas corpus "on the ground of his [Tubbs] being one of this City's Watermen" was withdrawn, and replaced by a proposal which stated merely that he obtain a writ "for John Tubbs one of the City's Watermen." At this meeting, also, the City solicitor was ordered to retain several lawyers, including Arthur Lee.[96] It is an illuminating comment on surviving attitudes within the City corporation that an American, in the employ of the Continental Congress, should have been invited to prosecute a measure which favoured the American cause at the expense of the British.

The application for a writ of habeas corpus was made at the Court of King's Bench on 28 November 1776, when, after detailed legal presentations from both sides of the dispute, it was refused on the grounds that there was no precedent legally exempting the City's watermen from impressment. During the subsequent legal vacation, however, Lord Mansfield did grant the writ, following the submission of further affidavits from the City which indicated that in 1745 one Richard Underhill had been discharged from the fleet, with the navy's acquiescence, on the grounds that he was a City waterman. Mansfield added the rejoinder to the habeas corpus that Tubbs should appear in court if the Admiralty decided to make a return of the writ.[97] The Admiralty made no further attempts to secure Tubbs's services, however, and he remained at liberty. But the City had only secured a limited victory: Tubbs had won a conditional, not an absolute, discharge; the Admiralty had made no concessions as to whom it might press; and no progress was made in the Tubbs committee's original intention of disputing the general validity of press warrants.

The next legal wrangle resulted from City officials implementing the aldermanic instructions to detain naval personnel engaged in impressment activities. On 16 December 1776 the constables and beadles of Lime Street Ward seized four naval officers for attempting to impress two men; the officers were then brought before Thomas Wooldridge, Sir Watkin Lewes, William Plomer, and William Lee at the Guildhall. The naval functionaries refused to give bail to appear at the next sessions and were committed for assault. The aldermen stated that their purpose in prosecuting the case "was to gain, in a proper and regular course of proceeding, a legal determination of the grand question respecting press warrants." Next day the Admiralty bailed the naval officers, and the charge of assault was heard before a jury at the Old Bailey early the following year. The jury failed, however, to find grounds for an indictment.[98]

The case is especially noteworthy because it attracted the interest and involvement of two leading reformers and philanthropists – Granville Sharp and Gen. James Oglethorpe. Their motives in condemning impressment were primarily humanitarian and judicial, although Sharp was, of course, a vigorous defender of the Americans which probably coloured his judgment of the issue. For Sharp, pressing by Order of Council stood in the same light as "General warrants [and] Ship money."[99] Sharp and Oglethorpe even obtained affidavits which apparently proved that two of the sailors had forfeited their bail by engaging in impressment activities before their case was heard; the City took no steps as a result of this information, however.[100]

Granville Sharp was also involved in a further legal dispute between the City and the Admiralty. On 21 March 1777 John Millachip, a freeman of the Needlemakers' Company, was pressed. The Admiralty refused to release him following application by Alderman Bull and the case was referred to the Tubbs committee, which successfully secured a writ of habeas corpus from Lord Mansfield; Millachip was consequently discharged. On 26 April 1776, however, Millachip was pressed for the second time and another writ of habeas corpus was issued on the undertaking that Millachip would appear in court if a return of the writ was made by the Admiralty.[101] The Admiralty on this occasion did decide to make such a return. Granville Sharp meanwhile was busying himself among the City politicians to make sure there was no wavering in their stand. On 30 April he went with William Lee (who had obvious motives for opposing impressment) to the home of John Glynn, the City recorder, where Sharp delivered "some remarks on the force of the Habeas Corpus Laws of which it seems he [Glynn] had not before been aware." Sharp observed that "Alderman Lee seemed much pleased with what was said indeed the Recorder also." Two days later Sharp visited Mr Bates, the secretary of Lord Sandwich (first lord of the Admiralty), and informed him that the return to the writ of habeas corpus was improper, "and would endanger Lord Sandwich as well as Lord Mansfield."[102] On 7 May 1777 the return to the writ was read at the Court of King's Bench and, after a series of adjournments, Lord Mansfield adjudged it to be insufficient – a decision which Granville Sharp regarded as the result of his interventions. The Admiralty desisted from further legal action and Millachip, like Tubbs, gained conditional freedom, although not an absolute discharge.[103]

The Tubbs committee sought to bring matters to a conclusive judgment by commencing a suit for assault and false imprisonment against Captain Kirke, the naval officer responsible for Millachip's detention. The committee's intention was twofold: "to establish the right of Exemption of a Freeman and Liveryman of London being impressed as also to bring to a legal discussion and determination the grand & General question respecting the right of impressing."[104] Kirke subsequently was served with an action by the City solicitor but no further proceedings appear to have been taken by either party.

At the same time as Millachip was first taken by the press gang, John Maund, a constable of Queenhithe Ward, was also snatched. In the case of Maund, however, the Admiralty discharged its victim absolutely on delivery of a writ of habeas corpus. Thus the City was able to claim a legal immunity from impressment for its City constables.[105]

This victory, however, was an isolated one. Press gangs continued to operate within the City, and the inconclusive outcome of the Millachip case meant that the courts did not support the exemption from impressment of London's citizens. Individual naval officers occasionally recognized citizenship of London as conferring immunity,[106] but generally City resistance to impressment only provoked the Admiralty into extending its claims. The scale of impressment increased as the probability grew of a French entry into the war; and the press gang on one occasion reportedly seized an apprentice from the shop of William Axford, a Wilkite Common Councilman for Farringdon Without Ward.[107]

The City's stand against impressment constituted evidence of and grounds for a continuing hostility within the Common Council to the war policies of Lord North's government. It was not a campaign that achieved many solid successes. The Wilkite politicians were, however, backed in their opposition to the press gang by that section of the population who were its victims and by those merchants whose commercial operations were disrupted by impressment activities. These groups supported the parliamentary attempts of Temple Luttrell, a friend and supporter of John Wilkes, to introduce legislation enabling the navy to recruit volunteers humanely.[108]

In addition to opposing impressment, the Wilkite Common Councilmen successfully resisted attempts by the City loyalists to raise a body of troops subsidized by the corporation. In 1777 provincial towns such as Manchester and Liverpool raised regiments to fight in the king's service, and metropolitan loyalists intended that London should follow their example. A public meeting was called for 7 January 1778 to promote the scheme. This gathering, however, was thinly attended and those present evinced little enthusiasm for the business at hand. Possibly the news of General Burgoyne's defeat at Saratoga had dampened loyalist ardour. But, despite an apparent lack of public zeal, Sir James Esdaile hastily convened a Court of Common Council for 16 January 1778, and offered the motion "that a Subscription be forthwith opened ... for the paying Bounties to such able bodied men who shall present and enlist themselves ... to serve in his Majesty's Sea or Land service for the Term of three Years or until the end of the present War."[109]

The proposal prompted lively debate in a well-attended Court. The Wilkite Common Councilmen, the previous evening in the Half-Moon Tavern, had affirmed their opposition to the payment of civic subsidies to soldiers or seamen. The main thrust of the opposition's objection to the loyalist motion was that the City had previously denounced the government's coercive measures against America and it would thus be an absurd reversal of policy to support them by civic subsidies. The Wilkites severely criticized Sir James Esdaile. They censured him for summoning the Common Council at short notice – in contradistinction to his behaviour in December 1777 when he had refused to convene a Court, on requisition from the City MPs, to consider the American situation. The City opposition also claimed that Esdaile had been closeted with the king to plot the scheme for civic bounties and that as a supplier of military equipment he would personally profit if the City raised a body of troops. The loyalist motion was eventually negatived by a considerable margin, although it enjoyed the support of eleven of the twenty aldermen present. The Wilkites consolidated their victory by securing a motion which stated "that to give any Countenance to, or to be in any manner instrumental in the farther continuance of the present ruinous and destructive War, whilst offers of just and Honourable terms are withheld from America, will reflect dishonour upon their Humanity and in nowise advantage the commercial interests of this great City."[110]

The attitude of the Common Council was a considerable setback to the progovernment party. For the king, the loyalists' defeat was a "mortifying circumstance."[111] The City ministerialists partly rectified the situation, however, by opening a subscription in support of the war effort to which individuals could contribute. It was reported that £20,000 was very quickly subscribed for "raising men for his Majesty's service, in such manner as his Majesty in his wisdom shall think fit."[112] The venture was soon assailed by opposition newspapers and by radicals in Parliament. The *London Evening Post* of 22-

24 January 1778 commented that "the generality of the subscribers at the London Tavern are *Scotchmen, Jews, policy brokers, black legged underwriters* from New Lloyd's, and people who are dependent upon government." In the House of Commons, John Wilkes questioned the constitutionality of "giving private aids, benevolences, and subscriptions, for public purposes, to the Crown, without the sanction of Parliament." He argued that "if troops could be raised, kept up, and paid, without the concurrence of this House, the liberties of this country must be at the mercy of the military, and their commander in chief, perhaps an ambitious prince." Lord Abingdon, a radical peer, pursued a similar theme in the House of Lords.[113]

Loyalists and the City opposition thus demonstrated their opposed attitudes by respectively supporting, and attempting to undermine, Britain's military power. The two groups also vied with each other in raising charitable subscriptions for selected victims of the war. One example of such an enterprise was the attempt by John Horne and the Constitutional Society to derive political capital by donating money to the widows and orphans of American troops killed at Lexington and Concord. On 18 October 1776 the loyalists countered by opening a subscription "for such occasional Acts of Benevolence as may be useful to the Soldiers who are or may be employed in his Majesty's Service in America and for succouring the distressed Widows and Orphans of those brave Men who have fallen in defending the Constitutional Government of this Country." Among the members of the committee which organized this venture were the contractors Thomas Harley, James Bogle French, Thomas Burfoot, and J. Julius Angerstein (a supplier of shipping to the Navy Board). By the middle of January 1776 nearly £15,000 had been subscribed to the fund.[114]

The main charitable enterprise of the metropolitan opposition was the raising of money for American rebels incarcerated in England. The plight of colonial prisoners of war first claimed public attention in early 1776, following the capture, and temporary confinement in Pendennis Castle, of Col. Ethan Allen. Correspondents to opposition newspapers complained that Allen had been harshly treated by his British captors.[115] Then, in August 1776, Alderman William Lee became involved in a heated controversy about British attitudes towards American prisoners. It seems that he wrote a letter, under the pseudonym "Humanitas," to the *Public Ledger* of 5 August 1776, alleging that the sailors of an American privateer had been brutally treated by Captain Ross, master of the English ship which effected their capture. Captain Ross subsequently confronted Lee on the Royal Exchange and threatened "to do for him in another Place." Because of his menacing behaviour Ross was charged before the lord mayor,

John Sawbridge, for a breach of the peace, although it appears that the case was eventually allowed to drop.[116] Opposition writers, however, kept the issue of American prisoners before the public through 1777.[117]

Meanwhile Americans in Europe, such as Benjamin Franklin, attempted through their English contacts to organize the amelioration of prison conditions for captured rebels. By December 1777 moves were afoot among the opposition to raise subscriptions for American prisoners; Lord Shelburne mooted such a step in the House of Lords on 5 December. On 11 December Lord Abingdon, after successfully moving in the Lords for the papers relating to the custody of American prisoners to be laid before the House, stated his intention of raising a subscription on their behalf. The Rockingham Whigs also interested themselves in the plight of the incarcerated Americans. They sent "a Person to Visit & relieve on the Spot the Prisoners at Forton & Plymouth." William Baker pointed out to Lord Rockingham the political advantage to be derived from such enterprises: "They will throw some Damp on the Arrogance & Presumption with which the Tories now affect to carry everything before them."[118]

It was the metropolitan opposition, however, which first organized a subscription on behalf of the American prisoners. A meeting for this purpose was held at the King's Arms Tavern on 24 December 1777. In order to carry the "benevolent design into execution," a committee was appointed chaired by Robert Macky (a pro-American Common Council member for Cheap Ward) and including among its members the four City MPs.[119] Among the early subscribers to the relief fund were Lord Abingdon, Lord Shelburne, Lord Rockingham, and Sir George Savile. The project thus constituted a rare example of unanimity among the opposition in which the initiative had been assumed by the City over an issue concerning America. The subscription was temporarily closed on 9 January 1778 after £4,657.9.6 had been raised for the 924 American prisoners in English jails.[120]

The subscription for American prisoners and the successful resistance to a civic subsidy for troops were aspects of a reviving energy among the opposition following the news of Burgoyne's defeat at Saratoga. Opponents of the war pressed the government to conclude peace with the colonists before the anticipated intervention of France on the American side. On 17 February Lord North – already aware of a treaty between France and America – revealed to the House of Commons his own plans for conciliation; they essentially involved repealing the government's coercive legislation and dispatching commissioners to America to treat for peace.[121]

On 20 February 1778 a meeting was held in the King's Arms Tavern, Cornhill, with the original purpose of raising public support for Lord North's plan. One Mr Bourne – described by Horace Walpole as a "low tool" – proposed the establishment of "a Committee of Peace" to promote the conciliation of America; but he also moved that if the Americans did not accept conciliatory proposals, or rescind their vote for independence, then the meeting should raise a subscription to assist the continued prosecution of the war. The ministerial scheme, however, was thwarted by members of the metropolitan opposition present at the gathering: they elected a patriot alderman as chairman and secured the passage of resolutions denouncing the promotion of subscriptions in support of the British war effort.[122] When the meeting reconvened on 23 February, chaired by John Sawbridge, it was entirely dominated by pro-Americans. Those present denounced Lord North's conciliatory proposals as insincere and ineffectual and adopted petitions to the king and the House of Commons, blaming the loss of the colonies on the administration, and demanding that unconditional peace terms be offered to the Americans "to prevent the commerce and the strength of that country from being added to the crown of France."[123] According to the *London Evening Post* of 7–10 March 1778, "twelve hundred principal merchants and traders in the city" had signed these documents by 7 March.

The Common Council was also moved to action by the prospect of joint military undertakings by France and America against Britain. On 4 March 1778 the Court adopted a petition to the king, calling for the end of hostilities in order to prevent America from becoming "the most formidable and lasting accession to the constant Enemies of the power and prosperity of your Kingdom." The prayer of the petition was preceded by a long preamble which denounced the administration in such violent terms that the moderate pro-Americans, Aldermen Kirkman and Newnham, criticized the document as "an abusive compilation."[124] The City's petition was presented to the king, to receive the by now traditional snub, on 13 March 1778 – four days before the public was officially informed of a commercial and defensive alliance between France and America that had been concluded over a month before.

CHAPTER SIX

The Last Years of the Pro-American Movement, 1778–1782

FRANCE ENTERS THE WAR

British attitudes towards the American war were profoundly affected by the Franco-American alliance and the prospect of imminent hostilities between France and Britain.

In Parliament, the most fundamental change of heart occurred among the Rockingham Whigs, who in April 1778 collectively relinquished their adherence to Parliament's imperial supremacy and accepted the virtual inevitability of American independence. Even before the news arrived of British military failure in America, some of Lord Rockingham's more radical friends had expressed grave misgivings about their party's continued support for the principles of the Declaratory Act. David Hartley, MP, favoured an early recognition of full American legislative autonomy following the Declaration of Independence. From September 1777 the duke of Richmond corresponded with James Adair to formulate proposals for the repeal of the Declaratory Act (hitherto the main stumbling block to opposition unity over America) which the Rockingham Whigs as a whole would find acceptable.[1] But when John Wilkes, on 10 December 1777, moved in the House of Commons for its repeal, he failed to receive support from the main body of the parliamentary Whigs; Charles Fox, for example, denied Wilkes's contention "that the law was tyrannous and unjust; that it was the grand source of our present troubles."[2] Wilkes's motion was made only a week after the news of Burgoyne's surrender reached England. The implications of this military defeat, and the prospect of French intervention, however, eventually undermined Rockinghamite support for the Declaratory Act. On 7 April 1778 the duke of Richmond advocated in the House of Lords the unconditional withdrawal of British troops from North America and the recognition of American independence; and by now Richmond's views represented those of his party as a whole.[3]

The renunciation of the Declaratory Act by the Rockingham Whigs had important implications for the pro-American movement in England. Their change of attitude removed a major obstacle to cooperation between the Wilkites and the largest section of the parliamentary opposition. It also meant that the metropolitan opposition was no longer the only politically organized element which was prepared to concede American constitutional claims. The pro-American movement in London thus lost distinctiveness as it acquired potential allies.

The attitude of Lord Chatham and his supporters to the changing fortunes of war was more complex than that of the Rockingham Whigs. Lord Chatham had long resisted alliance with the Rockinghamites partly because of their adherence to the Declaratory Act; but their acceptance of American independence – involving as it did the destruction of an empire which he had been instrumental in building – was equally repugnant to him. Chatham declared he would "as soon subscribe to transubstantiation as to sovereignty (by right) in the colonies."[4] On 7 April 1778 he fiercely opposed the duke of Richmond's proposal to abandon the American conflict; Chatham appealed instead for the continuation of war, both in America and against the new enemy, France. The high drama of Chatham's speech – followed shortly as it was by his death – has tended to obscure the fact that it manifestly failed to influence the government's opponents. In the City of London, the Common Council diligently sought to make suitable burial arrangements for its erstwhile hero, while ignoring his last political testimony. And the opposition newspapers in London, in late 1778 and early 1779, were virtually unanimous in calling for war with France but peace with America.[5]

Lord Shelburne, Chatham's leading supporter, was Janus-faced in his attitude to American independence as with so many other aspects of policy. He quickly supported Chatham's appeal for a vigorous military effort to retain the colonies; this response, however, possibly derived, not from any genuine conviction, but from Shelburne's respect for his political mentor. After Chatham's death, Shelburne tended to avoid the issue of American independence by remaining silent about it, while at the same time implying that he would not oppose the removal of British troops from North America. Such a posture did not undermine the unanimity of opposition in favour of an early peace with America (although, later, there were

to be divisions about how such a settlement might be accomplished).
Charles Fox, in late 1778, approved of Lord Shelburne's attitude
concerning American policy.[6]

In the City, moreover, Shelburne was no longer incurring the
automatic hostility of Wilkite politicians. The bestowal of City
honours on Richard Price could be regarded as a muted compliment
to Lord Shelburne, who was Price's political patron, and whose
American policy Price had lauded in *Observations on ... Civil
Liberty*. Shelburne also apparently exercised some influence in the
production of the City's petition to the king, calling for an end to
American hosilities, in March 1778.[7]

The erosion of divisions between the Wilkites and the parliamentary opposition prompted some bizarre speculations and plans.
Beaumarchais, in Paris, thought that Wilkes, Sawbridge, and other
City politicians were planning to instigate a riot at Westminster in
support of the increasing number of parliamentarians who favoured
American independence.[8] His belief proved false, but in the summer
of 1779 the Shelburnites – victims of a crisis mentality engendered
by the fear of a French invasion – vaguely plotted to raise the City
and effect some kind of coup d'état.[9]

There also increasingly occurred more solid demonstrations of
unity between the Wilkites and the parliamentary opposition. One
remarkable instance of such unity was the enthusiasm manifested
by the London patriots in the cause of Admiral Augustus Keppel.
This naval officer was a leading figure in Rockinghamite circles;
of aristocratic lineage, he adhered to the conservative wing of his
faction. In these respects he was an unusual recipient of City favours.
But his attitude towards the war guaranteed his popularity with the
pro-Americans in London. While the British military effort was
directed exclusively against the Americans, Keppel refused to participate in a conflict which he strongly opposed; he did, however,
accept nomination as commander of the Channel fleet in the event
of war with France. On 17 March 1778 – the day on which news
of the Franco-American alliance was made public in London – it
was reported that Keppel had raised his flag on board the *Prince
George* at Portsmouth.[10]

The Channel fleet's first major engagement with the French was
fought off Ushant in July 1778. It was an indecisive affair in which
the British failed to press home an initial advantage. Recriminations
ensued between Keppel and Vice-Admiral Sir Hugh Palliser, one of
Keppel's senior subordinate officers and a protégé of Lord Sandwich.
Of the dispute between the two men Edmund Burke commented,
"I do not remember that any thing has in my time excited so much

indignation." As a result of Palliser's accusations Keppel was court-martialed at Portsmouth in January 1779 for failing in his duty. Lord Rockingham, the earl of Effingham, Edmund Burke, the duke of Richmond, and other members of the Whig opposition attended the trial – which was held on land because of Keppel's ill-health – in support of their naval friend. As Horace Walpole remarked, "The Rockingham squadron treated the trial of Keppel as an affair of party rather than as a national one."[11]

This attitude was shared by contributors to the patriot press. "Brevitas," writing in the *London Evening Post* of 9–12 January 1779, explained the circumstances of Keppel's prosecution in the following manner: "He [Keppel] is a Whig; he is an honest man; and his prosecution arose from the Board of Admiralty. As a Whig, he is certainly feared and hated by the present Tory Ministry; as an honest man, what can he expect from those who are not so? And as his prosecution arose from the Board of Admiralty, have not that Board the means, and can it not be supposed they will not make use of them, of procuring men proper to their designs?"

The pessimism implicit in this newspaper piece proved unfounded. On 11 February Keppel was honourably acquitted of the charge against him. News of this event was quickly conveyed to London, and in the evening the houses of the Whig magnates were illuminated in triumph. A London mob celebrated Keppel's acquittal in traditional style. It looted Sir Hugh Palliser's house and hanged him in effigy on Tower Hill. The rioters also attacked the houses of Lord Sandwich, Lord George Germain, and Lord North. (According to Horace Walpole, Charles Fox and some other young aristocratic rakes were responsible for provoking the riot, but there is no first-hand testimony to confirm this assertion.) On 16 February, the night of Keppel's return to London, there were further celebrations and riots.[12]

On 12 February the Common Council made its own tribute to Keppel. The Court voted thanks to the Admiral "for his judicious able and spirited behaviour ... in his attack on the French fleet [in the engagement off Ushant], for his Glorious and Gallant Efforts to renew the Engagement in the afternoon of that day; Efforts rendered unsuccessful thro' the want of obedience to his Orders by the Vice Admiral of the Blue [Palliser]." The Court also resolved "that the Freedom of this City be presented [to Keppel] in a Box made of Heart of Oak ornamented and embellished with Gold."[13]

The thanks of the City were formally handed to Keppel on 20 February at his home in Audley Square. He was then entertained at a dinner held in his honour at the London Tavern in the company of a committee of the Common Council and the City MPs. The affair was elaborately prepared. James Sharp organized a musical band to accompany the procession from Keppel's house to the London Tavern. The official participants in the celebration were provided by Mr Sainsbury Sibley (a haberdasher) with blue cockades, each decorated with an anchor and cable and displaying the words "Keppel, freedom, virtue, triumphant." At the dinner, toasts were drunk to Lord Shelburne's party, as well as to the Americans and the Rockingham Whigs, in order to emphasize, presumably, the unanimity of opposition in the new cause of "Keppel and Liberty."[14] The occasion generated further popular excitement. A crowd of Londoners drew Keppel's coach to the London Tavern "amidst the general acclamation," according to the *London Evening Post* of 20–23 February 1779, ". . . of a greater number of persons than almost ever remembered." In the evening there were again illuminations, and a mob of fifteen hundred people, headed by "ringleaders . . . armed with Cutlasses and Lighted Flambeaux," broke lamps and unilluminated windows.[15]

The cause of Admiral Keppel presented an ideal opportunity for the metropolitan opposition to demonstrate its attitude towards the war after the intervention of France. When, however, the pro-American Common Councilmen considered what further steps to take in view of the new military situation, they were confronted with a dilemma. There was, on the one hand, considerable pressure to support a war against the traditional enemy, especially in the summer of 1779 when Britain was threatened with invasion by France and her ally, Spain. On the other hand, it was difficult for the pro-Americans to support British military action, *per se*, while in part it was still directed against America.

This dilemma helps to explain some complex manoeuvres by the Wilkites in two Common Council meetings held in June 1779. On 22 June William Saxby, seconded by Alderman Sawbridge, proposed that the "Court . . . present an humble Address to his Majesty on the present alarming state of public affairs; assuring his Majesty, that his loyal Citizens of London were ever ready to support the dignity of the Crown, and the constitutional interests of the country." The motion was phrased in such a way that it compelled loyalist support: John Jones and William Judd spoke in support of it. Aldermen Kirkman and Newnham, both moderate pro-Americans, opposed the proposal on the grounds that the City would be further degraded if the political requests contained in an address were again refused; both men favoured active measures by the corporation to improve the defence of the kingdom, Kirkman, for example, proposing that the City donate to the king a well-manned ship-of-war.[16]

The motion for an address was carried, despite the objections of

Newnham and Kirkman, and one was duly prepared in a committee dominated by Wilkites and pro-Americans. The content of this document revealed the tactics of the City opposition. The address implied that the corporation would support the war against the Bourbon powers only if the king first dismissed his ministers; it despaired "of any Success from the most vigorous exertions of your Majesty's loyal and dutiful Subjects, if the Public Measures of Government are continued to be conducted by the same unfortunate and incapable hands." John Sawbridge on the previous day had given prior notice of Wilkite tactics: he told Lord North in the House of Commons that the members of the Common Council would only raise money and men for the war on a conditional basis – "not a shilling nor a man would they grant while he and his colleagues were in office."[17]

The dictatorial language of the proposed Common Council address was unacceptable to the loyalists; so, in cooperation with those who opposed an address *per se*, they secured rejection of the committee's petition, and passed motions deferring the question of an address, and the related issues of civic subsidies for the war effort, until the next meeting of the Common Council.[18]

When the Court reconvened on 29 June the Common Councilmen and aldermen appointed to prepare an address produced a document which scarcely moderated the tone or content of their previous one. The second draft was strongly defended in committee by Aldermen Townsend, Bull, and Sawbridge; but when it was laid before the Court a curious reversion occurred: the Wilkites accepted a motion by John Merry, a loyalist of independent judgment, that the resolution to address the throne be rescinded. Most of the loyalists for their part continued to press for an address – "unclogged with any condition to restrain his Majesty from the choice of his servants" – as a first step towards securing the Common Council's financial support for the war.[19]

The outcome of this division was that the motion to address the throne and assist the war effort by opening the City chamber was narrowly defeated.[20] It was a partial, and distinctly hollow, victory for the Wilkites. Their original intention was clearly to have presented a petition to the king which offered financial support for the British war effort in return for political concessions that the king could only reject. They could then have argued that their patriotic endeavours to assist the struggle against the Bourbon powers had been thwarted by a vindictive and stubborn executive. The Wilkites' initial plan, however, was successfully resisted by the ministerialists in the Court. The Wilkites then adopted defensive tactics and, in turn, prevented the loyalists from securing an address offering the king the unqualified financial support of the corporation. The Wilkites gained no public credit by their behaviour and were left even more susceptible to the charge of factious and disloyal behaviour: "That in short they presumed to assert in public," as one anonymous pamphleteer charged, "... that the tyranny of France and Spain would be more welcome to them than the continuance of their rivals in power."[21]

In July 1779 the proponents of metropolitan assistance for national defence pursued their goal outside the City corporation. In Westminster and Middlesex, the duke of Northumberland and the Westminster MPs organized subscriptions for promoting military and naval recruitment and raised volunteer companies to help in the protection of the capital. Both projects generated considerable enthusiasm, although the inhabitants of the parish of St George's, Hanover Square, collectively refused to contribute to the subscriptions in support of the war effort. The initiative of Westminster and Middlesex was soon followed in London itself. A meeting of merchants and traders at the London Tavern on 27 July agreed to organize the formation of a body of volunteers to support "peace and legal government" in London and the kingdom.[22] The committee chosen to implement the project included – alongside loyalists such as Thomas Wellings, Samuel Beachcroft, and John Wombwell – a few pro-Americans, among them Nathaniel Newnham (deputy chairman of the committee) and John Kirkman, both of whom had earlier opposed the devious tactics of the orthodox Wilkites in Common Council.[23] The project for a City volunteer force lapsed in September as the danger of invasion diminished, but the breach in the unity of the pro-American party in London, which the issue engendered, lingered on.

ASSOCIATIONS AND THE AMERICAN ISSUE

The metropolitan opponents of government were thus distracted by internal dissension at the very time that extraparliamentary opposition to the administration was developing in the country as a whole. This surge of national discontent found its chief expression in the petitioning and Association movements led by the Yorkshire freeholders. The nature and significance of this important political development have been elaborated in a number of detailed works;[24] it remains here to emphasize the implications of the movement for the extraparliamentary agitation of the American issue.

In one sense there was a direct connection between events in America and the form of domestic discontent in 1779–80: the establishment of committees of correspondence and associations to promote political change was inspired to an extent by similar practice in America.[25] The Association movement, however, was not primarily concerned with questions of imperial policy; its main goals were to reduce administrative spending, curb the influence of the crown, and secure parliamentary reform. The relative importance of these elements, and their ultimate purpose, were subjects of considerable debate within the movement. Its more conservative adherents – including the followers of Lord Rockingham – felt that "economical reform," by simultaneously reducing government expenditure and curbing the power of the executive to corrupt MPs, constituted a sufficient political demand; other associators – including Rev. Christopher Wyvill (the effective leader of the Yorkshire freeholders), Charles Fox, and the metropolitan radicals – favoured parliamentary reform as the only effective means of securing domestic economy and correcting the alleged imbalance of the constitution.[26]

There was clearly an implicit connection at least between the domestic impact of the American war and the various purposes of the Association movement. The desire for government economy was prompted by the increase of taxation at a time when war was having a progressively deleterious effect on British commerce. The country's economic health in the early months of the American conflict proved only a temporary phenomenon. Two letters written by Samuel Curwen depicted the shift in the country's economic situation. On 8 August 1775 he wrote: "The manufactories are in full employ, and one of the warmest of the friends of America told me that letters from Manchester expressed joy that no American orders had been sent, otherwise there must have been disappointment somewhere." On 23 March 1778 Curwen witnessed a different situation: "The subject that at most employs and oppresses my mind," he wrote, "... is the critical and dangerous situation that the kingdom seems to be in"; his fears derived partly from "the tottering condition of national credit ... and the low price of stocks, as low as the end of the last eight years' war [sic], when the nation was almost drained of its specie."[27] Other economic parameters justified the pessimism expressed by Curwen: a shortage of circulating cash produced on one day, 5 March 1777, over twenty-six bankruptcies in London, which exceeded the highest number recorded in one day during the financial crisis of 1772; and in 1779 – as a concomitant of Britain's military and diplomatic isolation – the level of British exports was at its lowest since 1745.[28]

The press was naturally full of complaints about Britain's dire commercial straits. Many newspaper contributors made explicit associations between specific economic grievances and the American war. For example, "Reflector," writing in the *London Evening Post* of 20-23 June 1778, attributed the country's shortage of circulating cash to the fact that very little of the money sent to America for the payment of troops had found its way back to England. A paragraph in the *London Evening Post* of 2-4 March 1779 asked why taxes were so high and proceeded to answer the question thus: "To support a most contemptible ministry in their places, and to carry on the most bloody, expensive, and impracticable war, that the nation ever was involved in."

Hard times thus confirmed the iniquity of the war for those who had originally opposed the ministry's colonial policy. For Richard Neave, an Atlantic trader and Wilkite Common Councilman for Tower Ward, economic disaster constituted the final disillusionment. In 1777 he and his son were bankrupted and they quit the country for Europe. After bitterly denouncing the government and their creditors, they declared allegiance to the United States in the presence of Benjamin Franklin.[29] There were few, of course, who were prepared to go as far as the Neaves; yet, as Herbert Butterfield has observed, economic hardships engendered by the American conflict eroded support for Lord North's administration among those groups which had once supported it, notably the country gentlemen who were caught between rising taxes and falling land rents. These economic victims of the war were naturally among the foremost supporters of political crusades, such as the Association movement, which offered remedy for their misfortunes.[30]

The connection between the war and pressure for government economy seemed clear enough, but it was not normally explicated by those associators who had no prior objections to the government's American measures. Similarly, the connection between parliamentary reform and the American cause, while stressed by a number of associators, including John Cartwright and John Jebb, was downplayed by other reformers, notably Christopher Wyvill, who, for tactical reasons, sought to mute criticism of the administration's imperial policy. Although Wyvill himself can be described as a pro-American, he was reluctant to offend the country gentlemen who constituted his most respectable supporters, yet who also included a great many former advocates of American coercion. In addition, Wyvill was anxious to prevent clamour for an early peace from diverting public attention from the central issue of reform.[31]

Hence - despite the apparent links between the issues of reform, economy, and America - the American cause was not consistently upheld in the formal pronouncements of the Association movement.

The first Yorkshire petition to the House of Commons, prepared on 30 December 1779, cursorily blamed the economic ills of the country on the "expensive and unfortunate war" with the colonies, but it did not include any direct indictment of the government's American policy.[32] The Middlesex freeholders followed Yorkshire's example at a county meeting on 7 January 1780. George Byng (soon to become an MP for the county) proposed that the electors adopt a petition identical to that of Yorkshire. One freeholder, Colonel Miles, offered an amendment accusing the administration of driving the Americans to independence. He was answered by George Grieve, a Wilkite who would shortly emigrate to America, who said that he

for his own part, was convinced, as well as the Colonel, that the Americans were driven to independency by the present Administration. Many others thought so, but all might not think so. Many good men had differed in the outset of this unhappy war, and though they were generally convinced at last of its iniquity and madness it [i.e., reference to the alleged cause of American independence] might now be offensive to the feelings of some gentlemen who had been misled by the hired writers of the Court, who had been paid immense sums from the money extorted from the people for the abominable purpose of deceiving them into their own destruction.[33]

Grieve's views prevailed with the meeting; Colonel Miles withdrew his amendment. The freeholders then adopted the "Yorkshire petition" and established a committee of correspondence. In February 1780 the corporation of London and the electors of Westminster also followed Yorkshire's lead and avoided any direct censure of the government's American policy in their petitions.[34]

In March 1780 deputies for the electors of the petitioning counties, cities, and boroughs met in the capital to formulate plans for nationwide political associations. The deputies for the metropolitan constituencies included James Townsend, the Reverend Dr Bromley, John Kirkman, Brass Crosby, and Thomas Brand Hollis (the heir of Thomas Hollis); other representatives included John Jebb (a Huntingdonshire deputy), Major Cartwright, and Richard Price (both deputies for Nottinghamshire). The meeting agreed that the associations should have three objectives: public economy and a concomitant reduction in crown influence; the addition of at least one hundred county members to the House of Commons; and the adoption of annual parliaments.[35] The pursuit of an early peace with America was thus not one of the avowed goals of the deputies, despite the number of pro-Americans among them. They did, however, relate the issue of the American war to that of public economy and crown influence in a memorial justifying their activities;

For us ... it is reserved to feel ourselves bowed down under that intolerable oppression, which, to a British Mind in any past generation, could appear but as a fearful speculation – The enormous, the compactly-accumulated, the all devouring, Influence of the Crown. By an unhappy war with America, begotten in the first influence of this despotic system, and nursed with a view of giving completion to it, this fatal influence has been armed with more ample means, than ever it enjoyed before, for enslaving Parliament in the private application of no small part of those monies which have far exceeded the supplies of former wars ... whilst the nation itself, in every species of its property, in every department of its commerce, in every description of its people (those only excepted who have become great on the spoils of the public) hath visibly sunk almost into beggary.[36]

At the end of March 1780 the committee of Yorkshire freeholders adopted the proposals of the deputies with one exception: triennial rather than annual parliaments were agreed upon as a proper objective of the county association. The question of America was dealt with in a separate resolution. The meeting agreed "that the prosecution of an offensive war in America, is most evidently a measure which, by employing our great and enormously expensive operations against the inhabitants of that country, prevents *this* from exerting its united, vigorous, and firm efforts, against the powers of France and Spain, and has no other effect upon America than to continue, and thereby to increase the enmity which has so long and so fatally subsisted betwixt the arms of both, can be productive of no good whatever."[37]

This resolution appeased those Yorkshire freeholders who were developing misgivings about the war and its conduct. They included General Hale, who moved the resolution, and Rev. Henry Zouch, the author of a pamphlet which proposed a general inquiry, conducted by the associating counties, to evaluate the domestic impact of the war. Wyvill temporarily forsook his tactical neglect of the American cause and seconded General Hale's motion, in order to win the support of those who followed Lord Rockingham and his parliamentary lieutenants in disapprobating other aspects of the association's emerging political posture.[38] The resolution relating to America was mildly expressed, however, and could scarcely have caused offence to those early advocates of American coercion whom Wyvill was so anxious to conciliate.

The metropolitan constituencies based their own forms of association on the Yorkshire model. A committee of the Common Council adopted the Yorkshire plan with only one modification: on Granville

Sharp's urging the committee opted to press for annual, not triennial, parliaments.[39] An incidental, though important, effect of the Association movement, therefore, was to erode further the political autonomy and separate identity of extraparliamentary opposition in London. The popular movement of the capital was also continuing to lose distinctiveness in relation to the parliamentary opposition. On 16 December 1779 the Common Council sent a letter of thanks to each member of the minority in the House of Lords who had supported motions in favour of "economical reform"; the group included Lord Shelburne, Lord Rockingham, the duke of Portland, and the duke of Richmond. Then, in March 1780, the committees of correspondence of London and Middlesex expressed their gratitude to Edmund Burke for his project of government economy.[40] The Common Council which met on 7 April continued to show appreciation of the activities of the leaders of parliamentary opposition: John Dunning received the official thanks of the City for his famous motion of the previous day that "the influence of the Crown has increased, is increasing, and ought to be diminished," and Lord Shelburne – who by now, apparently, was politically rehabilitated as far as the City opposition was concerned – was congratulated on his recovery from a wound sustained in a duel. The letter conveying this message addressed Lord Shelburne thus: "This City feels a peculiar degree of Gratitude and affection to your Lordship on account of the constant assistance which you have afforded her whenever the Property or Priviledges of this Corporation have been attacked or her motives misrepresented."[41]

The most important manifestation, however, of cooperation between parliamentary opponents of government and metropolitan opposition "out of doors" was the Westminster Committee chaired by Charles Fox, who was emerging as a radical reformer and "man of the people." Early signs of Fox's new popularity began to appear in late 1779; his health was toasted at a meeting to celebrate Wilkes's election as chamberlain, and in December it was reported that he was a candidate for the freedom of the City. At the meeting of Westminster electors on 2 February 1780, at which the Westminster Committee was instituted, John Wilkes, following the recommendation of John Jebb, moved that Fox offer himself as a parliamentary candidate for the constituency – a proposal that was unanimously accepted by those present.[42]

The Westminster Committee itself incorporated a wide range of opposition sentiment from within Parliament and outside it. Its active political core included Fox himself and two of his parliamentary allies, Richard Fitzpatrick and R.B. Sheridan; two radical intellec-

tuals, John Jebb and Thomas Brand Hollis; and a few veterans of
the Wilkite movement. The situation in Westminster was thus different
from that in Yorkshire where Christopher Wyvill resisted the direct
involvement of the parliamentary Whigs in the affairs of the county's
association. Unlike Wyvill, moreover, the leading members of the
Westminster Committee – notably Fox and John Jebb – had few
tactical inihibitions about relating the causes of America and domestic
reform. On 30 November 1780, for example, the committee officially
thanked John Wilkes and others for opposing a parliamentary vote
of thanks to Generals Clinton and Cornwallis (who had both achieved
some passing successes in America) on the familiar grounds that a
British victory in America would be followed by the extirpation of
liberty in the mother country.[43]

The willingness of London's radical politicians to cooperate with
the parliamentary Whigs coincided with, and was probably encouraged by, the renewal of antagonistic factions within the metropolitan
opposition. The new disruptive issue was that of Catholic relief. By
an act of 1778 certain disabilities were removed from Roman Catholics;
it became possible, for example, for them to join the army simply
by taking an oath of obedience to the crown. This legislation,
inoffensive as it superficially appeared, upset Protestant zealots, many
of whom sought to reestablish the connections previously expressed
during the passage of the Quebec Act between antipopery and the
cause of America. The *London Evening Post* of 20–23 March 1779
solemnly reported: "The Pope hath lately written a circular letter
to the Papists in England, commanding them to *yield* the most
unlimited obedience to the Ministry, and to support them by all
the means in their power. He also further orders them, to encourage
their youth of all ranks to enter into the army designed for the
American crusade, granting them a dispensation to take any oaths
which may be administered to them, and finally an indulgence of
20 days for every rebel heretic they shall destroy."

At a meeting of the Middlesex freeholders on 11 April 1780, some
of those present attempted unsuccessfully to make Catholic relief an
issue of the Association movement. The Reverend Dr Bromley called
"the Quebec bill a most wicked and pernicious piece of business,
and thought the late act to take off restraints from Papists an arrow
shot from the same quiver."[44]

Within the corporation of London, hostility to Catholic relief ran
high. Aldermen Crosby and Bull were both members of the Protestant
Association, led by the fanatical Lord George Gordon, which sought
repeal of the legislation removing disabilities from Roman Catholics.
On 31 May 1780 the Common Council followed the lead of Crosby

and Bull and officially condemned Catholic relief. Two days later Alderman Bull seconded Gordon's parliamentary motions that the petition of the Protestant Association should be brought up and heard by the House of Commons.[45]

The disruptive potential of the Catholic issue for London politics might have remained unrealized had not the presentation of this petition triggered a week of looting and destruction in London – the so-called Gordon Riots – for which antipopery provided an ostensible justification. On 8 June 1780 the Common Council, at the height of the disturbances, agreed to petition Parliament against Catholic relief for the purpose of "quieting the minds of the People."[46]

The Court's formal unanimity over this issue, however, could not disguise the disparate positions that its members were adopting over the question of Catholic toleration and the riots in the streets. Some City magistrates, including the lord mayor, Brackley Kennett, were rendered inactive by the civil disorders, unwilling to order the military to fire on the rioting crowds in case they should be incited further. The Protestant zealots for their part virtually sanctioned the mob's activities. The constables in Alderman Bull's ward continued to wear blue cockades – the adopted symbol of the Protestant Association – and voiced support of the rioters as national heroes. Bull's protégé, the incorrigible Henry Maskall, was prosecuted at the Old Bailey for allegedly participating in the destruction of Lord Mansfield's house on 7 June 1780, though during the course of Maskall's trial the veracity and motives of the prosecution witnesses were questioned and he was acquitted.[47]

The role of John Wilkes during the Gordon Riots was diametrically opposed to that of his former close ally, Bull. Wilkes played a vigorous part in the suppression of public disorder. He shot down rioters attempting to storm the Bank of England and secured the arrest of William Moore (the suspected author of *The Crisis*) for publishing incendiary material before and during the riots. Other pro-Americans also helped to quell the disturbances. Alderman Kirkman, for example, commanded a corps of light horse volunteers to combat the rioters.[48]

The different responses of pro-Americans during the Gordon Riots demonstrate that there was no simple relationship between the issues of popery and America. For some – such as Frederick Bull, Henry Maskall, the Reverend Dr Bromley, and William Moore – support for America and Lord George Gordon (himself a pro-American) were aspects of a single crusade: the defence of Protestantism against the menace of Roman Catholicism and its alleged concomitant, political tyranny. Public response to the Quebec Act had previously shown the importance of such an attitude. But an ideological connection between intolerant Protestantism and the political goals being sought by the American revolutionaries was far from being axiomatic for many English friends of America. The Rockingham Whigs included some of the foremost proponents of Catholic relief – notably Sir George Savile and Edmund Burke – and their attitude was shared within the metropolitan opposition by John Wilkes, for whom civil liberty and religious toleration were intrinsically associated.[49]

The Gordon Riots had a damaging effect on the continued promotion of reform and pro-American causes in London. Many of the "middling sort" were permanently deterred from further engagement in opposition politics. And recriminations inevitably ensued between former allies within the popular movement. In the House of Commons, Wilkes joined Edmund Burke in attacking Frederick Bull for his role during the riots.[50] For his part, John Wilkes was greeted at the midsummer Common Hall of 1780 with cries of "No Popish Chamberlain" according to the *London Evening Post* of 22–24 June 1780.

Internal dissensions, it is true, did not prevent the metropolitan opposition from enjoying successes in the parliamentary elections called by the administration in September 1780 to profit from the conservative backlash to the Gordon Riots. Charles Fox wrested a Westminster seat from the government. In the City, the successful candidates were Frederick Bull, George Hayley, John Kirkman, and Nathaniel Newnham (who enjoyed the secret support of the administration in the hope that he would replace John Sawbridge as a City member). Kirkman died, however, at the conclusion of the poll and Sawbridge later replaced him unopposed. In Middlesex, the radical George Byng was returned with John Wilkes. Most of the triumphant candidates in the metropolitan constituencies were involved in the Association movement and pledged to support its aims in Parliament.[51]

In contrast to 1774, however, the issue of America was scarcely mentioned in the electoral campaign. This may partly have been because many of the candidates were so well known that there was little need for them to reaffirm their political attitudes; but a further explanation is that the repercussions of the Gordon Riots continued to dominate political debate in the capital. In Middlesex, Wilkes was forced to devote his energies replying to those freeholders who condemned him for appeasing popery. John Sawbridge possibly lost his parliamentary seat on the first ballot because of public misunderstanding about his attitude to the Catholic question.[52]

In Common Council, the distraction of the metropolitan opposition in the aftermath of the Gordon Riots enabled the City loyalists to secure some notable triumphs. On 8 July 1780 the Court agreed to present an address to the king "expressing ... grateful thanks ... for his Majesty's care and attention to the citizens of London, in granting them such an aid as became necessary to subdue the late dangerous riots, they being too formidable for the control of the civil authority."[53] The form of the address was finally agreed on 24 July by a margin of ten votes. Then, on 15 March 1781, Common Council agreed to deny use of Guildhall facilities to delegates of county and borough associations then gathered in London. At the same Court, the loyalists succeeded, after long debate, in dissolving the corporation's committee of correspondence and association.[54]

The reassertion of loyalism in London was part of a national reaction that temporarily strengthened the authority of Lord North's government. The American issue largely ceased to be agitated outside London in the eighteen months following the Gordon Riots. The success of Generals Clinton and Cornwallis in their campaign in the southern colonies in 1780 even encouraged the transitory delusion that America might after all be militarily subjugated.[55] In London, the only group to uphold consistently the American cause in the wake of the June disturbances was the Society for Constitutional Information. The group was formed in April 1780 by Major Cartwright, John Jebb, and other reformers, "to diffuse throughout the kingdom, as universally as possible, a knowledge of the great principles of Constitutional Freedom, particularly such as respect the election and duration of the representative body."[56] America did not figure in the group's original prospectus, but the society's second address to the public, written by Thomas Day, drew a lively, if unhistorical, parallel between the fall of Rome and the collapse of the first British Empire, and predicted that future historians would

execrate the authors of the American war as equally devoid of policy, public spirit, and humanity; and while he beholds on one side the rights of nature, the interests of mankind, a rising empire formed upon the noblest principles of equity and reason, and destined to prove a common refuge from European tyranny, he may see nothing on the other, but the low illiberal aims of selfishness, avarice, and cruelty, that would, if possible, counteract the designs of Providence itself, engross its blessings, or convert them into curses for all the rest of the species ... such were the aims of the British ministry, but the weakness of their measures were equal to the iniquity of their councils.[57]

Other publications of the society argued similar themes, and in

December 1780 its members drank a toast to "America in our arms and Despotism at our feet."[58]

It should be emphasized, however, that the function of the Society for Constitutional Information was essentially limited to the dissemination of polemical tracts. It did not engage in active politics, although its members included some prominent members of the City opposition, such as Aldermen Crosby, Sawbridge, and Turner. Those of the "middling sort" were perhaps deterred from joining the society by its membership subscription of one to five guineas a year.[59]

A resurgence of articulated popular opposition to the American war was delayed until the end of November 1781, when news of General Cornwallis's surrender at Yorktown arrived in England. Few people, inside Parliament or outside it, could have reasonably expected in the light of this event that Britain could retain by force its American possessions, especially when the country was now at war with the Dutch, as well as with the French and Spanish. In London, Charles Fox and the Westminster Committee met on 3 December to organize renewed metropolitan opposition to the North administration. Christopher Wyvill opposed the exploitation of the news from Yorktown for the purpose of toppling the government, because he felt it would distract attention from the necessity of reform; but he was unable to halt the march of events in London. It was probably the result of prompting by the Westminster Committee that a Common Hall was convened on 6 December 1781 in order to promote an address, remonstrance, and petition to the king praying that he discontinue military action in America and dismiss his ministry. John Wilkes and William Hurford spoke in support of the proposed address, and a letter was read from the absent Frederick Bull urging the livery to make a decisive stand against the administration.[60]

The address, remonstrance, and petition accepted by the livery was adopted shortly afterwards in identical form by the other metropolitan constituencies. The author of the document was John Jebb – a hint at the dominant role the Westminster Committee was coming to exercise in London politics.[61] The address was simply and dramatically composed. It stated: "Your Majesty's fleets have lost their wonted superiority. Your armies have been captured. Your dominions have been lost." Continuation of the war, the address went on, "can tend to no other purpose than that of alienating and rendering irrecoverable the confidence of our American brethren with whom we hope to live upon the terms of intercourse and friendship so necessary to the commercial prosperity of this kingdom."[62]

The king, as in April 1775, refused to receive Common Hall's address on the throne, which prompted the livery to reconvene on

31 January 1782, when a resolution was carried "that the unequal Representation of the people, the corrupt state of Parliament and the perversion thereof ... have been the principal causes of the War with America, of the consequent dismemberment of the British Empire, and of every grievance of which we complain."[63] Despite his refusal to receive Common Hall's petition, neither the king nor his administration could resist the growing tide of opposition of which the renewed wave of protest from the livery was only a part. After the Christmas recess the parliamentary opposition continued the attack on the government initiated in the metropolis. On 27 February 1782 General Conway's motion condemning any further prosecution of hostilities in North America was carried by nineteen votes; MPs accepted an additional motion for an address to the king informing him of the changed attitude of the House of Commons to the American war.[64] These motions were immediately preceded by the reading of a petition from Common Council, adopted unanimously the same day, praying that the House of Commons "interpose in such manner as to their wisdom shall seem most effectual for preventing the continuance of the War with America."[65] It is doubtful whether the City's intervention exercised a critical influence on the course of parliamentary events, but the timing of the corporation's petition was a further indication of the coordination now established between opposition "out of doors" and in Parliament to the government's American policy. In London, on the evening of 28 February, houses were illuminated, and firecrackers were exploded, in celebration of the opposition's parliamentary triumphs.[66]

The coup de grâce was will to come. On 15 March 1782 the House of Commons ominously deliberated a motion of no confidence in Lord North and his government. Five days later Lord North only averted passage of a motion calling for the removal of the ministers by announcing his administration's collective resignation. The triumph of the opposition had at last arrived, and a new ministry headed by Lord Rockingham, and including Charles Fox and Lord Shelburne as its principal secretaries of state, received the mantle of power from a reluctant king.[67]

Afterword

The political events of February and March 1782 did not formally terminate the war between America and Britain; preliminary articles of peace between the English-speaking combatants were not signed until 30 November 1782. But the change of administration entailed the removal from office of those men whom the erstwhile opposition designated as the authors of Britain's imperial calamity and guaranteed that military action in mainland North America would not be resumed. The raison d'être of the pro-American movement in London thus disappeared.

For the remainder of the year extraparliamentary political forces in the capital manifested loyal, and largely indiscriminate, support for the king and his new ministers. On 9 April 1782 the Common Council agreed upon an address to George III thanking him for "having graciously complied with the wishes of his People in making a Change in his Councils." James Adair reported to Lord Rockingham that the address was adopted "without one dissentient voice. Everybody vied with each other in expressions of confidence in, and approbation of our new administration, and even those whose sentiments did not appear to concur with real cordiality, found themselves obliged to fall in with the general voice." The electors of Westminster and Middlesex quickly followed the City's lead and adopted similar loyal addresses to the throne.[1]

The loyalist mood in London was sustained by a series of British naval victories against the Bourbon powers in the West Indies, which the City acknowledged by bestowing its thanks and freedom on the victorious commanders. In May the Common Council expressed its unaccustomed loyalty in a more material way: the Court responded to Lord Shelburne's attempt to augment the domestic forces of the kingdom by ordering that £5,000 be spent on refurbishing the City's militia.[2]

The dispute between Lord Shelburne and Charles Fox over the conduct of peace negotiations – a disagreement that continued when Fox left office after Rockingham died and Shelburne assumed the premiership in July 1782 – evoked little partisan response from the population of the capital. Fox and his ally John Jebb attempted to rally opposition to Lord Shelburne among the Westminster electors, on the grounds that Shelburne was attempting to deny independence to the Americans and was unnecessarily protracting the war with the continental powers. Despite the efforts of the Foxites, however, there seems to have been little popular criticism of Shelburne's supervision of the peace talks. His determination to secure debts owed to British merchants in North America probably enhanced his popularity with the commercial community.[3]

Certainly Common Council expressed no censure of Lord Shelburne or his administration. In November and December 1782 the corporation conveyed its satisfaction with the government by seriously considering a proposal to donate a man-of-war to the king.[4] The termination of hostilities with the Bourbon powers rendered the prosecution of the scheme unnecessary, but the changed attitude of the Common Council which the incident displayed stands in significant contrast to the Council's stubborn refusal to support the war effort while it was still in part directed against the Americans. So it was that at the end of the Anglo-American conflict the patriotism of the City was once more in correspondence with national loyalty, as it had been during the Seven Years' War.

While it lasted, the pro-American movement constituted an important demonstration of the extent, coherence, and vigour of disaffection among independent tradesmen in the capital. In terms of their immediate objectives, however, the pro-Americans met with only limited success. In one sense, by denying to the king and Lord North's administration the national unanimity that they sought in the face of colonial rebellion, the pro-Americans justified their own assertion that the American War of Independence was in fact a civil war; and by so doing they helped to establish a vibrant tradition of domestic dissent over British foreign policy that has survived until the present century.[5] But though a telling political gesture, Wilkite obstruction of the war effort was scarcely an immediate factor in Britain's defeat. Lord North's government was ultimately thwarted, not by a diffusion of pro-American sentiment, but by a combination of military failure

in North America and a mounting domestic opposition induced by
weariness with the war and its damaging economic effects.

During the war London's pro-Americans patently failed to over-
come their isolation in the national context. The political and
economic preoccupations of London's independent tradesmen were
not shared by other socioeconomic groups in the capital, and outside
London loyal blandishments proved generally persuasive. Crucially,
there did not exist in the provinces, as there did in London, the
kind of political infrastructure necessary for encouraging and sus-
taining incipient pro-American sentiment.[6]

Despite, however, their negligible impact on the course of imperial
events, the pro-Americans should not be regarded merely as a group
whose historical significance was to illuminate the character and
intensity of popular protest in eighteenth-century London. Their
movement signified more than that. For through their sympathetic
response to events in America, the pro-Americans helped to effect
a transformation in the movement for political reform in Britain.
From the beginnings of the pro-American movement, those friendly
to the colonists viewed the imperial controversy through the lens
of country-party ideology. In this perception, the persecution of the
colonists was a predictable consequence of a growing tendency to
ministerial despotism and parliamentary corruption. Hence appeals
for colonial relief were characteristically made in conjunction with
the traditional country-party demands for shorter parliaments and
the exclusion of pensioners and placemen from the House of Commons. But as the imperial crisis intensified the emphasis of metropolitan reformers shifted and became more modern. While retaining
their desire for a more virtuous Parliament, these reformers began
stressing changes that would have guaranteed a more representative
one. In part, this shift was generated by a sense that the state of
parliamentary representation was inappropriate for the governance
of a large empire. The Stamp Act crisis helped to initiate this attitude
among British reformers, and it was given exaggerated expression
in John Wilkes's parliamentary motion for franchise reform in 1776.

But the American Revolution did more than focus critical attention
on the inadequacies of Parliament as a representative body and agency
of imperial government. It also served to direct the attention of London
radicals to American representative institutions, compared to which
domestic practice seemed egregiously deficient. (Americans in the
capital, such as Arthur Lee, naturally encouraged such comparisons.)
Despite the lack of uniformity among late colonial legislatures and
emerging state constitutions, they were based firmly on the principle
of actual representation. Thus their endorsement by domestic

reformers involved a categorical break with the idea of virtual representation, which, prior to the revolutionary crisis, was not just some specious invention of authoritarian ministers, but an implicit corollary of the country-party precept that the virtuous citizen should rise above personal or sectional interests in his political behaviour.

The circumstances of the Anglo-American conflict temporarily retarded, as we have seen, the practical possibility of reform, while at the same time shifting its theoretical asssumptions and goals. But the American Revolution left an enduring impression on British reform. In the 1790s the artisan members of the London Corresponding Society were quite explicit in acknowledging an integral connection between their earlier support for America and their later political demands. They testified that the conduct of the war had helped induce disillusionment with the government, while at the same time the revolution had taught them the necessity of, and the proper basis for, representative government. English libertarian values had helped shape the ideological perspective of colonial radicals; now the American adaptation of these values in the crucible of revolutionary change was, in turn, nourishing and reviving the domestic reform tradition.[7]

Appendixes

A NOTE ON SOURCES AND
METHOD

Appendixes A, B, and C list and tabulate information concerning
the signers of a pro-American petition and two progovernment
addresses, all from London, delivered to the throne in October 1775.
The identified pro-American petitioners are listed in full in Appendix
A. In Appendix B, the information concerning the pro-American
petitioners of 11 October is tabulated and compared in a number
of categories with a tabulation of information on those who signed
the loyal address of 14 October and the loyal livery address of 20
October. The two loyal addresses are combined in this appendix in
order to facilitate their comparison with the pro-American petition.
Those loyal addressers who were in, or who during the war would
enter, a contractual relationship with the administration – as royal
purveyors, placemen, loan subscribers, and contractors for war supplies – are listed in full in Appendix C.

The pro-American petitioners of 11 October are named in the
London Evening Post, 14-17 October 1775. The signers of the loyalist
address of 14 October 1775 and of the loyal livery address of 20 October
are given in the *London Gazette*, 10-14 October 1775 and 24-28
October 1775.

Information on occupations and company directorships is derived
mainly from the *New Complete Guide*, 1775; *Kent's Directory*, 1775
and 1776; F.G. Hilton Price, *A Handbook of London Bankers* (London
1890-1); and William Bailey, *List of Bankrupts, Dividends and
Certificates, from the Year 1772, to 1793*, 2 vols. (London 1794).
Directories only occasionally categorize the regional trading interests
of merchants; the identification of merchants trading to North America

is therefore partly based on the lists in "London Merchants on the Stamp Act Repeal," *Proceedings of the Massachusetts Historical Society* 55 (1923): 215-23, and three petitions to the House of Lords of merchants, traders, and others involved in North America commerce: those of 5 March 1766 (supporting Stamp Act repeal), 7 February 1775, and 15 March 1775, Main Papers, House of Lords Record Office. Not all of these petitioners to the House of Lords were North America merchants (some were manufacturers or wholesalers of one commodity) and such is taken to have been their primary interest only if they are listed as merchants in the directories. Corroborative evidence to establish the identity of North America merchants is derived from Katharine A. Kellock, "London Merchants and the pre-1776 American Debts," *Guildhall Studies in London History* 1 (1974): 109-49, Edward C. Papenfuse, *In Pursuit of Profit: The Annapolis Merchants in the Era of the American Revolution* (Baltimore: Johns Hopkins University Press 1975), and from an exceptionally detailed directory, *Mortimer's Universal Director*, 1763. This latter source also helps in discovering the regional trading interests of other individuals whose merchant status is established from the more up-to-date, though less detailed, directories. A petition from "The Planters of the [West Indian] Colonies and the Merchants of London trading thereto," 7 February 1775, Main Papers, supplies supplementary information on West India planters and merchants.

Protestant Dissenting Deputies have been located in the minutes of their organization: Guildhall MSS 3083/vol. 2, fols. 186-7. Lewis Namier and John Brooke, *The History of Parliament: The House of Commons*, vols. 2 and 3, has been used to find MPs among the petitioners and addressers.

Information on contractors is derived from the following sources: Treasury contractors and their agents, Norman Baker, *Government and Contractors: The British Treasury and War Supplies, 1775-1783*; subcontractors to the Treasury contractors, T 1/518, fols. 118-34, T 1/534, fols. 225-33; regular recipients of army extraordinary payments, Add. MSS 38375; Navy and Victualling Board contractors, Adm. 106/2593-606, Adm. 112/162-8, Adm. 20/273-91; Ordnance Board contractors, WO 47/86-96. Subscribers to the loans of 1780 and 1781 are taken from [Almon's] *Parliamentary Register* 17: 416-23, and *The Remembrancer* 11: 240-51. Royal purveyors and placemen have been located in *Royal Kalendar*, 1775. W.T. Laprade, ed., *Parliamentary Papers of John Robinson*, Publications of the Camden Society, 3d ser., 33 (London 1922): 135-91, and Add. MSS 37836 have been searched for recipients of secret and special service funds. The latter source runs only from 1779, but it is likely that a loyalist addresser on the list, John Lind, was in receipt of a pension when he signed the document in view of his pamphleteering activities around this time.

Voting patterns of petitioners and addressers in the mayoral election of 1772 are based on *A List of the Persons who have polled for Messieurs Wilkes and Townsend* (London 1772) and *A Number Extraordinary of Miller's London Mercury* (containing lists of persons polling for Hallifax and Shakespear), 16 October 1772. These lists also supply the livery company of voters in the election. Figures on livery company membership have been obtained from George F.E. Rudé, *Wilkes and Liberty: A Social Study of 1763 to 1774*, 212–13. Rudé, "Anti-Wilkite Merchants of 1769," *Guildhall Miscellany*, 2 (1965): 283–304, has been used to identify petitioners and addressers who also signed a loyal address to the king in 1769.

Only petitioners and addressers for whom biographical details can be established with a fair degree of certainty are included in Appendices A, B, and C. Signatories with common names are often impossible to identify as the same name may recur two or more times in directories and poll books. But discretionary judgment has been exercised. To take one example: the name John Reynolds occurs twice on the pro-American petition and three times in directories and poll lists; it is fairly safe to assume that one John Reynolds on the list is the Wilkite and known pro-American of that name. (The identity of the other petitioning John Reynolds is uncertain and he is perforce omitted from Appendix A.) In such cases, a question-mark has been added to denote the possibility of error. Of the pro-American petitioners, 622 have been identified in one or more category; no trace can be found of 260; and 218 cannot be adequately distinguished from others of like name. Of signatories to the two loyalist addresses, the identities of 1,091 can be established; 264 cannot be traced; and 299 cannot be distinguished from others of the same name. Approximately 316 individuals signed both loyal addresses, but they are accorded only one entry each in the various tables.

Appendix D lists aldermen and Common Councilmen for the period 1775–9, a timespan during which there were recorded divisions over issues involving America. The list of Common Councilmen is taken from the *Royal Kalendar*, 1775 (new edition), 1776, 1777, 1778, 1779, and 1780, and the list of aldermen from Alfred B. Beaven, *The Aldermen of the City of London, temp. Henry III–1908*. The sources of information on occupations, votes cast in the mayoral election of 1772, and petitioning behaviour in October 1775, are the same as those for Appendixes A, B, and C. The fact that Common Councilmen were resident in the wards they represented helps identification in directories, where addresses are generally given. Journals of Common Council, vols. 66 and 67, while giving exact numbers for divisions, do not specify how individuals voted. This information has been obtained from the following newspapers: 7 July 1775 vote: *Gazetteer*, 11 July 1775, with correction, ibid., 12 July 1775 (for votes of Common Councilmen), *Morning Chronicle*, 8 July 1775 (for full list of the minority), and *London Chronicle*, 6–8 July 1775 (for votes of aldermen); 21 July 1775 vote: *London Evening Post*, 20–22 July 1775 (list of motion's opponents only); 29 June 1779 vote: *London Evening Post*, 29 June–1 July 1779, *Public Advertiser*, 1 July 1779, and *Morning Chronicle*, 30 June 1779. The division lists of 7 July 1775 contain a few discrepancies; hence the occasional query about how some votes were cast in this division.

APPENDIX A
The Pro-American Petitioners of 11 October 1775

Name	Occupation, contracts, directorships	Signatory of 1769 loyal address (indicated by "A")	Vote in 1772 mayoral election, with livery co.[1]	Bank-ruptcy during war (years of)	Elected position when petition signed[2]
William Addis	Watchmaker & Goldsmith				
Agacis & Wallis	£1,000 Loan Sub. (1781)				
Tho. Ainsley	Potter & Glass-seller			1776, 1781	
Charles Aldridge					CC: Aldersgate
Ed. Aldridge	Wine Mercht		W-T Goldsmiths		
Edmund Barker Allen	Notary Public				
Richard Anderson	Mercht			1778	
William Anderson?	North Am. Mercht		W-T Mercht Taylors		CC: Bridge
James Ansell	Cooper		W-T Coopers		CC: Tower
Anstie & Worstead	Tea-dealers				
Paul Archer			W-T Joiners		
Wm. Archer	Weaver				
Ashton, Hodgson & Co.	Bay Factors				
Tho. Ashton	Tea-dealer		W-T Musicians		
Sam Athawes	North Am. Mercht				
Atkins & [Robert] Wyatt	Curriers & Leather Cutters				[Wyatt]: CC: Walbrook
Robert Atkinson	Hemp Mercht				
Tho. Atkinson & Co.	Warehousemen; £20,000 Loan Sub. (1780)				
Samuel Austen	Man's Mercer & Button-seller				
Edward Austin	Mercht & Drysalter				
John Austin	Mercht & Drysalter; £5,000 Loan Sub. (1781)		W-T Fishmongers		
George Bague	North Am. Mercht; Victualling Contract (Rice)				
Wm. Baily			W-T Coach-makers		

Name	Occupation, contracts, directorships	Signatory of 1769 loyal address (indicated by "A")	Vote in 1772 mayoral election, with livery co.[1]	Bank-ruptcy during war (years of)	Elected position when petition signed[2]
Richard Baker?	Distiller; £10,000, £2,000 Loan Subs, (1780, 1781)				
William Baker	North Am. Mercht; £1,000 Loan Sub. (1781)?				
William Baker	Notary Public				
Oliver Banks	Hatter & Hosier				
Henry Banner			W–T Joiners		CC: Cripplegate Without
John Barber	Sugar Baker		W–T Drapers		
Jos. Barber	Stationer		W–T Drapers		
Solomon Barber	Grocer		W–T Drapers		
Wm. Barber	Sadler & Harness-maker		W–T Curriers		
Thomas Barke	Mercht; £4,000 Loan Sub. (1781)				
Joseph Barlow			H–S Tallow Chandlers		
Jos. Barnes	Floor Cloth Manufacturer		W–T Painter-stainers		
Thomas Barrow	Sadler			1781	
Charles Bartrum	Hardwareman				
Jos. Baughan			W–T Feltmakers		
Sam. Baughan	Hatmaker		W–T Dyers		CC: Bridge
Stephen Beck	Brazier		W–T Armourers & Braziers		
Thomas Beetson	Mercer				
William Belch	Leather-seller		W–T Haberdashers		
Wilfred Bell	Timber Mercht			1777	
Peter Bellamy	Mercer				
John Bellett	Upholders' Warehouseman		W–T Upholders		CC: Aldgate
John Bennett	Worsted-maker				
J.W. Benson			W–T Apothecaries		CC: Lime Street
Wm. Bentley	Feltmonger		W–T Feltmakers	1776	
James Birch	Manchester Warehouseman				
Jn. Francis Blache	Wine Mercht				

Name	Occupation, contracts, directorships	Signatory of 1769 loyal address (indicated by "A")	Vote in 1772 mayoral election, with livery co.[1]	Bank-ruptcy during war (years of)	Elected position when petition signed[2]
George Blakesley	Sadler		W-T Sadlers		
Foster Bland	Banker				
Wm. Board	Chemist & Druggist				
Thomas Boddington	Linen Draper; £30,000 Loan Sub. (1780)		W-T Cloth-workers		CC: Cheap; PDD
G. Bodley			H-S Fishmongers		
John Boldero	Banker; £50,000, £60,000 Loan Subs. (1780, 1781)				
William Bond	Grocer		W-T Grocers		
William Bonham	Packer		H-S Salters		
Thomas Bord					CC: Cordwainer
F. Bouchet			W-T Founders		
John Bourke	"West Indian"[3]		W-T Mercht Taylors		
Thomas Bourke	"West Indian"				
Josiah Bowden			W-T Coopers		
Thomas Bowlby	Currier		W-T Curriers		
John Bowles	Print-seller		H-S Joiners		
George Bowley	Oil & Colourman				
John Boydell	Print-seller	A	H-S Stationers		CC: Cheap
Jos. & James Boydell	Insurance & Ship-brokers	[James]: A			
John Boylston	North Am. Mercht				
John Bradney	Apothecary		H-S Weavers		PDD
R.C. Bradshaw & Sons	Weavers				
Rich. Brewer	Callico-printer			1782	CC: Farring-don Without
Wm. Brewer	Draper			1779	
Lancelot Brewer			W-T Tallow Chandlers		
Edward Bridgen	North Am. Mercht				
Samuel Briggs	Indigo-maker				
John Briscoe	North Am. Mercht				
John Bristow	Engine-maker		W-T Carpenters		

Name	Occupation, contracts, directorships	Signatory of 1769 loyal address (indicated by "A")	Vote in 1772 mayoral election, with livery co.[1]	Bankruptcy during war (years of)	Elected position when petition signed[2]
Tho. Bromfield	North Am. Mercht				
John Bromhead			T Skinners		
Ro. Bromley	Clergyman				
R. Haning Brooks	Tea-dealer		W–T Curriers		
Jos. Browning	Hardwareman				
William Bruton			W–T Butchers		
James Buchanan	North Am. Mercht				
Henry Buckley			W–T Blacksmiths		
Robert Bullcock & Son	Haberdashers		W–T Tin-plate-workers		CC: Bishopsgate
John Burges	Mercht				
H. Burgess			W–T Wax Chandlers		
John Burnett	Brewer				
Benj. Burnley	Beer Mercht		W–T Innholders		CC: Bread Street
Atkinson Bush	Rum & Brandy Mercht				
R. Bush	Mercht				
John Bushnell	Cabinet-maker & Upholder		W–T Upholders		
Henry Butler, Sr	Hatmaker		W–T Feltmakers		
John Button	Glass-grinder & Cabinet-maker			1778	
Tho. Plumer Byde	Banker			1779	
Carey, [John] Moorey & Welch	North Am. Merchts				[Moorey]: CC: Bread Street
Tho. Carrington			W–T Clockmakers		
Henry Carter	Leather-seller				
Nath. Cartwright	Threadlaceman				
Govert Cassau	North Am. Mercht				
Cawthorn & Watson	Factors				
Jarvis Chambers	Warehouseman				
James Chapple	Stuff-weaver				
Bar. John Cheale	Pin-maker			1782	
Charles Childs			W–T Weavers		
Fr. Clarke & Co.	Ribbon Manufacturers				

Name	Occupation, contracts, directorships	Signatory of 1769 loyal address (indicated by "A")	Vote in 1772 mayoral election, with livery co.[1]	Bank-ruptcy during war (years of)	Elected position when petition signed[2]
Richard Clarke?			W-T Musicians		CC: Queenhithe
Samuel Clarke			W-T Carpenters		
Wm. Clifford & Co.	Warehousemen			1782	
John Cobb	Hatter				
Joseph Cockfield	Russia Mercht				
William Colhoun	"West Indian"				
James Collins			W-T Glovers		
William Compton	£500 Loan Sub. (1781)				
Edward Colson	Hosier			1778	
Cooper, Garratt & Taddy	Tobacconists & Tea-dealers				
Tho. Copping			W-T Coopers		
Edmund Cork			W-T Joiners		
William Corrock	Chinaman				
Wm. Cotterell	Chinaman				
Christopher Court	North Am. Mercht				
Wm. Cowland			W-T Armourers & Braziers		
Wm. Cowley	£5,000 Loan Sub. (1780)				
Wm. Cragg			W-T Butchers		
Robert Craston	Hosier			1778	
Joshua Crickett	Ribbon-weaver				
John Crisp	Oilman				
J. Crompton	Mercer			1783	
John Crompton	Paper-hanging maker & Upholder				
James Croome	Cheesemonger		W-T Glovers		
Brass Crosby, Esq.			W-T Goldsmiths		A: Bread Street
[Henry] Crosley & Lambley	Warehousemen			1780	
Richard Cumming			W-T Tin-plate-workers		
Benjamin Curtis	Linen Draper				
Timothy Curtis	Biscuit-maker				
Charles Dale	Hardwareman				
Samuel Dales	Wholesale Linen Draper		W-T Goldsmiths		

Name	Occupation, contracts, directorships	Signatory of 1769 loyal address (indicated by "A")	Vote in 1772 mayoral election, with livery co.[1]	Bank-ruptcy during war (years of)	Elected position when petition signed[2]
Wm. Davenhill	Bookseller & Stationer		W–T Stationers		
John Davis			W–T Mercht Taylors		CC: Aldgate
Richard Davis	Rope & Coal Mercht				
Tho. Dealtry			W–T Cutlers		
Dennis deBerdt	North Am. Mercht				
John Deighton	Linen Draper				
Henry Dekar			W–T Feltmakers		
Thomas Delafield	Grocer				
Benjamin Dell			W–T Upholders		
Richard Dell	Hosier				
Wm. Denham			W–T Joiners		
Dennis & Woodward	Sadlers				
T. Dennis			W–T Coopers		
John Dering	Linen Draper				
Quinton Dick	Irish Factor				
Charles Dilly	Bookseller		W–T Stationers		
Edward Dilly	Bookseller		W–T Stationers		
Wm. Domville	Stationer		W–T Stationers		
Josiah Dornford	Mercht				
Mat. Dove	Salter & Oilman		W–T Drapers		
John Dowley			W–T Blacksmiths		
Dowling, Brett & Hardingham	Norwich Manufacturers				
John Dunkin, Sr			W–T Plaisterers		PDD
Math. Dupont			W–T Sadlers		
Abraham Dupuis	Hardwareman				
Thomas Dutton	Sugar Cooper		W–T Coopers		
James Dyer	Broker		T Ironmongers		
Robert Dyke	Mercht			1782	
Richard Eaton	Mercht				
Thomas Eden	North Am. Mercht; £10,000, £7,000 Loan Subs. (1780, 1781)				
A. Edmonds & Harper	Stationers				
George Elderton	Coal Mercht				

Name	Occupation, contracts, directorships	Signatory of 1769 loyal address (indicated by "A")	Vote in 1772 mayoral election, with livery co.[1]	Bankruptcy during war (years of)	Elected position when petition signed[2]
James Elderton	Blackwell Hall Factor				
Richard Ellis	Upholder				
Robert Ellison	Mercht				
Robert Emerton			W–T Barbers		
Sam. Enderby	Oil Mercht; Victualling Contract (Oil); £5,000, £1,000 Loan Subs. (1780, 1781)				
Tho. Entwisle	Cabinet Founder				
Samuel Estwick	"West Indian"				
Eben. Evans	Wholesale Leather-seller		W–T Leathersellers	1780	
Benjamin Farmer	Lighterman & Coal Mercht				
Henry Fawconer	Linen Draper		W–T Barbers		
Burket Fen	Hosier		H–S Ironmongers		
John Finch	Ironmonger: £500 Loan Sub. (1781)		W–T Grocers		
William Finch	Hatter				
[Joseph] Fisher & Surgay	Hosiers		[Fisher]: W–T Cutlers		
William Fleming	Carpet Warehouseman		W–T Glovers		
Joseph Flight	Banker				PDD? (or below)
Joseph Flight	Linen Draper				PDD? (or above)
William Floyd			W–T Vintners		
Alex Forbes	Broker				
James Ford			W–T Joiners		
John Fox	Mercht		W–T Grocers		CC: Farringdon Without
James Freeman	Mercer			1777	
John French			W–T Stationers		
Robert French					CC: Cripplegate Without
Tho. Furnass	Broker			1782	
Gadsden & Johnson	North Am. Merchts				

Name	Occupation, contracts, directorships	Signatory of 1769 loyal address (indicated by "A")	Vote in 1772 mayoral election, with livery co.[1]	Bankruptcy during war (years of)	Elected position when petition signed[2]
Mat. Gale	North Am. Mercht; Navy Contract (Petersburgh Hemp)	A			
Tho. Gardner, Esq.	Sun Fire Office Dir.				
T. Garner	Corn Factor				
Geo. Gaskin	Clergyman				
Jos. Gattey	Druggist				
James Gautier	Broker			1777	
Henry George	Threadman & Haberdasher		W–T Weavers	1781	CC: Bishopsgate
Ed. Gibbs			W–T Carpenters		
Wm. Hassell Gibbs	Ironmonger			1778	
[Edward] Gilbert & Wilkinson	Stationers		[Gilbert]: T Stationers		
George Gimber	Fish-hook & Needle-maker		T Blacksmiths		
Samuel Goadbey	Stationer		W–T Drapers		
David Godfrey?	£9,000, £2,000 Loan Subs. (1780, 1781)				
Richard Goodall	Mercht				
James Goodier	Mercht				
Thomas Gorst	Cooper		W–T Coopers		CC: Billingsgate
Jo. Asgill Gosling	"West Indian"		W–T Goldsmiths		
Francis Gough	Paper-hanging Manufacturer				
Grace & Kennedy	Linen Drapers				
Henry Grace			W–T Grocers		
Richard Gravatt	Banker			1778	
Wm. Greaves	Silkman				
Edmund Green	Mercht				
Richard Green	Ironmonger		W–T Farriers		
Charles Greenwood	Upholder & Cabinet-maker				
Robert Gregory, Esq.	E. Ind. Co. Dir.				MP: Rochester
Richard Griffiths	Surgeon				

Name	Occupation, contracts, directorships	Signatory of 1769 loyal address (indicated by "A")	Vote in 1772 mayoral election, with livery co.[1]	Bankruptcy during war (years of)	Elected position when petition signed[2]
Silvanus Grove	North Am. Mercht; Lond. Ass. Dir.				
Robert Gyfford	Stationer				
John Haddon	Mercer			1782	
Hagger & Allis	Brewers				
Eng. Hake & Co.	Merchts				
John Hamilton	Wharfinger				
Benjamin Hamnet	North Am. Mercht				CC: Farringdon Within
Thomas Hankin	Coal Mercht				
Sam. Hanning			W-T Carpenters		CC: Cordwainer
Benjamin Hanson	Mercht		W-T Joiners		
Samuel Hanson	Orange Mercht		W-T Joiners		CC: Billingsgate
Nath. Hardcastle	Tallow Factor & Hop Mercht				
Tho. Harden			H-T Goldsmiths		
John Harford	North Am. Mercht				
Thomas Harland	Ironmonger				
Harris & Prescott	Linen Drapers				
Harris & [John] Readhead			[Readhead]: W-T Needlemakers		
Jos. Harrison	Wharfinger & Coal Mercht				
Tho. Harrisons	North Am. Mercht				
Daniel Harrop	Haberdasher			1777	
Joseph Harrop	Haberdasher				
Tho. Hartley & Co.	Wholesale Glover				
William Hartley	Cabinet-maker			1783	
Benj. Hawes	Blue Maker				
William Hawes	Grocer		H-S Ironmongers		
Hawkins & Sayer	Wholesale Linen Draper				
George Hayley, Esq.	North Am. Mercht		W-T Armourers & Braziers		A: Cordwainer; MP: London
Amos Hayton	North Am. Mercht				
Samuel Heartley					PDD

Name	Occupation, contracts, directorships	Signatory of 1769 loyal address (indicated by "A")	Vote in 1772 mayoral election, with livery co.[1]	Bank-ruptcy during war (years of)	Elected position when petition signed[2]
Charles Heath	Mathematical Instrument Maker				
Job Heath	Shoe Warehouseman				
John Henlock	Mercht		W–T Glovers		CC: Bread Street
Joseph Heylin	Gun-maker		W–T Vintners	1779	
Joseph Hickman	Watchmaker & Jeweller				
John Hill	M.D.				
William Hills			W–T Glaziers		
John Hinde	Grocer & Tea-dealer				
Samuel Hoare	Banker				
Samuel Hoare, Jr	£89,000 Loan Sub. (1780)				
Wm. Hodder	Apothecary				
Robert Hodgson	Druggist				
Peregrine Hog	Linen Draper		H–S Fletchers		
Robert Holden	Man's Mercer				CC: Cheap
Wm. Holland	Oilman		W–T Drapers		
Thomas Holloway	Engraver				
Joseph Holmes	Silk & Gauze Weaver				
Thomas Hopkins	Throwster				
John Horton	Dyer		W–T Dyers		CC: Cripplegate Within; PDD
Thomas Houston	Packer				
John Howell	Hosier				
Charles Howse	Clock & Watch Maker				
Edward Howse	Distiller		W–T Tin-plate-workers		CC: Farring-don Without
John Hubbard	Coal Mercht		W–T Haberdashers		
William Hubbard	Russia Mercht				
[David] Hudson & Worthington	Merchts		[Hudson]: W–T Feltmakers		
Thomas Hudson	Mercht; £1,000 Loan Sub. (1781)		H–S Carpenters		
R. Humphreys	Chemist & Druggist				

Name	Occupation, contracts, directorships	Signatory of 1769 loyal address (indicated by "A")	Vote in 1772 mayoral election, with livery co.[1]	Bankruptcy during war (years of)	Elected position when petition signed[2]
James Hunt	Gold-worker		H–S Goldsmiths		CC: Cheap
William Hunt	Distillers			1783	
William Hunter	Exchange Broker		W–T Upholders		
William Hurford & Co.	Coal Merchts & Wharfingers		W–T Barbers		CC: Castlebaynard; PDD
Tho. Hutchinson			W–T Barbers		
John Hyndman & Co.	North Am. Merchts; £10,000, £2,000 Loan Subs. (1780, 1781)				
William Inge	Cheesemonger			1778	
Edw. Jackson	Man's Mercer				CC: Bridge
Geo. Jackson & Co.	Hatmakers: £1,000 Loan Sub. (1781): [George Jackson]		[Geo. Jackson, Sr & Geo. Jackson, Jr]: W–T Feltmakers		
Samuel Jackson	Brewer				
Wm. Jacobson	Linen Draper				
Hugh James	Grocer				
Joseph James	Raisin Wine Maker		W–T Vintners		
Montague James	"West Indian"				
Richard James	Cooper		W–T Coopers		
Rich. James, Jr	Wine Cooper				
Rt. Jamieson	Factor				
Henry Janson	Bottle Warehouseman		W–T Fishmongers		CC: Dowgate
S.T. Janssen, Bart.			W–T Stationers		City Chamberlain
William Jarvis			W–T Curriers		
Mark Jefferson			W–T Bricklayers & Tylers		
Edward Jefferyes	Timber Mercht				
Geo. Jeffrey, Jr	Linen Draper				
William Jellicoe			H–S Skinners		
Issac Jemmett	Mercht				PDD
Joseph Jenkinson	Warehouseman				
Joseph Jennings	Hardwareman		W–T Drapers		PDD
John Jerman	Grocer				
Jos. Jewson	Hardwareman		W–T Turners		CC: Bridge

Name	Occupation, contracts, directorships	Signatory of 1769 loyal address (indicated by "A")	Vote in 1772 mayoral election, with livery co.[1]	Bank-ruptcy during war (years of)	Elected position when petition signed[2]
Thomas Joel	Schoolmaster				Secretary, London Association
Huge Johnston	Mercht				
Ph. Joling			W–T Joiners		
Josiah Jollands	Grocer				
George Keath			H–S Musicians		
Henry Keene	Coal Mercht; £500 Loan Sub. (1781)		W–T Fishmongers		PDD
John Keene			W–T Bakers		
John Keene			W–T Curriers		
Ant. Facer Kemp	Tobacconist & Brandy Mercht		W–T Distillers		
George Kemp	Glass-grinder & Cabinet-maker		W–T Upholders		
Luke Kendall	Jeweller				
[Henry] Kettle & Mandeville	Manchester Warehouseman		[Kettle]: H–S Tin-plate-workers		
James King	Hosier		H–T Frame-work-knitters		
William Kirby	Tobacconist		W–T Goldsmiths		
Joshua Kitson	Ship Chandler; Beer & Cider Mercht			1778	
Joseph Knowles	M.D.		W–T Leathersellers		
Thomas Lamb	Dyer & Buckram Stiffener		W–T Clothworkers		
John Landin	Weaver				
Tho. Langford	Hatter & Sword Cutler		W–T Cutlers		
Langkopf, Molling & Rasch	Merchts				
Sam. Lawford	Apothecary				
Sam. Lawrence			W–T Fishmongers		
Arthur Lee	Attorney				Agent for Mass. colony
William Lee, Esq.	North Am. Mercht				A: Aldgate
William Lee	Attorney				

Name	Occupation, contracts, directorships	Signatory of 1769 loyal address (indicated by "A")	Vote in 1772 mayoral election, with livery co.[1]	Bank-ruptcy during war (years of)	Elected position when petition signed[2]
Lever Legg	Woollen Draper; £5,000 Loan Sub. (1780)		W-T Mercht. Taylors		
Nicholas Leigh	Linen Draper & Manchester Warehouseman				
John Lewis	Stock-broker				
John Lodge	Packer		W-T Clothworkers		
Joseph Lomas	£500 Loan Sub. (1781)				
John Lomax			W-T Innholders		CC: Farring-don Within
Michael Lovell	"West Indian"		W-T Ironmongers		
Leonard Lowden	Hatter & Hosier		W-T Leather-sellers		
Thomas Ludlam	Linen Draper				
Jos. Lumley			W-T Joiners		
Wm. Lutwyche	Jeweller		W-T Embroiderers		
Ronold McAlleston			H-S Wax Chandlers		
George Makenzie Macaulay					CC: Vintry
Rt. Macky, Esq.	Mercht; £15,000 Loan Sub. (1781)	A			
John Maddocks	Broker		W-T Glovers	1780	
Eben Maitland	Mercht				
Rob. Maitland, Jr.	Mercht; £2,000 Loan Sub. (1781)				PDD
James Mangnall	Manchester Warehousman				
John Manship, Esq.	East India Mercht; E. Ind. Co. Dir.				
Sam. Margerum	Tin-plate-worker				
Henry Maskall	Apothecary		W Glass-sellers		President, London Association
William Markes	Glover		W-T Glovers		
Joseph Martin	Banker				MP: Tewkesbury
J. Massen	Mercht; £2,000 Loan Sub. (1780)				

Name	Occupation, contracts, directorships	Signatory of 1769 loyal address (indicated by "A")	Vote in 1772 mayoral election, with livery co.[1]	Bank-ruptcy during war (years of)	Elected position when petition signed[2]
Rich. Mathew			W-T Coopers		
Benjamin Maud					CC: Aldersgate
Charles Maynard			W-T Upholders		CC: Farring-don Within
Tobias Maynard	Confectioner		T Grocers		
Wm. Meadows	Silkman		W-T Dyers	1779	
John Meane			W-T Turners		
Wm. Merrick			H-S Vintners		
Stephen Mesnard	Shipwright				
Edward Minesie	"West Indian"			1776	
W[illiam] & R. Molleson	North Am. Merchts	[William]: A			
Philip Morgan	Mercer		H-S Wax Chandlers		
Tho. Morley	Broker			1777	
Richard Morson	Goldsmith & Jeweller				
James Moxham	Sugar-refiner				
John Munt	Hatmaker				
Edward Neale	Mercer				
James Neale	Staffordshire Warehouseman				
Rich. Neave	North Am. Mercht; Bank of Eng. Dir.		W-T Drapers	1777	CC: Tower
John Newman	Goldsmith & Jeweller				CC: Langbourn
Nat. Newnham, Esq.	Grocer				A: Vintry
Tho. Newnham	£2,500, £2,000 Loan Subs, (1780, 1781)				
Wm. Newnham	Grocer				
William Newton	Notary Public				
Jos. Nicholls	Currier & Leather Cutter		W-T Curriers		
Joseph Nicholson	North Am. Mercht				
Richard Norfolk	Pewterer		W-T Pewterers		
John North	Hat Warehouseman		H-S Drapers		
Thomas North	Leather Factor				
Wm. Northage	£500 Loan Sub. (1781)				

Name	Occupation, contracts, directorships	Signatory of 1769 loyal address (indicated by "A")	Vote in 1772 mayoral election, with livery co.[1]	Bankruptcy during war (years of)	Elected position when petition signed[2]
John Norton	North Am. Mercht	A			
Samuel Norton	Watch & Clock Maker				
Jacob Nortzell	Perfumer				
John Nunns	Haberdasher		H-S Blacksmiths		
Charles Ogilvie	North Am. Mercht				
Tho. Oliver	"West Indian"; £41,000 Loan Sub. (1781)				
Joseph Paice, Esq.	Mercht; £20,000 Loan Sub. (1781); South Sea Co. Dir.				PDD
Edward Parish	Mercer				CC: Farringdon Within
Joseph Parker	Linen Draper		W-T Mercers		
Mary Parker & Son	Wine & Brandy Merchts			1781	
S. Parson	Grocer				
J. Patchings			W-T Coopers		
J.L. Paulhan	Sugar Baker		H-S Ironmongers		CC: Tower
William Payne	Coal & Hop Mercht				
George Peacock	Watchmaker				
Samuel Peacock	Mercht		W-T Pewterers		
Thomas Peacock	Glass Warehouseman		W-T Carpenters		
Tho. Peake			W-T Plumbers		
James Pearson	Linen Draper		W-T Fishmongers	1779	PDD
Michael Pearson	Man's Mercer				
Jere. Percy			H-W Plumbers		CC: Aldersgate
Samuel Petrie	Mercht				
Richard Peyton	Stationer				
Charles Phillips	"West Indian"				
Jos. Phillips	Wine Cooper				
Francis Philpott	Glass-maker				
J. Warner Phipps	Coal Mercht		W-T Fishmongers	1781	
James Palmer	Wine Mercht		H-S Plaisterers		

Name	Occupation, contracts, directorships	Signatory of 1769 loyal address (indicated by "A")	Vote in 1772 mayoral election, with livery co.[1]	Bank-ruptcy during war (years of)	Elected position when petition signed[2]
Nich. Phipps	Upholder & Auctioneer				
William Pickett	Jeweller & Goldsmith		W–T Goldsmiths		
Tho. Pickford	Sadler & Ironmonger; £500 Loan Sub. (1781)		W–T Sadlers		
John Piper	Packer				CC: Queenhithe; Treasurer, London Association
John Place	Linen Draper				
William Plomer, Esq.			W–T Bricklayers & Tylers		A: Bassishaw
Thomas Plumer, Esq.	Mercht; Bank of Eng, Dir.	A			
Samuel Plummer	Woollen Draper				CC: Tower
Edward Polhill	Upholder				CC: Bread Street
Barth. Pomeroy	Linen Draper		H–S Mercht Taylors		
John Popplewell	Tea-broker		W–T Grocers	1777	
James Potts	Corn Factor & Biscuit Baker				
James Poyas	North Am. Mercht				
Tho. Wm. Preston	North Am. Mercht				
Robert Prettyman			W–T Barbers		
Liscomb Price	Scrivener		W–T Joiners	1776	
Rice Price			W–T Drapers		
James Pritt	Hosier				
Jos. Proctor	Grocer & Teaman			1781	
Pryor & Harford	North Am. Merchts				
Stephen Purdeau			W–T Barbers		
Sam. Randall?	Shoe-maker; Treasury Subcontract (Shoes)				
John Ratray	Woollen Draper				
John Reynolds, Esq.?	Attorney		W–T Frame-work-knitters		

Name	Occupation, contracts, directorships	Signatory of 1769 loyal address (indicated by "A")	Vote in 1772 mayoral election, with livery co.[1]	Bank- ruptcy during war (years of)	Elected position when petition signed[2]
T. Rhodes	Stock-broker		W–T Fishmongers		
David Richardson	Slop-seller & Hosier				
Robert Richardson	Innholder			1780	
Tho. Richardson	Factor				
Tho. Richardson	Mercht				
Wm. Richardson			W–T Stationers		CC: Farring- don Without
Ridgway & Rolleston	North Am. Merchts		[Ridgway]: W– T Skinners		
Tho. Roberts, Jr	Broker				
Wm. Robley	Linen Draper		W–T Musicians		
Thomas Rogers	Linen Draper		H–S Wax Chandlers		PDD
John Rooke	Spanish Mercht	A			
Benjamin Rosewell	Attorney				
Robert Ross			H–S Salters		CC: Billingsgate
John Routh	Grocer & Tea- dealer				
Thomas Rud	Mercht			1778	
John Runnington			W–T Grocers		
James Russell	North Am. Mercht				
James Rutherford			H–S Bakers		
Henry Rutt	Glover		H–S Clothworkers		
Jere. Rydout					PDD
Bateman Saddington	Apothecary & Chemist		W–T Apothecaries		
Robt. Saddington	Leather-seller				
Sam. Saloway	Tanner & Leather Factor				
Sam. & Wm. Salte	Linen Drapers				
John Sampson	Woollen Draper			1777	
Henry Sanders	Silk Dyer		W–T Dyers		
Stephen Sandwell	Gun-maker			1778	
John Satchell	Timber Mercht				
John Sawbridge, Esq.			W–T Frame- work-knitters		A: Langbourn; MP: London
William Saxby	Linen Draper; £2,000 Loan Sub. (1781)		W–T Painter- stainers		CC: Bread Street

Name	Occupation, contracts, directorships	Signatory of 1769 loyal address (indicated by "A")	Vote in 1772 mayoral election, with livery co.[1]	Bank-ruptcy during war (years of)	Elected position when petition signed[2]
Thomas Sayer			W-T Distillers		
Stephen Sayre	Banker			1776	
Richard Scott	Mercht				
William Scott	Hosier		W Barbers		
William Scullard	Mercht	A	H-S Vintners		
John Seaber			W-T Clothworkers		
Tho. Seamark	Mercht			1783	
James Searle	Mercht				
James Season	Trunk & Fire Bucket Warehouseman		H-S Leathersellers		
Wm. Sewell			W-T Fruiterers		
James Sharp	Ironmonger		W-T Drapers		CC: Lime Street
Tho. Sharrar	Silk Thrower				
Sam. Sharwood	Currier				
Lewis Shepheard			W-T Vintners		
Tho. Sherwood	Draper		W-T Drapers	1777	
Wm. Shrigley	Mercer				
Brigg Shrimpton, Jr			W-T Coopers		
Priest Shrubb			W-T Plumbers		CC: Vintry
Sainsbury Sibley	Haberdasher & Glover		W-T Joiners		CC: Cordwainer
Wm. Simpson	Mercht		W-T Joiners		
Thomas Slater	Warehouseman				
Wm. Slater	Linen Draper		W Apothecaries		
John Sloman	Linen Draper				
Smith, Harris, & Hatfield	Ribbon Manufacturers				
Charles Smith?	Linen Draper; £500 Loan Sub. (1781)		H-S Clothworkers		
Edward Smith	Laceman		W-T Weavers		
George Smith	Warehouseman		W-T Cordwainers		
Charles Sommers	Scale-maker		W-T Skinners		CC: Walbrook
Jos. Sparrow	Silk Dyer		W-T Clothworkers	1778	
Samuel Sparrow	North Am. Mercht				PDD
James Spence	Grocer			1775	

Name	Occupation, contracts, directorships	Signatory of 1769 loyal address (indicated by "A")	Vote in 1772 mayoral election, with livery co.[1]	Bank-ruptcy during war (years of)	Elected position when petition signed[2]
Henry Spencer	Tobacconist; £30,000, £3,000 Loan Subs, (1780, 1781)	A	H–S Musicians		
John Spicer			W–T Farriers		
Godfrey Springhall	Wine Broker			1778	
William Stagg	Stock-broker		W–T Barbers		
Richard Stanier	Insurer			1783	
Tho. Staton	Gun-maker				
[Luke] Stavely & [Robert] Turner	Linen Drapers			1777	Both CC: Bread Street; [Turner]: Treasurer, London Association
Benjamin Stead	North Am. Mercht				
Robert Stead			H–S Mercht. Taylors		
Henry Sterry	Currier & Leather Cutter		H–S Curriers		
Wm. Stevens, Jr	Malt Factor			1778	
Joseph Stevenson	Cooper				CC: Dowgate
Joseph Stonard	Corn Factor				
Wm. Stone					CC: Cordwainer
Story & Alderson	North Am. Merchts				
William Straphan	Potter				
[John] Stratton & Rodbard	North Am. Merchts		[Stratton]: T Haberdashers		
John Strettell	North Am. Mercht				
John Stringer	Warehouseman				
Thomas Swanson	Pewterer				CC: Bassisshaw
Shield Swanston	Mercht			1781	
J. Tappenden & Co.	Ironmongers; Treasury Subcontract (Tools)				
John Taverna	Packer				
Ed. Farmer Taylor	Brazier		W–T Braziers & Armourers		CC: Tower
James Tew			W–T Bakers		

Name	Occupation, contracts, directorships	Signatory of 1769 loyal address (indicated by "A")	Vote in 1772 mayoral election, with livery co.[1]	Bank-ruptcy during war (years of)	Elected position when petition signed[2]
Samuel Thorne			W–T Girdlers		
Wm. Thornthwaite	Woollen Draper				
H. Thorowgood			W–T Farriers		
J. Thorowgood			W–T Stationers		
Samuel Thorpe	Wholesale Haberdasher				CC: Aldgate
Thomas Thorpe			W–T Vintners		CC: Farring-don Without
Harrison Thwaites	Birmingham Warehouseman				
Thomas Tilson	Grocer				
Thomas Todd	Druggist		W–T Salters		
Ben Tomkins	Stationer		W–T Butchers		
Edward Tomlin	Clock & Watch Maker				
Samuel Toulmin	Clock & Watch Maker		W–T Joiners		PDD
John Towers	Haberdasher		W–T Fishmongers		PDD
Samuel Towers	Hardwareman				
Matthew Towgood	Mercht		W–T Fishmongers		
Thomas Tredway	Glove-seller		W–T Merct Taylors		
Edw. Trelawny	Coal Mercht				
John Trelawny	Haberdasher, Hosier & Button-seller		W–T Skinners		
John Trevanion	Mercht				MP: Dover
Edw. Grant Tuckwell	Coal Mercht				
Samuel Turner, Jr	"West Indian"; Lond. Ass. Dir.				
Wm. Turner	Linen Draper; £2,000 Loan Sub. (1780)		W–T Musicians		
Oman Turpin	Bookseller				
Edward Tutet	Clock & Watch Maker		W–T Clockmakers		CC: Langbourn
Stephen Tyers	Broker		W–T Coopers		CC: Billingsgate
John Underwood	Grocer		W–T Glovers		
Stephen Unwin	Hardwareman				CC: Cripplegate Within

Name	Occupation, contracts, directorships	Signatory of 1769 loyal address (indicated by "A")	Vote in 1772 mayoral election, with livery co.[1]	Bank- ruptcy during war (years of)	Elected position when petition signed[2]
Edward Upton	Broker		W-T Glovers		CC: Farring- don Within
Thomas Vardon	Ironmonger				
Goodson Vines	Mercht				
John Vowell	£3,000 Loan Sub. (1781)				PDD
John Vowell, Jr	Stationer			1779	
Geo. Waddington	Exchange Broker		W-T Innholders		
John Wager			W-T Poulterers		
James Waghorn	Threadman				
Ja. Walker & Son	Weavers				
William Walker	Grocer & Tea- dealer		W-T Vintners		
Wallace, Davidson & Johnson	North Am. Merchts				
James Waller	Gun-maker				
John Wansey	£1,000 Loan Sub. (1781)				
Tho. Warboys	Brandy Mercht				
Matthew Warr			W-T Barbers		
George Warren			T Feltmakers		
James Warren	Wine Mercht				
John Warren	Cooper; £500 Loan Sub. (1781)		W-T Coopers		
William Warren	Mercht				
Samuel Waterman	North Am. Mercht				
Jonathan Wathen	Hatmaker; £3,000 Loan Sub. (1780)		H-S Haberdashers		
Robert Watkins					CC: Bread Street
Daniel Watkinson	Tallow Mercht				
Tisdale Webb	Wholesale Upholsterer				
Joseph Welch	Wire-worker		W-T Girdlers		
Richard Weld	Mercht; £3,000 Loan Sub. (1781)				
Richard Welles	Stationer				
John Wenham			W-T Vintners		
West & Hobson	North Am. Merchts				
Wm. West	Hop Factor				
Owen Weston	Cooper				

Name	Occupation, contracts, directorships	Signatory of 1769 loyal address (indicated by "A")	Vote in 1772 mayoral election, with livery co.[1]	Bankruptcy during war (years of)	Elected position when petition signed[2]
Richard Weston			W–T Butchers		
Tho. Weston & Son	Tobacconists				
Tho. Wetherell			W–T Painter-stainers		
[Geo.] Wheatley & Risdale	Wholesale Upholsterers; [Wheatley]: £10,000 £13,000 Loan Subs, (1780, 1781)		[Wheatley]: W–T Wax Chandlers		
Richard Wheeler	Distiller		W–T Joiners		
Tho. Whitehorne	Fan-dealer				
Enor Whitely	Woollen Draper			1780	
Tho. Whittell	Tobacconist		W–T Grocers		
Tho. Whywall	Tobacconist				
Wm. Wilbraham	Weaver				
Heaton Wilkes	Malt Distiller				
John Wilkes, Esq.					A: Farringdon Without; MP Middlesex
John Wilkie	Bookseller		H–S Stationers		
James Wilkins	Blackwell Hall Factor				
Reader Wilkinson	Druggist				
James Williams, Esq.	"West Indian"				
John Williams	Tea-dealer & Wine Mercht; £8,000 Loan Sub. (1781)				
Theo. Williams	Broker				
Robert Willis	Broker				
Joseph Wilson	Hop Mercht				
Rd. Wilson & Son	Warehousemen		[Richard]: W–T Founders		
Thomas Wilson, D.D.	Clergyman		W–T Joiners		
Jos. Windsor	Linen Draper				
Henry Winstanley	Silkman				
Joseph Wise	Linen Draper		W–T Drapers		CC: Portsoken

Name	Occupation, contracts, directorships	Signatory of 1769 loyal address (indicated by "A")	Vote in 1772 mayoral election, with livery co.[1]	Bank-ruptcy during war (years of)	Elected position when petition signed[2]
[Jn.] Withers, [Robert] Birch & Rivers	Linen Drapers		[Withers]: H-S Bricklayers & Tylers; [Birch]: W-T Dyers		
Robert Withers			W-T Carpenters		
Simon Wooding	Wine Mercht		W-T Vintners		
Wm. Woodnorth	Refiner			1777	
Tho. Wooldridge	North Am. Mercht			1777 and 1781	
Edward Worsley			W-T Joiners		
Keith Wray	Mercht				
John Wren	Satin-weaver				
William Wright	Wine Mercht			1782	CC: Farring-don Without
Wm. Wright	Orange Mercht				
Edward Yates	Stationer & Playing-card Maker			1776	
Ch. Yoxall	Wharfinger				
Daniel Zuchoft	Mercht				

APPENDIX B

A Comparison of the Pro-American Petitioners of 11 October 1775 with the Progovernment Addressers of 14 and 20 October 1775

TABLE 1
Occupations
(In parentheses, percentage of petitioners or addressers whose occupations can be determined; percentages are calculated to the nearest whole number)

Pro-American Petitioners		*Progovernment Addressers*
(a) PROFESSIONALS		
3 (1%)	Clergy	0 (–)
3 (1%)	Doctors	1 (–)
7 (1%)	Lawyers	5 (1%)
1 (–)	Schoolmasters	0 (–)
14 (3%)		6 (1%)
(b) OVERSEAS MERCHANTS, FACTORS, BROKERS, WAREHOUSEMEN, FINANCIERS		
44 (9%)	General or Unspecified Merchts	196 (25%)
43 (9%)	North Am. Merchts	5 (1%)
2 (–)	North Eur. Merchts	33 (4%)
3 (1%)	South Eur. Merchts	15 (2%)
1 (–)	Oriental Merchts	9 (1%)
12 (2%)	"West Indians"	4 (1%)
16 (3%)	Warehousemen	18 (2%)
16 (3%)	General or Unspecified Factors/Agents/ Brokers	22 (3%)
7 (1%)	Commodity Brokers/Factors	19 (2%)
5 (1%)	Stock-exchange Brokers	7 (1%)
2 (–)	Insurers/Insurance Brokers	13 (2%)
7 (1%)	Bankers	14 (2%)
158 (31%)		355 (45%)
(c) WHOLESALERS IN SPECIFIC COMMODITIES, RETAILERS, CRAFTSMEN, PACKERS		
4 (1%)	Arms Dealers	4 (1%)
11 (2%)	Chemists/Druggists	18 (2%)
7 (1%)	Clock/Watch Makers	12 (2%)
76 (15%)	Cloth/Silk Trade	74 (9%)
12 (2%)	Coal Dealers	5 (1%)
9 (2%)	Coopers	5 (1%)
2 (–)	Engineers/Instrument Makers	2 (–)
5 (1%)	Equestrian & Carrying Trades	7 (1%)
21 (4%)	Household Construction & Supplies	40 (5%)

Pro-American Petitioners		Progovernment Addressers
8 (2%)	Jewellers/Workers in Precious Metal	29 (4%)
13 (3%)	Leather Trade	8 (1%)
23 (5%)	Alcoholic Beverages Trades	42 (5%)
21 (4%)	Non-Precious Metal Trade	26 (3%)
7 (1%)	Oil/Colourmen	21 (3%)
41 (8%)	Outfitters/Haberdashers	28 (4%)
5 (1%)	Packers	14 (2%)
29 (6%)	Provisions/Food Processing	29 (4%)
2 (-)	Ship Construction/Supplies	4 (1%)
18 (4%)	Stationery/Book & Print Trade	27 (3%)
3 (1%)	Timber Merchts	4 (1%)
7 (1%)	Tobacconists	5 (1%)
10 (2%)	Miscellaneous	17 (2%)
334 (66%)		421 (54%)

TABLE 2
Directorships of Companies

Pro-American Petitioners		Progovernment Addressers
2	Bank of England	14
2	East India Company	12
2	London Assurance	7
0	Royal Exchange Assurance	10
1	South Sea Company	6
1	Sun Fire Office	3
8		52
(1% of identified petitioners)		(held by 50 [5%] of identified addressers)

TABLE 3
Contractors, Loan Subscribers, Pensioners, Placemen

Pro-American Petitioners		Progovernment Addressers
40	Loan Subscribers	167
0	Treasury Contractors & Their Agents	15
2	Treasury Subcontractors	8
3	Navy & Victualling Board Contractors	70
0	Ordnance Contractors	19
0	Agents for Prize Cargoes Sold by Admiralty	6
0	Regular Recipients of Army Extraordinary Payments	6
0	Crown Placemen/Purveyors/Pensioners	25
45		316
(held by 44 [7%] of identified petitioners)		(held by 263 [24%] of identified adressers)

TABLE 4
Elected Representatives
(In parentheses, percentages of identified petitioners and addressers)

Pro-American Petitioners		Progovernment Addressers
7 (1%)	Aldermen	7 (1%)
67 (11%)	Common Councilmen	54 (5%)
6 (1%)	MPs	10 (1%)
19 (3%)	Protestant Dissenting Deputies	16 (1%)
99 (16%)		87 (8%)

TABLE 5
Petitioners' and Addressers' Votes in Mayoral Election of 1772 by Livery Company
(In parentheses, company membership in 1756)

Pro-American Petitioners				Progovernment Addressers		
Wilkes and/or Town-send	Hallifax and/or Shakes-pear	Split Vote[1]		Wilkes and/or Town-send	Halifax and/or Shakes-pear	Split Vote[1]
3	1	–	Apothecaries (145)	–	13	–
4	–	–	Armourers & Braziers (74)	2	2	–
2	1	–	Bakers (139)	1	13	–
8	–	–	Barbers (295)	3	12	–
4	1	–	Blacksmiths (169)	1	8	–
–	–	–	Bowyers (36)	–	4	–
–	–	–	Brewers (115)	–	2	–
2	1	–	Bricklayers & Tylers (92)	6	8	1
4	–	–	Butchers (173)	8	9	1
6	–	–	Carpenters (100)	1	6	–
2	–	–	Clockmakers (60 in 1766)	2	12	–
5	2	–	Clothmakers (138)	–	21	–
1	–	–	Coachmakers (92)	–	5	–
–	–	–	Cooks (54)	1	4	–
12	–	–	Coopers (248)	3	10	–
1	–	–	Cordwainers (79)	–	8	–
6	1	–	Curriers (87)	1	1	–
3	–	–	Cutlers (62)	1	2	–
2	–	–	Distillers (103)	–	3	–
12	1	–	Drapers (156)	1	11	–
5	–	–	Dyers (96)	–	9	–
1	–	–	Embroiderers (74)	–	3	–
3	–	–	Farriers (66)	1	3	–
8	–	–	Feltmakers (100)	1	1	–
9	1	–	Fishmongers (159)	3	11	–
–	1	–	Fletchers (31)	–	1	–
2	–	–	Founders (100)	2	9	–
2	–	1	Frame-work-knitters (51)	–	2	–
1	–	–	Fruiterers (41)	1	–	–
2	–	–	Girdlers (71)	–	2	–
1	–	–	Glaziers (78)	1	4	–
1	–	–	Glass-sellers (49)	–	3	–
7	–	–	Glovers (206)	5	13	–
7	1	1	Goldsmiths (162)	–	17	–
8	–	–	Grocers (125)	–	12	–
3	1	–	Haberdashers (312)	3	14	–
3	–	–	Innholders (111)	1	8	–
16	1	–	Joiners (370)	6	18	–
2	3	–	Ironmongers (88)	–	14	–
3	1	–	Leathersellers (118)	–	4	–

Pro-American Petitioners				Progovernment Addressers		
Wilkes and/or Town-send	Hallifax and/or Shakes-pear	Split Vote[1]		Wilkes and/or Town-send	Hallifax and/or Shakes-pear	Split Vote[1]
–	–	–	Lorimers (97)	–	4	–
–	–	–	Masons (78)	1	5	–
1	–	–	Mercers (146)	–	2	–
5	2	–	Mercht Taylors (275)	2	17	–
4	2	–	Musicians (100)	–	9	–
1	–	–	Needlemakers (46)	1	2	–
3	–	–	Painter-stainers (99)	1	7	–
–	–	–	Pattenmakers (54)	–	–	–
2	–	–	Pewterers (96)	1	10	1
1	1	–	Plaisterers (74)	–	4	–
2	–	1	Plumbers (55)	1	4	–
1	–	–	Poulterers (91)	–	4	–
3	–	–	Sadlers (65)	–	6	1
1	2	–	Salters (125)	–	15	–
–	–	–	Scriveners (52)	–	3	–
4	1	–	Skinners (117)	–	8	–
9	2	–	Stationers (199)	2	21	–
–	–	–	Surgeons (89)	–	–	–
1	1	–	Tallow Chandlers (159)	1	2	1
3	1	–	Tin-plate-workers (60 in 1766)	1	5	–
2	–	–	Turners (133)	4	11	–
6	–	–	Upholders (95)	2	4	1
8	2	–	Vintners (186)	3	15	1
2	3	–	Wax Chandlers (104)	3	3	–
3	–	–	Weavers (203)	1	8	1
223	34	3		79	471	8

% of petitioning voters:				% of addressing voters:		
86	13	1		14	84	2

APPENDIX C

Progovernment Addressers of 14 and 20 October 1775, who had or would have a Contractual, Financial, or Occupational Link to the Administration[1]

Name	Occupation, directorship	Place, pension, contracts, loan subs.	Signatory of 1769 loyal address (indicated by "A")	Vote in 1772 mayoral election[2]	Elected position when address signed[3]
Will. Adair	Mercht	£25,000 Loan Sub. (1780)			
James Adam?	Architect	Architect to H.M. Board of Works			
R. Aislabie	Mercht	£5,000 Loan Sub. (1780)			
Alexander Anderson	Mercht	£1,000 Loan Sub. (1781)			
J.W. Anderson	Mercht; Agent and Commission-ary for the City of Dantzig; Royal Exchange Assur. Dir.	Agent to owners of prize cargo sold to navy	A		
David André	Italian Mercht	£10,000, £5,000 Loan Subs. (1780, 1781)	A		
J. Lewis André	Mercht	£2,000 Loan Sub. (1781)	A		
J. Jul. Angerstein	Insurer	Navy Contract (Shipping); £3,000 Loan Sub. (1781)			
John Jacob Appach	Mercht	£1,000 Loan Sub. (1781)			
Hugh Atkins	Russia Mercht	Navy Contract (Petersburgh Hemp)	A		
Chr. Atkinson	Corn Factor	Victualling Contract (Wheat Malt); £10,000 Loan Sub. (1781)			H-S
Richard Atkinson	"West Indian"	Treasury Contract (Rum, Provisions); Navy Contract (Shipping); Victualling Contract (Sourkraut); £200,000 Loan Sub. (1781): [Mure, Son, and Atkinson]			

Name	Occupation, directorship	Place, pension, contracts, loan subs.	Signatory of 1769 loyal address (indicated by "A")	Vote in 1772 mayoral election[2]	Elected position when address signed[3]
William Ayres	Harness-maker	Ordnance Contract (Equestrian Equipment)		W–T	
John Baril	Mercht	£1,000 Loan Sub. (1781)			
Francis Baring	Mercht; Royal Exchange Assur. Dir.	Navy Contract (Hemp); £100,000, £50,000 Loan Subs. (1780, 1781)			
Joseph Barr	Mercht	Navy Contract (Archangel Tar)	A		
Isaac Barrett	Wax Chandler	Wax Chandler to H.M. Household		H–S	
John Barrow		£25,000 Loan Sub. (1781)			
E.B. Batson	Banker	£40,000, £60,000 Loan Subs. (1780, 1781)	A		
Alex. Baxter, Esq.	Russian Counsul & Mercht	£12,000, £140,000 Loan Subs. (1780, 1781)	A		
Sam. Beachcroft	Italian Mercht; Gov., Bank of Eng.	£3,000 Loan Sub. (1781)	A		
James Benson	Mercht	Victualling Contract (Irish Beef, Rum, Iron Hoops)			
Charles Best	Russia Mercht	£500 Loan Sub. (1781)	A		
Wm. Beverley		£8,000 Loan Sub. (1781)			
John Bickerton		Purveyor of Poultry to H.M. Household			
John Bigge	Mercer	Mercer to the Great Wardrobe	A	H–S	
Edm. Boehm	Hamburgh Mercht; South Sea Co. Dir.	£10,000, £15,000 Loan Subs. (1780, 1781)	A		
Dan. Booth	Mercht; Bank of Eng. Dir.	£30,000 Loan Sub. (1781)	A	H–S	
Peter Bostock	Mercht	£1,000 Loan Sub. (1781)			

Name	Occupation, directorship	Place, pension, contracts, loan subs.	Signatory of 1769 loyal address (indicated by "A")	Vote in 1772 mayoral election[2]	Elected position when address signed[3]
Richard Bowen		£2,000 Loan Sub. (1781)			
James Bowles	Stationer	£3,000 Loan Sub. (1781)			
Ralph Bressey		Ordnance Contract (Powder Barrels)			
U. Bristow	Packer	Treasury Subcontract (Blankets, Rugs)		H–S	
Tho. Bromwich	Paper-hanging-maker	Paper-hanging-maker to the Great Wardrobe	A	H–S	
Edw. Bull	Blackwell Hall Factor	£3,000, £500 Loan Subs. (1780, 1781)			
Richard Buller	Mercht	£10,000 Loan Sub. (1781)			
John Bullock?	Stationer	Ordnance Contract (Stationery)		H–S	
Tho. Burfoot	Packer	Packer for the Great Wardrobe; Treasury Contract (Rum, Packaging); Treasury Subcontract (Blankets, Rugs); £8,000 Loan Sub. (1781)		H–S	
James Calvert	Vinegar Mercht	Victualling Contract (Vinegar)	A		
Matt. Carrett	Mercht	£20,000, £15,000 Loan Subs. (1780, 1781)			
Peter Cazalet	Mercht	£10,000 Loan Sub. (1781)			
Matthew Chalie		£1,000 Loan Sub. (1781)			
James Chapman	Whalebone Mercht	£4,000, £1,000 Loan Subs. (1780, 1781)			CC: Bread Street
Lewis Chauvett	Mercht	Army Extraordinary Contract (Supplying Negroes to British Govt in the W. Indies)	A		

Name	Occupation, directorship	Place, pension, contracts, loan subs.	Signatory of 1769 loyal address (indicated by "A")	Vote in 1772 mayoral election[2]	Elected position when address signed[3]
Gabriel Clarmont	Mercht	£5,000 Loan Sub. (1780)			
Rich. Clay	Mercht & Manufacturer	£2,000 Loan Sub. (1781)	A		
Thomas Cooper?	Warehouseman	Victualling Contract (Mutton)	A		
Walter Cope	Ship & Insurance Broker	Navy Contract (Shipping); Victualling Contract (Oil)		H-T	
John Cornwall	Russia Mercht	Navy Contract (Petersburgh Hemp); [John] Cornwall and [Godfrey] Thornton, £200,000 Loan Sub. (1781)	A		
John Cottin	Mercht	£40,000 Loan Sub. (1781)	A		
Jukes Coulson	Iron Mercht	Victualling Contract (Iron Hoops); Ordnance Contract (Iron-work)	A	H-S	
J.N. Coussmaker	Mercht	£5,000 Loan Sub. (1781)	A		
Richard Crawshay	Ironmonger	Ordnance Contract (Gun-casting)		W-T	
Fr. Creuzé	Jeweller	£1,000 Loan Sub. (1781)			
Colin Currie?	Mercht	£2,000 Loan Sub. (1781): [Currie, Lefevre and Co.]			
Will Curtis?		Victualling Contract (London Bisket)			
Carter Daking	Cheesemonger	Treasury Subcontract (Cheese)		H-S	
Charles Dalbiac	Weaver	£8,000, £3,000 Loan Subs. (1780, 1781)			
James Dalbiac	Weaver	£4,000, £2,000 Loan Subs. (1780, 1781)	A		

Name	Occupation, directorship	Place, pension, contracts, loan subs.	Signatory of 1769 loyal address (indicated by "A")	Vote in 1772 mayoral election[2]	Elected position when address signed[3]
Edward Darell	Mercht	£10,000 Loan Sub. (1781): [Edward and Rob. Darell]	A		
Rob. Darell	Mercht; South Sea Co. Dir.	See above	A		
Thomas Deane		Coal Porter in Wood Yard of H.M. Household			
Daniel de St. Leu	Watchmaker	Watchmaker to Her Majesty; £1,000 Loan Sub. (1781)			
Jeremiah Devall	Plumber	Navy Contract (Plumber's Work at Admiralty in 1777)			
Wm. Devaynes	Mercht, Banker; East Ind. Co. Dir.	Treasury Contract (Provisions); £47,000, £500 Loan Subs. (1780, 1781)			MP: Barnstaple
Richard Dixon?	Cooper	£500 Loan Sub. (1781): [Richard and Robert Dixon]		W-T	CC: Walbrook
Robert Dixon	Wine Mercht	See above		H-S	
John Dolignon	Wine Mercht	Purveyor of Wine to H.M. Household			
John Dorrien	Mercht	£100,000, £100,000 Loan Subs. (1780, 1781)			
Alexander Douglas		£2,000 Loan Sub. (1781)			
Drew Drury?		Cutler to H.M. Household			
William Duncan	Agent	£10,000 Loan Sub. (1781)			
John Durand	Mercht	Pewterer to H.M. Household; Navy Contract (Shipping); Treasury Contract (Provisions); £10,000, £10,000 Loan Subs. (1780, 1781)	A		

Name	Occupation, directorship	Place, pension, contracts, loan subs.	Signatory of 1769 loyal address (indicated by "A")	Vote in 1772 mayoral election[2]	Elected position when address signed[3]
John Duval	Mercht & Jeweller	£8,000, £50,000 Loan Subs, (1780, 1781): [John Duval and Son]			
John Duval, Jr	Mercht & Jeweller	See above	A		
Sir James Esdaile	Military Outfitter, Banker	Ordnance Contract (Military Equipment); £10,000, £10,000 Loan Subs. (1780, 1781)		H-S	A: Cripplegate
James Esdaile, Jr.	Military Outfitter	Ordnance Contract (Military Equipment)			
Peter Esdaile	Military Outfitter	Ordnance Contract (Military Equipment)		H-S	
George Evans	Hop Factor	£1,000 Loan Sub. (1781)		W-T	
Tho. Ewer	Turkey Mercht	£20,000, £12,000 Loan Subs. (1780, 1781)	A		
Charles Eyre	Printer	Printer to H.M.			
Thomas Fenn	Factor & Warehouseman	£8,500, £5,000 Loan Subs. (1780, 1781)	A		
George Field		Army Extraordinary Contract (Blankets); £10,000, £5,000 Loan Subs. (1780, 1781)			
Henry Fletcher	East Ind. Co. Dir.	Navy Contract (Slops); Victualling Contract (Pincheons, Barrels, Hogheads	A	H-S	MP: Cumberland
Tho. Fletcher	Packer	£9,000 Loan Sub. (1780)	A		
Z.P. Fonnereau	Hamburgh Mercht	Army Extraordinary Contract (Victualling Gibraltar)			

Name	Occupation, directorship	Place, pension, contracts, loan subs.	Signatory of 1769 loyal address (indicated by "A")	Vote in 1772 mayoral election[2]	Elected position when address signed[3]
Thomas Fordham		Purveyor of fish to H.M. Household		H-S	
Charles Foreman	Hop Mercht	Victualling Contract (Hops)		H-S	
Simon Fraser	Mercht	Navy Contract (Shipping); £100,000, £10,000 Loan Subs. (1780, 1781)			
James Bogle French	"West Indian"	Treasury Contract (Rum, Provisions); £8,000 Loan Sub. (1780, 1781)	A	H-S	PDD
J.V. Gandolfi	Italian Mercht	£1,000 Loan Sub. (1781)			
John Garsed	Ribbon Weaver	£2,000 Loan Sub. (1781)	A		
R. Gathorne	Mercht	Victualling Contract (Wine)			
Peter Gaussen	Italian Mercht; Bank of Eng. Dir.	£100,000 Loan Sub. (1780)			
Thomas Gaysers	Mason	Victualling Contract (Mason's Work at Victualling Office in 1776)		H-S	
Richard Gimbert		Cork Cutter to H.M. Household			
And. Giradot	South Sea Co. Dir.	£25,000, £10,000 Loan Subs. (1780, 1781)	A		
John Goodchild		Linen Draper to H.M. Household			
Thomas Gorman	Mercht	Navy Contract (Russia Bar Iron)			
Francis Gosling	Mercht	£30,000, £60,000 Loan Subs. (1780, 1781): [Francis and Robert Gosling]			
Robert Gosling	Goldsmith, Jeweller, Hardwareman	See above		H-S	

Name	Occupation, directorship	Place, pension, contracts, loan subs.	Signatory of 1769 loyal address (indicated by "A")	Vote in 1772 mayoral election[2]	Elected position when address signed[3]
Robert Grant?	North Am. Mercht	Treasury Contractor's Agent; Victualling Contract (Provisions); £6,000 Loan Sub. (1781)	A		
John Gray?	Packer	£5,000 Loan Sub. (1780)			
Tho. Greenough		£1,000 Loan Sub. (1781)		H-S	
John Grier	Hamburgh Mercht	£5,000 Loan Sub. (1780)	A		
John Hainsworth	Handkerchief Weaver	£2,000 Loan Sub. (1780)			
A.F. Haldimand	Mercht	£50,000, £5,000 Loan Subs. (1780, 1781)			
Henry Hall		£2,000 Loan Sub. (1781)			
Philip Hall	Grocer	£30,000 Loan Sub. (1781)	A		
Charles Hamerton	Pavior	Navy Contract (Pavior's Work); Ordnance Contract (Pavior's Work)		H-S	
Thomas Hanbey?		£60,000 Loan Sub. (1781)		H-S	
Thomas Hardy?		Purveyor of the Works and Building, H.M. Board of Works			
Thomas Harley	Mercht, Banker	Treasury Contract (Specie, Clothing, Blankets): £100,000 Loan Sub. (1781): [Harley, Raymond and Co.)		H-S	A: Portsoken
James Harris		£2,000 Loan Sub. (1781)		H-S	
John Harrison?	Chairman, East Ind. Co.	£8,000 Loan Sub. (1781)	A		
David Harvey	Mercht	£1,000 Loan Sub. (1781)	A		
George Harvey	Mercht	£1,000 Loan Sub. (1781)			

Name	Occupation, directorship	Place, pension, contracts, loan subs.	Signatory of 1769 loyal address (indicated by "A")	Vote in 1772 mayoral election[2]	Elected position when address signed[3]
Thomas Hawes	Coal Mercht	Navy Contract (Coal)		H-S	
John Hayward	Ironmonger	£4,000, £500 Loan Subs. (1780, 1781)		H-S	
Thomas Heming	Goldsmith	Goldsmith to H.M. Jewel Office			
John Henniker	America & Baltic Mercht; London Assur. Dir.	Treasury Contract (Provisions); Navy Contract (Ships, Norway Goods, Riga Masts); £60,000, £10,000 Loan Subs. (1780, 1781)	A		MP: Dover
Benjamin Higgs	Mercht	Victualling Contract (London Bisket Bags, Canvas)		H-S	
Edmund Hill	Gunpowder Mercht	Ordnance Contract (Gunpowder); £4,000 Loan Sub. (1780)			
Peter Hodgson	Mercht	Navy Contract (Oil, Tallow, Tar, Shipping)	A		
Josiah Holford	Mercht	£5,000 Loan Sub. (1781)	A		
Henry Holland	Bricklayer	Bricklayer at the Tower, Mews, and Kensington; Navy Contract (Bricklaying at Admiralty)			
Henry Holland, Jr		£10,000, £6,000 Loan Subs. (1780, 1781)			
Richard Holland	Bricklayer	Navy Contract (Bricklaying at Admiralty)			
John Huddy	Ropemaker	Ordnance Contract (Rope)			
Isaac Hughes	Turkey Mercht	Agent to owners of prize cargoes sold to navy: [John and Isaac Hughes]	A		

Name	Occupation, directorship	Place, pension, contracts, loan subs.	Signatory of 1769 loyal address (indicated by "A")	Vote in 1772 mayoral election[2]	Elected position when address signed[3]
John Hughes	Turkey Mercht	See above	A	H-S	
John Hume		Treasury Subcontract (Shoes)		H-S	
Walter Humfrys	Mercht	Army Extraordinary Contract (Blankets)			
William Innes	Mercht	£30,000 Loan Sub. (1780)	A		
Charles James	Mercht	Navy Contract (Slop Cloth)			
Mich. James	Mercht	Navy Contract (Shipping)			
Thomas James		£1,000 Loan Sub. (1781)		H-S	
Wm. James	East Ind. Co. Dir.	Treasury Contract (Provisions); £150,000, £100,000 Loan Subs. (1780, 1781)	A		MP: West Looe
James Johnson?	Mercht	Ordnance Contract (Sandbags); £3,000, £2,000 Loan Subs. (1780, 1781)			
Tho. Johnson		Treasury Subcontract (Tinplate)			
James Jones	Iron-founder	Ordnance Contract (Shot and Shell); £5,000 Loan Sub. (1781)			
Sam Justice	Mercht	Navy Contract (Hemp)			
G. Farqu. Kinloch	Mercht	£5,000 Loan Sub. (1781): [Kinloch and Hogg]	A		
Robert Knox	Mercht	£30,000, £10,000 Loan Subs. (1780, 1781)			
Marmaduke Langdale		£1,000 Loan Sub. (1781)			
William Langley?		Treasury Subcontract (Shirts)			

Name	Occupation, directorship	Place, pension, contracts, loan subs.	Signatory of 1769 loyal address (indicated by "A")	Vote in 1772 mayoral election[2]	Elected position when address signed[3]
J.H. Langston	Portugal Mercht; Dep. Gov., Bank of Eng.; Sun Fire Office Dir.	£2,000 Loan Sub. (1781)			
Ab. Lara	Broker	£4,000 Loan Sub. (1781)			
Edw. Layton	Backmaker	Victualling Contract (Backmaker's Work)			H-S
J. Rob Le Cointe	Mercht & Jeweller	£10,000, £40,000 Loan Subs. (1780, 1781)	A		
Noah Le Cras	Mercht	Navy Contract (Shipping)			
J. Le Messurier		Navy Contract (Shipping)			
Geo. Lempriere	Mercht	£5,000, £1,000 Loan Subs. (1780, 1781)			
John Lind		Pension from Secret Service Fund			H-S
Andrew Lindegren	Swedish Mercht	Navy Contract (Iron, Archangel Tar): [And. and Cha. Lindegren]; £2,000 Loan Sub. (1781): [Lindegren and Co.]; Agents to owners of prize cargoes sold to navy: [And. and Cha. Lindegren]	A		
Cha. Lindegren	Swedish Mercht; Royal Exchange Assur. Dir.	See above	A		
Edward Lloyd		The Mews Keeper, under the Master of the Horse			
Colin Mackenzie	Insurance Broker	£8,000, £10,000 Loan Subs. (1780, 1781)			
John Maddison		£5,000, £10,000 Loan Subs. (1780, 1781)			

Name	Occupation, directorship	Place, pension, contracts, loan subs.	Signatory of 1769 loyal address (indicated by "A")	Vote in 1772 mayoral election[2]	Elected position when address signed[3]
Tim. Mangles	Mercht; London Assur. Dir.	Navy Contract (Shipping)	A		
Joseph Manwaring		One of King's Honourable Band of Gentleman Pensioners			
William Maskall	Calendar	£5,000 Loan Sub. (1781)		H-S	CC: Cripplegate Within
John Mason?	Sun Fire Office Dir.	£500 Loan Sub. (1781)			
Arnold Mello	Mercht; London Assur. Dir.	Navy Contract (Timber)	A		
Henry Meriton	Pitch & Tar Mercht	Victualling Contract (Pitch, Iron Hoops)			
John Merry	Stationer	£8,000 Loan Sub. (1781)		W-T	CC: Bishopsgate
John Michie	East Ind. Co. Dir.	£8,000 Loan Sub. (1781)			
William Mills	Brandy Mercht; Banker	Treasury Contract (Provisions)		H-S	
Nath. Modigliani	Mercht	£70,000, £8,000 Loan Subs. (1780, 1781)	A		
Andrew Moffatt	Insurance Broker	Navy Contract (Shipping); £10,000 Loan Sub. (1780)			
John Mount	Stationer	Navy Contract (Stationery)	A		
R.R. Mure	"West Indian"	Navy Contract (Rum, Provisions); Loan Sub.: see entry for Richard Atkinson			
James Oliphant	Hatmaker	Treasury Subcontract (Hats)			PDD
Mark Ord	Broker	Navy Contract (Shipping)			
Alexander Ougston	Mercht	£3,000 Loan Sub. (1780)			
Tho. Page	Stationer	Navy Contract (Stationery)	A	H-S	

Name	Occupation, directorship	Place, pension, contracts, loan subs.	Signatory of 1769 loyal address (indicated by "A")	Vote in 1772 mayoral election[2]	Elected position when address signed[3]
John Painter?		Assistant Scowerer in Kitchen of H.M. Household		H-S	
J. Pardoe	Mercht	£5,000 Loan Sub. (1780)	A		
Samuel Peach	Mercht	£10,000 Loan Sub. (1781)			MP: Crickdale
George Peters	Mercht; Bank of Eng. Dir.	Navy Contract (Petersburgh Hemp)			
Thomas Phillips	Pavior	Pavior to H.M. Household; £4,000 Loan Sub. (1780)			
Abr. Pitches	Brandy Mercht	Navy Contract (Rum)		H-S	
Samuel Plumbe		£5,000 Loan Sub. (1781)		H-S	A: Castlebaynard
Will Power	Broker	£5,000 Loan Sub. (1780)		W-T	
Thomas Prickett		Ordnance Contract (Shot and Shell)			
David Pugh	Grocer	£2,000 Loan Sub. (1781)	A	H-S	
Evan Pugh	Oil Mercht & Soap-maker	£5,000 Loan Sub. (1781)		H-S	CC: Bishopsgate
Thomas Raikes	Mercht	Navy Contract (Petersburgh Hemp); £15,000, £5,000 Loan Subs. (1780, 1781): [W and T. Raikes]	A		
William Raikes	Mercht; Royal Exchange Assur. Dir.	Navy Contract (Petersburgh Hemp); Loan Sub., see above	A		
John Rea	Mercht	Army Extraordinary Contract (Rice)			
John Read		Navy Contract (Limes); £2,000 Loan Sub. (1780)			
John T. Reade		£60,000 Loan Sub. (1781)			
Daniel Richards	Stationer	£5,000 Loan Sub. (1781)		H-S	

Name	Occupation, directorship	Place, pension, contracts, loan subs.	Signatory of 1769 loyal address (indicated by "A")	Vote in 1772 mayoral election[2]	Elected position when address signed[3]
J.L. Richter	Mercht	Victualling Contract (Staves)			
John Rigg	Mercht	£5,000 Loan Sub. (1781): [J. Rigg and Son]	A		
John Rigg, Jr.	Mercht	See above	A		
Isaac Rimington	Haberdasher	£8,000 Loan Sub. (1780)			
John Roberts?	Mercht; Dep. Chairman, East Ind. Co.	Treasury Contract (Provisions); £18,000 Loan Sub. (1780)	A	H-S	
Richard Robinson		£2,000, £500 Loan Subs. (1780, 1781)		H-S	
Ciprien Rondeau	Mercht	Treasury Subcontract (commodity unknown)			
Gilbert Ross	Agent	£3,000 Loan Sub. (1781)			
Wm. Ross	Mercht	£3,000, £2,000 Loan Subs. (1780, 1781)			
John Anth. Rucker	Mercht	Victualling Board (Beef); £10,000 Loan Sub. (1781)	A		
J.P. Rucker	Mercht	Victualling Board (Beef)			
Henry Russell		Navy Contract (Painter's Work and Materials for Repair of Admiralty Office)		H-S	
Thomas Sabe	Tin-plate-worker	Navy Contract (Tin and Turnery Wares); Ordnance Contract (Candlesticks)		H-S	
Sam. Sanders	Timber Mercht	Navy Contract (Norway Goods)		W-T	
Arthur Scaise	Brazier & Coppersmith	Navy Contract (Cast Iron Ballast); Ordnance Contract (Shot and Shell)			

Name	Occupation, directorship	Place, pension, contracts, loan subs.	Signatory of 1769 loyal address (indicated by "A")	Vote in 1772 mayoral election[2]	Elected position when address signed[3]
Edward Seward	Scarlet Dyer	£6,000, £5,000 Loan Subs. (1780, 1781)		H-S	
Alex. Shairp	Russia Mercht	Navy Contract (Petersburgh Hemp)			
Walter Shairp	Russia Mercht	Navy Contract (Petersburgh Hemp)	A		
Wm. Sheldon	Mercht	£2,000 Loan Sub. (1781)	A		
John Shoolbred	Mercht	Navy Contract (Transporting Navy Stores)	A		
Caleb Smith		£5,000 Loan Sub. (1781)			
John Smith, Esq.?	East Ind. Co. Dir.	£500 Loan Sub. (1781)			
John Spiller	Dyer	£10,000 Loan Sub. (1781)	A	H-S	
John Stables	Mercht	£2,000 Loan Sub. (1781)			
George Stainforth	Wine Mercht	Purveyor of Wine to H.M. Household; £10,000 Loan Sub. (1781)	A		
Peter Stapel	Mercht	£10,000 Loan Sub. (1780)			
John Staples	Mercht & Insurer; East Ind. Co. Dir.	Navy Contract (Pit sand); £3,000 £1,000 Loan Subs. (1780, 1781)			
John Stephenson	Mercht	Treasury Contract (Provisions); £20,000, £10,000 Loan Subs. (1780, 1781)	A		MP: Mitchell
Row Stephenson	Banker	£20,000 Loan Sub. (1781)			
Robert Stevenson	Scotch Mercht	£15,000, £10,000 Loan Subs. (1780, 1781)			
John Stock	Timber Mercht	Navy Contract (Painter's Work); £2,000, £2,000 Loan Subs. (1780, 1781)	A	H-S	

Name	Occupation, directorship	Place, pension, contracts, loan subs.	Signatory of 1769 loyal address (indicated by "A")	Vote in 1772 mayoral election[2]	Elected position when address signed[3]
Jonathan Stonard	Corn Factor	£1,000 Loan Sub. (1781)		H–S	PDD
Will. Strahan	Printer	Printer to H.M.; Navy Contract (Printer's Work); £10,000, £10,000, Loan Subs. (1780, 1781)	A	H–S	MP: Malmesbury
Peter Thelluson	Mercht	Agent to owners of prize cargo sold to navy; £350,000, £250,000 Loan Subs. (1780, 1781)	A		
James Thomas	Wine mercht	£2,000 Loan Sub. (1781)			
Harry Thompson	Mercht	£25,000, £30,000 Loan Subs. (1780, 1781)			
Isaac Thompson	Mercht	£4,000, £500 Loan Subs. (1780, 1781)			
And. Thomson		Navy Contract (Hemp); £20,000 Loan Sub. (1781)	A		
Godf. Thornton	Russia Mercht; Bank of Eng. Dir.	Navy Contract (Petersburgh Hemp); Loan Sub.: see entry for John Cornwall	A		
Robert Thornton	Russia Mercht	Victualling Contract (Malt, Hops)	A		
Richard Till		£5,000 Loan Sub. (1780)			
Kirkes Townley		One of King's Honourable Band of Gentleman Pensioners		H–S	
John Trotter	Upholder	Treasury Contract (Hospital Bedding); Army Extraordinary Contract (Hospital Bedding); £10,000 Loan Sub. (1781)	A	H–S	

Name	Occupation, directorship	Place, pension, contracts, loan subs.	Signatory of 1769 loyal address (indicated by "A")	Vote in 1772 mayoral election[2]	Elected position when address signed[3]
James Upchurch	Blacksmith	Navy Contract (Smith's Work); Victualling Contract (Iron Hoops)		H-S	
Charles Vere	Chinaman	Navy Contract (Slops)			
Isaac Walker		£20,000, £4,000 Loan Subs. (1780, 1781)		H-S	
Thomas Walker	Brazier & Ironmonger	Ordnance Contract (Iron Ordnance)		H-S	
James Walton	Powdermaker	Ordnance Contract (Powder)		H-S	CC: Cornhill
Wm. Ward?		Navy Contract (Shipping)			
John Warren	Sugar Broker	Victualling Contract (Casks); £1,000 Loan Sub. (1781)	A	H-S	
Joseph Watkins	Mercht	£8,000 Loan Sub. (1781)	A		
Joseph Waugh	Drysalter & Mercht	£25,000 Loan Sub. (1781)	A	H-S	
David Webster	Druggist	£10,000, £3,000 Loan Subs. (1780, 1781): [David and James Webster]	A	H-S	
George Webster	Drug Mercht	£1,000 Loan Sub. (1781)	A	H-S	
James Webster	Druggist	Loan Sub.: see entry for David Webster		H-S	
William Webster		£2,000, £500 Loan Subs. (1780, 1781)			
Tho. Wellings	Druggist & Chemist	£10,000 Loan Sub. (1781)		H-S	PDD
William Weston?	Tea Dealer & Hop Mercht	£1,000 Loan Sub. (1781)		H-S	
Mark Weyland	Mercht; Bank of Eng. Dir.	£10,000 Loan Sub. (1781)	A		
Matthew Wiggins	Cooper	Victualling Board (Tight Butts, Iron Hoops)		W	

Name	Occupation, directorship	Place, pension, contracts, loan subs.	Signatory of 1769 loyal address (indicated by "A")	Vote in 1772 mayoral election[2]	Elected position when address signed[3]
John Wilkinson	Broker	Navy Contract (Shipping)	A		
Charles Wilsonn	Laceman	£5,000, £5,000 Loan Subs. (1780, 1781)			
Rob. Wilsonn	Stationer	£10,000, £1,000 Loan Subs. (1780, 1781)	A		
Benj. Winthrop	Mercht	£10,000 Loan Sub. (1780)			
George Wombwell	Mercht; East Ind. Co. Dir.	Treasury Contract (Provisions)			MP: Huntingdon
James Worsdale		Ordnance Contract (Painter's Work)			
Wm. Worsfold	Packer	Packaging (Treasury)		H-S	
Thomas Wright	Printer	£10,000, £5,000 Loan Subs. (1780, 1781)		H-S	CC: Candlewick
John Yates	Stationer & Playing Card-maker	£1,000 Loan Sub. (1781)			
Tim Yeats	Hop Mercht	£15,000, £8,000 Loan Subs. (1780, 1781)			

APPENDIX D
The Court of Common Council, 1775–1779 (incl.)

Name & Ward (date of joining or leaving ward in relevant period)	Occupation	Company	Vote in 1772 mayoral election[1]	Petition signed in Oct. 1775[2]	7 July 1775 vote on address against war[3]	21 July 1775 vote on reply to New York Assoc.[4]	29 June 1779 vote on address and support for war
ALDERMEN							
Aldersgate							
Sir Thomas Hallifax		Goldsmiths	H-S				
Aldgate							
John Shakespear (–May 1775)	Embroiderers						
William Lee (May 1775–)	Mercht	Haberdashers		A	A		
Bassishaw							
William Plomer	Oilman	Bricklayers & Tylers	W-T	A	A		A
Billingsgate							
Richard Oliver (–Nov. 1778)	"West Indian"	Drapers					
Thomas Sainsbury (Nov. 1778–)	Tobacconist & Snuff-maker	Bowyers	W-T				A
Bishopsgate							
James Townsend		Mercers					A
Bread Street							
Brass Crosby		Musicians	W-T[5]	A			A
Bridge							
John Hart (–May 1776)	Dry salter	Skinners		G/GL	G	G	
Thomas Wooldridge (May 1776–)	Mercht	Musicians		A			G
Bridge Without							
Robert Alsop		Ironmongers	H-S	G/GL			
Broad Street							
Benjamin Hopkins (–March 1776)	Mercht	Drapers			G	G	
Richard Clark (March 1776–)	Mercht	Joiners	H-S				G
Candlewick							
Sir Charles Asgill (–July 1777)		Skinners					

Name & Ward (date of joining or leaving ward in relevant period)	Occupation	Company	Vote in 1772 mayoral election[1]	Petition signed in Oct. 1775[2]	7 July 1775 vote on address against war[3]	21 July 1775 vote on reply to New York Assoc.[4]	29 June 1779 vote on address and support for war
Thomas Wright (July 1777-) *Castlebaynard*	Printer	Stationers	H-S	GL			
Samuel Plumbe *Cheap*		Goldsmiths	H-S	GL	G		
John Kirkman *Coleman Street*		Fishmongers			A		A
Robert Peckham *Cordwainer*	Mercht	Wheelwrights					
George Hayley *Cornhill*	Mercht	Armourers & Braziers	W-T	A			A
Brackley Kennett *Cripplegate*	Wine Mercht	Vintners	H-S	G/GL	G		G
Sir James Esdaile *Dowgate*	Arms Manufacturer & Banker	Coopers	H-S	G/GL	G	G	G
Walter Rawlinson (-May 1777)		Grocers				G	
John Hart[6] (May 1777-) *Farringdon Within*	Dry salter	Skinners		G/GL			
William Bridgen (-Oct. 1779)	Mercht	Cutlers					
Henry Kitchin (Oct. 1779-) *Farringdon Without*	Leather Cutter	Curriers	H-S	G/GL			
John Wilkes *Langbourn*		Joiners		A			A
John Sawbridge *Lime Street*		Frame-work-knitters	W-T	A			A
Sir Watkin Lewes *Portsoken*		Joiners			A		A
Thomas Harley *Queenhithe*	Mercht	Goldsmiths	H-S	G/GL	G	G	G
Frederick Bull *Tower*	Tea-dealer	Salters	W-T		A		A
Samuel Turner (-Oct. 1775)	Mercht	Clothworkers	H-S				

Name & Ward (date of joining or leaving ward in relevant period)	Occupation	Company	Vote in 1772 mayoral election[1]	Petition signed in Oct. 1775[2]	7 July 1775 vote on address against war[3]	21 July 1775 vote on reply to New York Assoc.[4]	29 June 1779 vote on address and support for war
Hugh Smith (Oct. 1775–Sept. 1777)	Physician	Salters					
Evan Pugh (Sept. 1777–)	Oil Mercht & Soap-maker	Skinners	H–S	G/GL			G
Vintry							
Nathaniel Newnham	Grocer	Mercers		A	A		A
Walbrook							
Nathaniel Thomas	Mercht	Wax Chandlers	H–S	G/GL		G	G

COMMON COUNCILMEN[7]

Aldersgate

Name & Ward	Occupation	Company					
Charles Aldridge[8]		Goldsmiths		A	A		A
John Bailey (1777–)		Joiners					A
James Brogden	Watchmaker	Goldsmiths					A
Robert Fisher (–1777)	Attorney	Goldsmiths					
Wm. Fouch (–1777)		Joiners	H–S	GL		G	
Thomas Isherwood (1777–)	Distiller	Stationers		GL			G
Benj. Maud		Goldsmiths		A	A		A
John Mott (1776–)		Innholders					A
Philip Oriel	Stationer	Mercht Taylors	H–S				
Jeremiah Percy		Plumbers	H–W	A	A		A
John Robins (–1775)	Cheesemonger	Goldsmiths	H–S	GL			
Nat. Wright		Carpenters	W–T		A		
Edward Yates (1775–6)	Stationer & Playing-card maker	Cardmakers					
Aldgate							
John Bellett	Upholder's Warehouseman	Upholders	W–T	A			

Name & Ward (date of joining or leaving ward in relevant period)	Occupation	Company	Vote in 1772 mayoral election[1]	Petition signed in Oct. 1775[2]	7 July 1775 vote on address against war[3]	21 July 1775 vote on reply to New York Assoc.[4]	29 June 1779 vote on address and support for war
John Davis (-1778)		Mercht Taylors	W–T	A	A		
Gab. Heath (1778-)		Bricklayers & Tylers					A
Tho. Holdsworth		Vintners	H–S		A		A
Cha. Lincoln	Optician	Fletchers			A		A
Jos. Partridge	Packer	Clothworkers					
S. Thorpe	Wholesale Haberdasher	Tin-plate-workers		A			
Bassishaw							
John Firth		Glovers	W–T				
Sam Knight		Clothworkers	W–T				A
Gab. Leekey	Watchmaker	Skinnres	H–S	G/GL	G	G	G
Tho. Swanson	Pewterer	Pewterers		A			
Billingsgate							
R. Barneveit	Cheesemonger	Mercht Taylors					
Wm. Deane	Stationer	Mercht Taylors	W–T				A
Thomas Dunnage	Mercht	Cutlers	W–T		A		A
Josiah Dornford (1775-)	Mercht	Clothworkers		A			A
Charles Easton	Stone Mercht	Masons	W–T			G	
Tho. Gorst	Cooper	Coopers	W–T	A	A		A
Samuel Hanson	Orange Mercht	Joiners	W–T	A			A
John Kittermaster	Mercht	Fishmongers	H–S		G?		
William Oliver (-1775)		Coopers	W–T				
Tho. Wm. Preston	North Am. Mercht	Wheelers		A			A
Robert Ross (-1776)		Salters	H–S	A			
Stephen Tyers	Broker	Coopers	W–T	A	A		A
Bishopsgate							
Wm. Bamford, Sr (-1776)	Shoe-warehouse	Cordwainers	H–S		G?		
Richard Blackall	Apothecary	Musicians	W–T		G?	G	G
Tho. Brown (-1775)		Mercht Taylors	H–S				
R. Bullcock	Haberdasher	Tin-plate-workers	W–T	A	A		A

Name & Ward (date of joining or leaving ward in relevant period)	Occupation	Company	Vote in 1772 mayoral election[1]	Petition signed in Oct. 1775[2]	7 July 1775 vote on address against war[3]	21 July 1775 vote on reply to New York Assoc.[4]	29 June 1779 vote on address and support for war
William Cooke (1775-)	Tyre-smith	Blacksmiths	H-T	G/GL			
Richard Draper (1776-)	Grocer	Glovers		GL			G
Michael Eaton (1775-)		Mercht Taylors					
John Fasson	Pewterer	Pewterers	W-T		G?	G	
Edw. George (-1777)	Thread-maker	Mercht Taylors	W-T		A		
Henry George	Threadman & Haberdasher	Weavers	W-T	A	A		A
Wm. Judd	Hop Mercht	Joiners		G/GL	G	G	G
John Merry	Stationer	Drapers	W-T	G/GL	G	G	A
John Miles (-1775)	Coach-maker	Wheelwrights		GL			
Samuel Nelme (1776-)		Vintners	H-S	GL			G
George Paillet (-1775)		Upholders	W-T				
John Pinhorn (1776-)	Teaman	Wax Chandlers					A
Sam. Provey	Weaver	Clothworkers	W-T				A
Evan Pugh[9] (-1776)	Oil Mercht & Soap-maker	Skinners	H-S	G/GL	G	G	
John Ward (1777-)		Clothmakers	H-S	G/GL			G
Edward Wix		Bricklayers & Tylers	T-S	G/GL	G		G
Bread Street							
Ja. Archer (-1776)	Meal-factor	Frame-work-knitters	W-T				
Wm. Bedford (1777-)	Linen Draper	Drapers					A
Peter Ja. Bennett (1777-)	Silk, Gauze & Ribbon Weaver	Goldsmiths					
Benj. Burnley (-1776)	Beer Mercht	Innholders	W-T	A	A		
James Chapman (1776-)	Whalebone Mercht	Innholders		G/GL			G
John Ewer (1776-)	Linen Draper	Skinners	H-S				G

Name & Ward (date of joining or leaving ward in relevant period)	Occupation	Company	Vote in 1772 mayoral election[1]	Petition signed in Oct. 1775[2]	7 July 1775 vote on address against war[3]	21 July 1775 vote on reply to New York Assoc.[4]	29 June 1779 vote on address and support for war
W. Hallier	Tin-plate-worker	Tin-plate-workers	H-S	G/GL	G	G	G
John Hemans	Handkerchief & Buckram Warehouseman	Glovers			A		G
John Henlock (-1776)	Mercht	Glovers	W-T	A			
John James (1778-)	Weaver	Dyers					
John Moorey	North Am. Mercht	Salters	H-S	A[10]			
Henry Parker (1777-)		Armourers & Braziers					
Edw. Polhill (-1778)	Upholder	Upholders		A	A		
Wm. Saxby	Linen Draper	Painter-stainers	W-T	A			A
Luke Stavely (-1777)	Linen Draper	Frame-work-knitters		A	A		
Robert Turner (-1777)	Linen Draper	Bowyers		A[11]			
John Walker	Sugar Baker	Ironmongers					A
Robert Watkins (-1777)		Bricklayers & Tylers		A			
Thomas Wright (1776-) *Bridge*	Wine Mercht	Innholders					
William Anderson	North Am. Mercht?	Mercht Taylors	W-T	A			A
Sam. Baughan	Hatmaker	Dyers	W-T	A			A
Coles Child	Wholesale Toyman	Weavers	W-T				A
John Cobb (1777-)	Hatter	Barbers		A			A
George Cooper	Tobacconist & Teaman	Goldsmiths	H-S				A
C. Corderoy	Sadler's Ironmonger	Haberdashers	W-T				G
Edward Coster	Oil Cooper	Coopers	H-S	G	G		
Henry Crosley (1775-)	Warehouseman	Frame-work-knitters		A			A

Name & Ward (date of joining or leaving ward in relevant period)	Occupation	Company	Vote in 1772 mayoral election[1]	Petition signed in Oct. 1775[2]	7 July 1775 vote on address against war[3]	21 July 1775 vote on reply to New York Assoc.[4]	29 June 1779 vote on address and support for war
John Dowley (1776-)		Blacksmiths	W-T	A			A
Tho. Escutt (-1775)	Wine Mercht	Dyers		G/GL	G?	G	
Tho. Hartley (1775-6)	Wholesale Glover	Haberdashers		A			
Tho. Horne (-1777)	Stock-broker	Fishmongers	H-S	G/GL	G	G	
Edw. Jackson (-1775)	Man's Mercer	Spectacle-makers		A			
Joseph Jewson	Hardwareman	Turners	W-T	A			A
Tho. Norman (-1777)	Hatter	Wheelwrights					
Will. Post (-1776)	Goldsmith	Embroiderers	H-S	G/GL			
John Rowlatt (1776-)	Oilman	Glovers					G
Wm. Rowlatt	Oilman	Glovers	W-T		A		
M. Thompson	Coal Mercht	Fishmongers	W-T				
Jos. Wilson (1777-)	Hop Mercht	Frame-work-knitters		A			
Jacob Wrench	Seedsman	Drapers	W-T				A
Broad Street							
Wm. Acton		Painter-stainers	H-S	GL	G	G	
J. Ellis	Scrivener	Scriveners	H-S	GL	G	G	G
James Evans	Watchmaker	Skinners			G		G
Pet. Nich. Frisquett	Jeweller	Haberdashers	H-S	GL	G	G	G
John Gibson	Broker	Painter-stainers	H-S	G/GL	G	G	G
John Harris	Hatter & Tea-dealer?	Painter-stainers			G	G	
John Sealy	Grocer & Tea-dealer	Grocers	H-S		G	G	G
Geo. Sharpe (1778-)	Agent	Girdlers					A
Dav. Stuart		Spectacle Makers			G	G	G
Henry White (-1778)	Weaver?	Painter-stainers	H-S		G	G	
Theo. Williams (1776-)	Broker	Wheelwrights		A			

Name & Ward (date of joining or leaving ward in relevant period)	Occupation	Company	Vote in 1772 mayoral election[1]	Petition signed in Oct. 1775[2]	7 July 1775 vote on address against war[3]	21 July 1775 vote on reply to New York Assoc.[4]	29 June 1779 vote on address and support for war
Richard Windsor (-1776)	Undertaker	Mercers	H-S		G		
Candlewick							
William Bagster (1776-7)		Apothecaries					
Thomas Davies (1776-)		Feltmakers					
Wm. Gaskarth (-1775)	Warehouseman	Musicians	H-S	G	G?	G	
William Gill		Stationers	H-S		G	G	G
John Hotham (1778-)		Mercht Taylors					
Philip Milloway (-1777)	Mercht	Clothworkers	H-S	G	G	G	
Mathias Palling (1777-)	Oil & Colourman	Joiners	W-T				G
Matt. Perchard (-1775)	Mercht	Goldsmiths	H-S	G/GL	G?	G	
Peter Perchard (1777-)	Mercht & Goldsmiths	Goldsmiths	H-S	G/GL			G
Cha. Rashfield		Coopers	H-S		G	G	G
Robert Ward (1775-)	Watch & Clock Maker	Goldsmiths					A
Edw. Watson	Mercht	Founders	H-S	G/GL	G	G	G
Wm. Wightwick (1775-8)		Leathersellers	H-S				
Wm. Wilson (-1776)		Needlemakers					
Thomas Wright[12] (-1776)	Printer	Stationers	H-S	GL	G		
Castlebaynard							
Philip Bell (-1775)	Cabinet-maker & Upholder	Vintners	H-S	G/GL			
George Bellas, Esq. (-1775)	Attorney	Carpenters					
William Box (1775-)		Apothecaries					G
Rob. Harris	Druggist & Chemist	Tin-plate-workers	W-T		A		

Name & Ward (date of joining or leaving ward in relevant period)	Occupation	Company	Vote in 1772 mayoral election[1]	Petition signed in Oct. 1775[2]	7 July 1775 vote on address against war[3]	21 July 1775 vote on reply to New York Assoc.[4]	29 June 1779 vote on address and support for war
T. Harrison		Stationers	H-S	G/GL			G
John Hopkins	Hosier	Grocers	H-S	G/GL	G		G
William Howard (1775-)		Vintners		GL			
Wm. Hurford	Coal Mercht & Wharfinger	Barbers	W-T	A	A		
Hen. Major, Esq.		Haberdashers	H-S	GL	G	G	G
R. Manning		Drapers	W-T		A		A
John Pittway (-1775)		Fishmongers	H-S	G/GL	G?		
Tipping Rigby (1775-)		Drapers		G/GL			G
Mid. Young	Attorney	Tin-plate-workers			A	G	
Cheap							
John Allen (1775-)		Goldsmiths					
Tho. Boddington (-1778)	Linen Draper	Clothworkers	W-T	A	A		
John Boydell	Print-seller	Stationers	H-S	A			G
Rich. Bristow	Attorney	Goldsmiths	W-T				A
Wm. Cawne (-1775)		Clothworkers					
William Cooper (-1778)	Silkman	Weavers				G	
N. Foster	Hardwareman	Mercht Taylors					A
Robert Holden	Man's Mercer	Mercer		A	A		A
James Hunt	Gold-worker	Goldsmiths	H-S	A	A		
Rob. Macky, Esq. (1778-)	Mercht	Joiners		A			
John Marlar		Haberdashers	H-S		G		
Tho. Nalder (-1775)	Wholesale Glovers	Leathersellers	W-T				
Hen. Nettleship (1777-8)	Hardwareman	Grocers					
John Salt (-1775)	Paper-hanging Manufacturer	Grocers					
John Smith		Ironmongers	H-S	G/GL?			G
James Stamp (1775-)	Goldsmith & Jeweller	Goldsmiths					A

Name & Ward (date of joining or leaving ward in relevant period)	Occupation	Company	Vote in 1772 mayoral election[1]	Petition signed in Oct. 1775[2]	7 July 1775 vote on address against war[3]	21 July 1775 vote on reply to New York Assoc.[4]	29 June 1779 vote on address and support for war
Robert Taggart (1775-7)		Clothworkers					
Tho. Vezey (1778-)		Glovers					A
Jn. Withers (1778-)	Linen Draper	Bricklayers & Tylers		A[13]			A
Coleman Street							
Henry Cothery		Innholders		GL			
John Jacob (1775-)	Druggist & Chemist	Carpenters					
Wm. Lewis	Mercht	Carpenters			G?		
Tho. Russel		Carpenters	H-S	GL	A?		G
John Sassory	Jeweller	Haberdashers	H-S	G/GL	A	G	
Thomas Smith (-1775)		Distillers		GL	G		
Robert Winbolt		Goldsmiths	H-T		A		
Cordwainer							
Edward Aldridge	Wine Mercht	Goldsmiths	W-T	A			A
John Barnes (1778-)	Grocer	Goldsmiths					
Edward Beynon (1778-)		Glovers					A
Tho. Bord (-1776)		Tallow Chandler		A	A		
Rob. Hanning Brooks (1776-7)	Tea-dealer	Curriers	W-T	A			
John Chapman (1775-)	Grocer	Glovers	W-T				A
Sam. Hanning		Carpenters	W-T	A			A
John Peart		Upholders	W-T		A		
William Poole (-1776)	Haberdashers	Weavers	W-T	GL	G		
Sainsbury Sibley (-1775)	Haberdasher & Glover	Joiners	W-T	A	A		
William Stone (-1778)		Joiners		A	A	G	
Thomas Tilson (1777-)	Grocer	Glovers		A			A

Name & Ward (date of joining or leaving ward in relevant period)	Occupation	Company	Vote in 1772 mayoral election[1]	Petition signed in Oct. 1775[2]	7 July 1775 vote on address against war[3]	21 July 1775 vote on reply to New York Assoc.[4]	29 June 1779 vote on address and support for war
Stephen Yates (-1778)		Haberdashers	W-T		A		
Lake Young	Glass-cutter	Glaziers	W-T		A		A
Cornhill							
Wm. Bythesea	Woollen Draper	Salters			G		G
T. Cogan, Esq.	Haberdasher	Plaisterers	H-S	G/GL	G	G	G
Henry Parker		Stationers	H-S		G	G	G
Wm. Shenton	Stationer	Mercht Taylors	H-S		G?	G	G
J. Walton, Esq.	Powdermaker	Mercht Taylors	H-S	G/GL	G	G	G
Henry Wright	Ironmonger & Brazier	Drapers	H-S	G/GL	G	G	G
Cripplegate Within							
Cha. Birkhead (1776-8)		Haberdashers					
Edw. Dowling (1778-)	Norwich Manufacturers	Cutlers		A[14]			A
Henry Fawconer (1778-)	Linen Draper	Barbers	W-T	A			A
Wm. Gifford		Leathersellers					
John Hanforth (1775-7)	Innholder & Agent	Innholders	H-S	GL			
Benj. Holdsworth (1777-)		Dyers					A
John Horton (-1778)	Dyer	Dyers	W-T	A	A		
Wm. Maskall (-1778)	Calendar	Glovers	H-S	GL	G?	G	
Richard Mathew (1775-7/1778-)		Coopers	W-T	A			
Isaac Mather (1777-)		Plumbers	W-T	GL			
John Moore (-1775)	Stocking Trimmer	Glovers	H-S	G			
John Roake (-1775)	Ironmonger & Brazier	Ironmongers					
Cha. Turner (-1776)		Carpenters	W-T				
Stephen Unwin	Hardwareman	Grocers		A	A		
Henry White		Fishmongers			G	G	G
Cripplegate Without							
Henry Banner		Joiners	W-T	A	A		A

Name & Ward (date of joining or leaving ward in relevant period)	Occupation	Company	Vote in 1772 mayoral election[1]	Petition signed in Oct. 1775[2]	7 July 1775 vote on address against war[3]	21 July 1775 vote on reply to New York Assoc.[4]	29 June 1779 vote on address and support for war
J. Banner		Plumbers	W-T		A		A
Rob. French		Tallow Chandlers		A			A
John Jones	Wine & Brandy Mercht	Founders	H-S	G/GL	G	G	G
Dowgate							
Wm. Clemmons (1777-)		Barbers	H-S	GL			G
William Gates		Masons	W-T	GL			
Jn. Greenwood (-1775)	Wharfinger & Broker	Ironmongers					
Francis Hilton	Scarlet Dyer	Dyers		G/GL	G?A?	G	
R. Holder		Musicians					A
Henry Janson (-1777)	Bottle Warehouse	Fishmongers	W-T	A	A		
Jn. Packman		Tallow Chandlers	W-T				
John Salter (1775-)	Plumber	Plumbers	H-S	GL			G
George Smirthwaite	Mercht	Mercht Taylors		G			
Jos. Stevenson	Cooper	Coopers		A			A
Farringdon Within							
W. Carter		Mercht Taylors					
Thomas Caslon	Bookseller	Stationers	H-S				A
Thomas Chawner (1776-8)	Goldsmith	Tin-plate-workers					
Charles Clavey (-1777)	Linen Draper	Masons	W-T				
John Clements		Pewterers	H-S			G	G
John Cooke		Musicians		GL?			
Stan. Crowder	Bookseller	Stationers	H-S				
Gadaliah Gatfield	Hat Warehouse	Musicians	H-S				G
Sylvanus Hall		Curriers	H-S		A	G	A
Benj. Hamnett	North Am. Mercht	Basketmakers		A			A
Tho. Hyde	Goldsmith	Fishmongers	W-T				A
John Lokes (-1776)	Wax Chandler	Wax Chandlers	W-T				
John Macquiston	Floor-cloth Warehouse	Turners	H-S			G	
Cha. Maynard		Upholders	W-T	A			A
Edward Parish	Mercer	Wheelwrights		A	A		A

Name & Ward (date of joining or leaving ward in relevant period)	Occupation	Company	Vote in 1772 mayoral election [1]	Petition signed in Oct. 1775 [2]	7 July 1775 vote on address against war [3]	21 July 1775 vote on reply to New York Assoc. [4]	29 June 1779 vote on address and support for war
Thomas Patrick (1776-)	Tin-plate-worker	Goldsmiths		G/GL			
Daniel Pinder		Dyers			A		A
Wm. Powell (1778-)		Painter-stainers	H-S				G
Joseph Speck (1777-)	Wine Cooper	Coopers	W-T				
Edward Upton (-1776)	Broker	Glovers	W-T	A	A		
Tho. Vanhagen		Joiners	H-S		A		
Farringdon Without							
John Adams (-1778)	Hatter & Sword-cutler	Feltmakers	W-T		A		
Row. Atkinson	Hemp Mercht	Wheelwrights					A
Wm. Axford	Grocer	Musicians	W-T				
Richard Brewer	Callico-printer	Joiners		A	A		A
John Burnell (1776-7)		Carpenters	H-T				
Tho. Burnell (1778-)		Masons	H-S	GL			G
Lambeth Case (1775-6)		Joiners	H-S				
John Champion (1777-)	Grocer	Carpenters					A
John Crockett (-1778)		Mercht Taylors	T	GL			
Ezekiel Delight (1778-)		Vintners		GL			G
John Fox (-1775)	Mercht	Grocers	W-T	A			
Thomas Goodwin (1778-)	Gold-beater	Painter-stainers					
Tho. Harder (1778-)		Painter-stainers	H-S				A
Richard Hearne (-1777)		Upholders					
Ed. Howse (-1776)	Distiller	Tin-plate-workers	W-T	A			
Hugh James (1777-8)	Grocer	Cordwainers		A			

Name & Ward (date of joining or leaving ward in relevant period)	Occupation	Company	Vote in 1772 mayoral election[1]	Petition signed in Oct. 1775[2]	7 July 1775 vote on address against war[3]	21 July 1775 vote on reply to New York Assoc.[4]	29 June 1779 vote on address and support for war
John Lomax		Innholders	W-T	A	A		
John Mansfield		Joiners	W-T				
John Marsh (1777-)	Sugar-broker	Dyers	H-W				A
William Newman (1778-)		Curriers	H-S				
Richard Oakes	Case & Cabinet Maker	Leathersellers				G	A
Wm. Richardson (-1777)		Stationers	W-T	A			
Tho. Sainsbury[15] (-1778)	Tobacconist & Snuff-maker	Bowyers	W-T				
William Sharpe (1777-)		Weavers	H-S	G/GL			G
Ben Stephenson (-1777)		Goldsmiths			A		
William Stiles (1776-)		Cooks	W-T				
Tho. Thorpe		Vintners	W-T	A	A		
Wm. Wright	Wine Mercht	Innholders		A	A?		
Geo. Wyatt	Attorney?	Drapers		G/GL	G		G
Edw. Yorke (-1775)		Pewterers					
Langbourn							
George Bodley (1776-)		Fishmongers	H-S	A			
Thomas Burrow	Oil & Colourman	Vintners	W-T		A		A
Christopher Corral	Gold & Silver Laceman	Goldsmiths	H-S		G?	G	
Ingham Foster	Ironmonger	Ironmongers	H-S			G	A
Thomas Hudson (1778-)	Mercht	Carpenters	H-S	A			
William Lem (-1778)	Wine Mercht	Salters			A		
Geo. Maynard	Hosier	Vintners	H-S		G	G	G
John Newman	Goldsmith & Jeweller	Joiners		A			A
Matthias Palling (-1776)	Oil & Colourman	Joiners	W-T		G	G	

Name & Ward (date of joining or leaving ward in relevant period)	Occupation	Company	Vote in 1772 mayoral election[1]	Petition signed in Oct. 1775[2]	7 July 1775 vote on address against war[3]	21 July 1775 vote on reply to New York Assoc.[4]	29 June 1779 vote on address and support for war
Peter Pope	Hosier	Haberdashers	H–S		G	G	
Edward Tutet	Watch & Clock Maker	Clockmakers	W–T	A	A		A
T. Witherby *Lime Street*	Stationer	Coopers	H–S	G/GL	G	G	G
J.W. Benson		Apothecaries	W–T	A	A		A
Samuel Browne		Drapers	H–S			G	G
John Hardy	Hardwareman	Musicians					
James Sharp *Portsoken*	Ironmonger	Drapers	W–T	A	A		A
Abra. Brecknock (–1776)	Grocer	Innholders	H–S				
Ph. Grafton (–1775)	Oilman	Turners	H–S	G/GL	G	G	
Robert Harding	Exchange Broker & Auctioneer	Salters	H–S	G/GL	G	G	G
Ant. Facer Kemp (1775–)	Tobacconist & Brandy Mercht	Distillers	W–T	A			
Cha. Parnell (1776–)		Bricklayers & Tylers					
Wm. Wilson	Gun-maker	Gunmakers		G	G	G	G
Joseph Wise *Queenhithe*	Linen Draper	Drapers	W–T	A	A		A
John Ball	Hoop-bender	Coopers	W–T				
Wm. Beswick	Grocer	Paviors					
Richard Clarke		Musicians	W–T	A?			
Robert Exam (1777–)	Coppersmith	Leathersellers	T				G
Wm. Humfrys	Grocer	Coopers	H–S	G/GL	G	G	G
J. Piper (–1777)	Packer	Mercht Taylors		A	A		
Benjamin Shaw (1775–)	Mercht	Coopers	H–S				
Wm. Tarver (–1775) *Tower*	Malt Factor	Haberdashers	W–T				
James Ansell	Cooper	Coopers	W–T	A	G	G	G
Wm. Bagster (1778–)		Apothecaries					
Wm. Chivers (–1777)	Wine Mercht	Coopers					

Name & Ward (date of joining or leaving ward in relevant period)	Occupation	Company	Vote in 1772 mayoral election[1]	Petition signed in Oct. 1775[2]	7 July 1775 vote on address against war[3]	21 July 1775 vote on reply to New York Assoc.[4]	29 June 1779 vote on address and support for war
John Close	Broker	Wheelwrights					G
Humphry Jeffries (1778-)	Ironmonger	Fletchers					
Alex Kinnier (1777-8)	Mercht	Coopers					
Richard Neave (-1777)	North Am. Mercht	Drapers		A	A		
John Nodin (1777-8)		Wheelwrights					
J.L. Paulhan (-1776)	Sugar Baker	Ironmongers	H-S	A			
Gregory Pember (-1778)	Wine Mercht	Coopers	W-T		A		
S. Plummer	Woollen Draper	Clothworkers		A	A		
Anderton Poole (1778-)	Oil & Colourman	Coachmakers					G
Ben Robertson	Mercht	Glovers	W-T				
William Shone (1776-)	Wine, Beer & Cyder Mercht	Glass-sellers	W-T				G
Joseph Speck (1776-7)	Wine Cooper	Coopers	W-T				
Edw. Far. Taylor (-1777)	Brazier	Armourers & Braziers	W-T	A			
John Taylor (1777-)		Mercht Taylors	W-T				
John Townshend (-1777)	Maltster & Coal Mercht	Stationers	H-S	GL		G	
Cha. Wilkins	Oilman	Salters				G	G
John Woodcock (1777-)		Vintners	W-T				
William Worth (1777-)		Butchers					G
Vintry							
Robert Benson (-1775)	Wharfinger?	Needlemakers					
John Elmes		Bricklayers & Tylers					
Robert Evered		Glovers	W-T		A		
Thomas Furnell	Coal Mercht	Goldsmiths	W-T				A
James Haslam (1775-)		Fruiterers					

Name & Ward (date of joining or leaving ward in relevant period)	Occupation	Company	Vote in 1772 mayoral election[1]	Petition signed in Oct. 1775[2]	7 July 1775 vote on address against war[3]	21 July 1775 vote on reply to New York Assoc.[4]	29 June 1779 vote on address and support for war
Lau. Holker		Ironmongers					
G.M. Macaulay		Bowyers		A			A
Priest Shrubb (-1778)		Plumbers	W-T	A			
John Walford (1778-)	Buckram-stiffener & Dyer	Apothecaries		G/GL			
Godfrey Wilson	Coal Mercht	Farriers	H-S		A		A
Wm. Wryghte	Wine Mercht	Glovers					
Walbrook							
Rich. Alsager	Packer	Clothworkers			G	G	
Tho. Axford	Broker	Musicians	W-T		A		A
Richard Dixon	Cooper	Coopers	W-T	GL			
Tho. Harrison	Mercht	Blacksmiths			A		
Christopher Parker (1778-)	Distiller & Tobacconist	Glovers					
Cha. Sommers	Scale-maker	Skinners	W-T	A	A		
Jona. Turner		Leathersellers	H-S	GL			
Nich. Warrington (-1778)		Goldsmiths	W-T				
Robert Wyatt	Currier & Leather-cutter	Skinners	W-T	A[16]			

Notes

ABBREVIATIONS

City Addresses	*Addresses, Remonstrances, and Petitions to the Throne, presented from the Court of Aldermen, the Court of Common Council, and the Livery in Common Hall Assembled . . .* (London 1865)
CSM Pubs	*Publications (Transactions) of the Colonial Society of Massachusetts*, Boston
JCC	Journals of Common Council, Corporation of London Record Office
MHS Colls	*Collections of the Massachusetts Historical Society*, Boston
MHS Procs	*Proceedings of the Massachusetts Historical Society*, Boston
Wilkes's Speeches	*The Speeches of Mr. W[ilkes] in the House of Commons* (London 1786)
WMQ	*The William and Mary Quarterly*, 3d series

CHAPTER ONE

1 J.M. Bumsted, "'Things in the Womb of Time': Ideas of American Independence, 1633 to 1763," *WMQ* 31 (1974): 533–64; Alan Rogers, *Empire and Liberty: American Resistance to British Authority, 1755–1763* (Berkeley: University of California Press 1974).

2 Jack P. Greene, *The Quest for Power: The Lower Houses of Assembly in the Southern Royal Colonies, 1689–1776* (Chapel Hill: University of North Carolina Press 1963); Charles M. Andrews, *The Colonial Background of the American Revolution*, 2d ed. rev. (New Haven, Conn.:

Yale University Press 1931), 3–66; Bernard Bailyn, *The Ideological Origins of the American Revolution* (Cambridge, Mass.: Belknap Press of Harvard University Press 1967), 22–54; H. Trevor Colbourn, *The Lamp of Experience: Whig History and the Intellectual Origins of the American Revolution* (Chapel Hill: University of North Carolina Press 1965).

3 D.C. Douglas et al., eds., *English Historical Documents*, 12 vols. (London: Eyre and Spottiswoode 1953–77), 9: 696.

4 For the way in which American acceptance of trade regulations came to be misinterpreted by British ministers as acceptance of external taxation, see Edmund S. and Helen M. Morgan, *The Stamp Act Crisis: Prologue to Revolution* (Chapel Hill: University of North Carolina Press 1953), 272–6.

5 Pauline Maier, *From Resistance to Revolution: Colonial Radicals and the Development of American Opposition to Britain, 1765–1776* (New York: Knopf 1972), 169–70.

6 Ibid., 175–6; Bailyn, *Ideological Origins*, 105–9.

7 Maier, *From Resistance to Revolution*, 142–3, 171–8; Oliver M. Dickerson, *The Navigation Acts and the American Revolution* (Philadelphia: University of Pennsylvania Press 1951), 208–56.

8 Franklin to Lord Kames, London, 25 Feb. 1967, Leonard W. Labaree et al., eds., *The Papers of Benjamin Franklin* (New Haven, Conn.: Yale University Press 1959–), 14: 65.

9 Paul Langford, *The First Rockingham Administration* (London: Oxford University Press 1973), 149–99.

10 Douglas et al., eds., *English Historical Documents* 9: 695.

11 Paul Langford, "The Rockingham Whigs and America, 1767–1773," in Anne Whiteman et al., eds., *Statesmen, Scholars and Merchants: Essays in Eighteenth-Century History presented to Dame Lucy Sutherland* (Oxford: Clarendon Press 1973), 135–52; Peter D.G. Thomas, *British Politics and the Stamp Act Crisis: The First Phase of the American Revolution* (Oxford: Clarendon Press 1975), 358; G.H. Guttridge, *English Whiggism and the American Revolution*, new ed. (Berkeley: University of California Press 1966), 66–8. For a comment from an American in London on the dilatoriness of the Rockingham Whigs, see Arthur Lee to R.H. Lee, 27 Dec. 1768, Paul P. Hoffman, ed., *Lee Family Papers, 1762–1795*, University of Virginia microfilm (Charlottesville, Va. 1966), reel 1.

12 "London Merchants on the Stamp Act Repeal," *MHS Procs* 55 (1923): 218.

13 [Cobbett's] *Parliamentary History of England* 16 (1813): 103, 108.

14 Ibid., 178.

15 Chatham to Lord Shelburne, 3, 7 Feb. 1767, W.S. Taylor and J.H., Pringle, eds., *Correspondence of William Pitt*, 4 vols. (London 1838–40), 3: 188,

193-4; Robert J. Chaffin, "The Townshend Act of 1767," *WMQ* 27 (1970): 90-121; Robert E. Toohey, *Liberty and Empire: British Radical Solutions to the American Problem* (Lexington: University of Kentucky Press 1978), 114-5; P.G. Walsh Atkins, "Shelburne and America, 1763-1783" (D. Phil. diss., Oxford University, 1971).

16 The standard work on the intellectual antecedents and social relations of this group is Caroline Robbins, *The Eighteenth-Century Commonwealthman: Studies in the Transmission, Development and Circumstances of English Liberal Thought from the Restoration of Charles II until the War with the Thirteen Colonies* (Cambridge, Mass.: Harvard University Press 1959).

17 Ibid., 329-30, 479-91; Walter Wilson, *The History and Antiquities of Dissenting Churches and Meeting Houses in London, Westminster and Southwark*, 4 vols. (London 1808-14), 2: 283-9, 3: 479-91; Verner W. Crane, "The Club of Honest Whigs: Friends of Science and Liberty," *WMQ* 23 (1966): 210-33; "English Journal of Josiah Quincy, Jr., 1774-1775," *MHS Procs* 50 (1917): 443.

18 See, for example, Horace Walpole, *Memoirs of the Reign of George III*, ed., G.F. Russell Barker, 4 vols. (London 1894), 3: 320, and Ian R. Christie, *Wilkes, Wyvill and Reform: The Parliamentary Reform Movement in British Politics, 1760-1785* (London: Macmillan 1962), 15.

19 Basil Cozens-Hardy, ed., *The Diary of Sylas Neville, 1767-1788* (London: Oxford University Press 1950), 90, 149, 196, 301.

20 Catharine Macaulay to John Wilkes [1769?], Add. MSS 30870, fol. 242, British Library.

21 Lord Viscount Molesworth, *The Principles of a Real Whig; contained in a preface to the famous Hotoman's Franco-Gallia, and now reprinted at the request of the London Association to which are added their Resolutions and Circular Letter* (London 1775), 6.

22 Caroline Robbins, "The Strenuous Whig: Thomas Hollis of Lincoln's Inn," *WMQ* 7 (1950): 420.

23 Corinne C. Weston, *English Constitutional Theory and the House of Lords, 1556-1832* (London: Routledge and Paul 1965), 23-4; Isaac Kramnick, *Bolingbroke and His Circle: The Politics of Nostalgia in the Age of Walpole* (Cambridge, Mass.: Harvard University Press 1968), 121-7.

24 Catharine Macaulay, *The History of England from the Accession of James I to that of the Brunswick Line*, 8 vols. (London 1763-83), 1: xv.

25 Ibid., 8: 334.

26 Ibid., 334-5; Robbins, *Eighteenth-Century Commonwealthman*, 338-9, 357, 364-6, 370-5.

27 Cozens-Hardy, ed., *Neville Diary*, 59, 244-5.

28 Thomas Hollis to Jonathan Mayhew, 4 March 1765, Bernhard Knollenberg, ed., "Hollis-Mayhew Correspondence, 1759–1766," *MHS Procs* 69 (1956): 166; Catharine Macaulay to James Otis, London, 27 April 1769, "Warren-Adams Letters," *MHS Colls* 72 (1917); 7–8.

29 [Francis Blackburne], *Memoirs of Thomas Hollis, Esq., F.R.S. and A.S.*, 2 vols. (London 1780), 1: 73, 161–2, 241; Robbins, *Eighteenth-Century Commonwealthman*, 262–4; Robbins, "The Strenuous Whig," 434; Colin C. Bonwick, "An English Audience for American Revolutionary Pamphlets," *Historical Journal* 19 (1965) 365–6.

30 Francis Blackburne, "A Critical Commentary on Archbishop Secker's Letter to the Right Honourable Horatio Walpole, concerning Bishops in America," in Francis Blackburne, *The Archdeacon of Cleveland: The Works, Theological and Miscellaneous of Francis Blackburne … with some account of the Life and Writings of the Author by Himself, completed by his son, Francis Blackburne* 7 vols (Cambridge 1805), 2: 25, hereafter cited as Blackburne, *Works and Life*.

31 [Francis Blackburne, ed.], *A Collection of Letters and Essays in Favour of Public Liberty, first published in the News-papers in the Years 1764, 65, 66, 67, 68, 69, and 1770. By an Amicable Band of Wellwishers to the Religious and Civil Rights of Mankind*, 3 vols. (London 1774). Blackburne's role in the publication of these letters is revealed in Blackburne, *Works and Life* 1, unpaginated advertisement.

32 Frederick J. Hinkhouse, *The Preliminaries of the American Revolution as Seen in the English Press, 1763–1775*, Columbia University Studies in History, Economics and Public Law, no. 276 (New York 1926), 146.

33 [Blackburne], *Hollis Memoirs* 1: 280–3; Thomas Hollis, MS Diary, Houghton Library, Harvard University. Strahan, a friend of Benjamin Franklin, was at this time sympathetic toward American grievances. He later switched to the government camp.

34 [Blackburne, ed.], *Letters and Essays* 1: 219.

35 "The Stamp Act in Contemporary English Cartoons," with a note by Douglass Adair, *WMQ* 10 (1953): 538–42, plus illustrations. Hollis sponsored the English circulation of similarly pro-American tracts and prints following the Boston Massacre. M. Dorothy George, "America in English Satirical Prints," *WMQ* 10 (1953): 522.

36 Hollis Diary, entries for 24 July, 25 Aug. 1768; Cozens-Hardy, ed., *Neville Diary*, 17.

37 On the reason's for Bute's unpopularity, see John Brewer, "The Misfortunes of Lord Bute: A Case Study in Eighteenth-Century Political Argument and Public Opinion," *Historical Journal* 16 (1973): 3–44.

38 [Blackburne], *Hollis Memoirs* 1: 299; Thomas Hollis to Lord Chatham, 19 April 1773, Chatham Papers, PRO 30/8/40, pt. 2, fol. 274, Public Record Office, London; Cozens-Hardy, ed., *Neville Diary*, 14, 31.

39 Thomas, *Stamp Act Crisis* 233–4; Samuel and Thomas Fluyder to James Beekman, London, 31 March 1766, Philip L. White, ed., *The Beekman Mercantile Papers*, 3 vols. (New York: New York Historical Society 1956), 2: 706; Pomeroy and Hodgkin to James Beekman, 31 March 1766, ibid., 908.

40 *Gentleman's Magazine* (1768), 124.

41 Alfred B. Beaven, *The Aldermen of the City of London, temp. Henry III – 1908*, 2 vols. (London: Fisher 1908–13), 1: 280. See a bitter letter on Trecothick's unpopularity from William Samuel Johnson (the Connecticut agent) to William Pitkin, 12 March 1768, "Letters of William Samuel Johnson to the Governors of Connecticut," *MHS Colls*, 9 (1885): 267.

42 See letters from "Liveryman" and "No Bostonian," *St. James's Chronicle*, 23–26 Jan., 4–6 Feb. 1768; and from "No Bostonian" and "An Ancient Liveryman," *Public Advertiser*, 18 March 1768.

43 *Political Register*, Extraordinary Number, 2 (1768): 216.

44 On the political utility of patriotism, see Quentin Skinner, "The Principles and Practice of Opposition: The Case of Bolingbroke versus Walpole," in Neil McKendrick, ed., *Historical Perspectives: Studies in European Thought and Society in Honour of J.H. Plumb* (London: Europa 1974), 93–128.

45 Kramnick, *Bolingbroke*, 39–83; Peter G.M. Dickson, *The Financial Revolution in England: A Study in the Development of Public Credit, 1688–1756* (London: Macmillan 1967), esp. 15–38.

46 Lucy S. Sutherland, "The City of London in Eighteenth-Century Politics," in Richard Pares and A.J.P. Taylor, eds., *Essays Presented to Sir Lewis Namier* (London: Macmillan 1956), 49–56. This article lucidly distinguishes "the City" in its civic and financial senses.

47 Lord John Hervey, *Some Materials towards Memoirs of the Reign of George II*, ed. Romney Sedgwick, 3 vols. (London: Eyre and Spottiswoode 1931), 1: 138.

48 George F.E. Rudé, *Hanoverian London, 1714–1808* (London: Secker and Warburg 1971), 149–58; Reginald R. Sharpe, *London and the Kingdom*, 3 vols. (London 1895), 3: 27–9; Kramnick, *Bolingbroke*, 49–50.

49 The population figures are taken from M. Dorothy George, *London Life in the XVIIIth Century* (New York: Knopf 1925), 329. The ten MPs comprised four for the City and two each for Middlesex, Westminster, and Southwark. On a per capita basis, London should have had nearly sixty members. In 1741 there was some agitation in the London press for a redistribution of seats (see for example *Gentleman's Magazine* [1741], 343); but it was not until the 1760s that the inequities of the parliamentary structure began to be attacked in any sustained campaign for a reform of representation.

50 For contemporary comment on this tendency, see *Annual Register*, 1765, History of Europe, 46–7, and an anonymous pamphlet, *A Letter to the Common Council of London, on their late extraordinary Address* (London 1765). See also George F.E. Rudé, "The Anti-Wilkite Merchants of 1769," *Guildhall Miscellany* 2 (1965): 289–91, and George, *London Life*, 2–3.

51 Lucy S. Sutherland, *The City of London and the Opposition to Government, 1768–1774* (London: Athlone Press 1959), 8–11; Sutherland, "City of London," in Pares and Taylor, eds., *Essays presented to Sir Lewis Namier*, 64–7.

52 George F.E. Rudé, *Wilkes and Liberty: A Social Study of 1763–1774* (Oxford: Clarendon Press 1962), 22–34.

53 *Gentleman's Magazine* (1768), 124.

54 Ibid., 187–8; Rudé, *Wilkes and Liberty*, 57; Maier, *From Resistance to Revolution*, 165–6.

55 Rudé, *Wilkes and Liberty*, 39–70, 105–34; Maier, *From Resistance to Revolution*, 177–8.

56 Rudé, *Wilkes and Liberty*, 49–59.

57 Ibid., 59–61; Maier, *From Resistance to Revolution*, 173–4.

58 For such antimonarchy sentiment as there was in London in the late 1760s, see John Brewer, *Party Ideology and Popular Politics at the accession of George III* (Cambridge: Cambridge University Press 1976), 153, 190.

59 On this point, see an interesting letter in the *Middlesex Journal*, 30 May–1 June 1769, from "A Firm Friend to the Laws Liberties and Ancient Constitution of Our Country," calling for joint petitions to the throne from England and the colonies.

60 [Stephen Sayre], *The Englishman Deceived* (London 1768), 21; *Annual Register*, 1769, Chronicle, 116.

61 Pauline Maier, "John Wilkes and American Disillusionment with Britain," *WMQ* 20 (1963): 373–95.

62 [Blackburne], *Hollis Memoirs* 1: 290.

63 Thomas Somerville, *My Own Life and Times* (Edinburgh 1861), 146.

64 Cozens-Hardy, ed., *Neville Diary*, 30–1. Neville later visited Wilkes in prison. Ibid., 61–2.

65 *City Biography*, 2d ed. (London 1800), 88.

66 On Granville Sharp's family ties and their significance, see John A. Woods, "James Sharp: Common Councillor of London in the Time of Wilkes," in Whiteman et al., eds., *Essays Presented to Lucy Sutherland*, 276–7. Granville Sharp was an orthodox Anglican, but his political

principles placed him in the Real Whig camp. Colin C. Bonwick, "Contemporary Implications of the American Revolution for English Radicalism," *Maryland Historian* 7 (1976): 35.

67 Rudé, *Hanoverian London*, 149-58; J.H. Plumb, *Sir Robert Walpole*, 2 vols. (London: Cresset Press 1956), 1: 31-2, 2: 107-9; Kramnick, *Bolingbroke*, 171-2; H.T. Dickinson, *Bolingbroke* (London: Constable 1970), 189-90, 225.

68 For a detailed discussion of the shifting applicability of the labels Whig and Tory, see Brewer, *Party Ideology*, 39-54.

69 John G.A. Pocock, *The Machiavellian Moment: Florentine Political Thought and the Atlantic Republican Tradition* (Princeton, NJ: Princeton University Press 1975), 466-7.

70 Marie Peters, "The 'Monitor' on the Constitution, 1755-65: New Light on the Ideological Origins of English Radicalism," *English Historical Review* 86 (1971): 706-27.

71 Kramnick, *Bolingbroke*, 169-70; [Arthur Lee], *A Second Appeal to the Justice and Interests of the People, on the Measures respecting America* (London 1775), 37-8; Gordon S. Wood, *The Creation of the American Republic, 1776-1787* (Chapel Hill: University of North Carolina Press 1969), 567-8.

72 John Cannon, *Parliamentary Reform, 1640-1832* (Cambridge: Cambridge University Press 1973), 24-53. The agitation in the press in 1741 for a redistribution of seats (see above, note 49) was not continued and cannot be designated as part of the traditional country-party program for parliamentary reform.

73 Ibid., 53. Many of these contributions are reproduced in [Blackburne, ed.], *Letters and Essays*, 2: 44-7, 60-6.

74 Evidence for the influence of the Stamp Act crisis on the development of parliamentary reform programs is largely inferential and not absolutely conclusive. Contemporaries rarely made an explicit connection, though Pitt did couple a repudiation of the virtual representation of America with an attack on the rotten boroughs which, he predicted, "cannot continue the century" and should be "amputated." [Cobbett's] *Parliamentary History* 16: 100. The case of a connection between the American crisis of the 1760s and domestic reform has been persuasively argued in Brewer, *Party Ideology*, 206-16, though, as succeeding chapters will show, it was in the 1770s that a clear link between the issues of America and parliamentary reform became most evident.

75 See, for example, the detailed proposals of "Regulus," *Political Register* 2 (1768): 222-6.

CHAPTER TWO

1 James L. Clifford, ed., *Dr. Campbell's Diary of a Visit to England in 1775* (Cambridge: Cambridge University Press 1947), 58.

2 Quoted in Christie, *Wilkes, Wyvill and Reform*, 9.

3 See, for example, "Lysander," *Middlesex Journal*, 6–8 Aug. 1771.

4 *An Apology for the Ministerial Life and Actions of a Celebrated Favourite* (London 1766), 17; *Remarks on the Importance of the Study of Political Pamphlets, Weekly Papers, Periodical Papers, Daily Papers, Political Music, etc.* (London 1765), 4. For other citations on the same theme, see Brewer, *Party Ideology*, 139–41.

5 William Henry Curran, *The Life of the Right Honourable John Philpott Curran*, 2d ed., 2 vols. (Edinburgh 1822), 1: 58; Brewer, *Party Ideology*, 148–50.

6 Christie, *Wilkes, Wyvill and Reform*, 7–8; Alexander Stephens, *Memoirs of John Horne Tooke*, 2 vols. (London 1813), 1: 161–3; *Middlesex Journal*, 14–16 Dec. 1769. For an important discussion of the way clubs - provincial as well as metropolitan - promoted political independency through mutual economic aid and provided crucial support to the cause of Wilkes, see John Brewer, "Commercialization and Politics," in Neil McKendrick, John Brewer, and J.H. Plumb, *The Birth of a Consumer Society: The Commercialization of Eighteenth-Century England* (Bloomington: Indiana University Press 1982), 203–62. Wilkes himself, before his exile, belonged to social clubs such as the Beefsteak, where he was observed dining by James Boswell: Frederick A. Pottle, ed., *Boswell's London Journal, 1762–1763* (New York: McGraw-Hill 1950), 52. After his return from France, he joined his social inferiors in such political clubs as the Friends of Freedom and the Antigallicans, who admitted him as grand master. Thos. Blair to Wilkes, 25 Jan. 1775, and Wilkes to Jean-Baptiste Suard, 13 April 1770, Wilkes MSS, 2, fol. 118, and 3, letter 32, William Clements Library, Ann Arbor, Mich.

7 Quoted in Dora Mae Clark, *British Opinion and the American Revolution* (New Haven, Conn.: Yale University Press 1930), 161.

8 Crane, "Club of Honest Whigs," *WMQ* 23 (1966): 230.

9 Rudé, *Wilkes and Liberty*, 61–2. For details of the society's original membership, see Arthur Lee to R.H. Lee, 23 March 1769, Hoffman, ed., *Lee Family Papers*, reel 1; and Sutherland, *City of London*, 19–21.

10 Rudé, *Hanoverian London*, 120–2. See Appendix D for occupations of Common Council members during the period.

11 Rudé, *Wilkes and Liberty*, 152–4; Christie, *Wilkes, Wyvill and Reform*, 33.

12 *Morning Chronicle*, 22 Feb. 1775.

13 [Almon's] *Parliamentary Register* (London 1775-80), 1: 227.

14 W.P. Treloar, *Wilkes and the City* (London: Murray 1917), 69-76; Sutherland, *City of London*, 20-1; Beaven, *Aldermen* 2: 134-5; Maier, "Wilkes and American Disillusionment," *WMQ* 20 (1963); 378.

15 *Lloyd's Evening Post*, 23-25 June 1773.

16 Walter P. Prideaux, ed., *Memorials of the Goldsmiths' Company*, 2 vols. (London 1896-7), 2: 255-63; Sharpe, *London and the Kingdom*, 3: 93-4, 138-9.

17 Treloar, *Wilkes and the City*, 63; Henry L. Phillips, ed., *Annals of the Worshipful Company of Joiners* (London 1915), 65; Frame Work Knitters Company Admissions Book, 1728-1784, MS 3445/2, Guildhall Library, London; *Middlesex Journal*, 18-20 June 1771, 15-17 June 1773.

18 P.D.G. Thomas, "John Wilkes and the Freedom of the Press," *Bulletin of the Institute of Historical Research* 33 (1960): 86-98; *Memoir of Brass Crosby, Esq. Alderman of the City of London and Lord Mayor, 1770-1771* (London 1829), 18-19; John A. Woods, "The City of London and Impressment, 1776-1777," *Proceedings of the Leeds Philosophical and Literary Society* 8 (1956-9): 111; *Annual Register*, 1771, History of Europe, 16, and Chronicle, 70-1.

19 Lawrence Stone, "Literacy and Education in England, 1640-1900," *Past and Present*, no. 42 (1969): 109.

20 *Remarks on the Importance of the Study of Political Pamphlets*, 4.

21 Thomas R. Adams, "The British Pamphlets of the American Revolution for 1774: A Progress Report," *MHS Procs* 81 (1969): 36, 41; Bonwick, "An English Audience," *Historical Journal* 19 (1976): 362.

22 Bonwick, "An English Audience," 360-1; Brewer, *Party Ideology*, 146-8.

23 Brewer, *Party Ideology*, 143-4; Robert L. Haig, *The Gazetteer, 1735-1797: A Study in the Eighteenth-Century English Newspaper* (Carbondale: Southern Illinois University Press 1960), 79.

24 Solomon Lutnick, *The American Revolution and the British Press* (Columbia: University of Missouri Press 1967), 2, 15-19; Brewer, "Commercialization and Politics," in McKendrick, Brewer, and Plumb, *Birth of a Consumer Society*, 252-60. At least one editor, Henry Bate of the *Morning Post*, received a substantial pension from government during the American Revolution. Add. MSS 37836, fols. 71, 77.

25 Brewer, *Party Ideology*, 174; Miller to Wilkes, [1769?], Add. MSS 30875, fol. 215.

26 For evaluations of the prodigious journalistic output of Franklin and Lee, see Verner W. Crane, *Benjamin Franklin's Letters to the Press* (Chapel Hill: University of North Carolina Press 1950), and A.R. Riggs, "Arthur Lee and the Radical Whigs, 1768-1776," (PHD diss., Yale University, 1967), 50-61.

27 See the statement of editorial policy on the front of the *London Chronicle*, 4–6 July 1769.

28 L.H. Butterfield, "The American Interests of the Firm of E. and C. Dilly, with their letters to Benjamin Rush, 1770–1795," *Papers of the Bibliographical Society of America* 45 (1951): 284–96.

29 Robbins, "The Strenuous Whig," *WMQ* 7 (1950): 436–8; *Memoirs of John Almon: Bookseller of Piccadilly* (London 1790), 35–51; Robert R. Rea, *The English Press in Politics, 1760–1774* (Lincoln: University of Nebraska Press 1963), 223; Lucyle Werkmeister, *The London Daily Press, 1772–1792* (Lincoln: University of Nebraska Press 1963), 112–21.

30 Werkmeister, *London Daily Press*, 109–49.

31 *Memoirs of … Almon*, 32–3.

32 Ibid., 93. The Almon correspondence in Add. MSS 20733 gives some indication of the range of Almon's contacts. His correspondents included Lord Camden, Thomas Pownall (an ex-governor of Massachusetts and an authority on colonial affairs), Ralph Izzard (a well-connected diplomat from South Carolina), and Samuel Wharton (an American promoter of land schemes). His correspondence indicates that he retained contact with many Americans even after the outbreak of war in 1775.

33 See, for example, [John Almon], comp. and ed., *A Collection of … Papers relative to the dispute between Great Britain and America: shewing the causes and progress of that misunderstanding from 1764 to 1775* (London 1777).

34 O.A. Sherrard, *A Life of John Wilkes* (London: Allen and Unwin 1930), 261–77; Raymond Postgate, *That Devil Wilkes* (London: Constable 1930), 186–98, 233–44.

35 Stephens, *Horne Tooke* 1: 178; C.R. Ritcheson, *British Politics and the American Revolution* (Norman: University of Oklahoma Press 1954), 117.

36 *The Controversial Letters of John Wilkes, Esq.; The Rev. John Horne and their principal adherents* (London 1771), 158.

37 John Almon, ed., *The Correspondence of the late John Wilkes and his friends [with] memoirs of his life*, 5 vols. (London 1805) 1: 60; Wilkes to [?], Paris, 4 Dec. 1765, Wilkes MSS, 1, fol. 91a, Clements Library. The seriousness of Wilkes's ambitions, however, may be questioned in the light of a letter to his brother, Heaton, of 17 Nov. 1765, in which he says: "If I am to be an exile from my native London, it shall not be in the new world: so far I can command." Ibid., fol. 91.

38 John Wilkes to Heaton Wilkes, 17 Nov. 1765, ibid.

39 Most of the correspondence between Wilkes and his colonial admirers is published in W.C. Ford, ed., "John Wilkes and Boston," *MHS Procs* 47 (1913–14): 190–215, and G.M. Elsey, ed., "John Wilkes and William

Palfrey," *CSM Pubs* 34 (1937–42): 411–88. For most of the original letters to Wilkes, see Add. MSS 30870.

40 Wilkes to Committee of Boston Sons of Liberty, King's Bench Prison, 19 July 1768, 30 March 1769, Add. MSS 30870, fols. 135–6; Wilkes to Palfrey, 14 April, 27 Sept. 1769, 24 July 1770, Elsey, ed., "Wilkes and Palfrey," 413, 415, 418.

41 Boylston to William Cooper, London, 27 April 1769, Samuel Adams Papers, box 1, New York Public Library, New York City.

42 L.H. Butterfield, ed., *Letters of Benjamin Rush, vol. 1, 1761–1792* (Princeton, NJ: Princeton University Press 1951), 72.

43 Elsey, ed., "Wilkes and Palfrey," 412. See also Wilkes to Jean-Baptiste Suard, King's Bench Prison, 12 Sept. 1768, Wilkes MSS, 3, letter 21, Clements Library.

44 Out of thirty-one reported speeches in the Commons, from his election in 1774 until the end of the war, thirteen were primaily concerned with supporting the revolutionary cause, while three others – two on reform and one on civil list expenditure – made frequent references critical of ministerial policy towards America. His other speeches tended to be shorter in length and more trivial in content. *Wilkes's Speeches.*

45 See, for example, letters of 1 Jan., 2 Sept. 1778, *Letters ... of John Wilkes ... to his daughter*, 4 vols. (London 1804), 2: 57–8, 104.

46 Wilkes to Jean-Baptiste Suard, London, 18 March 1774, Wilkes MSS, 4, Clements Library.

47 *Controversial Letters*, 161–9.

48 Riggs, "Arthur Lee and the Radical Whigs," 79–82, 93; Arthur Lee to R.H. Lee and Richard Parker, London, 23 Dec. 1768, and Arthur Lee to R.H. Lee, London, 15 Aug. 1769, Hoffman, ed., *Lee Family Papers*, reel 1; Franklin Bowditch Dexter, ed., *The Literary Diary of Ezra Stiles, D.D., Ll.D., January 1, 1769–March 13, 1776* (New York: Scribner's 1901), 318–21.

49 Quoted in A.R. Riggs, "Arthur Lee, a Radical Virginian in London, 1768–1776," *Virginia Magazine of History and Biography* 78 (1970): 273n25. Lee's name occurs frequently in Wilkes's dinner diary. Add. MSS 30866.

50 Lee to one of his brothers in Virginia, 1771 (wrongly dated in following as 1767), R.H. Lee, *Life of Arthur Lee*, 2 vols. (Boston 1829), 1: 186; Lee to R.H. Lee, 27 Dec. 1768, 18 Sept. 1769, Hoffman, ed., *Lee Family Papers*, reel 1.

51 Hoffman, ed., *Lee Family Papers*, reel 1.

52 Riggs, "Arthur Lee and the Radical Whigs," 121; Michael G. Kammen, *A Rope of Sand: The Colonial Agents, British Politics and the American Revolution* (Ithaca, NY: Cornell University Press 1968), 129; A. Matthews, ed., "Letters of Dennys De Berdt, 1757–70," *CSM Pubs* 13 (1910–11):

305n2; Dennis deBerdt (and others) to Robert Carter, London, 26 Jan. 1770, Emmet Collection, 7, MS 5865, New York Public Library, New York City.

53 William Bollan to Samuel Danforth and others, London, 23 June 1769, "The Bowdoin and Temple Papers," *MHS Colls*, 6th ser., 9 (1897): 148; W.S. Johnson to W. Pitkin, 23 March, 18 Sept. 1769, "Letters of William Samuel Johnson," ibid., 5th ser., 9: 267: Benjamin Franklin to William Franklin, London, 16 April, 5 Oct. 1768, Labaree et al., eds., *Papers of Benjamin Franklin* 15: 98-9, 224; Crane, ed., *Franklin's Letters to the Press*, 126; Kammen, *Rope of Sand*, 148-51.

54 *Public Advertiser*, 14, 26 Jan., 13 Feb. 1769.

55 Ibid., 2 March 1769; Sutherland, *City of London*, 27.

56 Rudé, *Wilkes and Liberty*, 70-1; *Middlesex Journal*, 27-29 April 1769.

57 *Public Advertiser*, 25 May 1769; *Annual Register*, 1769, Chronicle, 199. There has been much confusion concerning the drafting and presentation of this petition. George Rudé is right in pointing out that there were in fact two Middlesex petitions, one of which, from a section of the Middlesex freeholders, was presented to the House of Commons on 29 April. He would seem, however, to be wrong in concluding that the petition to the Commons was a drastic modification of that adopted by the county electors on 27 April, and that the petition of 24 May was the product of another meeting of which no mention exists. The meeting of 27 April clearly intended its petition to be presented to the king. Rudé is probably correct, however, in claiming that the petition of 29 April (which included no statement of American grievances) derived from collusion between the Rockingham Whigs and one of their City contacts, James Adair. See Rudé, *Wilkes and Liberty*, 71-2, 108-9, 200-2, which may be usefully compared with the newspaper references given above.

58 Lee, *Arthur Lee* 1: 245-6 and note.

59 Rudé, *Wilkes and Liberty*, 109-10; *Middlesex Journal*, 10-12 Aug. 1769; Thomas Copeland et al., eds., *The Correspondence of Edmund Burke*, 10 vols. (Cambridge: Cambridge University Press; Chicago: Chicago University Press 1958-78), 2: 31-5.

60 *City Addresses*, 16.

61 Ibid., 15.

62 Bollan to Samuel Danforth and others, 23 June 1769, "Bowdoin and Temple Papers," 148; Wilkes to Palfrey, 24 July 1769, Elsey, ed., "Wilkes and Palfrey," 414.

63 John Calcraft to Lord Chatham, 13 Sept. 1770, Chatham Papers, PRO 30/8/25, fol. 59.

64 *Middlesex Journal*, 28-30 Sept. 1769.

65 *Public Advertiser*, 12 Oct. 1769.

66 Malcolm Freiberg, "William Bollan, Agent of Massachusetts," *More Books* 23 (1948): 180; F.G. Walett, "Governor Bernard's Undoing: An Earlier Hutchinson's Letters Affair," *New England Quarterly* 38 (1965): 219–21; deBerdt to Thomas Cushing, 18, 30 Sept., 12 Oct. 1769, Matthews, ed., "Letters of Dennys De Berdt," 380–1; Elsey, ed., "Wilkes and Palfrey," 414–3.

67 Walett, "Governor Bernard's Undoing," 221–3; Riggs, "Arthur Lee and the Radical Whigs," 31–5.

68 De Berdt to Cushing, 16 Nov. 1769, 24 Feb. 1770, Matthews, ed., "Letters of Dennys De Berdt," 385, 404; Glynn to Wilkes, 20 Oct. 1769, Add. MSS 30870, fol. 210; Wilkes to Palfrey, 27 Sept. 1769, Elsey, ed., "Wilkes and Palfrey," 415.

69 Matthews, ed., "Letters of Dennys De Berdt," 410.

70 *Middlesex Journal*, 24–26 May 1770.

71 *Annual Register*, 1769, Appendix to Chronicle, 181–7; Maier, *From Resistance to Revolution*, 187.

72 *The Whisperer*, 24 March 1770.

73 William Bollan to Samuel Danforth, 28 April 1770, "Bowdoin and Temple Papers," 177.

74 See, for example, letters from P.C., "Decimus," and "Touchstone," *Middlesex Journal*, 1–3, 8–10, 24–26 May 1770; from "Brutus," *London Evening Post*, 12–15 May 1770; and from "Mentor," *The North Briton*, 28 April 1770. Some letters were clearly written by Americans, e.g., one from "Junius Americanus" [Arthur Lee], *Middlesex Journal*, 24–26 April 1770.

75 Macaulay to Town of Boston, 9 May 1770, MS. 195, Boston Public Library.

76 Robbins, "The Strenuous Whig," 433; George, "America in English Satirical Prints," 522. The tract was also published by William Bingley: see advertisement in the *Middlesex Journal*, 5–8 May 1770.

77 Boston town committee to Benjamin Franklin and others, 13 July 1770, Samuel Adams Papers, box 1.

78 Kammen, *Rope of Sand*, 194–200.

79 It has been convincingly shown that James Burgh, not Benjamin Franklin, was the main author of "The Colonist's Advocate" (although Franklin possibly collaborated on some of the pieces): Carla H. Hay, "Benjamin Franklin, James Burgh and the Authorship of the 'The Colonist's Advocate' Letters," with comments by William B. Willcox et al. and Verner W. Crane, *WMQ* 32 (1975): 111–24. For the relevant newspaper letters, see Crane, ed., *Franklin's Letters to the Press*, 167–207.

80 Hancock MSS, box 27, folder 1, New England Historic Genealogical Society, Boston.

81 *Middlesex Journal*, 10–12 Aug. 1769.

82 J.G.A. Pocock, "1776: The Revolution against Parliament," in J.G.A. Pocock, ed., *Three British Revolutions: 1641, 1688, 1776* (Princeton, NJ: Princeton University Press 1980), 278; Brewer, *Party Ideology*, 240–64; Rudé, *Wilkes and Liberty*, 107–11; Ross J. Hoffman, *The Marquis: A Study of Lord Rockingham, 1730–1782* (New York: Fordham University Press 1973), 217–22; Wilkes to Jean-Baptiste Suard, 2 March 1770, Wilkes MSS, 3, letter 30, Clements Library.

83 Rudé, *Wilkes and Liberty*, 151–2; Burke to Charles O'Hara, 9 Aug. 1770, Copeland et al., eds., *Burke Correspondence* 2: 240–1; Baker to W. Talbot, 13 Sept. 1770, William Baker MSS, c9/1, Hertfordshire Record Office, Hertford.

84 Copeland et al., eds., *Burke Correspondence* 2: 150.

85 Catharine Macaulay, *Observations on a Pamphlet, Entitled Thoughts on the Cause of the Present Discontents* (London 1770), 6, 12, 18–20.

86 [Debrett's] *History, Debates and Proceedings of both Houses of Parliament . . . 1743 to . . . 1774*, 7 vols. (London 1792), 5: 305–6; *Controversial Letters*, 217–19; Trecothick to Edmund Burke, 8 Oct. 1771, Copeland et al., eds., *Burke Correspondence* 2: 245.

87 A friendly correspondence between Chatham and Hollis continued after 1766: Chatham Papers, PRO 30/8/40, pt. 2, fols. 239–95, and in Stanhope MSS 736, Kent Record Office, Maidstone, Kent.

88 Quoted in D.S. Lovejoy, "Henry Marchant and the Mistress of the World," *WMQ* 12 (1955): 392. See also Dexter, ed., *Diary of Ezra Stiles* 1: 319.

89 *London Evening Post*, 27–29 Nov. 1770.

90 *Controversial Letters*, 221.

91 Beaven, *Aldermen* 1: 280, 2: 134. For Oliver's pro-American speech on becoming a City MP, see *Public Advertiser*, 12 July 1770.

92 John Norris, *Shelburne and Reform* (London: Macmillan 1963), 58–60, 76–9; Rudé, *Wilkes and Liberty*, 165; Lord Edmond Fitzmaurice, *Life of William, Earl of Shelburne, afterwards first Marquess of Lansdowne*, rev. ed., 2 vols. (London: Macmillan 1912), 1: 460–2.

93 *Controversial Letters*, 6–8. See also Walpole, *Memoirs* 3: 121–2.

94 Rudé, *Wilkes and Liberty*, 155–69; Mr Dayrell to Earl Temple [Sept. 27?, 1771], W.J. Smith, ed., *The Grenville Papers*, 4 vols. (London 1852–3), 4: 535–7; Treloar, *Wilkes and the City*, 126–7.

95 Junius to John Wilkes, 21 Aug. 1771, J. Wade, ed., *Letters of Junius*, 2 vols. (London 1850–5), 2: 63–70; [Draft] Adams to Henry Marchant, Boston, 7 Jan. 1772, Samuel Adams Papers, box 1.

96 Simon Maccoby, *English Radicalism, 1762–1785* (London: Allen and Unwin 1955), 171.

97 Horne, from the beginning of his exchange with Wilkes, virtually conceded that Wilkes was winning popular support. *Controversial Letters*, 26–7.

98 Riggs, "Arthur Lee and the Radical Whigs," 113-14.

99 Almon, ed., *Wilkes Correspondence* 5: 42-3. For an account of the impact of this incident in generating colonial opposition to government, see J.P. Greene, "Bridge to Revolution: The Wilkes Fund Controversy in South Carolina," *Journal of Southern History* 29 (1963): 19-52.

100 *English Liberty: being a collection of interesting tracts from the year 1762 to 1769, containing the private correspondence, public letters, speeches, and addresses of John Wilkes, Esq.* (London n.d.), with MS additions, Guildhall Library, MS 3332/1, 441; *Controversial Letters*, 157-69.

101 *Annual Register*, 1770, Appendix to Chronicle, 225.

102 Quoted in Maier, *From Resistance to Revolution*, 204n13.

103 7,8 Sept. 1770, Copeland et al., eds., *Burke Correspondence* 2: 157.

104 *Gazetteer*, 9 March 1771; *Annual Register*, 1771, Chronicle, 93-4. For an account of the secession favourable to Wilkes, see fragment in Arthur Lee's hand, Arthur Lee Papers, 6 MS Am. 811.7 (240), Houghton Library, Harvard University.

105 Hoffman, ed., *Lee Family Papers*, reel 2; Riggs, "Arthur Lee and the Radical Whigs," 138; *Annual Register*, 1771, Chronicle, 94; *Middlesex Journal*, 16-18 April 1771; *Gazetteer*, 24 April 1771.

106 Lee to R.H. Lee, 11 June 1771, Hoffman, ed., *Lee Family Papers*, reel 2; Lee to Samuel Adams, 14 June 1771, Samuel Adams Papers, box 1.

107 *Public Advertiser*, 13 June, 23 July 1771; Lee to R.H. Lee, 11 June 1771, Hoffman, ed., *Lee Family Papers*, reel 1; Lee to Samuel Adams, 14 June 1771, Samuel Adams Papers, box 1.

108 [Draft] Adams to Arthur Lee, 27 Sept. 1771, Samuel Adams Papers, box 1. I have followed Richard D. Brown, *Revolutionary Politics in Massachusetts: The Boston Committee of Correspondence and the Towns, 1772-1774* (Cambridge, Mass.: Harvard University Press 1970), 44-7, in locating the derivation of the Boston Committee of Correspondence in Adams's scheme for a colonial Bill of Rights society. That this scheme itself derived from Arthur Lee's plans in London is quite evident from the cited correspondence between Adams and Lee.

109 Thomas Hutchinson, *The History of the Colony and Province of Massachusetts Bay*, ed. L.S. Mayo, 3 vols. (Cambridge, Mass.: Harvard University Press 1936), 3: 261; Douglass Adair and J.A. Shutz, eds., *Peter Oliver's Origin and Progress of the American Revolution: A Tory View* (San Marino, Calif.: Huntingdon Library 1961), 78.

110 Arthur Lee to Samuel Adams, 25 Jan. 1773, Samuel Adams Papers, box 2; Samuel Adams to Arthur Lee, 9 April 1773, Lee, *Arthur Lee* 2: 202-3; W.L. Sachse, *The Colonial American in Britain* (Madison:

University of Wisconsin Press 1956), 186; *Public Advertiser*, 25 July 1771.

111 Wade, ed., *Letters of Junius* 2: 71–4, 84–5.

112 *Public Advertiser*, 25 July 1771.

113 Brown, *Revolutionary Politics*, 49–91; *London Chronicle*, 29 June–1 July 1773; *Gentleman's Magazine* (1773), 401–2.

114 Lucy S. Sutherland, *The East India Company in Eighteenth-Century Politics* (Oxford: Clarendon Press 1952), 240–68; Riggs, "Arthur Lee and the Radical Whigs," 154; duke of Richmond to Edmund Burke, 27 May 1773, Copeland et al., eds., *Burke Correspondence* 2: 436–7; duke of Richmond to James Adair, 25, 31 Oct. 1773, 16 Aug. 1774, Add. MSS 50829; JCC, 66 (1773–6), 18–19; Alison G. Olson, *The Radical Duke: Career and Correspondence of Charles Lennox, third Duke of Richmond* (London: Oxford University Press 1961), 38; Brown, *Revolutionary Politics*, 153–5.

115 Arthur Lee to R.H. Lee, 17 July 1772, Hoffman, ed., *Lee Family Papers*, reel 2.

116 *Middlesex Journal*, 8–10, 17–19, 22–24 June 1773.

117 23 June 1773, Samuel Adams Papers, box 2.

118 E.g., *Public Advertiser*, 2, 3 July 1773.

119 W.C. Ford, ed., *The Letters of William Lee, Sheriff and Alderman of London, 1766–1783*, 3 vols. (New York 1891), 1: 13–14; *Public Advertiser*, 5 July 1773; Purdie and Dixon's *Virginia Gazette*, 23 Dec. 1773.

120 *Middlesex Journal*, 2–4 Nov. 1773; North to king, 31 Oct. 1773, Sir John Fortescue, ed., *The Correspondence of George III, from 1760 to 1783*, 6 vols. (London 1927–8), 3: 20.

121 *Middlesex Journal*, 16–18, 20–23, 25–27 Nov. 1773; City Elections, 1768–1796: A Collection of Broadsheets in the Guildhall Library, fols. 42–9. The accusation that Roberts was a papist was freely bandied.

122 *Middlesex Journal*, 16–18 Nov. 1773.

123 Riggs, "Arthur Lee and the Radical Whigs," 160–1; *Public Advertiser*, 29 Nov. 1773.

124 City Elections, 1768–1796, fol. 41.

125 Ford, ed., *Letters of William Lee* 1: 17–18; Beaven, *Aldermen*, 1: 281.

126 *Middlesex Journal*, 21–23 Dec. 1773.

CHAPTER THREE

1 The opening three paragraphs of this chapter are based largely on the accounts in Benjamin Woods Labaree, *The Boston Tea Party* (New York: Oxford University Press 1964), 58–216, and Bernard Donoughue, *British Politics and the American Revolution: The Path to War, 1773–75* (London: Macmillan 1964), 21–126.

2 CO 5/118, fols. 69, 72, Public Record Office.

3 Kammen, *Rope of Sand*, 284–6; Donoughue, *British Politics and the American Revolution*, 27–9, 31–4; Jack M. Sosin, *Agents and Merchants: British Colonial Policy and the Origins of the American Revolution* (Lincoln: University of Nebraska Press 1965), 158–61; Bernard Bailyn, "The Central Themes of the American Revolution: An Interpretation," in S.G. Kurtz and J.H. Hutson, eds., *Essays on the American Revolution* (Chapel Hill: University of North Carolina Press 1973), 13–14.

4 See Edmund Burke to the Committee of Correspondence of the General Assembly of New York, 6 April 1774, Copeland et al., eds., *Burke Correspondence* 2: 528, and the duke of Manchester to Lord Rockingham, 20 April 1774, Wentworth-Woodhouse Muniments, R1-1486, Sheffield City Library, which advises against opposition to the Massachusetts regulation bill because of the prevailing state of public opinion.

5 Rockingham to Edmund Burke, 30 Jan. 1774, Copeland et al., eds., *Burke Correspondence* 2: 516.

6 Donoughue, *British Politics*, 73–101, 135–46.

7 [Debrett's] *Parliamentary Debates* 7: 74–5; A.F. Steuart, ed., *The Last Journals of Horace Walpole during the Reign of George III, from 1771–1783, with notes by Dr. Doran*, 2 vols. (London: Lane 1910) 1: 316, 338–9.

8 Lutnick, *American Revolution and the British Press*, 35–49.

9 Labaree, *Boston Tea Party*, 179.

10 [Lee] to Samuel Adams, 14 May 1774, Samuel Adams Papers, box 2.

11 *Lloyd's Evening Post*, 5–7 April 1775. Suspicions about the government's motives were also expressed by George Johnstone, an MP and director of the East India Company. Donoughue, *British Politics*, 22–3.

12 [?] to Chatham, 15 Nov. 1774, Chatham Papers, PRO 30/8/97, fols. 260–1; *London Evening Post*, 2–5 April 1774.

13 Donoughue, *British Politics*, 79; [Debrett's] *Parliamentary Debates* 7: 73.

14 [Debrett's] *Parliamentary Debates* 7: 215.

15 Kammen, *Rope of Sand*, 290.

16 Bollan to the Massachusetts Council, 11, 15 March 1774, "Bowdoin and Temple Papers," *MHS Colls*, 6th ser., 9: 353–7, 360–4.

17 Kammen, *Rope of Sand*, 290–1; Peter Force, ed., *American Archives*, 4th ser. (Washington, DC 1837–46), 1: 46.

18 Force, ed., *American Archives*, 4th ser., 1: 58, 60, 79, 81, 120.

19 Donoughue, *British Politics*, 105–26; Jack M. Sosin, *Whitehall and the Wilderness* (Lincoln: University of Nebraska Press 1961), esp. 239–55.

20 Quoted in Donoughue, *British Politics*, 122.

21 William Lee to R.H. Lee, 10 Sept. 1774, Ford, ed., *Letters of William Lee* 1: 91–2.

22 *Public Advertiser*, 6 June 1774; *London Evening Post*, 25–28 June 1774.

23 *Middlesex Journal*, 2–4 June 1774.

24 JCC, 66 (1773–6): 105–6.

25 Sayre to Samuel Adams, 15 Aug. 1774, Samuel Adams Papers, box 3.

26 JCC, 66 (1773–6): 106.

27 Steuart, ed., *Walpole's Last Journals* 1: 359–60.

28 Quoted in Maier, *From Resistance to Revolution*, 248.

29 *Public Advertiser*, 22 June 1774; *Middlesex Journal*, 21–23 June 1774; *London Evening Post*, 23–25, 25–28 June 1774. For George Grieve's interesting and multinational career in the cause of liberty, see John Brewer, "English Radicalism in the Age of George III," in Pocock, ed., *Three British Revolutions*, 332.

30 *London Evening Post*, 23–25 June 1774.

31 *Middlesex Journal*, 23–25 June 1774; Common Hall Book, 7 (1751–88): 182, Corporation of London Record Office.

32 *London Evening Post*, 30 July–2 Aug. 1774.

33 *Public Advertiser*, 16 June 1774. For the domestic impact of the Quebec Act on the American cause, see also Maier, *From Resistance to Revolution*, 248.

34 Donoughue, *British Politics*, 177–80. Inevitably Lord Bute was credited by the radical press with promoting dissolution. See, for example, *London Evening Post*, 29 Sept.–1 Oct. 1774.

35 Lee, *Arthur Lee* 1: 262; *London Evening Post*, 23–25 Aug. 1774; North to George III, 25 Sept. 1774, Fortescue, ed., *Correspondence of George III* 3: 133.

36 *London Evening Post*, 17–20 Sept. 1774.

37 Ibid., 24–27 Sept. 1774.

38 Accounts of the debate, which differ only in minor points of detail, are given in *Middlesex Journal*, 24–27 Sept. 1774; *Public Advertiser*, 27 Sept. 1774; *London Evening Post*, 24–27 Sept. 1774.

39 The pledge is printed in full in *Middlesex Journal*, 27–29 Sept. 1774.

40 Ibid., 24–27 Sept. 1774. Staples's outburst tends to confirm that direct trade relations with America were not conducive to feelings of sympathy with colonial grievances.

41 *London Evening Post*, 24–27 Sept. 1774; *Public Advertiser*, 27 Sept. 1774.

42 *Middlesex Journal*, 24–27 Sept. 1774.

43 [Draft] John Robinson to George III, 7 Oct. 1774, and George III to Robinson, 8 Oct. 1774, Add. MSS 37833, fols. 3–4; *London Evening Post*, 18–20 Oct. 1774.

44 Maccoby, *English Radicalism*, 202; *Middlesex Journal*, 13–15 Sept. 1774.

45 The first of these slogans – as well as referring generally to supporters of the Quebec Act – probably also referred to the alleged Roman Catholic

background of the ministerial candidate, John Roberts. See also City Elections, 1768–1796, fol. 48.

46 *Middlesex Journal*, 22–24 Sept. 1774.

47 The account of this Common Hall is based on reports in the *London Evening Post*, 1–4 Oct. 1774; *Middlesex Journal*, 1–4 Oct. 1774; *London Chronicle*, 1–4 Oct. 1774.

48 *London Chronicle*, 1–4 Oct. 1774. The clause relating to America was paraphrased from the original Bill of Rights pledge formulated in 1771. See above, 50.

49 *London Chronicle*, 1–4 Oct. 1774. William Baker had four years previously expounded his political philosophy in a letter to a friend: "I consult those whom I believe to be honest, and my own heart – to attend to the advice of the one, but to follow implicitly the dictates of the other." Baker to W. Talbot, 13 Sept. 1770, William Baker MSS C9/1.

50 John Robinson to George III, 7 Oct. 1774, Add. MSS 37833, fol. 3; *Middlesex Journal*, 8–11 Oct. 1774.

51 City Elections, 1768–1796, fol. 70; *Middlesex Journal*, 8–11 Oct. 1774; *London Chronicle*, 4–6 Oct. 1774.

52 Beaven, *Aldermen* 1: 281.

53 *London Evening Post*, 1–4 Oct. 1774; *London Chronicle*, 4–6 Oct. 1774; Ford, ed., *Letters of William Lee* 1: 20; Ian R. Christie, "The Wilkites and the General Election of 1774," *Myth and Reality in Eighteenth-Century British Politics and Other Papers* (Berkeley: University of California Press 1970), 244–60.

54 Handbill dated 1 Oct. 1774, Stanhope MSS, bundle 247, Kent Record Office, Maidstone, Kent.

55 Newspaper clippings, ibid., bundles 220, 247.

56 *London Evening Post*, 1–4 Oct. 1774; *London Chronicle*, 4–6 Oct. 1774; Donoughue, *British Politics*, 186.

57 Aubrey Newman, *The Stanhopes of Chevening* (London: Macmillan 1969), 135; Christie, "Wilkites and the General Election of 1774," *Myth and Reality*, 250; Donoughue, *British Politics*, 186; *Middlesex Journal*, 8–11 Oct. 1774.

58 *London Chronicle*, 13–15 Oct. 1774; *Middlesex Journal*, 8–11 Oct. 1774. There is evidence to suggest, however, that in fact Percy fully supported the government's American policy. Sir Lewis Namier and John Brooke, *The History of Parliament: The House of Commons, 1754–1790*, 3 vols. (London: Her Majesty's Stationery Office 1964), 3: 269–70.

59 Donoughue, *British Politics*, 195.

60 Christie, "Wilkites and the General Election of 1774," *Myth and Reality*, 252–4; *London Chronicle*, 4–6 Oct. 1774.

61 Donoughue, *British Politics*, 196–7; Christie, "Wilkites and the General

Election of 1774," *Myth and Reality*, 250–1, 255–8. For Mawbey's appeal to the electorate, see *Morning Chronicle*, 6 Oct. 1774.

62   Christie, "Wilkites and the General Election of 1774," *Myth and Reality*, 254; Stephen Sayre to John Wilkes, 29 Aug. 1769, Add. MSS 30870, fol. 185. Trevanion's name appears frequently in Wilkes's dinner diary, Add. MSS 30866.

63   Christie, "Wilkites and the General Election of 1774," *Myth and Reality*, 254–5; Donoughue, *British Politics*, 197n2; Bull to John Wilkes, Add. MSS 30871, fol. 229.

64   Namier and Brooke, *House of Commons* 1: 75–6.

65   For details of this election campaign, see P.T. Underdown, "Henry Cruger and Edmund Burke: Colleagues and Rivals at the Bristol Election of 1774," *WMQ* 15 (1958): 14–34, and Donoughue, *British Politics*, 197–8. Cruger's name appears in accounts of money disbursed on secret service warrants by John Robinson. Add. MSS 37836, fol. 63. See also Namier and Brooke, *House of Commons* 2: 280–2.

66   *London Chronicle*, 15–18 Oct. 1774.

67   It should be emphasized, however, that eighteenth-century elections in the provinces are not a reliable guide to public opinion. Where seats were contested, the divisive issues concerned patronage and local matters rather than questions of national policy. Of course, even had there been widespread support for the colonists, the unrepresentative structure of eighteenth-century Parliaments would have distorted its reflection in the House of Commons.

68   "Henry Ireton" [Josiah Quincy, Jr] to his wife, London, 24, 27 Nov. 1774, and 14 Jan. 1775, Josiah Quincy, Jr, Papers, Massachusetts Historical Society, Boston; William Lee to John Dickinson, London, 19 Aug. 1774, John Dickinson Papers, 22–2, Historical Society of Pennsylvania, Philadelphia.

69   Sosin, *Agents and Merchants*, 184; Force, ed., *American Archives*, 4th ser., 1: 186–7.

70   William Lee to Thomas Cushing [?], 1 June 1774, CO 5/118, fol. 26. See also Lawrence Henry Gipson, *The British Empire before the American Revolution*, 15 vols. (New York: Knopf 1936–70) 12: 134–5, and Arthur Lee to John Dickinson, 2 April 1774, John Dickinson Papers, 22–1. As a North American merchant himself, Lee had a vested interest in denouncing his fellow traders as a way of persuading colonial merchants to do business exclusively with him (Ford, ed., *Letters of William Lee* 1: 28–30), but, as will be shown, his judgments are supported in the main by evidence from other quarters.

71   18, 25 Sept. 1774, Copeland et al., eds., *Burke Correspondence* 3: 31.

72   See, for example, Clark, *British Opinion*, 65–6, 70, 78–9.

73 The statistics on exports are derived from John J. McCusker, "The Current Value of English Exports, 1697-1800," *WMQ* 28 (1971): 621. See also R.B. Sheridan, "The British Credit Crisis of 1772 and the American Colonies," *Journal of Economic History* 20 (1960): 161-86, and Ralph Davis, "English Foreign Trade, 1700-1774," *Economic History Review*, 2d ser., 15 (1962): 285-303.

74 Davis, "English Foreign Trade," 300-1.

75 Fluyder, Marsh, Hudson, and Streatfield to James Beekman, London, 3 Feb. 1775, and B. Pomeroy and Son to James Beekman, London, 2 Nov. 1774, White, ed., *Beekman Mercantile Papers* 2: 755, 947.

76 Joseph Albert Ernst, *Money and Politics in America: A Study in the Currency Act of 1764 and the Political Economy of Revolution* (Chapel Hill: University of North Carolina Press 1973), viii.

77 *The Interest of the Merchants and Manufacturers of Great Britain, in the Present Contest with the Colonies, stated and considered* (London 1774), 49-50. See also unsigned pieces on the same theme in *Lloyd's Evening Post*, 2-4 Jan. 1775, and *Gazetteer*, 3 Jan. 1775.

78 *Middlesex Journal*, 30 April-3 May 1774. See also *Morning Chronicle*, 2 Jan. 1775.

79 Steuart, ed., *Walpole's Last Journals* 1: 427.

80 William Molleson to Lord Dartmouth, 31 Aug. 1774, Dartmouth Papers, D(W) 1778/II/America/953, William Salt Library, Stafford, Eng.; William Lee to R.H. Lee, 25 Feb. 1775, Ford, ed., *Letters of William Lee* 1: 131-3; "Journal of Josiah Quincy, Jr.," *MHS Procs* 50: 466-7.

81 Letters from deBerdt to Dartmouth, 17 June, 6 July, 31 Aug. 1774, 19 March 1776, Dartmouth Papers, D(W) 1778/I/ii/987, D(W) 1778/I/ii/994, D(W)/1778/I/ii/1011, D(W) 1778/II/1665.

82 The dilemma of the merchants was accurately summarized by a pseudonymous essayist, "Boston Saint," in the *Gazetteer*, 7 Jan. 1775.

83 S.M. Rosenblatt, "The Significance of Credit in the Tobacco Consignment Trade: A Study of John Norton and Sons, 1768-1775," *WMQ* 19 (1962): 383-99; Jacob M. Price, "Who was John Norton? A Note on the Historical Character of Some Eighteenth-Century Virginia Firms," ibid., 400-7; Namier and Brooke, *House of Commons* 2: 42.

84 W.T. Baxter, *The House of Hancock: Business in Boston, 1724-1775* (Cambridge, Mass.: Harvard University Press 1945), 285; *Middlesex Journal*, 24-26 June 1773. Hayley appears to have had a more harmonious relationship with Nicholas Brown of Rhode Island. James B. Hedges, *The Browns of Providence Plantation*, 2 vols. (Cambridge, Mass.: Harvard University Press 1952), 1: 182-5.

85 Norman Baker, *Government and Contracts: The British Treasury and War Supplies, 1775-1783* (London: Athlone Press 1971), 27, 163, 232.

86 Ibid., 28, 190–1, 194–5; L.B. Namier, "Anthony Bacon, M.P., An Eighteenth-Century Merchant," *Journal of Economic and Business History* 2 (1929–30): 37–63; WO 47/89, fol. 734, Public Record Office.

87 *A Short Address to the Government, the Merchants, Manufacturers, and the Colonists in America and the Sugar Islands, on the Present State of Affairs* (London 1775).

88 This attempt at reconciliation was apparently initiated by Lord Hyde, chancellor of the Duchy of Lancaster, probably with the approval of Lord Dartmouth. Donoughue, *British Politics*, 214–5, 244–7; Betsy C. Corner and Christopher Booth, *Chain of Friendship: Selected Letters of Dr. John Fothergill of London, 1735–1780* (Cambridge, Mass.: Belknap Press of Harvard University Press 1971), 27–30.

89 William Lee to R.H. Lee, 10 Sept. 1774, Ford, ed., *Letters of William Lee* 1: 91; Arthur Lee to F.L. Lee, 2 April 1774, and to R.H. Lee, 13 Dec. 1774, Lee, *Arthur Lee* 1: 39, 209–11; Josiah Quincy, Jr, to his wife, 7 Jan. 1775 (wrongly dated 1774), Josiah Quincy, Jr, Papers; Dunlop and Wilson to Joseph Pemberton, London, 5 April 1775, Pemberton Papers, 27: 117, Historical Society of Pennsylvania, Philadelphia; Kammen, *Rope of Sand*, 294; Maier, *From Resistance to Revolution*, 251–3.

90 *Public Advertiser*, 22, 23 Dec. 1774.

91 Blackburn to Lord Dartmouth, 22 Dec. 1774, Dartmouth Papers, D(W) 1778/II/1033.

92 Blackburn to Lord Dartmouth, [4 Jan. 1775?], ibid., D(W) 1778/II/1025; *Lloyd's Evening Post*, 4–6 Jan. 1775.

93 *Lloyd's Evening Post*, 4–6 Jan. 1775; Mildred to James Pemberton, 13 Feb. 1775, Pemberton Papers, 27: 73.

94 Douglas et al., eds., *English Historical Documents* 9: 696; Burke to Lord Rockingham, 12 Jan. 1775, Copeland et al., eds., *Burke Correspondence* 3: 98. According to John Blackburn, the petition was actually drafted by William Lee and William Baker, who were "interdicted [by the rest of the merchants' committee] from interfering with any Political Question, or desiring any Repeal of the Laws." Blackburn to Dartmouth, [Jan. 4, 1775?], Dartmouth Papers, D(W) 1778/II/1025.

95 Woods, "James Sharp," in Whiteman et al., eds., *Essays presented to Lucy Sutherland*, 279–80.

96 *Lloyd's Evening Post*, 11–13 Jan. 1775.

97 *Journals of the House of Commons* 35: 71–2, 83; [Almon's] *Parliamentary Register* 1: 107; James Clark to Charles Jenkinson, 25 Jan. 1775, Add. MSS 38208, fols. 127–8; *London Chronicle*, 24–26, 26–28 Jan. 1775.

98 Lillian M. Penson, *The Colonial Agents of the British West Indies* (London: University of London Press 1924), 203–4. Throughout the eighteenth century the interests of the West India planters and the West

India traders frequently diverged, but they were brought together by the common threat to their survival posed by the imperial crisis. They had grounds for their anxiety; the outbreak of the American revolutionary war created enormous problems for the islands' trade and widespread famine among the slave population. Richard B. Sheridan, "The Crisis of Slave Subsistence in the British West Indies during and after the American Revolution," *WMQ* 33 (1976): 615-41; Lowell J. Ragatz, "The Sugar Colonies during the Revolution," in Charles W. Toth, ed., *The American Revolution and the West Indies* (Port Washington, NY: Kennikat Press 1975), 75-85.

99 Namier and Brooke, *House of Commons* 2: 407, and 3: 224-5. See also Samuel Estwick, *A Letter to Josiah Tucker* (London 1776), in which Estwick denounces successive governments' pursuit of an American revenue.

100 *Gentleman's Magazine* (1774), 404-5; Sheridan, "Crisis of Slave Subsistence," 617-18.

101 Penson, *Colonial Agents*, 204; J.H. Parry and P.M. Sherlock, *A Short History of the West Indies*, 2d ed. (London: Macmillan 1963), 135. Twelve "West Indians" were, or became, government contractors. Baker, *Government and Contractors*, 228-9.

102 Burke to Lord Rockingham, 12 Jan. 1775, Copeland et al., eds., *Burke Correspondence* 3: 98.

103 *London Chronicle*, 17-19 Jan. 1775; *Morning Chronicle*, 15 Feb. 1775.

104 [Almon's] *Parliamentary Register* 2: 35-9.

105 *The Evidence delivered on the Petition presented by the West India Planters and Merchants to the House of Commons as it was introduced at the Bar and summ'd up by Mr. Glover* (London 1775). In late 1775 the "West Indians" again petitioned against the economic consequences of the government's American policy, specifically the prohibitory bill (*Annual Register*, 1775, Chronicle, 170; *London Evening Post*, 5-7 Dec. 1775, and 12-14 Dec. 1775; *Public Advertiser*, 12 Dec. 1775). After that their representations were mainly devoted to seeking better protection for the islands and their sea traffic (e.g., Petitions of the West India Planters and Merchants to the king, 16 Dec. 1778, and Dec. 1781, *Annual Register*, 1778, Chronicle, 312, and 1781, Chronicle, 319-20; Representation from the Committee of West India Planters and Merchants to Lord George Germain, 2 Dec. 1778, CO 5/249, fol. 72).

106 *London Chronicle*, 9-11 Feb. 1775; *Morning Chronicle*, 15 Feb. 1775.

107 Donoughue, *British Politics*, 243, 251-4; *Morning Post*, 23 Feb. 1775.

108 William Lee to F.L. Lee, 25 Feb. 1775, Hoffman, ed., *Lee Family Papers*, reel 2; *Lloyd's Evening Post*, 27 Feb.-1 March 1775.

109 JCC, 66 (1773-6): 189-90; Meeting for Sufferings, 34: 20-2, Friends' Library, London.

110 *Lloyd's Evening Post*, 27 Feb.-1 March 1775; Donoughue, *British Politics*, 251-2.

111 *London Chronicle*, 11-14, 14-16, 21-23, 23-25 March 1775; JCC 66 (1773-6): 191-2; William Lee to F.L. Lee, 11 March 1775, Hoffman, ed., *Lee Family Papers*, reel 2.

112 Meeting for Sufferings, 34: 23-7; Dartmouth Papers, D(W) 1778/II/1237; Barclay to Pemberton, 18 March 1775, Pemberton Papers, 27: 103.

113 From the Meeting for Sufferings in London to the Friends of the Meeting for Sufferings in Philadelphia, 24 March 1775, Pemberton Papers, 27: 110; Yearly Meeting Minute Book, 15: 261-2, Friends' Library; Daniel Mildred to John Pemberton, 13 July 1775, Pemberton Papers, 28: 4; David Barclay to James Pemberton, 13 July 1775, ibid., 5.

114 See, for example, Namier and Brooke, *House of Commons* 1: 17; Lewis Namier, *England in the Age of the American Revolution*, 2d ed. (London 1961), 39.

115 James E. Bradley, "Whigs and Nonconformists: 'Slumbering Radicalism' in English Politics, 1739-89," *Eighteenth-Century Studies* 9 (1975): 23n80.

116 Anthony Lincoln, *Some Political and Social Ideas of English Dissent, 1763-1800* (Cambridge: Cambridge University Press 1938), 10-12; Carl B. Cone, *Torchbearer of Freedom: The Influence of Richard Price on Eighteenth-Century Thought* (Lexington: University of Kentucky Press 1952), 15, 70; Robbins, *Eighteenth-Century Commonwealthman*; Crane, "Club of Honest Whigs," *WMQ* 23 (1966): 210-33; C.C. Bonwick, "English Dissenters and the American Revolution," in H.C. Allen and Roger Thompson, eds., *Contrast and Connection: Bicentennial Essays in Anglo-American History* (London: Bell 1976), 88-109.

117 Kammen, *Rope of Sand*, 204.

118 J.T. Rutt, *Life and Correspondence of Joseph Priestley, Ll.D., F.R.S.*, 2 vols. (London 1831), 1: 75.

119 *An Address to Protestant Dissenters of All Denominations* (London 1774), 5. In this pamphlet Priestley repeated many of the themes he had earlier expressed in *The Present State of Liberty in Great Britain and her Colonies, by an Englishman* (London 1769).

120 Steuart, ed., *Walpole's Last Journals* 1: 409; letter from "Hystaspes" [Thomas Joel] to Protestant Dissenters, *London Evening Post*, 8-10 Dec. 1774; Bradley, "Whigs and Nonconformists," 23; Colin C. Bonwick, *English Radicals and the American Revolution* (Chapel Hill: University of North Carolina Press 1977), 86; Minute Books of the Body of Protestant Dissenting Ministers in and about the Cities of London and Westminster, 2, MS 38.106, Dr. Williams's Library, London; Minutes of the Protestant Dissenting Deputies, Guildhall MS 3083/2, 70-210. On French's ties to government, see Baker, *Government and Contractors*, 30, 163.

On Wellings's political ties, see an advertisement signed by Wellings on behalf of a loyalist society in *New Morning Post*, 14 Dec. 1776, and below, 115, 150.

121 Rudé, *Wilkes and Liberty*, 191; Sutherland, *City of London*, 32-3.

122 *Wilkes's Speeches*, 2-6. Wilkes's brief period of political inactivity was the subject of press comment. See, for example, *Morning Chronicle*, 25 Jan. 1775.

123 *Wilkes's Speeches*, 7-19.

124 JCC, 66 (1773-6): 170-2, 177-9.

125 *Morning Chronicle*, 22 Feb. 1775; JCC 66 (1773-6): 185.

126 *Lloyd's Evening Post*, 27-29 March 1775; William Lee to R.H. Lee, 3 April 1775, Hoffman, ed., *Lee Family Papers*, reel 2; ibid., for a fragment of the petition in Arthur Lee's hand; *Lloyd's Evening Post*, 3-5 April 1775.

127 Lee to [Josiah Quincy, Jr, or Samuel Adams], 6 April 1775, Samuel Adams Papers, box 2; letter from B.C., *London Chronicle*, 25-27 April 1775.

128 *Gazetteer*, 8 April 1775. See also *London Chronicle*, 4-6 April 1775.

129 Common Hall Book, 8 (1751-88): 186-7.

130 *London Evening Post*, 11-13 April 1775; *London Chronicle*, 8-11 April 1775.

131 Steuart, ed., *Walpole's Last Journals* 1: 456-7; Common Hall Book, 8 (1751-88): 189.

132 *Lloyd's Evening Post*, 20-22 Feb., 22-24 March 1775.

133 *Public Advertiser*, 18 Feb. 1775; *London Chronicle*, 21-23 Feb. 1775; *Morning Post*, 23 Feb. 1775.

134 SP 37/12, fols. 345-6, Public Record Office; TS 11/209/884, Public Record Office.

135 A useful summary of the contents of *The Crisis* is contained in J.B. Sanders, "The Crisis of London and American Revolutionary Propaganda, 1775-1776," *Social Studies* 58 (1967): 7-11,

136 *The Crisis*, no. 3 (4 Feb. 1775), and no. 5 (18 Feb. 1775).

137 Ibid., no. 6 (25 Feb. 1775), no. 15 (29 April 1775), no. 17 (13 May 1775), no. 18 (20 May 1775), and no. 34 (9 Sept. 1775).

138 Ibid., no. 1 (20 Jan. 1775).

139 Ibid., no. 4 (11 Feb. 1775).

140 *Journals of the House of Lords* 34 (1774-6): 330-1. The parliamentary resolution also authorized the attorney-general to commence prosecution against the printers of the paper. Accordingly, a case was built up against Samuel Axtell, the printer, and in April 1776 the Court of King's Bench sentenced him to three months in prison for libel. Another publisher must have been found, however, because the publication of *The Crisis*

was not interrupted. SP 37/12, fols. 345–6; TS 11/209/884; *London Evening Post*, 27–30 April 1776.

141 Cited in Lutnick, *American Revolution and the British Press*, 3.

142 *Morning Post*, 8 March 1775. There is a similar, though less detailed, account in the *Gazetteer*, 8 March 1775.

143 Lindsey to Rev. W. Turner, 2 Feb. 1775, Lindsey MSS 12.44, letter 26, Dr. Williams's Library; Hutchinson to Mr Green, 10 Jan. 1775, P.O. Hutchinson, ed., *The Diary and Letters of His Excellency Thomas Hutchinson*, 2 vols. (London 1883–6), 1: 355.

144 *London Chronicle*, 14–16 March 1775.

145 G.H. Guttridge, ed., *The American Correspondence of a Bristol Merchant, 1766–1776: Letters of Richard Champion*, University of California Publications in History, 22, no. 1 (Berkeley, Calif. 1934), 4; Burke to Lord Rockingham, 18,25 Sept. 1774, Copeland, et al., eds., *Burke Correspondence* 3: 29–32; *Lloyd's Evening Post*, 24–27 March 1775; Steuart, ed., *Walpole's Last Journals* 1: 450.

146 Donoughue, *British Politics*, 133; Guttridge, *English Whiggism*, 77–8. Chatham had, of course, countenanced the Townshend duties, but these could be casuistically regarded as trade regulators rather than taxes.

147 For letters from Stephen Sayre to Lord Chatham, see Taylor and Pringle, eds., *Chatham Correspondence* 4: 359–68, and Chatham Papers, PRO 30/8/6, fols. 87–8, and PRO 30/8/55, fols. 114–33. For letters from Arthur and William Lee to Chatham, see Chatham Papers, PRO 30/8/48, fols. 56–72.

148 Chatham Papers, PRO 30/8/55, fol. 118.

149 Quoted in Riggs, "Arthur Lee and the Radical Whigs," 214.

150 Donoughue, *British Politics*, 232–7; Douglas et al., eds., *English Historical Documents* 9: 805–11; Sayre to John Dickinson, 5 Feb. 1775, John Dickinson Papers, 13.

151 JCC, 66 (1773–6): 179; Common Hall Book, 8 (1751–88): 188; *Wilkes's Speeches*, 13–15.

152 William Lee to Lord Chatham, 16 Feb. 1775, Chatham Papers, PRO 30/8/48, fol. 69; Chatham to Lee, n.d., ibid., PRO 30/8/6, fols. 56–7; William Lee to R.H. Lee, 10 Sept. 1774, Ford, ed., *Letters of William Lee* 1: 93.

153 Beaven, *Aldermen* 1: 14.

154 Ford, ed., *Letters of William Lee* 1: 26–7.

155 Arthur B. Tourtellot, *Lexington and Concord: The Beginning of the War of the American Revolution* (New York: Norton 1963), 237.

156 *London Evening Post Extraordinary*, 29 May 1775.

157 Donoughue, *British Politics*, 273; *London Gazette*, 6–10 June, 27–30 May 1775; *London Chronicle*, 30 May –1 June 1775; *Public Advertiser*, 31 May 1775; *London Evening Post*, 30 May–1 June 1775.

158 W.S. Lewis et al., eds., *The Yale Edition of Horace Walpole's Correspondence*, 48 vols. (New Haven, Conn.: Yale University Press 1937-83), 24: 111; Lee to John Dickinson, 12 July 1775, John Dickinson Papers, 22-2; Germain quoted in Lutnick, *American Revolution and the British Press*, 63.

159 *Public Advertiser*, 9 June 1775; *The Trial (at large) of John Horne, Esq. . . . for a Libel* (London 1777), 15.

160 TS 11/1079/5378-90; *Annual Register*, 1776, Chronicle, 197; *Morning Chronicle*, 18 Dec. 1776, 8, 13 Feb. 1777; *Gazetteer*, 18 Dec. 1776, 13 Feb. 1777.

161 *Trial of John Horne; Further Proceedings on the Trial of John Horne, Esq.* (London 1777); *Annual Register*, 1777, Appendix to Chronicle, 234-45.

162 *Morning Chronicle*, 8 Feb. 1777; Horne to Lee, Lee Papers, 1, folder 24, William Clements Library.

163 *London Evening Post*, 20-22 June 1775; *Public Advertiser*, 21 June 1775; Riggs, "Arthur Lee and the Radical Whigs," 231-2.

164 *City Addresses*, 41-2.

165 For accounts of this Common Hall, see *Public Advertiser*, 26 June 1775, and *London Chronicle*, 24-27 June 1775.

166 *City Addresses*, 39-40.

167 Common Hall Book, 8 (1751-88): 191-2. See *Lloyd's Evening Post*, 1-4 Sept. 1775, for a copy of Effingham's resignation from the army.

168 *City Addresses*, 43.

169 Ibid., 43-4; *Public Advertiser*, 5 July 1775.

170 *Public Advertiser*, 5, 6 July 1775; W. Brummell to [Lord North?], 4 July 1775, Fortescue, ed., *Correspondence of George III* 3: 231-2.

171 King to Lord North, 5 July 1775, Fortescue, ed., *Correspondence of George III*, 3: 233; *Public Advertiser*, 5 July 1775.

172 JCC, 66 (1773-6): 236-7.

173 Hutchinson to Lord Hardwicke, 24 June 1775, Add. MSS 35427, fol. 22.

174 *London Chronicle*, 6-8, July 1775; JCC, 66 (1773-6): 239-40. See Appendix D for the division on the motion to address.

175 *City Addresses*, 45; king to Lord North, 9 July 1775, Fortescue, ed., *Correspondence of George III* 3: 233; Thomas Hutchinson to Lord Hardwicke, 17 July 1775, Add. MSS 35427, fols. 28-9.

176 See letter from "Hystaspes" (Thomas Joel) to the Common Council of London and a letter from "An Old Staunch Whig," *London Evening Post*, 11-13 July 1775; and an anonymous paragraph denouncing the "poor, timid, languid Address to the Throne," ibid., 20-22 July 1775.

177 JCC, 66 (1773-6): 241; *London Evening Post*, 22-24 July 1775; [?] to Henry Cruger, Jr, Kinderhook, New York, 6 Nov. 1775, CO 5/134, fol. 33; JCC, 66 (1773-6), 259-60; *Morning Chronicle*, 26 Oct. 1775.

178 *London Evening Post*, 27–29 July 1775.

179 Douglas et al., eds., *English Historical Documents* 9: 850; *London Evening Post*, 26–29 Aug. 1775.

180 *London Evening Post*, 23–26 Sept. 1775.

181 Ibid., 9–12, 16–19 Sept. 1775.

182 Ibid., 23–26 Sept. 1775. See also *Public Advertiser*, 27 Sept. 1775.

183 *Middlesex Journal*, 23–26 Sept. 1775; *Lloyd's Evening Post*, 2–4 Oct. 1775; William Lee to F.L. Lee, 25 Sept. 1775, CO 5/40, fols. 35–6.

184 *Public Advertiser*, 30 Sept. 1775; Common Hall Book, 8 (1751–88): 194.

185 Common Hall Book, 8 (1751–88): 193–4.

186 Burke to Rockingham, [22,] 23 Aug., 1 Oct. 1775, Copeland et al., eds., *Burke Correspondence* 3: 194, 224; Yonge to Thomas Townshend, 8 July 1775, Sydney Papers, 8, William Clements Library; William Lee to Lord Chatham, 24 June 1775, Chatham Papers, PRO 30/8/48, fol. 70; Sayre to the duke of Manchester, 7 Sept. 1776, Portland MSS PWF 8218, University of Nottingham Library: Manchester to Sayre, [n.d.], ibid., PWF 8219; Hoffman, *The Marquis*, 337–8.

187 Bull to John Wilkes, 19 Nov 1775, Add. MSS 30871, fol. 249; [Almon's] *Parliamentary Register* 3: 215–30; Steuart, ed., *Walpole's Last Journals* 1: 496–7; *Public Advertiser*, 28 Nov. 1775; Lord North to George III, [27 Nov. 1775], Fortescue, ed., *Correspondence of George III* 3: 296.

CHAPTER FOUR

1 William Lee to Edward Browne, 17 Jan. 1775, and William Lee to R.H. Lee, 17 Jan. 1775, Ford, ed., *Letters of William Lee* 1: 111 note, 114; Arthur Lee to Thomas Cushing, 6 Jan. 1771, Lee, *Arthur Lee* 1: 247–8; Arthur Lee to John Dickinson, 10 April 1775, John Dickinson Papers, 25–2. Arthur Lee's initial pessimism was shared by Josiah Quincy, Jr. Quincy to his wife, 14 Jan. 1775, Josiah Quincy, Jr, Papers, and Maier, *From Resistance to Revolution*, 250.

2 [?] to Dickinson, 29 July 1775, John Dickinson Papers, 25–1; Maier, *From Resistance to Revolution*, 257–8, and note 58; Lords of Admiralty to Lord Dartmouth, 21 Sept. 1775, enclosing a copy of a letter from a person at Philadelphia, 29 July – 1 Aug. 1775, R.A. Roberts, ed., *Calendar of Home Office Papers of the Reign of George III, 1773-1775, preserved in the Public Record Office* (London 1899), 409–11; *Morning Chronicle*, 28 Sept. 1775.

3 L. de Loménie, *Beaumarchais et Son Temps*, 2d ed., 2 vols. (Paris 1873), 2: 94. Beaumarchais sometimes exaggerated the instability of British politics, but his report of Rochford's remark seems credible in the light of the Sayre affair discussed below.

4 H.B. Wheatley, ed., *The Historical and Posthumous Memoirs of Sir Nathaniel Wraxall*, 5 vols. (London 1884), 1: 98.

5 SP 37/12, fols. 5-6, 12-20, 36-7; Steuart, ed., *Walpole's Last Journals* 2: 3; M.J. Sydenham, "Firing His Majesty's Dockyard: Jack the Painter and the American Mission to France, 1776-1777," *History Today* 16 (1966): 324-31; T.B. Howell, ed., *A Complete Collection of State Trials*, 33 vols. (London 1809-26), 20: 1318-67.

6 Francis Richardson's Information, TS 11/542/1758.

7 Nicholas Nugent's Information, ibid.; Steuart, ed., *Walpole's Last Journals* 2: 482.

8 Warrant for seizing and apprehending Sayre, warrant for committing Sayre to the Tower, and Col. Rainsford's memorandum, TS 11/542/1758; *London Evening Post*, 21-24, 24-26 Oct. 1775.

9 Examination of Stephen Sayre taken before the earl of Rochford, 23 Oct. 1775, TS 11/542/1758. Reynolds and Sayre, in May 1775, jointly purchased some land in Dominica: Indenture of Sale, Hewitt Papers, MS 552/464/2, University of London Library, Senate House, London.

10 *London Evening Post*, 26-28 Oct. 1775; *Public Advertiser*, 28 June 1776; Stephen Sayre vs. Lord Rochford, before Lord Chief Justice de Grey, 27 June 1776, TS 11/542/1758.

11 Quoted in Maier, *From Resistance to Revolution*, 260.

12 Steuart, ed., *Walpole's Last Journals* 1: 482; Hutchinson, ed., *Hutchinson's Diary and Letters* 1: 547.

13 Anthony Storer to Lord Carlisle, 17 Dec. 1775, HMC *15th Report, Appendix, part 4, The Manuscripts of the Earl of Carlisle, Preserved at Castle Howard*, ed. R.E.G. Kirk (London 1897), 311 ("Eyre" not "Sayre" is printed in this transcript, but the context makes it clear that this is an error); *Morning Post*, 3 Oct. 1775; *London Evening Post*, 21-24 Oct. 1775.

14 Steuart, ed., *Walpole's Last Journals* 1: 481; Horace Walpole to Rev. William Mason, 27 Oct. 1775, and Walpole to Sir Horace Mann, 28 Oct. 1775, Paget Toynbee, ed., *The Letters of Horace Walpole, fourth Earl of Orford*, 26 vols., (Oxford: Clarendon Press 1903-25), 9: 273, 277-8; Lord Macclesfield to Charles Jenkinson, 27 Oct. 1775, Add. MSS 38208, fol. 192; *Morning Post*, 31 Oct. 1775.

15 Riggs, "Arthur Lee and the Radical Whigs," 210; Edmund, baron de Harold, to William Knox, 13 Sept. 1774, HMC *Report on Manuscripts in Various Collections*, vol. 6, *The Manuscripts of Captain Howard Vicente Knox*, ed. S.C. Lomas (Dublin 1909), 113.

16 Wilkes's dinner diary, Add. MSS 30866, entries for 11 Sept., 9, 25 Oct. 1775, 19 Jan., 5, 10, 11 Feb., 28 April, 19 May 1776; Maier, *From Resistance to Revolution*, 256-7; Lord Stormont to Lord Weymouth, Paris, 20 Nov. 1776, SP/78/300, fol. 249.

17 Horace St. Paul to Weymouth, Paris, 1 May 1776, SP/78/299, fol. 68; see also Stormont to Weymouth, Paris, 25 Sept. 1776, ibid., fol. 536.

18 Roberts, ed., *Calendar of Home Office Papers, 1773-1775*, 473.

19 Lee to Wilkes, 17 June 1779, Add. MSS 30872, fols. 101-4; James Adair to Lord Rockingham, Jan. 1778, enclosing two papers from John Wilkes, George, earl of Albemarle, ed., *Memoirs of the Marquis of Rockingham and His Contemporaries*, 2 vols. (London 1852), 2: 334-5; Treloar, *Wilkes and the City*, 210-9.

20 Lee to Josiah Quincy, Jr, 17 March 1775, enclosing "Address to the Soldiers," Dartmouth Papers, D(W) 1778/II/1190; Riggs, "Arthur Lee and the Radical Whigs," 209.

21 The following account is based on the material in SP 37/11, fols. 79-129b, except where otherwise stated. There is a secondary account of the affair (based on the Wedderburn Papers in the Clements Library), H.B. Van Tyne, "A British Strike in 1775," *Michigan Alumnus Quarterly Review* 45 (1938-9): 157-64. This article contains a number of errors, however. William Lee, for example, is confused with his brother, Arthur.

22 Letter from *"Patriae Amicus," Morning Post*, 23 Sept. 1775. It is possible that the speech attributed to Richardson was fabricated in order to embarrass Chatham.

23 SP 37/11, fol. 97.

24 Ibid., fols. 86, 90, 95, 117.

25 Ibid., fol. 95.

26 Robinson to Wedderburn, 26 Aug. 1775, and notes in Wedderburn's hand on back of letter from John Pownall to Wedderburn, 23 Aug. 1775, Wedderburn Papers, 2, folders 13 and 10, Clements Lib.

27 Rumours of the association's impending formation began in June 1775 (*London Evening Post*, 13-15 June 1775). The society should not be confused with the London Military Association (sometimes called the London Association) which helped in the suppression of the Gordon Riots.

28 SP 37/11, fol. 136.

29 *London Evening Post*, 14-16 Sept. 1775; [James Burgh], *Political Disquisitions*, 3 vols. (London 1774-5), 3: 429, 433-5.

30 "An Officer in the East India Company" to Lord Dartmouth, London, 9 Sept. 1775, with enclosed tract headed "Sidney's Exhortation ...," Dartmouth Papers, D(W) 1778/II/1503.

31 *St. James's Chronicle*, 2-4 Nov. 1775. See also the association's lengthy resolution in support of press freedom generally: *London Evening Post*, 25-27 Jan. 1776.

32 *London Evening Post*, 25-27 Jan., 27 Feb.-1 March 1776.

33 Ibid., 2-5 Sept. 1775.

34 William Mathers (mayor of Worcester) to earl of Suffolk, 31 Aug. 1775, and Craven to Suffolk, 2 Sept. 1775, SP 37/11, fol. 135. See also Charles Simpson (town clerk of Lichfield) to Lord Dartmouth, 9 Sept. 1775, and John Osbaldeston to Dartmouth, Blackburn, 10 Sept. 1775, Dartmouth Papers, D(W) 1778/II/1504 and 1507.

35 *Public Advertiser*, 4 Sept. 1775.

36 *Morning Post*, 5 Sept. 1775.

37 *Public Advertiser*, 12 Oct. 1775.

38 Ibid., 6 Sept. 1775; *London Evening Post*, 26–28 Oct. 1775, 2–4 May 1776, 27 Feb.–1 March 1777; *St. James's Chronicle*, 2–4 Nov. 1775.

39 SP 37/11, fol. 136.

40 Letter from "Cassius," *Public Advertiser*, 11 Oct. 1775; *Kent's Directory*, 1775, 47.

41 *Middlesex Journal*, 27–30 April, 2–4 May 1771, 15–17 Sept. 1774; Appendix A; letter from "Cincinnatus," *Public Advertiser*, 22 April 1775.

42 Ninetta S. Jucker, ed., *The Jenkinson Papers, 1760–1766* (London: Macmillan 1949), 69; letter from *"Patriae Amicus," Morning Post*, 23 Sept. 1775; letter from "Cassius," *Public Advertiser*, 11 Oct. 1775; *Royal Kalendar*, 1771, 119; Richardson to Jenkinson, March 1777, 15 Dec. 1777, Add. MSS 38209, fols. 104, 109.

43 *Public Advertiser*, 28 Sept. 1775; *Morning Chronicle*, 26, 28 Sept. 1775. Maskall lived on Oxford St., which was literally "on the road to Tyburn."

44 *Public Advertiser*, 19 Oct. 1775.

45 *London Chronicle*, 15–17 Sept. 1774; *London Evening Post*, 23–26 Sept. 1775.

46 See above, 83–4; *Lloyd's Evening Post*, 27–29 March 1775; letter from B.C., *London Chronicle*, 25–27 April 1775; letter from "Cincinnatus," *Public Advertiser*, 22 April 1775.

47 *London Chronicle*, 24–27 June 1775; *Public Advertiser*, 19 Oct. 1775; and see above, 95.

48 *Public Advertiser*, 15 July 1773, 26 Sept. 1775.

49 *London Evening Post*, 28–30 Sept. 1775; *Public Advertiser*, 21 March 1776; Appendix D. *London Evening Post*, 20–22 June 1775, reported that in Common Council, "Piper spoke well in favour of America."

50 Appendixes A and D; *Kent's Directory*, 1775, 162.

51 Robbins, "The Strenuous Whig," *WMQ* 7 (1950): 439n112.

52 *London Evening Post*, 24–26 Nov. 1774. Thomas Joel admitted to the pseudonym "Hystaspes" in a letter to John Wilkes, [1775?], Add. MSS 30871, fol. 231.

53 *London Evening Post*, 17–20 June, 23–25 Feb., 27–29 June, 11–13 July 1775.

54 Thomas Joel, *Poems with Letters Moral and Political in Prose*, 2d ed. (London 1775), 211–36. Another of Thomas Joel's publications indicates

his profession; he wrote *An Easy Introduction to the English Grammar*, printed for the Use of Mr. T. Joel's school by W. Andrews (Chichester 1770). In 1774 Joel's school apparently went bankrupt: P.C. Yorke, ed., *The Diary of John Baker* (London: Hutchinson 1931), 277.

55 Letter from "Harpagus" to "Hystaspes," *London Evening Post*, 29–31 Dec. 1774. I can find no subsequent repudiation of these charges in the press.

56 Letter from "Quidam," *Public Advertiser*, 18 Oct. 1775; letter from "Laywer," *Gazetteer*, 30 Sept. 1775; Joel to Wilkes [1775?], and 15 Dec. 1775, Add. MSS 30871, fols, 231, 261.

CHAPTER FIVE

1 *London Evening Post*, 3–5, 14–17 Oct. 1775; *Gazetteer*, 5 Oct. 1775; Edmund Burke to duke of Portland, 2 Oct. 1775, Copeland et al., eds., *Burke Correspondence* 3: 225–6, and appended editorial notes. Some accounts state that the petition contained 1,171 signatures (e.g., Maccoby, *English Radicalism*, 218); this figure, however, can be arrived at only by counting individually partners in firms which signed the petition collectively. Only seventy-three of the petitioners of 11 Oct. had signed previous petitions of London merchants and tradesmen etc. involved in the Atlantic trade.

2 *Public Advertiser*, 5 Oct. 1775; *London Gazette*, 10–14 Oct. 1775; Maccoby, *English Radicalism*, 218. In November, there was a similar clash in Southwark between a pro-American petition and a loyal address: *Public Advertiser*, 10, 13 Nov., 4 Dec. 1775.

3 *London Evening Post*, 5–7 Oct. 1775.

4 *London Gazette*, 24–28 Oct. 1775; *Public Advertiser*, 7 Oct. 1775.

5 Appendix B, table 3.

6 Ibid. It seems that during wartime credit became so restricted that government was not in a position to choose its creditors on political grounds. It has been shown, for example, that loans in wartime had to be raised without regard to questions of parliamentary patronage: Lewis Namier, *The Structure of Politics at the Accession of George III*, 2d ed. (London: Macmillan 1957), 47–8, and I.R. Christie, *The End of North's Ministry, 1780–1782* (London: Macmillan 1958), 182–3.

7 Appendix B, table 2; A.H. John, "Insurance Investment and the London Money Market of the Eighteenth Century," *Economica*, new ser., 20 (1953): 137–58. Over 10 per cent of the loans of 1780 and 1781 were subscribed by the directors of moneyed companies: [Almon's] *Parliamentary Register* 17: 416–23, and *The Remembrancer* 11: 240–51.

8 Appendix B, table 3; Appendix C.

9 Appendix C. The figure 263 excludes company directors who had no (ascertainable) personal links with the administration.

10 Appendix A; T 1/518, fol. 130, Public Record Office.

11 Appendix A; Appendix B, table 2; Sutherland, *East India Company*, 109, 228, 241, 347.

12 Appendix A; Appendix B, table 1.

13 Yearly Meeting Minute Book, 15 (1774–7): 61, Friends' Library.

14 11 Oct. 1775, Dartmouth Papers, D(W) 1778/II/1560. Fifteen of the petitioners, or their heirs, pressed the British government to settle their debt claims in 1790. Many claims had been settled before this. Katharine A. Kellock, "London Merchants and the pre-1776 American Debts," *Guildhall Studies in London History* 1: (1974): 116–49.

15 Appendix A; Appendix B, table 1; Appendix D; see above, 109–12.

16 Appendix B, table 1; Appendix C.

17 Appendix B, table 1; Clark, *British Opinion*, 100–2; *The West India Merchant: being a series of papers originally printed under that signature in the London Evening Post* (London 1778); Robert Greenhalgh Albion, *Forests and Sea Power: The Timber Problem of the Royal Navy, 1652–1862* (Cambridge, Mass: Harvard University Press 1926), 284–9; Kustaa Hautala, *European and American Tar in the English Market during the Eighteenth and Early Nineteenth Centuries* (Helsinki: Suomalainen tiedeakatemia 1963), 105–7.

18 William Bailey, *List of Bankrupts, Dividends and Certificates, from the Year 1772, to 1793*, 2 vols. (London 1794); *London Evening Post*, 14–17 Oct. 1775; *London Gazette*, 10–14, 24–28 Oct. 1775.

19 Appendix A; Appendix C; D.M. Joslin, "London Bankers in Wartime, 1739–84," in L.S. Pressnell, ed., *Studies in the Industrial Revolution presented to T.S. Ashton* (London: Athlone Press 1960), 173–4. The special circumstances relating to Sayre's bankruptcy are described above, 101.

20 Appendix B, table 5; Appendix A.

21 Rudé, "Anti-Wilkite Merchants of 1769," *Guildhall Miscellany* 2 (1965): 283–304; *London Gazette*, 10–14, 24–28 Oct. 1775; Appendix C; Appendix A.

22 Baker, *Government and Contractors*, 218–21.

23 *London Evening Post*, 18–21 May, 22–24 Aug., 14–17 Sept. 1776.

24 Baker, *Government and Contractors*, 221–3.

25 *Annual Register*, 1778, History of Europe, 35–6, 81–2.

26 Ibid., 82; *Public Advertiser*, 25 Oct. 1776; Intelligence Extraordinary, *London Evening Post*, 17–19 Dec. 1776; *Morning Chronicle*, 12 Oct. 1776.

27 *London Evening Post*, 28 Feb.–2 March, 2–4 July 1776.

28 Lee to Wilkes, 29 Nov. 1779, Add. MSS 30872, fol. 132; Granville Sharp Papers, box 28 (a) "D", Hardwicke Court MSS, Gloucestershire Record Office, Gloucester; Burke to Lord Rockingham, [22,] 23 Aug. 1775, Copeland et al., eds., *Burke Correspondence* 3: 191.

29 Nicholas Rogers, "Aristocratic Clientage, Trade and Independency: Popular Politics in Pre-Radical Westminster," *Past and Present*, no. 61 (Nov. 1973): 70-106.

30 Lord North to George III, 6 Oct. 1775, W.T. Laprade, ed., *Parliamentary Papers of John Robinson*, Publications of the Camden Society, 3d ser., 33 (London 1922), 45; [Draft], John Robinson to the king, 13 Sept. 1780, and Charles Jenkinson to Robinson, 14 Sept. 1780, MS Facsimiles, 340-1, fols. 171-2, British Library.

31 Baker, *Government and Contractors*; David Syrett, *Shipping and the American War, 1775-83* (London: Athlone Press 1970).

32 Main Papers, 19, 29 April 1776, House of Lords Record Office; [Almon's] *Parliamentary Register* 4: 1-104; *London Evening Post*, 7-9, 11-14 May 1776; *Public Advertiser*, 10, 16 May 1776; *Annual Register*, 1776, History of Europe, 142-3.

33 Baker, *Government and Contractors*, 175-8, 201-3, 209-12.

34 T 1/518, fols. 118-34, and T 1/534, fols. 225-33; *A List of the Persons who have polled for Messieurs Wilkes and Townshend* (London 1772); Electoral Roll of the Livery, 1781, Guildhall Library MS 1583.

35 Appendix C; Electoral Roll of the Livery, 1781, Guildhall Library MS 1583. Wiggins, Sanders, and Crawshay were in receipt of their first contracts before October 1775; Ayres received his first contract in 1779. The career of Richard Crawshay, the founder of a dynasty of Welsh ironmasters, is a remarkable "rags-to-riches" story. Leaving his Leeds home at the age of sixteen, Crawshay arrived in London virtually penniless. Having sold his pony for £15, he obtained employment in a warehouse selling flat-irons. He eventually became sole proprietor of the establishment and rich. Later he invested in a newly established ironworks in South Wales where he became associated with Anthony Bacon; the two of them received contracts during the American war for casting cannon. The shift in Crawshay's political allegiances could well have been related to the rise of his business fortunes. It should be stressed, however, that his career is worthy of comment, not because it was characteristic, but rather because it was exceptional. *The Dictionary of Welsh Biography down to 1940* (London: Cymmrodorian Society 1959), 86; WO 47/89, fol. 734, Public Record Office.

36 See above, 11. On 12 Nov. 1768, Sylas Neville recorded in his diary that his friend, Timothy Hollis, "knows 4 or 5 only (his cousin [Thomas Hollis], Mr Strahan, Mr Brand, Mr Price, etc) who thinks as he does concerning the Americans." Cozens-Hardy, ed., *Neville Diary*, 51.

37 Appendix C; [Facsimile] Franklin to Strahan, Philadelphia, 5 July 1775, Vaux Papers, Historical Society of Pennsylvania. (It is likely that this letter was never actually sent.)

38 Note the consistently anti-Wilkite theme in the "Correspondence between William Strahan and David Hall, 1763-1777," *Pennsylvania Magazine of History and Biography* 10, 11, 12 (1886-8).

39 wo 47/86-90; Add. mss 38208, fol. 34.

40 wo 47/86, fol. 327; wo 47/89, fol. 197; Adm. 20/278, Public Record Office; Adm. 20/281; Appendix D. Peter Perchard, who was elected to the Common Council for Candlewick Ward in 1777, received £1327.18.11½ for the hire of the ship "Snow Friends" (Add. mss 38208, fol. 24), but this transaction could hardly be construed as a regular contract.

41 Baker, *Government and Contractors*, 162, 212; T 1/518, fol. 133; *Royal Kalendar*, 1775, 74; Add. mss 37836, fols. 71, 77. Burfoot continued to play an active, though obscure, role in the electoral politics of the City after his retirement from the City corporation. See Burfoot to John Robinson, 30 Aug. 1781, and Lord North to Robinson, 1 Sept. 1781, ms Facsmilies, 340-2, fols. 242, 244, British Library. Note also the cases of Thomas Bromwich (an ex-Common Councilman of Farringdon Without Ward) and James Walton, who received his Ordnance contract for gunpowder in 1780, very shortly after retiring as Common Councilman for Cornhill Ward. Appendix C; Appendix D; wo 47/95, fols. 85, 155.

42 Cozens-Hardy, ed., *Neville Diary*, 3-4; Riggs, "Arthur Lee and the Radical Whigs," 99; John Jebb to Dr Chalmers, 16 July 1775, John Disney, ed., *The Works Theological, Medical, Political, and Miscellaneous of John Jebb, M.D., F.R.S., with Memoirs of the Life of the Author*, 3 vols. (London 1787), 1: 92; Richard Price to Charles Chauncey, "Price Letters," *MHS Procs*, 2d ser., 17 (1903): 278-81; "Lucius Junius Brutus," *London Evening Post*, 24-27 Aug. 1776; "Julian" to Lord G[eorge] G[ermain], *Public Advertiser*, 20 Nov. 1776.

43 E.g., Cone, *Torchbearer of Freedom*, 79-80.

44 *Observations on ... Civil Liberty*, 18, 78-87, 98-9.

45 Cone, *Torchbearer of Freedom*, 77-9, 88-9.

46 See his *Additional Observations on the nature and value of Civil Liberty, and the War with America*, 3d ed. (London 1777), and *Two Tracts on Civil Liberty, the War with America, and the debts and finances of the kingdom, with a general introduction and supplement* (London 1778).

47 *A Sermon Delivered to a Congregation of Protestant Dissenters at Hackney* (London 1779), 17.

48 Burgh, *Political Disquisitions* 2: 274-81; Cartwright, *A Letter to Edmund Burke, Esq.* (London 1775), 16.

49 *Wilkes's Speeches*, 66-7.

50 Ibid., 66; Christie, *Wilkes, Wyvill and Reform*, 63–7.

51 28 Jan. 1775, John Dickinson Papers, 359.

52 Priestley to Rev. T. Lindsey, 8 July 1776, Rutt, *Life and Correspondence of Joseph Priestley* 1: 291–2; Price, *Observations on ... Civil Liberty*, 59–60.

53 Cozens-Hardy, ed., *Neville Diary*, 244–5.

54 "Old Officer" to Lord G[eorge] G[ermain], *Public Advertiser*, 11 May 1776.

55 This is what Major Cartwright had argued for in his rather misleadingly titled *American Independence: The Interest and Glory of Great Britain* (1774). See also Granville Sharp, *A Declaration of the People's Natural Right to a Share in the Legislature*. It has been pointed out in Bonwick, *English Radicals*, 97, that the central purpose of Price's *Observations on ... Civil Liberty* was to promote reconciliation of Britain and America on a federal basis.

56 Sharp, *People's Natural Right*, 21; Cartwright, *American Independence*, new ed. (London 1775), 13.

57 JCC, 66 (1773–6): 300; [Almon's] *Parliamentary Register*, 4: 107.

58 Major Cartwright, *Take Your Choice!* (London 1776), 43; Granville Sharp Papers, box 21 (b), parcel 5 (i, Letters, Political); Hoare, *Memoirs of Granville Sharp* 1: 261–6.

59 Granville Sharp Papers, Diary, vol. G, 58.

60 *The Crisis*, no. 84 (24 Aug. 1776), published the Declaration of Independence in full, prefaced by this statement: "The following is the Declaration of INDEPENDENCE of the BRAVE, FREE, and VIRTUOUS Americans, against the most dastardly, slavish, and vicious TYRANT, that ever disgraced a Nation." See also an advertisement for a forthcoming political paper (the first issue to appear on 9 Nov. 1776), entitled "The Fall of Britain," which expresses strongly antimonarchical sentiments. Dartmouth Papers, D(W) 1778/II/1711.

61 *Wilkes's Speeches*, 89, 186; Price, *Additional Observations*. See also a letter from "Brutus," *London Evening Post*, 11–13 June 1776.

62 [Almon's] *Parliamentary Register* 3: 359–60.

63 Douglas et al., eds., *English Historical Documents* 9: 851.

64 Benjamin W. Labaree, "The Idea of American Independence: The British View, 1774–1776," *MHS Procs* (1969): 3–20; [James Macpherson], *The Rights of Great Britain asserted against the claims of America*, 4th ed. (London 1776); John Wesley, *Some Observations on Liberty occasioned by a late tract* (Edinburgh 1776).

65 Curwen to Dr Charles Russell, 10 June 1776, G.A. Ward, ed., *Journals and Letters of Samuel Curwen* (London 1842), 59; Walpole to Franklin, 1 Feb. 1777, Franklin Papers, 5, fol. 47, American Philosophical Society, Philadelphia.

66 E.g., Hutchinson, *The History of ... Massachusetts Bay* 3: 261; Adair and Schutz, eds., *Peter Oliver's Origin and Progress of the American Revolution*, 78, which states that Wilkes trained the colonists "in the way they should not have gone," although the Americans "having outdone *his* Outdoings" by establishing independence, "piqued his Pride as a *Briton*."

67 Labaree, "The Idea of American Independence," *MHS Procs*, 81 (1969): 9-10.

68 Steuart, ed., *Walpole's Last Journals* 1: 515.

69 *The Patriot* (London 1774), 22.

70 J.H. Plumb, "British Attitudes to the American Revolution," *In the Light of History* (London: Allen Lane The Penguin Press 1972), 78-86.

71 *Public Advertiser*, 11 Oct. 1776; Lutnick, *American Revolution and the British Press*, 77; Ritcheson, *British Politics and the American Revolution*, 229, 232-3; Sir George Savile to Lord Rockingham, 15 Jan. 1777, Albemarle, ed., *Rockingham Memoirs* 2: 305.

72 Newspaper clipping, Noble Collection, c. 78 (Hallifax), Guildhall Lib.

73 *London Evening Post*, 1-3 May 1777.

74 Ibid., 29 Sept.-1 Oct. 1777.

75 See the advertisement on behalf of the Associated Livery in *New Morning Post*, 14 Dec. 1776.

76 The figures are based on Appendix D. Common Councilmen who left the court only to rejoin it as aldermen are not included in this computation.

77 JCC, 66 (1773-6): 296; *Gazetteer*, 15 March 1776; *City Addresses*, 46.

78 JCC, 66 (1773-6), 296, 299-300, 354. The Drapers also admitted Price to the freedom of their Company. Rev. Arthur H. Johnson, *The History of the Worshipful Company of the Drapers of London*, 4 vols. (Oxford: Clarendon Press 1914-22), 3: 363n1.

79 Dr William King, *An Essay on Civil Government ... to which is added a Remonstrance with the Court of Common Council* [by Dr Samuel Johnson] (London 1776), 13-52; letter from "An Englishman," *Public Advertiser*, 9 May 1776.

80 *Lloyd's Evening Post*, 13-15 March 1776; letter to William Saxby from "A Liveryman," *Gazetteer*, 3 April 1776.

81 JCC, 67 (1776-9): 42; *Wilkes's Speeches*, 97.

82 "On the Practice of Pressing," 27 Oct. 1770, by "A captain in the Royal Navy," reprinted in *Public Advertiser*, 11 Dec. 1776; *Annual Register*, 1770, Chronicle, 163; ibid., 1771, History of Europe, 16.

83 JCC, 67 (1776-9): 13.

84 *London Evening Post*, 23-25 Jan. 1777.

85 Christopher Lloyd, *The British Seaman* (London: Collins 1968), 147; Adm. 1/5117, fol. 241; *London Evening Post*, 29-31 Oct. 1776.

86 Adm. 7/299, fol. 342; *London Evening Post*, 29-31 Oct. 1776.

87 *Wilkes's Speeches*, 83-4.

88 *London Evening Post*, 31 Oct.-2 Nov. 1776.

89 Adm. 1/5117, fols. 363, 379; *Annual Register*, 1770, Appendix to Chronicle, 225.

90 Adm. 1/5117, fol. 379.

91 JCC, 67 (1776-9), 160; *London Evening Post*, 7-10 March, 29 Sept.-1 Oct., 19-21 Nov. 1778.

92 Newspaper clipping, Noble Collection, C. 78 (Hallifax).

93 Granville Papers, PRO 30/29/3, bundle 6, fol. 552, Public Record Office; *London Evening Post*, 23-26, 26-28 Nov., 10-12 Dec. 1776.

94 *London Evening Post*, 7-10, 10-12 Dec. 1776, 21-23 Jan. 1778; JCC, 67 (1776-9): 13.

95 Woods, "City of London and Impressment," *Proceedings of the Leeds Philosophical and Literary Society* 8: 113-14; JCC, 67 (1776-9): 12-13; Repertory [of Aldermanic Bench], 181 (1776-7): 21-2, Corporation of London Record Office; Adm. 7/299, fol. 243.

96 JCC, 67 (1776-9), 13; Minute Papers of Committee appointed to obtain a habeas corpus for John Tubbs, 22 Nov. 1776-15 Jan. 1777, Misc. MS 114-3, Corporation of London Record Office.

97 Woods, "City of London and Impressment," 114-5; JCC, 67 (1776-9): 120-1; Lloyd, *British Seaman*, 143-4.

98 *London Evening Post*, 14-17, 17-19 Dec. 1776; Woods, "City of London and Impressment," 116.

99 Oglethorpe to Sharp, [n.d.], Granville Sharp Papers, box 28 (a), "C".

100 Woods, "City of London and Impressment," 116.

101 JCC, 67 (1776-9), 43, 121.

102 Granville Sharp Papers, Diary, vol. G, 60.

103 Woods, "City of London and Impressment," 118-9; JCC, 67 (1776-9): 121.

104 JCC, 67 (1776-9), 121.

105 Ibid., 121-2; Woods, "City of London and Impressment," 117.

106 For example, it was reported that Joseph Knight was released by the captain of a naval tender for receiving pressed men, specifically because he was a liveryman. *London Evening Post*, 27-30 Sept. 1777. See also the statement by Capt. Lloyd, before the City aldermen, that "he should pay respect to the copy of a man's freedom." Ibid., 14-17 Dec. 1776.

107 *Annual Register*, 1777, History of Europe, 28; *London Evening Post*, 6-8, 17-19 March, 2-5 May 1778.

108 *London Evening Post*, 29-31 Oct., 28-31 Dec. 1776, 4-6 March, 1-3 May 1777.

109 *Annual Register*, 1778, History of Europe, 81–3; *London Evening Post*, 6–8 Jan. 1778; JCC, 67 (1776–9): 107.

110 *London Evening Post*, 15–17 Jan. 1778; *Annual Register*, 1778, History of Europe, 83–5; JCC, 67 (1776–9): 107.

111 King to Lord North, 17 Jan. 1778, Fortescue, ed., *Correspondence of George III* 4: 20.

112 *Annual Register*, 1778, History of Europe, 85.

113 *Wilkes's Speeches*, 233; [Almon's] *Parliamentary Register* 10: 181–6.

114 *Public Advertiser*, 25 Oct. 1775, 18 Jan. 1776. A number of individual livery companies contributed to the fund. Prideaux, *Goldsmiths* 2: 263–4; William Meade Williams, ed., *Annals of the Worshipful Company of Founders* (London 1867), 158; J.S. Watson, *A History of the Salters' Company* (London: Oxford University Press 1963), 111.

115 *London Evening Post*, 6–9, 16–18, 23–25 Jan. 1776; letter from "An Old Officer," *Public Advertiser*, 22 Feb. 1776. On the circumstances of Allen's incarceration, see Charles A. Jellison, *Ethan Allen: Frontier Rebel* (Syracuse, NY: Syracuse University Press 1969), 162–3.

116 *Gazetteer*, 13 Aug. 1776; letters from "Plain Truth" and James Hodge, ibid., 14, 19 Aug. 1776; *Public Advertiser*, 16 Aug. 1776.

117 E.g., see two letters from "Humanitas," *London Evening Post*, 1–4 March, 9–11 Dec. 1777. The opposition MP, David Hartley, probably wrote these letters.

118 G.H. Guttridge, *David Hartley, M.P.: An Advocate of Conciliation, 1774–1783*, University of California Publications in History, 14, no. 3 (Berkeley, Calif. 1926), 275–6; editorial note, Copeland et al., eds., *Burke Correspondence* 3: 411; [Almon's] *Parliamentary Register* 10: 104–6; Baker to Lord Rockingham, 4 Jan. 1778, Wentworth-Woodhouse Muniments, R1–1756.

119 *London Evening Post*, 23–25 Dec. 1777; Appendix D.

120 Lord Rockingham to Lord Effingham, 25 Dec. 1777, Wentworth-Woodhouse Muniments, R1–1748; *London Evening Post*, 25–27 Dec. 1777, 8–10, 13–15 Jan., 5–7 May 1778.

121 Guttridge, *English Whiggism*, 97–105; Ritcheson, *British Politics and the American Revolution*, 244; J. Steven Watson, *The Reign of George III, 1760–1815* (Oxford: Clarendon Press 1968), 210–12.

122 *London Evening Post*, 19–21 Feb. 1777; Steuart, ed., *Walpole's Last Journals* 2: 119–20.

123 *London Evening Post*, 21–24 Feb. 1778. The quotation is from ibid., 24–26 Feb. 1778. The petition to the House of Commons was presented on 16 March. *Commons Journals* 36: 824–5.

124 JCC, 67 (1776–9), 126–7; *London Evening Post*, 3–5 March 1778. See also Steuart, ed., *Walpole's Last Journals* 2: 124–5.

CHAPTER SIX

1 Guttridge, *Hartley*, 257; David Hartley, *Substance of a Speech in Parliament upon the State of the Nation and the present Civil War with America* (London 1776); Richmond to Adair, 8 Sept. 1777, and Adair to Richmond, 11 Nov. 1777, Add. MSS 50829.

2 [Almon's] *Parliamentary Register* 8: 152.

3 Ibid., 10: 358–67; Ritcheson, *British Politics and the American Revolution*, 247–8.

4 Fitzmaurice, *Shelburne* 2: 10.

5 [Almon's] *Parliamentary Register* 10: 369–70; JCC, 67 (1776–9), 137–8, 148–50; Sharpe, *London and the Kingdom* 3: 170–1; Lutnick, *American Revolution and the British Press*, 129–31.

6 Walsh Atkins, "Shelburne and America," 261–2; Steuart, ed., *Walpole's Last Journals* 2: 161; Norris, *Shelburne*, 94.

7 Shelburne to Chatham [Dec. 1777?], and [Feb. 1778?], Chatham Papers, PRO 30/8/56, fols. 172–3; cf. Norris, *Shelburne*, 97–8.

8 Beaumarchais to the Comte de Vergennes, 12 Dec. 1777, Benjamin F. Stevens, ed., *Facsimiles of Manuscripts in European Archives Relating to America, 1773–83*, 25 vols. (London 1889–98), 20, no. 1770. Sawbridge was conferring with Old Whig leaders at this time. Ritcheson, *British Politics and the American Revolution*, 244.

9 Isaac Barré to Shelburne, [June?] 1779, Fitzmaurice, *Shelburne* 2: 34–5; Norris, *Shelburne*, 111.

10 Piers Mackesy, *The War for America, 1775–1783* (Cambridge, Mass.: Harvard University Press 1964), 171, 202–3; Namier and Brooke, *House of Commons* 3: 7–11; *London Evening Post*, 17–19 March 1778.

11 Mackesy, *War for America*, 209–11, 239–41; J.H. Broomfield, "The Keppel-Palliser Affair, 1778–1779," *Mariner's Mirror* 47 (1961): 195–203; Burke to Philip Francis, 24 Dec. 1778, Copeland et al., eds., *Burke Correspondence* 4: 34; Steuart, ed., *Walpole's Last Journals* 2: 237.

12 Broomfield, "The Keppel-Palliser Affair," *Mariner's Mirror* 47 (1961): 204–5; *Public Advertiser*, 13 Feb. 1779; *London Evening Post*, 11–13, 16–18 Feb. 1779; Steuart, ed., *Walpole's Last Journals* 2: 248; SP 37/13, fols. 261–2.

13 JCC, 67 (1776–9): 200.

14 Ibid., 209–11; Committees: Military and Naval Victories, Misc. MS 195.1, Corporation of London Record Office. The freedom of the City of London was not officially presented to Keppel until 16 Dec. 1779. JCC, 67 (1776–9): 329–31.

15 SP 37/13, fol. 262.

16 *Gazetteer*, 23 June 1779; *London Evening Post*, 22–24 June 1779; JCC, 67 (1776–9): 268.

17 JCC, 67 (1776–9), 268–9; *London Evening Post*, 19–22 June 1779.

18 *Gazetteer*, 23 June 1779; JCC, 67 (1776–9): 269.

19 *Gazetteer*, 30 June 1779; *London Evening Post*, 29 June –1 July 1779.

20 JCC, 67 (1776–9), 270–1. For the voting division, see Appendix D.

21 *A Short History of the Opposition during the Late Session of Parliament* (London 1779), 51.

22 *Public Advertiser*, 19, 28 July, 13, 18 Aug. 1779; *London Evening Post*, 29–31 July 1779.

23 George Hayley was included in the published list of committee members, but the public was later told that this was a mistake. *London Evening Post*, 17–19 Aug. 1779.

24 Notably, Herbert Butterfield, *George III, Lord North, and the People, 1779-80* (London: Bell 1949); Christie, *Wilkes, Wyvill and Reform*, 68–231; Eugene C. Black, *The Association: British Extraparliamentary Political Organization, 1769-1793* (Cambridge, Mass.: Harvard University Press 1963) 31–130.

25 Butterfield, *George III, Lord North* …, 209, 263; Bonwick, *English Radicals*, 141–2.

26 Butterfield, *George III, Lord North* …, 181–333; Christie, *Wilkes, Wyvill and Reform*, 68–153.

27 Curwen to Nathaniel Goodale, and Curwen to Judge Sewall, Ward, ed., *Letters of Samuel Curwen*, 35, 182–3.

28 *London Evening Post*, 6–9 March 1777; T.S. Ashton, *Economic Fluctuations in England, 1700-1800* (Oxford: Clarendon Press 1959), 62; George Chalmers, *An Estimate of the Comparative Strength of Great Britain*, new ed. (London 1794), 174; Phyllis Deane and W.A. Cole, *British Economic Growth, 1688-1959: Trends and Structure*, 2d ed. (Cambridge: Cambridge University Press 1967), 45–9.

29 SP 37/12, fols. 78, 87; Benjamin Franklin Papers, 74, fols. 26–7, American Philosophical Society.

30 Butterfield, *George III, Lord North* …, 24, 184; G.E. Mingay, *English Landed Society in the Eighteenth Century* (London: Routledge and Paul 1963), 261–2.

31 John Jebb to Christopher Wyvill, 27 Sept. 1781, Christopher Wyvill, ed., *Political Papers chiefly respecting the attempt of the County of York and other … districts commenced in 1779 … to effect a reformation of the Parliament of Great Britain*, 6 vols. (York 1794-1802), 4: 510–11; Bonwick, *English Radicals*, 110–11.

32 Wyvill, ed., *Political Papers* 1: 7.

33 *London Evening Post*, 6–8 Jan. 1780.

34 Ibid.; Wyvill, ed., *Political Papers* 1: 58–60; JCC, 67 (1776–9): 13.

35 Christie, *Wilkes, Wyvill and Reform*, 91; *London Evening Post*, 21–23 March 1780.

36 Wyvill, ed., *Political Papers* 1: 429.

37 Ibid., 148-9.

38 Ibid., 163; [Rev. Henry Zouch], *An English Freeholder's Address to his Countrymen* (London 1780); Black, *The Association*, 54-6.

39 Proceedings of Committee of Common Council for Corresponding with the Committees of the several Counties, Cities and Boroughs in the Kingdom, Misc. MS 115.6, Corporation of London Record Office; Christie, *Wilkes, Wyvill and Reform*, 107, 109-10.

40 JCC, 67 (1776-9), 331-3; Burke to William Rix, 6 March 1780, and Burke to James Townsend, 6 March 1780, and appended editorial notes, Copeland et al., eds., *Burke Correspondence* 4: 209-11.

41 JCC, 68 (1780-83): 46-7.

42 Butterfield, *George III, Lord North* ..., 222n1; Wyvill, ed., *Political Papers* 1: 90-3; *London Evening Post*, 1-3 Feb. 1780.

43 *London Evening Post*, 5-8 Feb. 1780; Christie, *Wilkes, Wyvill and Reform*, 108-9; Butterfield, *George III, Lord North* ..., 220-1, 227; Add. MSS 38593-4.

44 *London Evening Post*, 11-13 April 1780.

45 Ibid., 2-4 March 1780; JCC, 68 (1780-3): 61; Christopher Hibbert, *King Mob: The Story of Lord George Gordon and the Riots of 1780* (London: Longmans 1958), 43-4.

46 JCC, 68 (1780-3): 67.

47 Hibbert, *King Mob*, 58-61, 64-5; J. Gurney, ed., *The whole proceedings in the King's Commission of the Peace, Oyer and Terminer, and Gaol Delivery for the City of London ... held at Justice Hall in the Old Bailey, on Wednesday the 28th of June* (London 1780), 378-400.

48 Rudé, *Wilkes and Liberty*, 192; *St. James's Chronicle*, 10-13 June 1780; *London Evening Post*, 10-13 June 1780; Sharpe, *London and the Kingdom* 3: 192.

49 Hibbert, *King Mob*, 18, 38, 62; Postgate, *That Devil Wilkes*, 231, 252.

50 Black, *The Association*, 67; Steuart, ed., *Walpole's Last Journals* 2: 320.

51 Christie, *Wilkes, Wyvill and Reform*, 118-9; Christie, *End of North's Ministry*, 113-37; [Draft], John Robinson to the king, 13 Sept. 1780, MS Facsimiles, 340-1, fol. 171, British Library.

52 *London Evening Post*, 30 Aug.-1 Sept., 9-12 Sept. 1780; Steuart, ed., *Walpole's Last Journals* 2: 329.

53 *London Evening Post*, 8-11 July 1780.

54 JCC, 68 (1780-3): 70, 127-8; *St. James's Chronicle*, 15-17 March 1781.

55 Watson, *Reign of George III*, 214-15; Christie, *End of North's Ministry*, 231-66.

56 Douglas et al., eds., *English Historical Documents* 10: 220.

57 [Thomas Day], *A Second Address to the Public from the Society for*

Constitutional Information (London 1780), 11.

58 Quoted in Bonwick, *English Radicals*, 138. See also Butterfield, *George III, Lord North* ... , 351–2.

59 Douglas et al., eds., *English Historical Documents* 10: 220–2.

60 Christie, *Wilkes, Wyvill and Reform*, 136–7; Wyvill to F.F. Foljambe, 4 Jan. 1782, Wyvill, ed., *Political Papers* 4: 154–6; Common Hall Book, 8 (1751–88): 227–8; *St. James's Chronicle*, 6–8 Dec. 1781.

61 *St. James's Chronicle*, 8–11, 18–20 Dec. 1781; Jebb to Wyvill, 11 Dec. 1781, Wyvill, ed., *Political Papers* 4: 514–15, and ibid., 516–19.

62 *City Addresses*, 61–2.

63 Common Hall Book, 8 (1751–88): 229.

64 Christie, *End of North's Ministry*, 319–20.

65 JCC, 68 (1780–3), 217; *Commons Journals* 38: 860–1.

66 *Public Advertiser*, 2 March 1782.

67 Christie, *End of North's Ministry*, 352–69; Watson, *Reign of George III*, 242–4; Guttridge, *English Whiggism*, 135–7.

AFTERWORD

1 JCC, 68 (1780–3): 221; Adair to Rockingham, 9 April 1782, Wentworth-Woodhouse Muniments, R1–2038; *Public Advertiser*, 16, 31 May 1782.

2 JCC, 68 (1780–3): 239, 265–8.

3 Richard B. Morris, *The Peacemakers: The Great Powers and American Independence* (New York: Harper and Row 1965), 259–85, 351–2; Wyvill, ed., *Political Papers* 2: 159–81; Disney, ed., *Works of John Jebb* 3: 314–20; "The Memorial of the Merchants in behalf of themselves and others interested in the North American Trade previous to the year, 1776," 13 April 1782, Shelburne Papers, 87, fol. 177, Clements Lib.

4 JCC, 68 (1780–3): 273, 284, 293.

5 For the developing story, see A.J.P. Taylor, *The Trouble Makers: Dissent over Foreign Policy, 1792–1939* (London: Hamilton 1957).

6 This is not to say that the provinces lacked entirely the facilities for generating autonomous opposition to government. Recent studies have clearly shown otherwise. See, especially, Brewer, *Party Ideology*, 158–60, 174–80, and John Money, *Experience and Identity: Birmingham and the West Midlands* (Manchester: Manchester University Press 1977). Nonetheless, in the late eighteenth century there remained a considerable contrast between London and the provinces in terms of political awareness and opportunities for political expression.

7 "Notes respecting the London Corresponding Society," Add. MSS 27808, fols 113–14. See also Black, *The Association*, 28; Bonwick, *English Radicals*, 114–87, 216–66; and Arthur Sheps, "The American Revolution

and the transformation of English Republicanism," *Historical Reflec-tions/Reflexions Historiques* 2 (1975): 3–28.

APPENDIX A

1 W = Wilkes; T = Townsend; H = Hallifax; S = Skakespear.
2 A = Alderman; CC = Common Councilman; PDD = Protestant Dissenting Deputy. More detailed information on aldermen and Common Councilmen, for the period 1775–9, is contained in Appendix D.
3 The term is here used in its broadest sense, to cover West Indian merchants as well as planters.

APPENDIX B

1 I.e., Wilkes/Hallifax; Wilkes/Shakespear; Townsend/Hallifax; Townsend/Shakespear.

APPENDIX C

1 Company directors with no (ascertainable) personal links to the administration are not included in this table.
2 W = Wilkes; T = Townsend; H = Hallifax; S = Shakespear.
3 A = Alderman; CC = Common Councilman; PDD = Protestant Dissenting Deputy.

APPENDIX D

1 W = Wilkes; T = Townsend; H = Hallifax; S = Shakespear.
2 A = pro-American petitioner of 11 Oct. 1775; G = signer of progovernment address of 14 Oct. 1775; GL = signer of progovernment livery address of 20 Oct. 1775.
3 A = pro-American vote; G = progovernment vote. The same code is used for the other division lists.
4 List of majority only.
5 Erroneously listed under Goldsmiths in 1772 poll-book.
6 See also entry for Hart under Bridge Ward: Aldermen.
7 Elections to the Court took place in December each year.
8 Charles Aldridge is recorded in *Royal Kalendar*, 1777, as having joined the Court in December 1775, but he must have joined before as he voted in the 7 July 1775 division. *Gazetteer*, 11 July 1775.
9 See also entry for Pugh under Tower Ward: Aldermen.
10 Firm's signature on petition: Carey, [John] Moorey & Welch.
11 Firm's signature on petition: [Luke] Stavely & [Robert] Turner.

12 See also entry for Wright under Candlewick: Aldermen.
13 Firm's signature on petition: [Jn] Withers, Birch & Rivers.
14 Firm's signature on petition: [Edw.] Dowling, Brett & Hardingham.
15 See also entry for Sainsbury under Billingsgate Ward: Aldermen.
16 Firm's signature on petition: Atkins & [Robert] Wyatt.

Bibliography

PRIMARY SOURCES

Manuscript Material

Ann Arbor, Mich.: William L. Clements Library
  [John] Lee Papers
  Shelburne Papers
  Sydney Papers
  Wedderburn Papers
  Wilkes Manuscripts
Boston, Mass.: Boston Public Library
  Manuscripts
Boston: Massachusetts Historical Society
  Adams papers

Josiah Quincy, Jr, Papers
Boston: New England Historic Genealogical Society
  Hancock Manuscripts
Cambridge, Mass.: Houghton Library, Harvard
  Diary of Thomas Hollis
  Arthur Lee Papers
  Palfrey Family Papers
Gloucester, England: Gloucestershire Record Office
  Granville Sharp Papers (from Hardwicke Court, Gloucestershire)
Hertford, England: Hertfordshire County Record Office
  William Baker Manuscripts
London: British Library
  Additional Manuscripts:

20733	John Almon Correspondence
27808	Place Papers
30866, 30870-3, 30875, 30877, 30880-1, 30888, 30890-1	John Wilkes Papers
35427	Hardwicke Papers
37833-5	Correspondence of George III with John Robinson
37836	Accompts of John Robinson as Agent to George III
38208-11, 38343, 38374-5	Liverpool Papers
38593-4	Westminster Committee Papers
50829-30, 53808	Adair Papers

London: Corporation of London Record Office
  Common Hall Book
  Journals of Common Council
  Miscellaneous Manuscripts
  Repertory [of Aldermanic Bench]
London: Friends' Library
  Meeting for Sufferings, Minutes
  Yearly Meeting Minute Book
London: Guildhall Library
  Aldgate Ward, Wardmote Court Book, 1715-82
  Electoral Roll of the Livery, 1781
  Frame Work Knitters Company Admissions Book, 1724-84
  Minutes of the Protestant Dissenting Deputies
  Noble Collection
London: House of Lords Record Office
  Main Papers

London: Public Record Office

Admiralty Papers	Adm. 1/5117 (Miscellaneous Letters to Secretary's Department)
	Adm. 2/554 (Secretary's Out-Letters)
	Adm. 3/81-2 (Admiralty Minutes)
	Adm. 7/299 (Law Officers' Opinions)
	Adm. 20/273-91 (Victualling Board Accounts)
	Adm. 106/2593-606 (Navy Board Minutes)
	Adm. 112/162-8 (Contract Ledger)
Chatham Papers	PRO 30/8
Colonial Office Papers	CO 5/40 (Intercepted Letters)
	CO 5/115-7 (Petitions)
	CO 5/118 ("Dr. Franklin's Letters")
	CO 5/134 (Post Office)
	CO 5/249 (In-Letters Domestic, 1776-82)
	CO 5/251 (Out-Letters Domestic, 1776-80)
Granville Papers	PRO 30/29
State Papers, Domestic	SP 37/10-13
	SP 44/141
State Papers, Foreign	SP 78/299-300
Treasury Papers	T 1/518 (Miscellaneous)
	T 1/534 (Miscellaneous)
Treasury Solicitor's Papers	TS 11/24/62 (Prosecution of Parson Horne)
	TS 11/209/884 (Prosecution of printer of *The Crisis*)
	TS 11/1709/5378-90 (Prosecution of newspaper editors)
	TS 11/542/1758 (Case of Stephen Sayre)
War Office Papers	WO 47/86-96 (Minutes of Board of Ordnance)

London: University of London Library, Senate House
  Hewitt Papers
London: Dr. Williams's Library
  Theophilus Lindsey Manuscripts
  Minute Books of the Body of Protestant Dissenting Ministers of the Three Denominations in and about the Cities of London and Westminster
Maidstone, England: Kent Record Office
  Stanhope Manuscripts
New York: New York Public Library, Manuscripts Division
  Samuel Adams Papers
  Emmet Collection
Nottingham, England: University of Nottingham Library
  Portland Manuscripts

Oxford, England: Bodleian Library
  Richard Price Correspondence
Philadelphia, Pa.: American Philosophical Society
  Benjamin Franklin Papers
  Franklin Papers
Philadelphia: Historical Society of Pennsylvania
  John Dickinson Papers
  Pemberton Papers
  Vaux Papers
Sheffield, England: Sheffield City Library
  Wentworth-Woodhouse Muniments: Letters and Papers of Charles Watson-
    Wentworth, 2d marquess of Rockingham
Stafford, England: William Salt Library
  Letters and Papers of William Legge, 2d earl of Dartmouth
Facsimiles and Edited Microfilm of Manuscripts
  Hoffman, Paul P., ed. *Lee Family Papers, 1742–1795.* University of Virginia
    Microfilm. 6 reels. Charlottesville, Va., 1966. [Filmed from Lee Papers
    in Houghton Library; American Philosophical Society; and University
    of Virginia Library.]
  Robinson Papers in the possession of the marquess of Abergavenny: British
    Library Facsimiles, 340–1, 2.
  Stevens, Benjamin, F., ed., *Facsimiles of Manuscripts in European Archives
    Relating to America, 1773–83.* 25 vols. London 1889–98.

Printed Material

Official and Semi-Official Records, Calendars, Collections of Documents

*Addresses, Remonstrances, and Petitions to the Throne, presented from the
  Court of Aldermen, the Court of Common Council, and the Livery in
  Common Hall Assembled: Commencing the 28th October, 1760, with the
  answers thereto.* London 1865
[Almon, John, comp. and ed.]. *A Collection of ... Papers relative to the
  dispute between Great Britain and America: shewing the causes and
  progress of that misunderstanding from 1764 to 1775.* London 1777.
Bailey, William. *Lists of Bankrupts, Dividends and Certificates, from the
  Year 1772, to 1793.* 2 vols. London 1794.
Douglas, D.C. et al., eds., *English Historical Documents.* 12 vols. London:
  Eyre and Spottiswoode 1953–77. Vols. 9 and 10.
Force, Peter, ed. *American Archives,* 4th ser., 6 vols. Washington, D.C. 1837–
  46.
Further Proceedings on the Trial of John Horne, Esq. London 1777.

[Glover, Richard]. *The Evidence delivered on the petition presented by the West India Planters and Merchants to the House of Commons as it was introduc'd at the Bar and summ'd up by Mr. Glover.* London 1775.

Great Britain. Parliament. [Almon's] *Parliamentary Register.* 17 vols. London 1775-80.

- [Cobbett's] *Parliamentary History of England.* 36 Vols. London 1806-20. Vol. 16.

- [Debrett's] *History, Debates and Proceedings of both Houses of Parliament ... 1743 to ... 1774.* 7 vols. London 1792. Vols. 5-7.

- *Journals of the House of Commons.* Vols. 35-8.

- *Journals of the House of Lords.* Vols. 34-6.

Gurney, J. ed. *The whole proceedings in the King's Commission of the Peace, Oyer and Terminer, and Gaol Delivery for the City of London ... held at Justice Hall in the Old Bailey, on Wednesday the 28th of June.* London 1780.

Historical Manuscripts Commission. *11th Report, Appendix, Part 5. The Manuscripts of the Earl of Dartmouth.* Vol. 1. Edited by W.O. Hewlett. London 1887.

- *14th Report, Appendix, Part 10. The Manuscripts of the Earl of Dartmouth.* Vol. 2. Edited by B.F. Stevens, London 1895.

- *15th Report, Appendix, Part I. The Manuscripts of the Earl of Dartmouth.* Vol. 3. Edited by W. Page. London 1896.

- *15th Report, Appendix, Part 4. The Manuscripts of the Earl of Carlisle, Preserved at Castle Howard.* Edited by R.E.G. Kirk. London 1897.

- *Report on Manuscripts in Various Collections.* Vol. 6. *The Manuscripts of Captain Howard Vicente Knox.* Edited by S.C. Lomas. Dublin 1909.

- *Report on the Manuscripts of Mrs. Stopford-Sackville, of Drayton House, Northamptonshire.* Vol. 2. Edited by S.C. Lomas. London 1910.

Howell, Thomas B., ed. *A Complete Collection of State Trials.* 33 vols. London 1809-26. Vol. 20.

A List of the Persons who have polled for Messieurs Wilkes and Townsend. London 1772.

Phillips, Henry L., ed. *Annals of the Worshipful Company of Joiners.* London 1915.

Prideaux, Walter P. *Memorials of the Goldsmiths' Company.* 2 vols. London 1896-7.

Roberts, Richard A., ed. *Calendar of Home Office Papers of the Reign of George III, 1773-1775, preserved in the Public Record Office.* London 1899.

Schumpeter, Elizabeth B. *English Overseas Trade Statistics, 1697-1808.* Oxford: Clarendon Press 1960.

The Trial (at large) of John Horne, Esq. ... for a Libel. London 1777.

Wharton, Francis, ed. *The Revolutionary Diplomatic Correspondence of the United States.* 6 vols. Washington, DC 1889.

Williams, William Meade, ed. *Annals of the Worshipful Company of Founders.* London 1867.

Wyvill, Christopher, ed. *Political Papers chiefly respecting the attempt of the County of York and other ... districts commenced in 1779 ... to effect a reformation of the Parliament of Great Britain.* 6 vols. York 1794–1802.

Correspondence, Memoirs, Diaries, Contemporary Histories, Collected Works, and Speeches

Adair, Douglass and Schutz, J.A., eds. *Peter Oliver's Origin and Progress of the American Revolution: A Tory View.* San Marino, Calif.: Huntingdon Library 1961.

Albemarle, George, earl of, ed. *Memoirs of the Marquis of Rockingham and His Contemporaries.* 2 vols. London 1852.

Almon, John, ed. *The Correspondence of the late John Wilkes with his friends printed from the original manuscripts in which are introduced memoirs of his life.* 5 vols. London 1805.

– *Memoirs of John Almon: Bookseller of Piccadilly.* London 1790.

Anson, Sir William R., ed. *Autobiography and Political Correspondence of Augustus, Third Duke of Grafton, K.G.* London 1898.

Ballagh, James C., ed. *The Letters of Richard Henry Lee.* 2 vols. New York: Macmillan 1911–14.

Belsham, Thomas. *Memoirs of ... Theophilus Lindsey, M.A.* London 1812.

Bigelow, John, ed. *The Complete Works of Benjamin Franklin.* 10 vols. New York 1887.

Blackburne, Francis. *The Archdeacon of Cleveland: The Works, Theological and Miscellaneous of Francis Blackburne ... with some Account of the Life and Writings of the Author by Himself, completed by his son, Francis Blackburne.* 7 vols. Cambridge 1805.

[–] *Memoirs of Thomas Hollis, Esq. F.R.S. and A.S.* 2 vols. London 1780.

"The Bowdoin and Temple Papers." *Collections of the Massachusetts Historical Society,* 6th ser., 9 (1897).

Butterfield, L.H., ed. *Letters of Benjamin Rush.* Vol. 1. *1761–1792.* Princeton, NJ: Princeton University Press 1951.

Cartwright, F.D., ed. *The Life and Correspondence of Major Cartwright.* 2 vols. London 1826.

Chalmers, George. *An Estimate of the Comparative Strength of Great Britain.* New ed. London 1794.

City Biography. 2d ed. London 1800.

Clifford, James L., ed. *Dr. Campbell's Diary of a Visit to England in 1775.* Cambridge: Cambridge University Press 1947.

Copeland, Thomas W. et al., eds. *The Correspondence of Edmund Burke.* 10 vols. Cambridge: Cambridge University Press; Chicago: University of Chicago Press 1958–78.

Corner, Betsy C. and Booth, Christopher C., eds. *Chain of Friendship: Selected Letters of Dr. John Fothergill, 1735–1780.* Cambridge, Mass.: Belknap Press of Harvard University Press 1971.

Cozens-Hardy, Basil, ed. *The Diary of Sylas Neville, 1767–1788.* London: Oxford University Press 1950.

Crane, Verner W., ed. *Benjamin Franklin's Letters to the Press.* Chapel Hill, NC: University of North Carolina Press 1950.

[Crosby, Brass.] *Memoir of Brass Crosby, Esq. Alderman of the City of London and Lord Mayor, 1770–1771.* London, 1829.

Curran, William Henry. *The Life of the Right Honourable John Philpott Curran.* 2d ed. 2 vols. Edinburgh 1822.

Cushing, Harry A., ed. *The Writings of Samuel Adams.* 4 vols. New York: Putnam's 1904–8.

Dexter, Franklin Bowditch, ed. *The Literary Diary of Ezra Stiles, D.D., Ll.D., January 1, 1769–March 13, 1776.* New York: Scribner's 1901.

Disney, John. *Memoirs of Thomas Brand-Hollis, Esq. F.R.S. and A.S.* London 1808.

– ed. *The Works Theological, Medical, Political, and Miscellaneous of John Jebb, M.D., F.R.S., with Memoirs of the Life of the Author.* 3 vols. London 1787.

Elsey, G.M., ed. "John Wilkes and William Palfrey." *Publications (Transactions) of the Colonial Society of Massachusetts* 34 (1937–42).

English Liberty: being a collection of interesting tracts from the year 1762 to 1769, containing the private correspondence, public letters, speeches, and addresses of John Wilkes, Esq. London n.d. [with MS additions, Guildhall Library, London].

Fitzmaurice, Lord Edmond. *Life of William, Earl of Shelburne, afterwards first Marquess of Lansdowne.* 2d ed. 2 vols. London: Macmillan 1912.

Foner, Philip S., ed. *The Complete Writings of Thomas Paine.* 2 vols. New York: The Citadel Press 1945.

Ford, Worthington C., ed. *The Letters of William Lee, Sheriff and Alderman of London, 1766–1783.* 3 vols. New York 1891.

– ed. "John Wilkes and Boston." *Proceedings of the Massachusetts Historical Society* 47 (1913–14).

Fortescue, Sir John, ed. *The Correspondence of George III, from 1760 to 1783.* 6 vols. London 1927–8.

Guttridge, G.H., ed. *The American Correspondence of a Bristol Merchant: 1766–1776: Letters of Richard Champion.* University of California Publications in History, 22, no. 1. Berkeley, Calif. 1934.

Hervey, Lord John. *Some Materials towards Memoirs of the Reign of George II.* Edited by Romney Sedgwick. 3 vols. London: Eyre and Spottiswoode 1931.

Hoare, Prince. *Memoirs of Granville Sharp.* 2d ed. London 1828.

Hutchinson, Peter O., ed. *The Diary and Letters of his Excellency Thomas Hutchinson.* 2 vols. London 1883-6.

Hutchinson, Thomas. *The History of the Colony and Province of Massachusetts Bay.* Edited by L.S. Mayo. 3 vols. Cambridge, Mass.: Harvard University Press 1936.

[Johnson, W.S.] "Letters of William Samuel Johnson to the Governors of Connecticut." *Collections of the Massachusetts Historical Society*, 5th ser., 9 (1885).

Jucker, Ninetta S., ed. *The Jenkinson Papers, 1760-1766.* London: Macmillan 1949.

Knollenberg, Bernhard, ed. "Hollis-Mayhew Correspondence," *Proceedings of the Massachusetts Historical Society* 69 (1956).

Labaree, Leonard W. et al., eds. *The Papers of Benjamin Franklin.* In progress. New Haven, Conn.: Yale University Press 1959-.

Laprade, W.T., ed. *Parliamentary Papers of John Robinson.* Publications of the Camden Society, 3d ser., 33. London 1922.

Lee, Richard H. *Life of Arthur Lee.* 2 vols. Boston 1829.

Lewis, Wilmarth S., gen. ed. *The Yale Edition of Horace Walpole's Correspondence.* 48 vols. New Haven, Conn.: Yale University Press 1937-83.

"London Merchants on the Stamp Act Repeal." *Proceedings of the Massachusetts Historical Society* 55 (1923).

Macaulay, Catharine. *The History of England from the Accession of James I to that of the Brunswick Line.* 8 vols. London 1763-83.

Mason, Frances Norton, ed. *John Norton and Sons, Merchants of London and Virginia.* 2d ed. New York: A.M. Kelley 1968.

Matthews, A., ed. "Letters of Dennys De Berdt, 1757-70." *Publications (Transactions) of the Colonial Society of Massachusetts* 13 (1910-11).

Morgan, William. *Memoirs of the Life of the Rev. Richard Price, D.D., F.R.S.* London 1815.

Olson, Alison G. *The Radical Duke: Career and Correspondence of Charles Lennox, third Duke of Richmond.* London: Oxford University Press 1961.

Oliver, Andrew, ed. *The Journal of Samuel Curwen, Loyalist.* 2 vols. Cambridge, Mass.: Harvard University Press 1972.

Pottle, Frederick A., ed. *Boswell's London Journal, 1762-1763.* New York: McGraw-Hill 1950.

"Price, [Richard], Letters." *Proceedings of the Massachusetts Historical Society*, 2d ser., 17 (1903).

[Quincy, Jr, Josiah.] "English Journal of Josiah Quincy, Jr., 1774-1775." *Proceedings of the Massachusetts Historical Society* 50 (1917).

Ross, J.E., ed. *Radical Adventurer: The Diaries of Robert Morris, 1772–1774*. Bath: Adams and Dart 1971.

Russell, Lord John, ed. *Memorials and Correspondence of Charles James Fox*. 4 vols. London 1853–57.

Rutt, John T. *Life and Correspondence of Joseph Priestley, LL.D., F.R.S.* 2 vols. London 1831–2.

– ed. *The Theological and Miscellaneous Works of Joseph Priestley*. 25 vols. London 1817–32.

Smith, William J., ed. *The Grenville Papers: Being the Correspondence of Richard Grenville, Earl Temple, K.G., and the Right Hon. George Grenville, Their Friends and Contemporaries*. 4 vols. London 1852–3.

Somerville, Thomas. *My Own Life and Times*. Edinburgh 1861.

Stephens, Alexander. *Memoirs of John Horne Tooke*. 2 vols. London 1813.

Steuart, A.F., ed. *The Last Journals of Horace Walpole during the reign of George III*, with notes by Dr. Doran. 2 vols. London: J. Lane 1910.

[Strahan, William.] "Correspondence between William Strahan and David Hall, 1763–1777." *Pennsylvania Magazine of History and Biography* 10–12 (1886–8).

Taylor, W.S., and Pringle, J.H., eds. *Correspondence of William Pitt, Earl of Chatham*. 4 vols. London 1838–40.

Toynbee, Paget, ed. *The Letters of Horace Walpole, fourth Earl of Orford*. 26 vols. Oxford: Clarendon Press 1903–25.

Wade, J., ed. *Letters of Junius*. 2 vols. London 1850–5.

Walpole, Horace. *Memoirs of the Reign of George III*, ed. G.F. Russell Barker. 4 vols. London 1894.

Ward, George Atkinson, ed. *Journals and Letters of Samuel Curwen*. London 1842.

"Warren-Adams Letters." Vol. 1, 1743–77. *Collections of the Massachusetts Historical Society* 72 (1917).

Wheatley, H.B., ed. *The Historical and Posthumous Memoirs of Sir Nathaniel Wraxall*. 5 vols. London 1884.

White, Philip L., ed. *The Beekman Mercantile Papers, 1746–1799*. 3 vols. New York: New York Historical Society 1956.

[Wilkes, John.] *The Controversial Letters of John Wilkes, Esq.: the Rev. John Horne, and their principal adherents*. London 1771.

[–] *Letters . . . of John Wilkes . . . to his daughter*. 4 vols. London 1804.

[–] *The Speeches of Mr. W[ilkes] in the House of Commons*. London 1786.

Yorke, Philip C., ed. *The Diary of John Baker*. London: Hutchinson 1931.

Pamphlets and Pamphlet Collections

Almon, John, comp. *A Collection of Tracts on the Subjects of Taxing the British Colonies in America, and regulating their Trade*. 4 vols. London 1773.

An Apology for the Ministerial Life and Actions of a Celebrated Favourite. London 1766.

[Bacon, Anthony.] *A Short Address to the Government, the Merchants, Manufacturers, and the Colonists in America and the Sugar Islands, on the present state of affairs.* London 1775.

Bailyn, Bernard, ed. *Pamphlets of the American Revolution.* Vol. 1. Cambridge, Mass.: Belknap Press of Harvard University Press 1965.

[Bernard, Sir Robert?] *An Appeal to the Public; Stating and Considering the Objections to the Quebec Bill Inscribed and Dedicated to the Patriotic Society of The Bill of Rights.* London 1774.

Bertie, Willoughby, 4th earl of Abingdon. *Thoughts on the Letter of Edmund Burke, Esq.; to the Sheriffs of Bristol on the Affairs of America.* Oxford 1777.

[Blackburne, Francis, ed.] *A Collection of Letters and Essays in Favour of Public Liberty, first published in the News-papers in the Years 1764, 65, 66, 67, 68, 69, and 1770. By an Amicable Band of Wellwishers to the Religious and Civil Rights of Mankind.* 3 vols. London 1774.

[Burgh, James.] *Political Disquisitions.* 3 vols. London 1774-5.

Cartwright, John. *American Independence: The Interest and Glory of Great Britain,* new ed. London 1775.

- *A Letter to Edmund Burke, Esq.* London 1775.

- *A Letter to the Earl of Abingdon.* London 1778.

- *Take your Choice!* London 1776.

The Case stated, on philosophical ground, between Great Britain and her Colonies. London 1777.

City Elections, 1768-96: A Collection of Broadsheets in the Guildhall Library.

The Conduct of the Administration with regard to the Colonies. London 1776.

Day, Thomas. *Reflexions upon the Present State of England, and the Independence of America.* London 1782.

[-] *A Second Address to the Public from the Society for Constitutional Information.* London 1780.

Estwick, Samuel. *A Letter to Josiah Tucker . . .* London 1776.

Free Thoughts on the Continuance of the American War. London 1781.

Hampden [pseud.] *A Vindication of the Petition of the Livery of the City of London to his Majesty, as to the charge upon the ministry of raising a revenue in our colonies by prerogative.* London 1769.

[Hampson, Rev. John.] *Reflections on the present state of the American war.* London 1776.

Hartley, David. *Substance of a speech in Parliament upon the State of the Nation and the present Civil War with America.* London 1776.

[Hollis, Thomas, comp.] *The true sentiments of America contained in a collection of letters sent from the House of Representatives of the Province of Massachusetts Bay to several persons of high rank in this kingdom* ... London 1768.

[Horne, John.] *An Oration delivered by the Rev. Mr. Horne at a numerous meeting of the Freeholders of Middlesex, assembled at Mile-end assembly-room, March 30, 1770.* London 1770.

The Independent Freeholder's Letter to the People of England, upon the one thing needful at this final crisis. [London 1775?]

[Jebb, John.] *An Address to the Freeholders of Middlesex, assembled at Free-Masons Tavern ... the 20th of December 1779.* London 1779.

Joel, Thomas. *Poems with Letters Moral and Political in Prose.* 2d ed. London 1775.

Johnson, Samuel. *The Patriot.* London 1774.

[-] *Taxation no Tyranny; an answer to the Resolutions and Address of the American Congress.* London 1775.

King, Dr. William. *An Essay on Civil Government ... to which is added a Remonstrance with the Court of Common Council* [by Samuel Johnson]. London 1776.

[Knox, William.] *The Interest of the Merchants and Manufacturers, in the Present Contest with The colonies, stated and considered.* London 1774.

[Lee, Arthur.] *An Appeal to the Justice and Interests of the People of Great Britain in the present dispute with America. By an Old member of Parliament.* 2d ed. London 1775.

- *A Second Appeal to the Justice and Interests of the People, on the Measures respecting America.* London 1775.

- *A Speech intended to have been delivered in the House of Commons, in support of the petition from the General Congress at Philadelphia ...* London 1775.

A Letter to the Common Council of London, on their late extraordinary address. London 1765.

Macaulay, Catharine. *An Address to the People of England, Scotland, and Ireland on the present Important Crisis of Affairs.* Bath 1775.

- *Observations on a Pamphlet, Entitled Thoughts on the Cause of the Present Discontents.* London 1770.

[Macpherson, James.] *The Rights of Great Britain asserted against the claims of America.* 4th ed. London 1776.

Molesworth, Lord Viscount. *The Principles of a Real Whig; contained in a preface to the famous Hotoman's Franco-Gallia, and now reprinted at the request of the London Association to which are added their Resolutions and Circular Letter.* London 1775.

[Paine, Thomas.] *Common Sense*, and [Chalmers, James.] *Plain Truth.* Both published Philadelphia 1776; reprinted together, London 1776, prefaced with explanatory advertisement.

Price, Richard. *Additional Observations on the nature and value of Civil Liberty, and the War with America.* 3d ed. London 1777.

- *Observations on the Importance of the American Revolution, and the means of making it a benefit to the world.* London 1784.

- *Observations on the Nature of Civil Liberty, the Principles of Government, and the Justice and Policy of War with America.* London 1776.

- *A Sermon Delivered to a Congregation of Protestant Dissenters at Hackney.* London 1779.

- *Two Tracts on Civil Liberty, the War with America, and the debts and finances of the Kingdom, with a general introduction and supplement.* London 1778.

[Priestley, Joseph.] *An Address to Protestant Dissenters of All Denominations* ... London 1774.

- *The Present State of Liberty in Great Britain and her Colonies, by an Englishman.* London 1769.

[Quincy, Jr, Josiah.] *Observations on the Act of Parliament, commonly called the Boston Port-bill.* Boston 1774. Reprint. London 1774.

Remarks on the Importance of the Study of Political Pamphlets, Weekly Papers, Periodical Papers, Daily Papers, Political Music, etc. London 1765.

[Robinson-Morris, M., 2d baron Rokeby?] *Considerations on the measures carrying on with respect to the British Colonies in North America.* London 1774.

[Sayre, Stephen.] *The Englishman Deceived.* London 1768.

Sharp, Granville. *A Declaration of the People's natural right to a share in the Legislature.* London 1774.

[Shipley, Jonathan.] *A Speech intended to have been spoken on the bill for altering the charters of the colony of Massachusetts Bay.* 4th ed. London 1774.

A Short History of the Opposition during the Late Session of Parliament. London 1779.

Tucker, Josiah. *Four Tracts, together with Two Sermons on Political and Commercial Subjects.* Gloucester 1774.

- *An Humble and Earnest Appeal* ... 3d ed. London 1776.

- *A Series of Answers to certain Popular Objections, against Separating from the Rebellious Colonies and Discarding them Entirely* ... London 1776.

Wesley, John. *A Calm Address to our American Colonies.* London 1775.

- *Some Observations on Liberty occasioned by a late tract.* Edinburgh 1776.

The West India Merchant: being a series of papers originally printed under that signature in the London Evening Post. London 1778.

[Zouch, Henry.] *An English Freeholder's Address to his Countrymen.* London 1780.

Newspapers and Periodicals
(all published in London, except the *Virginia Gazette*)

Annual Register, 1768-83
The Crisis, January 1775-October 1776
Daily Advertiser, January 1775-April 1782, scattering
Gazetteer, March 1771-June 1779
Gentleman's Magazine, 1768-82
Lloyd's Evening Post, June 1773-August 1776
London Chronicle, June 1769-September 1775
London Evening Post, January 1770-December 1780
London Evening Post Extraordinary, 29 May 1775
London Gazette, April 1775-April 1782, scattering
London Magazine, 1769-82
London Museum of Politics, Miscellanies and Literature, 1770-1
London Packet, January-December 1776, scattering
Middlesex Journal, April 1769-September 1775
Monthly Review, 1769-82
Morning Chronicle, October 1774-July 1779
Morning Post, February 1775-July 1779
New Morning Post, 14 December 1776
The North Briton, 28 April 1770
A Number Extraordinary of Miller's London Mercury (containing lists of
    persons polling for Hallifax and Shakespear), 16 October 1772
Political Register, 1768-72
Public Advertiser, January 1769-December 1782
Public Ledger, January 1774-December 1776, scattering
The Remembrancer, 1775-81
St. James's Chronicle, January-December 1768, November 1775, January-
    December 1781
Virginia Gazette. Purdie and Dixon, 1773.
The Whisperer, March-June 1770

Directories, Registers, and Commercial Guides
(all published in London)

Campbell, R. *The London Tradesman*, 1747
Court and City Register, 1775-80
Kent's Directory, 1775, 1776
Lowndes' London Directory, 1774
Mortimer's Universal Director, 1763
New Complete Guide ... to London, 1775
Royal Kalendar, 1771, 1774-80

SECONDARY SOURCES: A SELECT
LIST

Bailyn, Bernard. *The Ideological Origins of the American Revolution.* Cambridge, Mass.: Belknap Press of Harvard University Press 1967.

- *The Origins of American Politics.* New York: Knopf 1968.

Baker, Norman. *Government and Contractors: The British Treasury and War Supplies, 1775-1783.* London: Athlone Press 1971.

Beaven, Alfred B. *The Aldermen of the City of London, temp. Henry III-1908.* 2 vols. London: E. Fisher 1908-13.

Black, Eugene C. *The Association: British Extraparliamentary Political Organization, 1769-1793.* Cambridge, Mass.: Harvard University Press 1963.

Bleackley, Horace. *Life of John Wilkes.* London: John Lane 1917.

Bonwick, Colin C. "An English Audience for American Revolutionary Pamphlets." *The Historical Journal* 19 (1976).

- *English Radicals and the American Revolution.* Chapel Hill, NC: University of North Carolina Press 1977.

Brewer, John. *Party Ideology and Popular Politics at the Accession of George III.* Cambridge: Cambridge University Press 1976.

Brown, Richard D. *Revolutionary Politics in Massachusetts: The Boston Committee of Correspondence and the Towns, 1772-1774.* Cambridge, Mass.: Harvard University Press 1970.

Cannon, John. *Parliamentary Reform, 1640-1832.* Cambridge: Cambridge University Press 1973.

Christie, Ian R. *Myth and Reality in Late Eighteenth-Century British Politics and Other Papers.* Berkeley, Calif.: University of California Press 1970.

- *Wilkes, Wyvill and Reform: The Parliamentary Reform Movement in British Politics.* London: Macmillan 1962.

Christie, Ian R., and Benjamin W. Labaree. *Empire or Independence, 1760-1776: A British-American Dialogue on the Coming of the American Revolution.* New York: Norton 1976.

Clark, Dora Mae. *British Opinion and the American Revolution.* New Haven, Conn.: Yale University Press 1930.

Dickson, Peter G.M. *The Financial Revolution in England: A Study in the Development of Public Credit, 1688-1756.* London: Macmillan 1967.

Donoughue, Bernard. *British Politics and the American Revolution: The Path to War, 1773-75.* London: Macmillan 1964.

George, M. Dorothy. "America in English Satirical Prints." *William and Mary Quarterly,* 3d ser., 10 (1953).

- *London Life in the XVIIIth Century.* New York: Knopf 1925.

Guttridge, George H. *English Whiggism and the American Revolution.* 2d ed. Berkeley, Calif.: University of California Press 1966.

Kammen, Michael G. *A Rope of Sand: The Colonial Agents, British Politics and the American Revolution*. Ithaca, NY: Cornell University Press 1968.

Labaree, Benjamin Woods. *The Boston Tea Party*. New York: Oxford University Press 1964.

Lutnick, Solomon. *The American Revolution and the British Press*. Columbia, Mo.: University of Missouri Press 1967.

Maier, Pauline. *From Resistance to Revolution: Colonial Radicals and the Development of American Opposition to Britain, 1765–1776*. New York: Knopf 1972.

McKendrick, Neil, John Brewer, and J.H. Plumb. *The Birth of a Consumer Society: The Commercialization of Eighteenth-Century England*. Bloomington: Indiana University Press 1982.

Namier, Lewis, and John Brooke. *The History of Parliament: The House of Commons, 1754–1790*. 3 vols. London: Her Majesty's Stationery Office 1964.

Plumb, J.H. "British Attitudes to the American Revolution." In *In the Light of History*. London: Allen Lane The Penguin Press 1972.

Pocock, John G.A. *The Machiavellian Moment: Florentine Political Thought and the Atlantic Republican Tradition*. Princeton, NJ: Princeton University Press 1975.

– ed. *Three British Revolutions: 1641, 1688, 1776*. Princeton, NJ: Princeton University Press 1980.

Riggs, A.R. "Arthur Lee and the Radical Whigs, 1768–1776." PH D dissertation, Yale University, 1967.

Ritcheson, Charles R. *British Politics and the American Revolution*. Norman, Okla.: University of Oklahoma Press 1954.

Robbins, Caroline. *The Eighteenth-Century Commonwealthman: Studies in the Transmission, Development and Circumstance of English Liberal Thought from the Restoration of Charles II until the War with the Thirteen Colonies*. Cambridge, Mass.: Harvard University Press 1959.

Rogers, Nicholas. "Aristocratic Clientage, Trade and Independency: Popular Politics in Pre-Radical Westminster." *Past and Present*, no. 61 (November 1973).

Rudé, George F.E. "The Anti-Wilkite Merchants of 1769." *Guildhall Miscellany* 2 (1965).

– *Hanoverian London, 1714–1808*. London: Secker and Warburg 1971.

– *Wilkes and Liberty: A Social Study of 1763 to 1774*. Oxford: Clarendon Press 1962.

Sharpe, Reginald R. *London and the Kingdom*. 3 vols. London, New York 1895.

Sheps, Arthur. "The American Revolution and the Transformation of English Republicanism." *Historical Reflections/Reflexions Historiques* 2 (1975).

Sosin, Jack M. *Agents and Merchants: British Colonial Policy and the Origins of the American Revolution*. Lincoln, Nebr.: University of Nebraska Press 1965.

Stevenson, John, ed. *London in the Age of Reform*. Oxford: Blackwell 1977.

Sutherland, Lucy S. *The City of London and the Opposition to Government, 1768-1774*. London: Athlone Press 1959.

– "The City of London in Eighteenth-Century Politics." In *Essays presented to Sir Lewis Namier*, edited by Richard Pares and A.J.P. Taylor. London: Macmillan 1956.

Timbs, John. *Clubs and Club Life in London*. London 1872.

Toohey, Robert E. *Liberty and Empire: British Radical Solutions to the American Problem, 1774-1776*. Lexington: University of Kentucky Press 1978.

Treloar, Sir William P. *Wilkes and the City*. London: J. Murray 1917.

Werkmeister, Lucyle. *The London Daily Press, 1772-1792*. Lincoln, Nebr.: University of Nebraska Press 1963.

Whiteman, Anne, J.S. Bromley, and P.G.M. Dickson, eds., *Statesmen, Scholars and Merchants: Essays in Eighteenth-Century History presented to Dame Lucy Sutherland*. Oxford: Clarendon Press 1973.

Woods, John A. "The City of London and Impressment, 1776-1777." *Proceedings of the Leeds Philosophical and Literary Society* 8 (1956-9).

Index

9-12/93

Please Do Not Remove Card From Pocket

YOUR LIBRARY CARD

may be used at all library agencies. You
are, of course, responsible for all materials
checked out on it. As a courtesy to others
please return materials promptly. A service
charge is assessed for overdue materials.

The SAINT PAUL PUBLIC LIBRARY